SRFLIS series in library science / ed. by Dr K P Singh ; no.11

PLAGIARISM:
An International Reader

PLAGIARISM:
An International Reader

Edited by
**M P Satija,
Daniel Martínez-Ávila**
and
Nirmal K Swain

Ess Ess Publications
New Delhi

PLAGIARISM
An International Reader

Copyright © by All Authors and Editors

All rights reserved. No part of this book may be reproduced in any form or by any electronic or mechanical means including information storage and retrieval systems without permission in writing from the publisher, except by a reviewer, who may quote brief passages in a review.

While extensive effort has gone into ensuring the reliability of information appearing in this book, the publisher makes no warranty, express or implied on the accuracy or reliability of the information, and does not assume and hereby disclaims any liability to any person for any loss or damage caused by errors or omissions in this publication.

ISBN: 978-93-87698-14-7

SRFLIS series in library science / ed. by Dr K P Singh ; no. 11

First Published 2019

Published by:
Ess Ess Publications
4831/24, Ansari Road,
Darya Ganj,
New Delhi-110 002, INDIA
Phones: 23260807, 41563444
Fax: 41563334
E-mail: info@essessreference.com
www.essessreference.com

Cover Design by *Maria José Vicentini Jorente and Stephanie Cerqueira*

Printed and bound in India

Plagiarism: an international reader / edited by M P Satija, Daniel Martínez-Ávila and Nirmal K Swain. – New Delhi : SRFLIS India, 2019.

p. ; cm. - (SRFLIS series in library science/ed. by K P Singh; no.11)

Bibliography : pp. 303-328

ISBN : 978-93-87698-14-7

1. Plagiarism I. Satija, M.P II. Martinez-Ávila, Daniel III. Swain, Nirmal K IV. series

Contents

Foreword	H. K. Kaul	
Preface	M.P. Satija	
	Daniel Martínez-Ávila	
1	Plagiarism: An Introduction M.P. Satija	1
2	The Problem of Plagiarism in Retractions of Published Articles John M. Budd	21
3	Plagiarism and High Politics: A Threat to Democracy Theodor Tudoroiu	29
4	Ethical Use of Information : The Contribution of the Academic Libraries in the Prevention of Plagiarism Helena Isabel Pereira Leitão Maria da Graça de Melo Simões Patrícia de Almeida Daniel Martínez-Ávila	49
5	Does Open Access Promote Plagiarism? Prabhash N. Rath Sanjaya Mishra	67
6	Plagiarism and the New Norm in Scholarly Communication: The New Information Professionals and Open Access Advocacy Groups' Perspective Stavroula Sant-Geronikolou	77 77
7	Measuring Plagiarism Research Output: A Bibliometric Analysis Suresh K Chauhan	95
8	Plagiarism : A Growing Menace Across Academia Ramesh Pandita Shivendra Singh	107

9	Beleaguered and Tousled Research: Murky Waters of Plagiarism and Retractions *Sumeer Gul* *Taufat Hussain*	127
10	Plagiarism in Research Publications and Violation of Law and Ethics *R Saha*	135
11	Plagiarism : An Academic Dishonesty. A Bibliometric Insight into the Spread of Problem *V. J. Suseela* *V. Uma*	143
12	Reflections about Research Ethics in Contemporary Society *Marta Ligia Pomim Valentim*	165
13	Role of Information Literacy in Curbing Plagiarism *Helen de Castro S. Casarin*	175
14	Policies and Guidelines for Academic Conduct in Universities: A Survey of the International Landscape *Manorama Tripathi* *Gayatri Dwivedi* *Parveen Babbar*	183
15	Plagiarism and Guides to Good Scientific Practices: The Brazilian Perspective *Eduardo Graziosi Silva* *João Carlos Gardini Santos* *José Augusto Chaves Guimarães*	201
16	Understanding the Concept of Plagiarism among Iranian Students *Asefeh Asemi* *Marzieh Sadat Hosseini*	209
17	Awareness and Attitude of Agricultural Students Towards Plagiarism *Nirmal Singh* *Sanjeev Kumar* *Dhiraj Kumar*	221
18	Academic Plagiarism : An Overview of the Policy and Preventive Measures in Pakistan *Kanwal Ameen* *Faiqa Mansoor*	231
19	Ethical Policies of LIS e-Journals Listed in the UGC Approved List *Dinesh K Gupta* *Vijendra Kumar*	239
20	Controlling Plague of Plagiarism in Indian Academic Institutions: Draft UGC Plagiarism Regulations 2018 *Ramesh C. Gaur*	249

Contents

21	The Pressures and Perils of Overachieving - An Inquiry into the Kaavya Viswanathan Case
	    Gurpartap S. Khairah
	    Nirmal Singh
		259

22	Anti-Plagiarism Software Check to the Doctoral Theses in Indian Universities and Institutions *S. T. Kale*	263
23	Information on Plagiarism at the University of Bradford *University of Bradford Library*	279

Appendix 1 : University Grants Commission (Promotion of Academic Integrity and Prevention of Plagiarism in Higher Educational Institutions) Regulations, 2018   291

Appendix 2 : IFLA Statement on Copyright Education and Copyright Literacy   299

Bibliography   303
    Nirmal Kumar Swain
    Harish Chander

Glossary   329

About the Authors: Author-Title Index   341

Title Index   359

Subject Index   361

Foreword

H. K. Kaul

Throughout the world students, researchers, authors and teachers are regularly engaged in searching and researching information which is already existing in manuscripts, print and digital forms inlibraries, museums, private collections, digital and online resources. And, this information on the Web is growing by the second. There is a big void existing between these large information resources and the precise requirements of students, researchers and writers who want to use quality resources. And, because of this void research on any topic is not full and final at any given time. Over and above, this large void facilitates some students, the upcoming researchers and authors, who are mostly ignorant about copyright rules, knowingly or unknowingly copy in part or fullany digital resource on the Web they like to use and make it their own work.This stealing of someone's content is not only immoral but this process has various ramifications on the worlds of scholarship, publishing, and the integrity of academic institutions. As a result of these unfair activities, wefind the samesentences and paragraphs by so-called authors popping up while searching information on the Web. That is mostly plagiarized content and their so-called authors are liable for penalties forcopyright violations.

Dr. M P Satija, UGC Emeritus fellow, Department of Library & Information Science, Guru Nanak Dev University, Amritsar, Prof. Daniel Martínez-Ávila, from Sao Paulo, Brazil and Dr. Nirmal K Swain of MDU Rohtak have collected useful contributions on plagiarism by experts from the USA, UK, Spain, Brazil, Pakistan, Iran and India. These papers in this volumehighlight the plague of academic plagiarism and the measuresbeing taken in several countries including India and Pakistan to curb its spread.

The academic atmosphere vitiated by plagiarism posesserious threat to original research and the creation of seminal works. Legal frameworks exist to punish the plagiarists but the spread is so large we also need to take other steps to curb it. Information literacy can play a great role in checking plagiarism. So can the lectures, discussions and workshops on plagiarismhelp in reducing it. We need tobring back the use of ethical values in research.

The role of antiplagiarism software in checking doctoral theses and dissertations in universities and institutions is important but as information is growing fast, the results of the anti-plagiarism software remain varying and we will have to have very high end software that will compare theses and dissertations with all ever-growing Web resources for plagiarism and deliver dependable results.

With the education of students, scholars and the public about the importance of copyright and the penalties that go with plagiarizing content and the infringement of copyright there could be substantial reduction in the cases of plagiarized contents. This is a global problem and needs to be tackled both at the global, national and institutional levels. This volume entitled Plagiarism: An International Reader so ably edited by Dr. Satija and his associates is a Commendable publication on plagiarism. I congratulate the editors for producing this useful volume. I am sure, if distributed well, it will help students, scholars and the public in understanding the demerits of the scourge of plagiarism that is prevalent in this day and age.

Preface

M.P. Satija
Daniel Martínez-Ávila

'*Nothing is quite so despised as the man who filches the credit which is the rightful due of another. Moreover, no form of thievery is sillier, for the truth always leaks out; everyone knows who the credit-snatcher is, and is skeptical of all credit to him?*' **- Vannevar Bush**

Plagiarism is thieving knowledge and other cerebral creations. With the advent of information technologies, the information explosion, and other changes affecting research, creativity and the academia, the research misconducts and frauds are becoming more and more the talk of the academic town. In the academic world and creative circles everybody is talking of it (see the select bibliography), as if all have become bitten now by this old bug.

Knowledge and creativity both are wealth and power generated by thinkers, researchers and innovators. Indeed, knowledge is superior power than the two other social powers, namely money and violence, as said by Alvin Toffler (1928-2016)1. Plagiarism is abusively stealing this power by some in many ways. This is happening without exception since antiquity in all societies. Knowledge which is the mother of all creativity is essential for survival of all societies, nay humankind. Societies and nations thrive on innovation, and become stagnant by the culture of imitations. A society can never progress and move further from the rut without new ideas and innovations in all fields of social life and professions. Plagiarism is not only inimical to research and innovation, but also a threat to democracy. We always need genuine innovations by the day to keep moving as a humanity and global society.

For some individuals in the modern world, creativity is a profession and essential for career promotion. But some individuals resort to stealing knowledge for various reasons and in many ways. Stealing knowledge is worse than stealing material property or money. People steal for various reasons: some are needy being bereft of ideas and skill of creative writing. Some are ignorant of the laws and norms of knowledge use and its recorded communication. Some have learnt the art of circumventing the law, though ethically they may be guilty of it. Some societies are lenient on plagiarism, or have different attitudes towards or perception of it. Most offenders do it as it is easier to steal than to create. They think they are smart enough not to be seen and caught stealing. Some do some pilfering to raise the standard of their writing. They are compulsive fraudsters. So all kinds of knowledge thieves are there with us to know. Laws against copyright infringement and plagiarism exist in every country of the modern world. But of late, especially in developing countries under pressure from the WTO regime, these laws are refurbished and geared to catch on such offenders. Law is the same for all—be it plagiarism for academic or commercial reasons.

Plagiarism must be curbed, though it cannot be eradicated. It must be controlled to provide security and encouragement to creators on whose creative labours the society moves onto the path of overall progress. The best means is to sensitize and educate people from early childhood against this menace and its devastating consequences for all of us.

Plagiarism may invite punishment depending upon the extent and nature of offence and also on against whom this offence has been committed. In the commercial world, the punishment could be a jail term, or some financial compensation for the litigant. In knowledge institutions, it may be some administrative and disciplinary action ranging from job dismissal to lighter warning, or anything in between. Journal editors usually retract the plagiarised article inducting the plagiarist to the hall of academic indictment, and the author may be blacklisted for some period.

This is an internationally commissioned compilation of articles from some of the known authorities in the field, and who have already some research to their credit. Papers fall mostly in three broader categories: theory of plagiarism and ways to curb it; attitudes towards plagiarism in different countries and various academic disciplines; and lastly, punishment for plagiarism by way of public exposure and trial of their crime and retraction of published articles. The topics include plagiarism policies, case studies, use of plagiarism machines and their limitations, consequences of plagiarism and how to avoid it. Some of the questions raised are: do the web and Open Access mode encourage plagiarism? Does prior warnings to students and researchers discourage and check plagiarism.

Special mention may be made of the papers by Dr. Theodor Tudoroiu dealing with plagiarism by the politically high-ups who usually escape punishment especially in authoritarian regimes, and of Dr. Ramesh Gaur who has been a member of the national committee on plagiarism constituted by the Government of India. Select bibliography may facilitate further to dive deeply into the sea of plagiarism studies. The home spun glossary may provoke interest in the nuances of the field.

We are thankful to all the contributors who, despite their very busy schedules, with alacrity accepted our invitation to write for the volume, and for forbearing our nagging reminders of deadline. This compilation entirely owes to them, their enthusiasm and scholarship. And many thanks to Dr H K Kaul, a librarian and a poet, for his encouraging Foreword.

Our aim is to promote an ethical culture, and high standards of integrity and transparency in the conduct of research and publications. We earnestly hope these papers based on research and reflections provide some grist to the mill of scholars and activists working against plagiarism – to make society free of this plague.

REFERENCES

Bush, Vannevar (1965). *Science is not Enough.* New York, N.Y.: Feffer and Simons, p.61

Toffler, Alvin (1990). *Powershift: Knowledge, Wealth and Violence at the Edge of the 21st Century.* New York: Bantam Books, 585 p.

1
Plagiarism: An Introduction

M.P. Satija

1. DEFINITION

It is difficult to define plagiarism due to its wide spread and varied use. Broadly speaking, plagiarism is any copyright infringement, yet every copyright infringement is not plagiarism. It is in the infamous company of unfair means such as piracy, data-fabrication, research falsification, evidence cooking, ghost-writing, proxy writing, research-recycling, literary-thefts, copying graphics, industrial designs and trademarks, and committing other frauds in research, writings, and artistic and industrial creations. Strictly speaking, it is any lack of giving proper, formal and adequate credit to the original source of ideas or their expression in any writing and all other forms and modes of creative expressions. Lack of proper attribution to the original source is plagiarism and a serious research misconduct.

2. WHAT CONSTITUTES PLAGIARISM?

It is using someone's intellectual or artistic creation without permission, acknowledgement and credit. According to the unabridged Oxford English Dictionary, the word has its roots in the classical Latin word *Plagirus* which means a person who abducts the child or slave of someone. A modern copycat plagiarist is an only brain-child kidnapper who, mercifully, does not ask for any ransom. Nevertheless, the act is illegal, unethical, and even criminal. Published works and other creative expressions are indeed for use of the public and benefit of the society at large. "Scientists and scholars want their ideas to be used and their words to be quoted", aptly writes Lafollette (2001, 304). But using them in a way what constitutes plagiarism is simply their abuse and an act of dishonesty. It is immoral. It is an academic or research fraud, and a criminal offence in business and industry.

Based on various dictionaries the Wikipedia makes a synthetic definition to describe it as "the wrongful appropriation, close imitation…and publication of another author's language, thoughts, ideas, or expressions, and representation of them as one's own original work" (Wikipedia contributors 2018a). Admitting that due to wide variations in its perception, practice and norms among nations, groups and disciplines, Lafollette (2001) identifies four elements present in most of the definition:

"1. The unattributed use of words, text, ideas, or illustrations created by someone other than the author listed;

"2. The failure to credit the original ("real") author in a manner appropriate to the communication;

"3. The implication (or statement) that the plagiarist is the original author; and

"4. The failure to obtain the original author's consent".

Any of these elements individually or collectively constitute plagiarism.

3. FORMS: OVERT, COVERT AND AMBIGUOUS

Plagiarism could be as obvious as blandly and blatantly copying a patch from a published text, or even the whole piece, or it is hidden, subtle or clever mixing, imitating, paraphrasing, pilfering phrases, adapting or translating someone else's language and thoughts and claiming them as original. Word-swapping, paraphrasing, style copying, un-permitted translation and many more such acts constitute copyright violations. Copyright abuse and plagiarism are inseparable twins.

4. PIRACY

Piracy, which is akin to daylight incognito robbery, is unauthorized reprinting or electronically copying and marketing a publication, print or electronic, as original imprint for commercial gains. It is just like printing fake currency notes. Publishers of best sellers, music and movie companies are blighted by this scourge more so in the digital environment where wholesale copying has become more than an easy game and a flourishing underground industry. Number one problem and worry of the music, movie and entertainment industry is piracy. But the musicians and movie makers themselves are not above board as far as plagiarism is concerned. Many Bollywood movies stories or scenes are stolen or closely copied from the Hollywood produce. Only recently many cases have been settled out of court. Now Hollywood agents have an office in Mumbai to keep tabs on such violations by the Indian film makers. The Indian industry is alerted and scared.

5. JUSTIFICATION: GREY AREAS AND MURKY WATERS

There are subtle stealers of ideas and phrases who subscribe to the theory that "there is nothing new under the sun". Everything is in everything and vice-versa, they say further. "An exceptional soul that 'creates from naught' is a *Brahma*. Others are humans" (Prasad, 2010). Research in social sciences and humanities is cynically taken as transfer of bones from one grave to another. Indeed, every new research depends upon the previous research. Every technology is evolutionary. In arts, imitation is mostly excused as a major part of learning the creative process. The saying 'imitation is the sincerest form of flattery' has some grain of truth in it. The great French artist Eugene Henri Paul Gauguin (1848-1903) once famously said that "Art is either plagiarism or revolution" (Tribune, 2013b). Copycats make some cosmetic changes and describe the original source as inspiration only. In the creative chain there is neither beginning nor any end. All science is cumulative: progressively building over the previous knowledge. Knowledge is a unity; a tremendously huge system. Isaac Newton (1643-1727) had famously said that only standing on the shoulders of giants he could look farther—and those shoulders were of Islamic science flourished seven centuries ago (al-Khalili, 2008). (This now much hackneyed phrase attributed to Newton was borrowed by him from Bernard of Chartres, a twelfth-century French Neo-Platonist philosopher, scholar, and administrator, (Perzanowski & Schltz, 2018, 145). Indeed, European science of 17th century owes much to Islamic scholars of Muslim civilization which in turn benefited much from Hindu science and mathematics (Sardar & Loon, 2002). S R Ranganathan (1892-1972) was of the views that ideas belong to none. They are in the cosmos, and the same idea may sometimes coincidentally strike simultaneously to two persons. History of science and inventions is replete with so many such stories of coincidences and priority claims (Satija, 1992). Bennett and Royle (2015, 103) doubt if there is anything as originality in creativity. A creative being is not a solitary person working on a deserted island. Indeed, no body is an island complete in himself. A creator is just like a bee who collects nectar from many flowers and makes its own honey. He is not a spider weaving sticky cobwebs from the abdomen. The French writer Michel de Montaigne (1533-1592), the best essayist the literary world has produced, drew consistently on other writers and thinkers, believe Bennett and Royle (2015). Being eclectic is not being plagiarist. Gorman (2008, 298) cites R. Clarke to say that many professions, especially journalism have a weak stand on plagiarism, and they fail to specify what exactly constitutes it. But for Gorman himself it is an offence of highly variable range.

To every one of us, ideas do come from some near or far off experiences and from known, forgotten or unknown sources. What matters is when and how you cultivate and shape it. John Milton (1608-1674) in *Eikonoklastes* wrote "for such kind of *borrowing*...if it is not bettered by the borrower, any good author is accounted as *Plagiare*". Therefore, many plead that copyright resides in expression of an idea, not the idea itself. Idea is open and free, but its expression is proprietary. It means that value additions to a creative work will not account to plagiarism. An acceptable academic dissertation by definition is discursive and synthesis of many viewpoints. In this vein, a character of the playwright Wilson Mizner (1876-1933) in a bantering tone but aptly says, "when you steal from one author, it's plagiarism; if you steal from many, it is research", quoted by McIver (1994). This has been best described by the poet laureate T S Eliot (1888-1965) in his book *The Sacred Wood* (1920) while writing on the playwright Philip Massinger (1583-1640). He says:

> We turn first to the parallel quotations from Massinger and Shakespeare collocated by Mr. Cruickshank to make manifest Massinger's indebtedness. One of the surest of tests is the way in which a poet borrows. Immature poets imitate; mature poets

steal; bad poets deface what they take, and good poets make it into something better, or at least something different. The good poet welds his theft into a whole of feeling which is unique, utterly different from that from which it was torn; the bad poet throws it into something which has no cohesion. A good poet will usually borrow from authors remote in time, or alien in language, or diverse in interest. Chapman borrowed from Seneca; Shakespeare and Webster from Montaigne. The two great followers of Shakespeare, Webster and Tourneur, in their mature work do not borrow from him; he is too close to them to be of use to them in this way. Massinger, as Mr. Cruickshank shows, borrows from Shakespeare a good deal.

6. WHAT DOES NOT CONSTITUTE PLAGIARISM?

In the modern world the plagiarism happens in the published or works in the public domain only. To make a case for copyright infringement or plagiarism both the original and copied work must be in the public domain. "The Copyright Act provides protection to an expressed or presentation of an idea, and not to the idea itself" writes Saha (2017, 2375). He further writes (p.2376) "… thoughts and ideas cannot be copyrighted under the law … raw data do not get protection in copyrights, but organisation of data in the form of a database is protectable." Writing degree exams, or delivering verbatim lectures, even if not attributed to the real author, do not make a case for plagiarism. Traditional knowledge or folklore for words and ideas do not come under copyright laws. Common facts, opinion, idioms and proverbs need no attribution (Monippally & Pawar, 2010,178). There is no need to cite any authority to say Mahatma Gandhi was born in so and so year, or he was an apostle of non-violence. You even need not quote John Keats to say "A thing of beauty is a joy forever"—every perceptive reader knows from whom it is! I need not explain the source to say that the full name of Mrs. Indira Gandhi is Indira Priyadarshni Gandhi. Any form change or genuine value addition is also exempted as it is considered as a new creation. For example, *Tales from Shakespeare* by Charles and Mary Lamb, which narrates plots of Shakespeare's plays in story forms is not a plagiarized work. Similarly, any parody of a poem, drama or speech is not plagiarism. Metamorphosis is certainly not an act of plagiarism: it is creation. Is mutating someone's ideas plagiarism? That is the question groping for a clear answer.

7. PLAGIARISM VS. PIRACY

Piracy is indeed intentional copyright violation, mostly for commercial purpose and financial gains. But it is not plagiarism, though a crime. Attribution is still there both to the author and publisher, but these are fake copies reproduced without any permission of the publisher. It is a serious criminal offence, just like printing fake currency, which may invite fine and jail term. Whereas in plagiarism, which is considered a non-cognizable offence, it is your institution which may punish you both in terms of your career and job. In India hardly any judicial court has awarded punishment for academic plagiarism. Nevertheless, many have ruined their career and reputation on being found guilty of it. Plagiarism in trade, commerce and industry is covered by the patent laws under the intellectual property rights. Thousands of national and international cases of patent violations are in judicial courts all over the world, and many have been settled out of court by paying huge money to the original patent holder by the accused party.

8. EVERY COPYRIGHT VIOLATION IS NOT PLAGIARISM

Copyright laws are intricate and paradoxical in a way. The law may allow you to take the entire document, but does unequivocally prohibit you to pilfer a portion from it. With attribution you may reprint and republish any publication which has either outlived its protection period, or has been permitted republication from the very beginning by the publisher. For example, religious, diplomatic, or propaganda literature is encouraged republication. Anyone, for example, can reprint and sell plays of Shakespeare, Kalidas, Diwan of Mirza Ghalib, or Diary of Anne Frank, or Das Kapital by Karl Marx. But no one is legally allowed a line without credit from these classics. If you copy from such sources there is no legal action, but you may surely provoke ridicule of your peers, and even administrative punitive action from your institution. To conclude, copying from copyleft publications is not a copyright violation, but surely is a punishable plagiarism. On the other hand, piracy is copyright infringement, but not plagiarism. Translating any copyrighted text without permission, even if fully attributed, is not plagiarism, but a serious copyright violation.

9. IT IS BENEFICIAL?

"Roger Clarke discounts its seriousness as a crime and finds it rather useful for better and wider circulation of knowledge", quotes Gorman (2008, 300). A plagiarized text does not matter with those who read for pleasure or to pass an examination. Musician Raghu Dixit feels piracy is a real boon for potential artists. He elaborates: "once a good song is downloaded, it is posted on the walls of so many Facebook users and is tweeted by hundreds of people so this way piracy is helping budding artists, who are promising…" (www.raghudixit.com). Author and journalist Andrlik (2012) detailing 'How plagiarism made America…' writes "250 years ago stealing another reporter's work without credit was an acceptable form of journalism. In fact, it was a practice that helped unite the colonies and win the Revolutionary War." He continues: "without professional writing staff of journalists or correspondents, eighteenth-century newspaper printers relied heavily on an inter-colonial newspaper exchange system to fill their pages. Printers often copied entire paragraphs or columns directly from other newspapers and frequently without attribution. As a result, identical news reports often appeared in multiple papers throughout America. This news-swappi2ng technique, and resulting plagiarism, helped spread the ideas of liberty and uphold the colonists' resistance to British Parliament." Powerful but ill-fated prime minister of Pakistan Mr. Zulfikar Ali Bhutto (1928-1979) to solve the problem of paucity of textbooks for university students publicly instigated publishers and printers of his country to freely reprint foreign textbooks and provide them at affordable rates to the students. Lo, listen! the great Bill Gates learned his first programing on an unauthorized software (Perzanowski & Schultz, 2016,123-124).

10. ONCE UPON A TIME KNOWLEDGE WAS FREE

Plagiarism is with us since antiquity and had prevailed unperceived until recently in every culture and in all ages. Its perception is mostly of Western origin. In the days of manuscripts in Europe, and ancient Indian tradition of gurukuls and ashrams for childhood schooling, rote learning was considered the best method of knowledge acquisition. A person with a sharp memory who could memorize and recite long patches of texts (whoso be their authors) was considered a scholar, and the master and owner of that knowledge. Real authors, many of them of distance past, could not be identified easily. Knowledge belonged to him who had it, who could memorise and use that. Being intangible and non-exclusive the concept of owning knowledge was just not there. Its unattributed use/reuse and propagation was not considered any theft, or unethical act. In that era, all knowledge had been, what in the information society and knowledge economy, we have come to term as, open access or knowledge commons. In fact, it was then more free and liberal than today's knowledge commons. Scholars and authors copied from others without acknowledgement or disclosing their sources except in case of religious scriptures. Any classical or revered writer was never quoted chapter and verse which usually resulted in misquotes. Scholars were few; diffusion of knowledge was slow; original and sourced ideas mingled promiscuously. That was all common and proper, an accepted norm. Tudoroiu (2017, 625) with many examples explains that concept of plagiarism is cultural. He writes, "China, with its tradition of collectivism, is frequently used as an example of a culture that devalues the Western concept of authorship while placing a greater value on imitation, which is encouraged and valued in the creation of new intellectual property. This results in a different system of values concerning plagiarism." He further quotes Bloch (2008, 219-220) who feels that "Chinese students neither understand Western concepts nor feel that such plagiarism is an unacceptable practice."

11. BEGINNINGS OF COPYRIGHT

The 19th century Industrial Revolution with its mass production methods ushered in the concept of authorial credit and subsequent passing on the accruing pecuniary benefits to the inventor or author. Printed books in the mid-15th century increased the volume of information and accelerated its flow in the society. It proved to be the game changer for learning, education, knowledge creation and dissemination. Abundance and easy availability of printed books led to a new type of knowledge which was based on evidence, reasoning and analysis called empirical knowledge (Kovac, 2008, 31-32). Format of books got standardized with title page, author's name, publisher/printer's imprint, colophon, sources, and index. That was the information transfer protocol of the day. Giving credit to the sourced authors became simplified. Authors of the books became known (some famous, too) and they asserted their rights as sole owners of the knowledge contained therein both for fame and financial benefits. It ultimately led to the concept of copyright for which the first ever law in the modern sense was enacted in England in the early 18th century.

12. IT IS A WIDESPREAD PLAGUE

Despite the national and international copyright and patent laws firmly in place everywhere in the civilized world, malpractices in research and creativity are on the increase, as in other fields. We are living in a culture of copying, claims Lynn Lampert (2008, 17-25). Plagiarism is getting rampant and worst by the day. Gorman (2008) aptly terms it a plague which is spreading uncontrolled like an epidemic. It has become pandemic in the academic world. Plagiarism is a snake, always tempting writers, editors, artists, storytellers, poets, films makers, fashion designers, architects, software engineers, researchers, students, and other creative beings. Many a mighty and famous like Shakespeare have been alleged to have fallen prey to it. In the contemporary world many a vice-chancellor, professor, director of research council, journalist, famed researcher has been found guilty of this crime (Wikipedia contributors 2018a). Incidents of academic cheating are on the rise in the UK, reveals a report. More than 17000 such incidents of academic cheating have been reported in more than eighty British universities including the Oxford (Times of India, 2011). Even the great Harvard University once tottered under its onslaught where more than one hundred cases of academic fraud came to light in 2012. The university had to admit that "magnitude of the case is unprecedented in anyone's living memory" (Tribune, 2013a). It is constantly in the news for the wrong reasons. According to Barry Gilmore, an American author on the subject, "... accusation of plagiarism plagued nominees for president, vice-president, writers and teachers, and those accusations were reported in the news across the nation and world. Plagiarism is a pervasive topic and challenge on college campus, and it's becoming more and more of a sore subject with many professors and administrators" (Gilmore 2009, 84).

13. ROUGES GALLERY

Whatsoever be the laws and efforts to curb this plague, its mutating virus keeps ahead of methods and medicines for its prevention and cure. A cop turned vice-chancellor of an Indian university was not wide of the mark when he recently stated candidly that 90% of the theses are a 'cut and paste work' (Lall, 2009). A university in the US rocked by plagiarism scandals formulated a policy to deal with the issue. Ironically, the very definition of plagiarism it adopted was plagiarized (Bartlett, 2009). A Japanese professor of anesthesiology Yoshitaka Fujii who faked 126 papers in a period of less than two decades (1993-2012) was dismissed from his job. He superseded the record of the infamous German anesthesiologist Joachim Boldt who fabricated only ninety from 1999 to 2011. Rudyard Kipling (1865-1936), a literary genius who was the youngest recipient of the Nobel Prize, admitted that he helped himself "promiscuously from other stories" (Tribune, 2013b). Other people charged with plagiarism are Oprah Winfrey, J.K. Rowling, Laurence Stern, S T Coleridge, Oscar Wilde, Vladimir Putin, Iranian President since 2013 Hassan Rouhani, to name a few. Shakespeare allegedly borrowed some of his plots from Raphael Holinshed. In 2012 the Time Columnist and CNN T.V. host Rafiq Zakaria admitted and apologized for some misappropriations in his article. He was suspended though soon his suspension was revoked. This is less than the tip of the iceberg. In India vice-chancellors, eminent professors and scientific advisors have been found guilty of this fraud (University Today, 2013). In 2017, Fernando Suárez, former president of King Juan Carlos University (URJC), in Spain, was also found guilty of decades of plagiarism and only forced to resign after a political scandal (Silió 2017). Suárez, who had plagiarized "hundreds, if not thousands, of paragraphs" in his publications (EFE 2016), claimed that they were actually "dysfunctions, because I'm human." It is a gold rush. Amazingly even the universities are not blameless on it (Bartlett, 2009). Everybody seems jumping on the plagiarism bandwagon.

14. WHY IT IS INDULGED IN?

It could be
- intentional and pre-planned,
- unintentional, incidental; ignorance of laws
- accidental.

Now we can access information in many innovative and numerous ways. Some of it happens due to ignorance and lack of awareness.

15. CRYPTOMNESIA, OR MEMORY LOSS

Indeed, some of it can be unintentional and accidental. A widely-read person might get some clues from previous and recent readings and some part of his/her composition may betray a close parallel with some previous compositions. An American-Indian teenager Kaavya Viswanathan in 2006 was accused of some plagiarized paragraphs in her maiden novel "How Opal Mehta Got Kissed...". Tendering an apology she pleaded it was totally unconscious and unintentional as she had widely read the accusing author Megan McCafferty - whose ardent fan Kaavya is. The alibi, of course, was not accepted and the little girl ruined her promising literary career and the huge sum of money she earned as the pre-publication deal (Lampert, 2008, 17-22). In psychological parlance it is known as Cryptomnesia to which anyone of us could fall prey to this memory bias. It is a memory loss and misattribution (Wikipedia contributors 2018b). We remember the facts or the ideas but forget their source, and after sometime treat it as our own creation(Taylor,1965). "You don't set out to try and steal anything, but it can happen" (Times of India, 28 Aug 2016). It does happen. The same piece quotes Gayle Dow who found out that "novices are more likely to commit accidental plagiarism." They steal inadvertently not knowing from where their ideas came (Gilmore, 2009, 35). The cryptomnesia may happen due to information overload or information anxiety. "It is true that plagiarists throughout history have claimed innocence by maintaining that they did not recall actually getting material from another source" (Gilmore, 2009, 35).

16. INTENTIONAL

Most of it is intentional due to necessity or habit. Some people are compulsive thieves, habitual offenders wanting to get everything quickly and easily. Some get into this bandwagon as everybody else is doing with ease and impunity.

17. PUBLISH OR PERISH SYNDROME

Intentional violations may be due to peer pressure and to aspire for fame without merit and hard work. "... plagiarism is easy, and anything that's easy is here to stay", aptly writes Gilmore (2009,84). Pandita and Singh (2018.23) have insightfully observed that "... to accomplish more in lesser time and to achieve new heights, people generally tend to engage themselves in many undesirable practices to achieve their ends." It is a theft and at times it seems the easy and smart way to escape hard and backbreaking labour and to circumvent many inevitable hassles in writing a paper - writing is tough and time taking. Writing to meet deadlines is an agony. Writing skill takes time to develop. The barbarian slogan in the academic world "Publish or Perish" is responsible for this crime as a surviving precept. In the course of meeting the pressure of deadlines some easily fall prey to this temptation. In an interview to the CNN-IBN channel on Kaavya Vishwanathan's case the celebrated Salman Rushdie stated that "I am sorry that this young girl, pushed by the needs of a publishing machine and, no doubt, by her ambition should have fallen into this trap so early in her career". Under pressure of work even teachers and supervisors indulge in this unethical practice which they otherwise would revile in their students (Hauptman, 2017). A star psychologist Diederik Stapel of Tilburg University, the Netherlands, who faked research published in peer reviewed journals, on being caught remorsefully said that he had been driven to falsifying research under constant pressure to perform (Bhattacharjee, 2013). Under pressure they resort to the *mantras* "pilfer and publish," or "copy but do not get caught" - but caught they are eventually. An editorial in the daily the Tribune (2013b) aptly put it "Ambitious artists and writers often suffer from acute self-doubt. They think by stealing other people's writings they can better an idea and its expression." Number of research publications is a key criterion for promotion of teachers in university and colleges under the 2010/2016 guidelines of University Grants Commission (2016). For some, this rule is counterproductive. "Faculties are under pressure to take an easy way to plagiarize and to meet their target," said one teacher. For another teacher, "UGC regulations are terrible as it is encouraging bad research and also affecting teaching" (Kumar, 2014). Pressure for numerical evidence spawns malpractices in academics, says the Academics for Creative Reform Group (2015). An editorial in an academic magazine fully endorsing this view writes, "UGC has done a singular dis-service by assigning a fix 'number of publications' without much regard to quality" (University Today, 2013). There is a mad rush for M.Phil/Ph.Ds for promoting academic career, earning a dignified title and, of course, for financial benefits that come with it. They forget that these exalted degrees, at the first instance, are training for a lifelong research. But many take it as the end, pinnacle of their research career.

18. GUIDE-STUDENT NEXUS

Many candidates, some even with the connivance of their guides, resort to unfair means to get these degrees awarded without duly earning them in the right way. Many of the unfair means in doctoral research had been going on undetected or were easily glossed over by the guide. Subsequent authorities only show concern if complained by some vindictive or jealous colleague. Research guides do not work enough on the research candidates either due to lack of time or commitment, or both. No wonder some of them flaunt to have successfully guided two dozen Ph.Ds and two scores of M.Phils even at the midpoint of their careers. A fortnightly academic newspaper satirically named an Indian professor having authored 144 research papers in five years only – that is apart from his other academic and research activities (University Today, 2013, p.1). It is difficult to find a guide who is competent and has time and will to sincerely supervise the research students. Pseudo guides are the order of the day (Satija, 2010). Not everyone having a Ph.D. degree and working as professor has competence or aptitude to be a research guide. A good guide is hard to find. Teachers (professors included) who have not even authored a single convincing research paper are always keen to guide research. It is these unscrupulous persons, more than anybody else, who are responsible for malpractices and deterioration in academics. In such an environment the students are left to fend for themselves. Without training, without due guidance restoring to plagiarism seems an easy option to them. This candidate-guide nexus has been lampooned by our native satirist late Jaspal Bhatti (1955-2012) in his nationally cast teleserial *Ulta Pulta*, Upside Down.

19. IGNORANCE

Web 2.0 very easily facilitates seamless access to information through wikis, blogs, tweets, live chats, YouTube and other social media. Today's students freely associate with information: hunt it, discover it and share it without much thought of copyright. The information technology, especially the web, and its social networking applications have multiplied this contagious practice. Some do not know the law; others misinterpret it. To majority of the new students there is no clarity on the ethical use of outside information by giving proper credits to the original sources in accordance with academic norms. A Pakistani study finds that students do not fully understand what constitutes plagiarism (Nirmal Singh, 2017, 901). Training component has been utterly lacking till recently on the part of the institutions. Students and learning researchers are untrained, ignorant and innocent as they think information is free for all. Its use is unconditional. Stealing anything intangible is not a theft for them, at the first instance—as it would still remain intact with the original owner. They have been doing it since their schooldays: copying from their class mates, or even expecting the doting parents to do the homework for them, or buying readymade projects from commercial shops for submission. Selling customized school projects to students is a sprawling business. Tudoroiu (2017, 623-624) stating that in Europe Ph.D ghost writing has become an open and big business reveals its rates varying from Euros 100,000 to 3000, the average being 30,000 Euros. To this we can safely add that in India it is US $1000 at the most. It is no wonder that many of the ghost-writers undertake this work resorting to plagiarism!

20. OPEN ACCESS VS. PLAGIARISM

For the uninitiated information or knowledge is not any proprietary resource. Gomez (2015, 173) finds three reasons to use information in any way they like. They think it, being in the open access, is free for all; they have paid to access it, and technically it can be copied. But they are confused between "ownership, copyright, fair use, plagiarism or even the basic idea that one can possess or own copies of information or media and still not own the rights to such material." It is all due to ignorance of the nuances of the copyright laws, especially the digital rights. Lack of training in research and writing, including referencing and citing is another cause. Peter Suber (2012, 23-24) makes it clear:

> OA isn't an attempt to relax rules against plagiarism. All the public definitions of OA support author attribution, even construed as a restriction on users. All the major open licenses require author attribution. Moreover, plagiarism is typically punished by the plagiarist's institution rather than by courts, that is by social norms rather than by law. Hence, even when attribution is not legally required, plagiarism is still a punishable offence and no OA policy anywhere interferes with those punishments.

Another study (Baruhson-Arbib and Yaari, 2004) confirms that students plagiarizing from the electronic resources find it less serious an offence than copying from print sources. Suseela and Uma (2017,295) cite a study by Schrimsher et al. (2011) who found that a section of students at the Samford University, Alabama, USA, "felt that internet knowledge need not be cited for academic purposes as it is a public information and hence free from intellectual property rights..." Perzanowski and Schultz (2018) aptly and timely remind that laws for owning a printed book are quite different than 'purchasing' an e-book. Your ownership rights of digital documents are limited and conditional.

21. UNCHECKED ACTIVITY

There is no check on plagiarism when college and university graduates are given some small research projects as assignments. In India, most of the conference papers compiled by copying lock, stock and barrel are accepted by the organizers only to swell participation in the conference. Some such authors even get published in the proceedings. They feel exalted and proud and later seek career benefits for it. No wonder many papers on a given theme look alike. Teachers and editors look the other way and take a very lenient view on copying and plagiarism. Journal editors in India till recently have been very linear or even indifferent on the issue.

22. ILL EFFECTS

It is a theft, a robbery and a crime. It is unethical to thrive on the produce and property of others. It is anti-social and anti-creativity. Plagiarism whether committed intentionally or happened accidentally, or did due to ignorance will invite the same legal action. Law is law, and its ignorance is no excuse. A blogger has aptly written that "a single instance of plagiarism can result in dramatic consequences" (Rothschild, 2011). In this gold rush you are more likely to strike shame than any fortune. In 2011, a very popular German Defense Minister Dr. Karl-Theodor Zu Guttenberg after some persuasion admitted copying passages from the work of others in his doctoral dissertation. He had to resign from the job though the German President Angela Markel argued that this has no effect on his job as the defence minister. He was mocked as Zu Googleberg. [Not surprisingly, a Pakistani well circulated newspaper reproduced this story copied verbatim from its American counterpart without any acknowledgement]. Another German minister Ms. Annette Schavan had her Ph.D. degree withdrawn by the university for the same reasons putting Angela Markel's government to embarrassment (Diehl, Jörg & Oliver Trenkamp, 2013). Saif al-Islam Gaddafi's doctorate earned from the London School of Economics in 2008 has now been retracted (Ray, 13). It had already taken its toll in the resignation of the Director of the LSE. In 2012 more than a hundred Harvard students were forced to withdraw from the university course for committing academic frauds including plagiarism (Tribune, 2013a). In cases of plagiarism and fraud even jail sentences have been awarded in the US when deliberate and intentional misconduct is proved (Deccan Herald). Joachim Boldt formerly considered a leading German anesthesiologist, having fabricated research data in most of his papers, has been dismissed from job and can be awarded ten years imprisonment along with a huge fine. Russian authorities have revoked doctorates of eleven persons accused of plagiarizing their dissertations (Tribune, 2013c).

24. SOCIAL, ACADEMIC AND ECONOMIC EFFECTS

For upstart researchers plagiarism is a great impediment to learning systematically the art of methodical research and its communication. It is bane of learning which discourages creativity and promotes imitation instead of innovation. Creativity is curbed. Progress of knowledge is thwarted; fake and fraudulent culture reigns supreme. Its prevalence undermines the rule of law, justice and fair-play. Writers would feel insecure. After all, you do not build a house to be occupied by thieves and profiteers. It also causes loss of trust and reputation. A nation indulging in technological imitations instead of innovations remains socially backward and economically poor. "As a consequence," writes Kumar (2014) "India's global share in research output continues to be low though it increased from 1.1 percent to 3.6 percent over the last 10 years." And regretfully, India's retraction rate of published research papers which is 44 per lac is much higher than the world average of 17 (Tripathi, 2014, 287). Retracting a publication is like convicting its author. Its elder brother, piracy has caused the downfall of many a corporate empire. Financial losses to commerce and industry are unaccountable. The cost of detecting and proving plagiarism for the institutions may be heavy. Pandita and Singh (2018, 24) and Saha (2017, 2377-2378) have listed a few more of its inimical effects.

25. WAYS TO PREVENT IT

There should be holistic, multipronged preventive and curative efforts to curb this menace. These can be spelled as:

1. Sensitizing students and the public on the issue: Legal and moral education: Awareness of ethics of research and the intellectual property laws
2. Education and training to avoid plagiarism: Explain copyright laws; its fair use clause, especially about the misconception that the use of open access information is unconditional; teach information literacy, and citation norms

3. Warning and administrative measures: use of technology such as Turnitin to detect such cases; to all stakeholders give prior and stern warning of likely punishment for plagiarism and other such malpractices.

First of all, the students and wannabe researchers should be rigorously taught research methods in a formal way. Further at some level they should be specifically taught the ethics of research and writing. Concept, operation and implications of copyright laws especially the "fair use" clause must be fully explained. Fair use clause is nuanced, ticklish and ambiguous. Devil lies in its details. It is a moral crime and unethical at best to reuse someone's (intellectual) property thus depriving someone of its paternity control and due credit. It is a dishonest behaviour in a civil society "... every plagiarized word is a malicious crime...You owe it to other people to give them credit where it's due", they need to be told (Gilmore, 2009,35). Once you commit it you always live under the fear of being caught and facing its dire consequences even long after. Whether it is due to ignorance, or happens accidentally, the long hands of the law wields its own stick.

Students going in for final written examination are given statuary warning against the use of unfair means and its consequences thereof. Every researcher must be reminded of it at different stages of the progress of research. Only research guides, teachers and editors can help to nip this evil in the bud. Various manifestations of unfair means must be explicitly and unambiguously spelled and watched out for its indulgence. It is a legal obligation of the respective institutions failing which the students would plead innocent and blameless (Gilmore, 2009, 38-39). This is what the law courts say and practice. Nirmal Singh (2012, 901) cites Kose and Arikin (2011) who made an experimental study of a Turkish university students. They observed that plagiarism level of the group decreased considerably who had been informed about the plagiarism check software. Another experimental study in the USA by Youmans (2011) endorses that sensitized and alerted students indulged less in it compared to those uninformed on the matter. Similarly, Zafarghandi et al. (2012) in a study of Iranian higher degree students found that indulgence in plagiarism is inversely correlated with its awareness as an unethical and consequently academically damaging activity.

26. EDUCATION AND TRAINING

Its best remedy is the adequate training of learners in the art and science of research and its communication and presentation. Tell them there is much excitement and real joy in original research and writing. If writing is an agony, it is ecstasy too. Writing makes an exact man, wrote Francis Bacon (1561-1626). True creativity is exalting and empowering. Information literacy has one strong component on the ethical and effective use of information taken from outside sources. Information literacy courses must be made compulsory to instruct students and researchers to locate, validate, evaluate evidences, synthesize and apply information and draw sound inferences and conclusion. Shenton (2016, 77-79) rightly believes that training in IL has become more necessary in face of the digital deluge. Teach them with real life examples to use and cite outside information correctly and incorrectly. Prescott (2016, 152-162) demonstrates collaborative learning in groups and then followed by individual learning curb plagiarism by developments of learning effective writing among young students. There are many citation management application such as *Endnote, RefWorks, Zotero, Mendeley*, and many more. Universities and research centers must subscribe to some of them and teach the researchers their practical use. Mandated by the UGC now universities have started pre-Ph.D courses. But candidates are hardly adequately taught the theory and practice of writing research. Mostly that is an eyewash, (University Today, 2015). In such courses writing research reports with citation of sources should be taught intensively and practically. Writing and presenting research is as much important as doing it. Knowledge, by definition, takes birth only when it is communicated to bring it to the public domain. Tacit knowledge *per se* is no knowledge. Only the public domain knowledge can be audited, verified and authenticated to become a justified true belief (JTB).

27. TECHNOLOGICAL SOLUTIONS

Every technology, always being Janus faced, can be equally used and abused, simultaneously. The web has boosted the culture of plagiarism, some say. It is like believing the T.V. is killing our reading habits. Nobody is certain. A survey research finds non-significant difference in plagiarism from electronic and print sources (Nirmal Singh, 2017, 907). He (p.910) confirms that "No evidence was found that the internet has caused a significant increase in plagiarism level..." Information technology might have worked as a catalyst, but certainly has not created plagiarism which was equally present but little known in the pre-web era of five millennia. Information technology indeed easily, instantly and abundantly facilitates cut-and-paste from the worldwide resources, and at the same time it also helps very easily in detecting plagiarism. Suber (2012,24) aptly points out "... if making literature digital makes plagiarism easier to commit, then OA [open access] makes plagiarism easier to detect. Not all plagiarists are smart, but the smart ones will not steal from sources indexed in every search engine. In this sense, OA deters plagiarism". Thus the IT is a tool for as well as a deterrent against plagiarism. Search engines can be used easily with the help of keywords to trace the original source of a suspected piece. But that is informal or improvisation. There are specifically designed web-based software systems, both free and proprietary, to help detect copying. Some of the non-proprietary systems are: Copytracker, JPlag, eTBLAST, Plagiarismcheck, etc. Some of the commercial systems are CopyCatch Gold, iThenticate, Gotcha, Plagiserve, Copyscape, Plagiarismscanner, Turnitin, Urkund, and many more.

28. SIMILARITY SCORE

These machines give data on what is called similarity score. Latter is defined as the percentage of text in the uploaded document that matches with texts in other published documents or web pages. In other words, it is the degree of similarity between two independent texts. Similarity detection is very simple and mechanical. The suspected piece is run through the large full text database of the detecting system which gives details of overlapping pieces of the text. But such a system has many inherent limitations. First of all, it will not be able to detect

Plagiarism : An Introduction

patches of texts copied from sources not included in the master database. Then of course, it will not know anything copied from print sources. Cleverly paraphrased works also go undetected in such systems. In fact, similarity is of two kinds: Semantic and Syntactic. For semantic similarity it is easily befooled as it can only spot fixed expression, not the basic idea. Worst of all it, is not able to distinguish between properly cited and unethically copied patches of a text. Results of detection vary from software to software for more than one reason. At best, all such systems only provide data; interpretation and judgment is always of human intelligence - not of the robots with AI.

29. WHOSE RESPONSIBILITY?

Plagiarism is a deep-rooted, widespread and ever spreading malaise. Its treatment should be diagnostic, preventive and curative clinically and legally. It has to be tackled both at the public level as well as individually. There should be a national level campaign to make students, researchers, writers and artists aware of the laws and ethics of research and creativity. If the apex law court can formulate guidelines against ragging in academic institutions and sexual harassment of women at work places then why this offence has not caught the attention of the nation as a whole and its lawmakers and dispensers? Some voluntary organizations such as "The Society for Scientific Values" (http://www.scientificvalues.org), in India, work as 'whistle blowers' and watchdogs to make the public aware of the malpractices in scientific research in India. There must be some national level policy for academic researchers for which the UGC should provide clear and concrete guidelines. The UGC through the Inflibnet of late has woken to this burning issue. In 2012, it mandated higher education institutions to check every M.Phil./Ph.D. thesis for plagiarism. UGC has provided software for this purpose to the universities. Further every such dissertation awarded degree must be submitted electronically to the ShodhGanga program executed by the Inflibnet, Ahmedabad (ShodhGanga). Similar program is ShodhGangotri for proposal submitted for Ph.D. registration. In the draft Policy of 2107 UGC while declaring zero tolerance in doctoral research has recommended the constitution of Plagiarism Disciplinary Authority (PDA) and Academic Misconduct Panel (AMP) in every research institution to monitor research and curb any research misconduct in the bud (Dwedi and Tripathi, 2017). But this policy is for research degrees. Plagiarism by teachers and other academician has to be tackled locally though now the "UGC panel has prescribed a range of punishments from salary cuts to dismissals for various types of malpractices" (Deccan Herald, 2014). New UGC policy against plagiarism is pending approval of the Ministry of Human Resources which proposes punishment to teachers in proportion to their percentage of plagiarism in their publication. More than 60 % of similarity score in a work may even lead to dismissal, reports Neelam Pandey (2018). Copyright infringement is a cognizable offense punishable with fine or imprisonment or both (Thomas, 2010). It is so ingrained in the academic culture that it cannot be eliminated altogether, though can be curbed with systematic and sustained efforts. Here are some suggestions:

Every university and research centre must adopt a zero tolerance policy for unfair means in research and writing. In my own university not many years ago, a cool but gutsy vice-chancellor when reported by an examiner of plagiarism in a Ph.D. thesis, not only he refused the aspired degree to the candidate, but also terminated him from the job. Earlier such cases were taken lightly as minor infractions, and the offenders were never even indicted. Similarly, a science researcher when found guilty of stealing data was divested of his already awarded degree later. Rare is such determination. Not long ago, in a mother university of the north India, a renowned D.Sc. degree holder paleontologist, when found guilty (first by foreigners) of fabricating research (a case which shook the nation and the entire science world in late 1980s) managed to go almost scot-free. Nevertheless, he was discredited by the academic and research world at large and the case became a textbook example of frauds in research. It brought a bad name to the university and the country. Gorman (2008, 298-299) regrets that the universities adopt "avoidance measures rather than tackling the issue head-on" for fear of litigation. This is strikingly true of India where "Many institutions do not even investigate complaints of plagiarism and fraud for fear of inviting adverse attention and loss of reputation" (Deccan Herald, 2014). Such frauds which come to light are aplenty. A few are investigated, but those who are deservedly punished are still fewer. Even the watch dogs are selective and biased in favour of the bigwigs (University Today, 2013). Institutions must have zero-tolerance policy towards any form of plagiarism by any one—high or low.

30. RESPONSIBILITY OF EDITORS

Journal editors and other compilers must use machine and human scanners to detect for such cases in all submissions. Any contributor found guilty of plagiarism should be reprimanded, and blacklisted for some period. In case of post-publication detection or reporting of a plagiarised piece of research, a future issue must report to the readers about the plagiarised article with full information to the authorities or employer of the guilty author. And such paper(s) should be declared withdrawn. Such retracted papers should not be cited for substance, but only as cases of misconducts in research. This has also been suggested by the committee which investigated Fujii's case: "The committee recommended several measures aimed at reducing the incidence of misconduct. They include regular seminars to raise awareness of the ethical aspects of medical research and to clarify the responsibilities of lead authors and co-authors. The report also said scientific societies, along with journals and institutions, should be prepared to investigate when questions are raised about publications by their members" (Nosowitz, Dan, 2012). There should be a regularly updated shame list of retractions to deter future misconduct.

As librarians we have to protect the rights of both the creators/copyright holders and our users (IFLA 2012). In the US public schools the librarians usually double as copyright officers to guide and provide fair-use access to library materials (Johnson, 2016, 26-32). Every university must establish what we can call "Centre for Ethical Research" with active involvement of librarians, department of library and information science, director of research, copyright experts and Deans of Students' Welfare. What could be a better welfare of the students than to teach them lifelong academic ethics to enable them to live and work honourably. Prevention is always better than cure.

REFERENCES

Academics for Creative Reform (2015). "Position paper on higher education" *University Today* 35(11) 1 June 2015: 8.

Al-Khalili, Jim (2008) "It's time to herald the Arabic science that prefigured Darwin and Newton" *The Guardian* (In ted) 30 Jan 2008 https://www.theguardian.com/commentisfree/2008/jan/30/religion.world (Accessed on 15 May 2018)

Andrlik, Todd (2012) "How plagiarism made America" *Huff Post Media*. 8 Sept. 2012. Available at <http://www.huffingtonpost.com/todd-andrlik/how-plagiarism-made-ameri_b_1772782.html?ir=India&adsSiteOverride=in> (Accessed 25 February 2018)

Bartlett, Thomas (2009). "2 universities' plagiarism policies look a lot alike" *The Chronicle of Higher Education*, January 28. Also available at<http://chronicle.com/article/2-Universities-plagiarism/117408/?key=T2x2IQY%2BYiVLbC1mNTcVY2lRbXdoMEl6YHFOYytxbl5UFg%3D%3D> (Accessed 25 February2018)

Baruhson-Arbib, S, & Yaari, E. (2004) "Printed versus internet plagiarism: A study of students' plagiarism" *Int. Jl. of Info Ethics* 1(6):1-7.

Bennett, Andrew, & Royale, Nicholas (2015) *This thing called literature: Reading, thinking, writing.* London: Routledge, ix, 160p

Bhattacharjee, Yudhijit (2013) "The mind of a con man" *New York Times*, 28 April 2013.

Bloch, J. (2008) "Plagiarism across cultures: Is there a difference?" In: C. Eisner, & M. Vicinus, (Eds.) *Originality, Imitation, Plagiarism: Teaching Writing in the Digital Age* Ann Arbor: The University of Michigan Press, pp. 220–221

Clarke, Roger (2008) "Plagiarism by academics: more complex than it seems" available at <www.anu.edu.au/people/Roger.Clarke/SOS/Plag0602.htmi> (Accessed 25 February 2018)

Deccan Herald (2014) "Editorial: Deal strongly with plagiarists" *Deccan Herald*, dated 9 Oct. 2014, p.10

Diehl, Jörg, & Oliver Trenkamp (2013), "Plagiarism Accusations: Merkel's Education Minister Has Ph.D. Title Revoked", *Spiegel Online International*, available at <http://www.spiegel.de/international/germany/education-minister-schavan-has-ph-d-revoked-in-plagiarism-scandal-a-881707.html> (accessed on 28 February, 2018).

Dwivedi, Gayatri, &Tripathi, Manorma (2017). "Stemming misconduct in higher education and research" *Annals of Library and Info Studies* 64(4): 282-284

EFE (2016). "Spanish college head beleaguered by decades-spanning plagiarism scandal." https://www.efe.com/efe/english/varios/spanish-college-head-beleaguered-by-decades-spanning-plagiarism-scandal/50000269-3127169 (accessed on 14 May, 2018).

Eliot, T.S. (1921). *The Sacred wood.* London: Methuen & Co., 1969. p. 125

Gilmore, Barry (2009) *Plagiarism: a how-not-to guide for students.* Portsmouth, NH: Heinemann.

Gomez, Gabriel (2015) "Do easily copied internet media in the library lead to plagiarism?" In Naga, Moses, et al (eds) *Librarianship redefined in knowledge society.* Bhubaneshwar: Open Page India, pp. 163-177.

Gorman, Gary (2008). "Editorial: The plague of plagiarism in an online world". *Online Information Review* 32(3):297-301

Hauptman, Robert (2017) "The decline and fall of academe" *Jl. of Info Ethics* 26(1):3-4

IFLA (2012). "IFLA Code of Ethics for Librarians and other Information Workers" available at <http://www.ifla.org/news/ifla-code-of-ethics-for-librarians-and-other-information-workers-full-version> (accessed on 28 February, 2018).

Jones, Barbara M. (2009) *Protecting intellectual freedom in your academic library.* Chicago: ALA

Johnson, Wendell G. (2016) "Copyright updates for K-12 librarians" *Knowledge Quest* 45(2): 26-32

Kose, O, & Arikin, A. (2011) "Reducing plagiarism by using online software: an experimental study", *Contemporary

Online Language Education Jl 1: 122-129

Kovac, Miha (2008). *Never mind the Web: here comes the book.* Oxford, U.K: Chandos.

Kumar, Prakash (2014) "Lack of regulatory mechanism promotes plagiarism" *Deccan Herald* 28 Oct, 2014, p.11.

Lafollete, Marcel (2001) "Scientific misconduct" in *Encyclopedia of Library and Information Science*/ed. by Allen Kent, et al New York: Marcel Dekker, Vol. 68, Supplement 31, pp. 303-304.

Lall, S.B. (2009). "Plagiarism in research is the bane of state universities" *University Today* 29(10),15 May, p8.

Lampert, Lynn (2008) *Combating student plagiarism: an academic librarian's guide.* Oxford, UK: Chandos.

McIver, Stuart B (1994) *Dreamers, Schemers and Scalawags.* Sarasota, Florida: Pineapple Press.

Monippally, Mathukutty M., & Pawar, Badrinaryan Shanker (2010*) Academic writing: a guide for management students and researchers.* New Delhi: Response Books, pp.176-187.

Nirmal Singh (2017) "Level of awareness among veterinary students of GADVASU towards plagiarism: a case study" *The Electronic Library* 35(5): 899-915.

Nosowitz, Dan. (2012). "Japanese Anesthesiologist completely faked 172 papers" available at <http://www.popsci.com/science/article/2012-07/japanese-anesthesiologist-completely-faked-172-papers> (accessed on 28 February, 2018).

Pandey, Neelam (2028). "Plagiarism in research could cost degrees, jobs" *The Hindustan Times* 3 April,p.8

Pandita, Ramesh, & Singh, Shivendra (2018). *Information literacy and plagiarism.* New Delhi: CBS Publishers & Distributors. 189p. ISBN 9789386827135.

Perzanowski, Aaron and Schultz, Jason (2016) *The end of ownership: personal property in the digital age.* Cambridge, MA: MIT Press, ix, 249 p.

Prasad, Ranganath (2011) *Chillibreeze* Nov. 2011 available at http://www.chillibreeze.com/articles_various/Recognizing-Plagiarism.asp

Prescott, Lynda (2016) "Using collaboration to further academic integrity" *Open Learning* 31(1): 152-162

Ray, Ashis (2011). "Copycat PhD? Gaddafison under LSE lens" *Times of India* (New Delhi) 3 March 2011, p.13

Rediff.com. (2006, May,02) "Kaavya a victim of her own ambition" http://www.rediff.com/news/report/kaavya/20060502.htm (accessed on 15 june,2018)

Rothschild, David (2011) "5 common excuses for plagiarism" available at http://www.ithenticate.com/plagiarism-detection-blog/bid/52928/5-Common-Excuses-for-Plagiarism#.VXQjENKqqko (Accessed 7 April, 2018).

Saha, R. (2017) "Plagiarism, research publications and law" *Current Science*, 112(12), 25 June 2017: 2375-2378 doi: 10.18520/cs/v112/i12/2375-2378

Sarrdar, Ziauddin, & Loon, Borin Van (2002). *Introducing science*; ed by Richard Appignanesi. Cambridge: Icon Books. ISBN 978-1-840-46358-3

Satija, M. P. (1992) *S R Ranganathan and the method of science.* New Delhi: Aditya.

Satija, M.P. (2010), "What ails doctoral research in library and information science" *Desidoc Journal of Library and Information Technology* 35(5), Sept. 61-66.

Schrimsher, R.H; Northrup, L.A., & Alverson, S.P. (2011) "A survey of Samford University students regarding plagiarism and scientific misconduct" *Int. Jl. of Educational Integrity* 7:3-17

"Scientific plagiarism in India"/Society for Scientific Values http://en.wikipedia.org/wiki/scientific_plagiarismin_in_india (Accessed 25 February 2018). Lists many cases of plagiarism in India.

Shenton, Andrew K. (2016) "A multifaceted approach to school pupil's evaluation of information" *The School Librarian* 64(2): 77-79.

Shodhganga http://shodhganga.inflibnet.ac.in It is Indian repository of electronic theses and dissertations (ETDs) submitted to Indian universities and other degree awarding institutions. It is maintained by the Inflibnet,

Ahmedabad, an inter-university center of the UGC.

Silió, Elisa (2017). "El rector de los piagios se despide con críticas a la justicia "a golpe de titular"" *El País*. https://politica.elpais.com/politica/2017/01/27/actualidad/1485557863_745427.html (accessed on 14 May, 2018).

Suber, Peter (2012) *Open access*. Cambridge,Mass.: MIT Press.

Suseela, V.J., &Uma,V (2017) " Plagiarism and academic dishonesty: study of users' perception in the University of Hyderabad" *SRELS Jl of Info Mgmt* 54(6): 293-301

Taylor, F. Kraupl (1965) "Cryptomnesia and plagiarism" *British Journal of Psychiatry* 3: 1111-1118.

Thomas, Zakir (2010) "Copyright act of 1957: an overview" In Satija, M.P. ed.: *Librarians as knowledge workers in the 21st century*. New Delhi: Ess Ess Publications, pp. 165-182.

Times of India (2011) "With 17,000 incidents, cheating on rise in UK universities" *Times of India* (New Delhi) 7 March 2011, p.11.

Tudoroiu, Theodor (2017) "No, prime minister: Ph.D plagiarism of high level public officials" *European Review* 25(4):623-641

University Grants Commission (2010/2016).Minimum Qualifications for Appointment of Teachers and other Academic Staff in Universities and Colleges and Measures for the Maintenance of standards in Higher Education 2010) Regulation 2016 (Forth Amendment) (No. F. 1-2/2016 (PS/Amendment) dt. 11.07.2016) Available at: https://www.ugc.ac.in/pdfnews/8377302_English.pdf (accessed on 5 April 2018)

University Grants Commission (2016) "Minimum standards and procedure for award of M.PHIL./PH.D degrees: Regulations, 2016" . Available at: https://www.ugc.ac.in/pdfnews/4952604_UGC-(M.PHIL.-PH.D-DEGREES)-REGULATIONS,-2016.pdf

Wikipedia contributors, (2018a) "Plagiarism," Wikipedia, The Free Encyclopedia, https://en.wikipedia.org/w/index.php?title=Plagiarism&oldid=840060936 (accessed May 9, 2018).

Wikipedia contributors, (2018b) " Cryptomnesia," Wikipedia, The Free Encyclopedia, https://en.wikipedia.org/w/index.php?title=Plagiarism&oldid=840060936 (accessed May 9, 2018).

Youmans, R.J. (2011) "Does adoption of plagiarism detection software in higher education reduce plagiarism?" *Studies in Higher Education* 36: 749-761.

Zafarghandhi, A.M.; Khosshroo, F., & Barkat, B. (2012) "An investigation of Iranian EFL students' perception of plagiarism" *Int. Jl. of Educational Integrity* 8: 69-8

2

The Problem of Plagiarism in Retractions of Published Articles

John M. Budd

1. INTRODUCTION

About four decades ago an Iraqi medical student named Elias Alsabti, who claimed to be a member of the Jordanian Royal family, gained positions in medical schools in the United States. Over a rather short period of time, Alsabti plagiarized approximately 50 to 60 papers. At times he apparently took papers from colleagues' mailboxes, copied them, and submitted them to lower-tier journals, where they were published. His prolific productivity was noticed and an exploration into the papers discovered the plagiarism. His reputation was utterly ruined (see Broad & Wade, 1982). The case of Alsabti might seem almost comical, but his plagiarized works made their way into the scholarly record.

The Alsabti case is extreme, especially when it comes to blatant plagiarism. That said, plagiarism is one of the prominent instances of scientific misconduct and is almost universally recognized as a cause for grave concern. For example, Wager and colleagues (2010) recount guidelines emanating from the Committee on Professional Ethics (COPE), a global group, representing thousands of institutional members (including most prominent biomedical journals). In referring to retractions, they (2010) state, "Retractions are also used to alert readers to cases of redundant publications (i.e. when authors present the same data in several publications), plagiarism, and failure to disclose a major competing interest likely to influence interpretations or recommendations" (p. 64). The authors continue, "Retracted articles should not be removed from printed copies of the journal (e.g. in libraries) not from electronic archives but their retracted status should be indicated as clearly as possible" (p. 65).

Retraction is an important phenomenon in all of the sciences, but is an especially pertinent action in the biomedical literature. Retraction is a serious action, taken when egregious misconduct is admitted to or shown to be the case. Editors may make statements of the retraction of a published work and, sometimes, third parties (including attorneys) may retract a paper. The most common (and, some say, the most serious) cause for retraction is the fabrication or falsification of data. Some researchers may create data from whole cloth, without the collection of legitimate data for legitimate analysis. Less common than fabrication of data, but still serious, is blatant plagiarism of substantial content from a previously published article. Similar to plagiarism is the duplication of publication—an author or set of authors publishing essentially the same paper in more than one journal. Retraction is not exactly a common occurrence; retractions represent a small portion of the published body of work; Van Steirteghem and Williams (2011) note that "The retraction of an article and hence its effective (but not physical) 'removal' from the scientific record is thankfully an uncommon occurrence; indeed there have only been three cases in the history of [*Human Reproduction*]" (p. 1940).

One other particular should be noted at this point in the discussion. Misconduct—and error, for that matter—is not always detected immediately. In an earlier study of the retractions of some works by John Darsee it was mentioned,

> Many of the cases of admitted or discovered fraud and misconduct were slow in being resolved. One possible explanation for the difficulty of discovery is the lack of replication of studies. It may be that actual or perceived rewards and funding do not work in favor of replication. The advancement of work in science does sometimes lead to the rooting out of invalid work through the process of building, or attempting to build, upon previous work (Kochan & Budd, 1992, p. 489).

In fact, it could take years before problems are discovered and papers retracted (although the time has shortened in recent years). It should be noted that, with the publicity and notoriety of misconduct, the time from publication to discovery has shortened in recent years.

2. RETRACTION TO PUBLISHED WORKS AND THE PLACE OF PLAGIARISM

As is evident, retraction of a published article can take place for any of a number of reasons, including plagiarism. Sometimes retraction can have notoriety attached to it. One of the most infamous instances concerned the claims of Andrew Wakefield, who purported to connect the measles, mumps, and rubella (MMR) vaccine to autism. His work was, after some time and controversy, retracted after originally being published in the medical journal, the *Lancet*. Eggerton (2010) notes, "In fact, as Britain's General Medical Council ruled in January, the children that Wakefield studied were carefully selected and some of Wakefield's research was funded by lawyers acting for parents who were involved in lawsuits against vaccine manufacturers. The council found Wakefield had acted unethically and had shown "callous disregard" for the children in his study, upon whom invasive tests were performed" (p. E199). Not only were Wakefield's results invalid, his method stretched the bounds of ethics.

For up-to-date information about retractions making news, the Retraction Watch (http://retractionwatch.com) blog may be the most complete single source. One their recent stories states,

The University of Illinois at Chicago (UIC) permanently suspended all research activities for a child psychiatrist years ago following an inquiry into her work, Retraction Watch has learned. In 2015, a UIC spokesperson told us the university had suspended Mani Pavuluri's clinical research in 2013, after a child in one of her studies had been hospitalized for exhibiting an increase in irritability and aggression. This prompted the university to launch a misconduct probe, and send letters to approximately 350 families of children participating in the research, notifying them of what happened. Now, a spokesperson has informed us that after the institution concluded its probe, it suspended her research "indefinitely" (accessed 12 April 2018).

Such action is rare, and is prompted only by extreme circumstances, including the mistreatment and maltreatment of human subjects. The fact that Pavuluri's work involved children was likely to be a factor in UIC's decision.

There has been an abundant amount written on retractions; it is neither possible nor desirable to cover all (or even a bare majority) of the articles that have been published. Mention of some selected items will serve the present purpose. For example, quite a lot of work has been done relating to examination of the growth in the number of retractions over time. Steen, Casadevall, and Fang (2013) summarize their analysis in simple and straightforward terms:

- The rate of publication has increased with a concomitant increase in the rate of retraction.
- Editors are retracting articles significantly faster now than in the past.
- The reasons for retraction have expanded to include plagiarism and duplicate publication (p. 6).

More will be said about the last observation shortly. Steen and colleagues provide sound evidence for each of their conclusions; attention to their work is highly recommended. In a similar vein, Loadsman and McCulloch (2017) editorialize that, "As a result of the recent cases, editors and other interested parties are now becoming far more aware of the potential for dishonest authors to submit fraudulent data. This follows a similar increase in awareness of the problem of plagiarism, and many editors are now taking a closer look at aspects like data distributions as well as textual similarity" (p. 931). Two things should be noted when it comes both to the existence of retractions and the increase in their numbers: (1) as far back as the 1970s people like John Darsee and Stephen Breuning noted that the pressure to publish in order to get promoted and earn tenure as well as to gain external research funding was a factor in their actions, and (2) there is the fact that data fabrication and plagiarism are easy and tempting. Never mind that the risk of such behavior is high and the penalties considerable; academia is no different from other walks of life in having some dishonest members inhabiting it.

In work on reasons for retraction done by Budd, Coble, and Abritis (2016), there is considerable detail as to why items do get retracted on the literature. While fabrication and falsification is a major category of reason for retraction, plagiarism appears quite frequently.

The body of literature in question covers the years 2010 through 2014. Of the 2,491 (in itself a large number, and approximately 65% were due to demonstrated or presumed misconduct) papers that were retracted during that period, 257 were removed explicitly for plagiarism (10.3%). The number and percentage may not appear to be great, but it is substantial. Budd, Coble, and Abritis (2016) quote from one statement of retraction: "This article has been retracted at the request of the editor as the authors have plagiarised part of several papers that had already appeared in several journals" (p. 6). There is another reason for retraction that, it would seem, is closed related to plagiarism—in particular, self-plagiarism. A total of 465 articles were retracted because of deliberate duplication of publication. That is, an author or set of authors willfully republished the same work in a different journal from the first appearance of the paper. These retractions are 18.7% of the overall number of retractions. When the two categories are combined, it becomes evident that more than a quarter of the retractions were due to deliberate copying of material. There is no doubt whatever that plagiarism is a serious problem. In the future, software that can detect plagiarism may lead to even more articles being retracted, or more papers that are submitted for possible publication not being published in the first place. For example, paper submitted to journals published by the University of Toronto Press can be subjected to a plagiarism check upon the beginning of the review process.

It should be noted that, while retraction is a formal action that should remove a paper from being considered valid, it is only one indicator that things can go wrong in the process of research and publication. In an important study of psychologists, John, Loewenstein, and Prelec (2012) found that substantial numbers of practicing psychologists and psychology researchers admit to falling short when it comes to ethical action. The numbers exceed those of retractions, which suggests that many more published articles could be retracted if the misprisions were found out. The authors (2012) conclude,

> the most egregious practices in our survey (e.g., falsifying data) appear to be less common than the relatively less questionable ones (e.g., failing to report all of a study's conditions). It is easier to generate a post hoc explanation to justify removing nuisance data points than it is to justify outright data falsification, even though both practices produce similar consequences. Given the findings of our study, it comes as no surprise that many researchers have expressed concerns over failures to replicate published results (p. 531).

3. CITATIONS TO RETRACTED PUBLICATIONS

My interest in scientific misconduct began when I watched an episode of the Public Broadcasting System (PBS) series, *Nova*. The title of the episode was, "Do Scientists Cheat," which aired in 1988. In that episode several cases were presented, including that of John Darsee, who was found to have fabricated the work reported in some of his publications. He was investigated by Harvard University and Emory University, with whom he was affiliated. A number of his publications were retracted, and the process and outcome of retraction of published work was explained. As a younger investigator I was fascinated by the possibility that an article that had been published in a journal could be retracted. I was also appalled that individuals would be guilty of such misconduct, but heartened that there is the possibility of discovery of the misconduct.

An outcome of pondering the phenomenon of misconduct—in all its forms, including plagiarism—was wondering if retracted articles continued to be cited post-retraction. A colleague and I decided to tackle the thorny problem of John Darsee's work, since there was evidence of retracted papers. The National Institutes of Health (NIH) in the US established the Office of Research Integrity (ORI). When questions about Darsee's work came to light, the NIH formed a committee to investigate the charges. In the aftermath of the NIH committee investigation, Woolf opined,

> The damage caused by falsification is not related merely to its frequency. Even if cases of fraud are infrequent, fraud has an impact on the research of other working scientists, on the reliability of the published literature, and on public attitudes that are vital to the future support of research. Greater understanding of these effects would allow the scientific community to take steps to minimize the adverse consequences within science and to reassure the public that its trust is warranted (pp. 12-13).

It is the effects that have concerned me over the years. As far back as the Darsee incident I began to wonder if the retracted works continued to be cited. Citations to Darsee's work from 1982-1990 were examined and 298 citations formed the basis for the investigation. Of those citations, only 5.7% acknowledged the misconduct. The vast majority of the citations, 85.9%, were classified as positive citations (see Kochan and Budd, 1992).

Colleagues and I have examined retractions and subsequent citations on later occasions. An examination of papers indexed in the MEDLINE database from 1966 through 1997 revealed that the 235 retracted articled were cited more than 2,000 times (Budd, et al., 1999). Again, very few of the citing works refer to the fact that what they were citing (usually as constituting valid work) had been retracted. A later work extended the examination to retractions appearing in MEDLINE to 2009. A total of 58% of those retractions were found to be due to misconduct. In keeping with the previous studies, few citing papers made mention of the retractions and most were positive (Budd, Coble, & Anderson, 2011). Most recently, as is mentioned above, citations to articles retracted from 2001-2005 were analyzed with regard to citations. An astonishing 6,341 citations were located (of which, 1,424 could not be studied for a variety of reasons). Only 4.15% acknowledged retraction. The remainder were either tacit (brief mention without negative implication) or substantive (treatment of the retracted articles as having something useful to contribute to the citing authors' works—and this category constituted 15.6% of the citations) (Budd, Coble, & Abritis, 2016).

The concern about citations to problematic work is not new, even though the active concern does not appear to lessen the frequency of citations to retracted works. For example, Thomasson and Stanley (1955) warned against citing just anything years ago:

The uncritical citation of disputed data by a writer, whether it be deliberate or not, is a serious matter. Of course, knowingly propagandizing unsubstantiated claims is particularly abhorrent, but just as many naive students may be swayed by unfounded assertions presented by a writer who is unaware of the criticisms. Buried in scholarly journals, critical notes are increasingly likely to be overlooked with the passage of time, while the studies to which they pertain, having been reported more widely, are apt to be rediscovered (pp. 610-611).

4. DISCUSSION

It is evident from this brief presentation that scientific misconduct represents a distinct cause for concern in the scientific community. The presence of fabrication, falsification, plagiarism, and duplication of content inhibit progress and the growth of knowledge. When researchers have to spend their time, not only search for work that has been reported, but also vetting the published work for legitimacy, there is less time to conduct the benchtop science that is the genuine goal of the inquiry. That said, the degree of citation of retracted work suggests that some scientists are less than diligent with the vetting process. "An implication for the literature of science and for scholarly literatures in general is that researchers need to take care how they retrieve information. The literature that has been cited in the past cannot be accepted uncritically. It must be treated with the same scrutiny that is accorded to new research; the fact that it is older and can be traced through the citations of former works is not necessarily evidence of its accuracy, validity, or honesty" (Kochan & Budd, 1992, p. 492). The extent of retractions and citations to retracted works should give scientists pause and should become integrated into the educational processes for graduate students who will ultimately be practicing researchers in many fields. Ethics instruction is a must for all curricula.

Why does misconduct take place? There are hints provided above with the specific cases of John Darsee and Stephen Breuning. Are these excuses the extent of the rationales that might be possible? "My own judgment is that scientists are most vulnerable to the temptation to fake data when (1) they are under career pressure to produce something; (2) they think they know what the answer is and feel that going to the trouble of taking the data is superfluous; and (3) they think they are somewhat protected because experiments are not expected to be precisely reproducible. This last point applies more to the biomedical sciences than to the physical sciences" (Goodstein, 1991, p. 513). The work of John and colleagues (2012) demonstrates quite clearly that the problem is not, by any means, limited to the biomedical or the physical sciences. A specific instance also help emphasize the reality that many disciplines are affected by misconduct. Budd (2013) reports on the case of Diederik Stapel, a social psychologist who had a large number of his publications retracted. His work came under scrutiny from multiple institutions and he was removed from his faculty position. The psychological sciences—whose work also carries profound implications for clinical practice—seem to be problematic as well. Retraction Watch reports also that hundreds of papers published by journals under the Institute of Electrical and Electronics Engineers (IEEE) umbrella have been retracted for a variety of reasons (see https://retractionwatch.com/2014/02/24/springer-ieee-withdrawing-more-than-120-nonsense-papers/). It is evident now that almost all scientific disciplines are vulnerable to misconduct.

When it comes specifically to plagiarism, there can be particular concern that extends beyond "traditional" textual plagiarism. "Authors must be aware that using published photos, images, art work, and tables without written permission is also plagiarism. . . . Plagiarism is basically intended to deceive the reader" (Juyal, et al., 2015, p. 77, 78). This statement implies that the humanities and the social sciences could also fall prey to plagiarized materials. Images are also essential communicative apparatus in almost all scientific disciplines. Imagine someone using duplicated electron microscopy in various published articles. The implications of plagiarizing images are extremely serious—as serious as textual plagiarizing (and self-plagiarizing) data. Again, the intention appears to be to deceive readers. Consequences can be apparent to anyone concerned with the ethics of practice and the purported cumulative aspect of science.

Can there be excuses for such actions as plagiarism? Fang and Casadevall (2011) answer this question: "Some have suggested that plagiarism is a culturally relative concept, which is less likely to be regarded as an unethical practice by some scientists in non-Western countries or those belonging to the younger generation. However, we do not share this view. Scientists must be explorers, and it is best if they do not precisely follow the wagon ruts left by their predecessors but instead strike out on their own paths, using their own words. The (American Society for Microbiology) journals strictly prohibit plagiarism and self-plagiarism" (p. 3857). Once again, education comes to the fore; young practitioners in all fields must be taught the ethical imperatives of their disciplines. Of course, this outcome necessitates that senior practitioners apply those ethical imperatives in their own work.

Fang and Casadevall (2011) address another matter; the correction and possible republication of problematic work: "In theory, a retracted article may be revised and republished, with removal of any erroneous, falsified, fabricated, or plagiarized content. In practice, however, authors of a retracted article may find republication to be a challenge. If misconduct has taken place, the authors may be subject to sanctions from the journal, which prohibit resubmission within a specified time frame" (p. 3856). Generally speaking, retraction because of unavoidable error tends to carry no negative repercussions for authors. If however, misconduct is indeed the cause for about 65% of retractions, there can indeed be consequences for the authors. And, as can be expected, multiple offenses tend to gain notoriety for the authors and editors are aware of the actions of the authors. There is no substitute for a finely tuned ethical sense among researchers everywhere; there is no excuse for deliberate commissions and omissions. Plagiarism, as we have seen, is a common form of commission and it should be treated as no less serious than any other causes for the retraction of published works.

REFERENCES

Broad, W., & Wade, N. (1982). *Betrayers of the truth: Fraud and deceit in the halls of science.* New York: Simon and Schuster.

Budd, J. M. (2013). The Stapel case: An object lesson in research integrity and its lapses. *Synesis: A Journal of Science, Technology, Ethics, and Policy* 4, G47-53.

Budd, J. M., Coble, Z., & Abritis, A. (2016).An investigation of retracted articles in the biomedical literature. *Proceedings of the 79th ASIS&T Annual Meeting,* assist.org/files/meetings/am16/proceedings/openpage16.html.

Budd, J. M., Coble, Z. C., & Anderson, K. M. (2011). Retracted publications in biomedicine: Cause for concern. Philadelphia, PA: Association of College & Research Libraries National Conference, http://www.ala.org/acrl/sites/ala.org/acrl/files/content/conferences/confsandpreconfs/national/2011/papers/retracted_publicatio.pdf.

Budd, J. M., Sievert, M. E., Schultz, T. R., & Scoville, C. (1999). Effects of article retraction on citation and practice in medicine. *Bulletin of the Medical Library Association* 87(4), 437-43.

Eggerton, L. (2010). Lancet retracts 12-year-old article linking autism to MMR vaccines. *CMAJ: Canadian Medical Association Journal* 182, E199-E200.

Fang, F. C. & Casadevall, A. (2011). Retracted science and the retraction index. *Infection and Immunity* 79(10), 3855-59.

Goodstein, D. (1991). Scientific fraud. *American Scholar* 60, 505-515.

John, L. K., Loewenstein, G., & Prelec, D. (2012). Measuring the prevalence of questionable research practices with incentives for truth telling. *Psychological Science* 23(5), 524-32.

Juyal, D., Thawani, V., & Thaledi, S. (2015). Plagiarism: An egregious form of misconduct. *North American Journal of Medical Science* 7(2), 77-80.

Kochan, C. A. & Budd, J. M. (1992). The persistence of fraud in the literature: The Darsee case. *Journal of the American Society for Information Science* 43(7), 488-93.

Loadsman, J. A. & McCulloch, T. J. (2017). Widening the search for suspect data—is the flood of retractions about to become a tsunami? *Anaesthesia* 72, 931-35.

Steen, R. G., Casadevall, A., & Fang, F. C. (2013). Why has the number of scientific retractions increased? *PLOS One* 8(7), 1-9.

Thomasson, P. & Stanley, J. C. (1955). Uncritical citation of criticized data. *Science* 121, 610-11.

Van Steirteghem, A. & Williams, A. C. (2011). Plagiarism, retraction and the future. *Human Reproduction* 26(8), 1940.

Wager, E., Barbour, V., Yentis, S. & Kleinart, S. (2010). Retractions: Guidance from the Committee on Professional Ethics (COPE). *Obesity Reviews* 11, 64-66.

Woolf, P. K. (1986). Pressure to publish and fraud in science. *Annals of Internal Medicine* 104, 254-56.

3

Plagiarism and High Politics: A Threat to Democracy

Theodor Tudoroiu[1]

1. INTRODUCTION

This chapter discusses a frequently ignored category of plagiarism that, at first view, might seem marginal. It concerns the doctoral plagiarism of high-ranking politicians, an issue that - unlike other forms of plagiarism explored in this book - involves a relatively small number of individuals and might therefore be assessed as an irrelevant case of infringement of academic rules. The following sections use a public office definition of corruption in order to show that, in fact, by shattering citizens' confidence in and respect for political class, political parties, state institutions, and rule of law, academic plagiarism of high-ranking politicians intertwines with and enforces the most serious democratic failures in their respective countries. As such, this specific type of plagiarism goes far beyond academia. It represents a direct, aggressive, and effective threat against democracy itself.

In early March 2011 it was revealed that the 2008 London School of Economics and Political Science (LSE) Ph.D. dissertation of Saif al-Islam Gaddafi, the second son and heir apparent to Libya's then dictator, was plagiarised. The LSE had 'been aware of the plagiarism claims *for some years*' (Sherwin, 2011; emphasis added) and 'was investigating' these claims (Vasagar & Sweney, 2011). At the same time, however, it had accepted a £1.5m donation from the Gaddafi International Charity and Development Foundation run by the new Ph.D. and used the £300,000 it had already received to finance a North Africa research program. Saif Gaddafi's

---

[1] The author acknowledges that this chapter has heavily drawn upon material from within Tudoroiu, Theodor. (2017). No, Prime Minister: PhD Plagiarism of High Level Public Officials. *European Review*, 25(4), 623-641, © Academia Europaea 2017, published by Cambridge University Press, reproduced with permission.

The author is grateful to Amanda Ramlogan and Mélissa E. Bryant for their useful suggestions.

academic adviser visited Libya in December 2009 on behalf of, and sponsored by, that program (*Ibid.*, 2011). Moreover, the prestigious Oxford University Press had signed a contract to publish the dissertation as a book after having it reviewed by 'scholars of the highest international standing' who acknowledged 'its scholarly quality and the author's credibility'. Incidentally, the author had offered to purchase 20,000 copies of the book (Baram, 2011).

This example stands out mainly due to the exaggerated amount of money involved in buying the degree. In Germany, a ghostwriter might charge as much as •100,000 for an excellent doctoral dissertation, but an average one in history does not cost more than •20,000 (Vitzthum, 2008). In Portugal, the price might be as high as •50,000 (Ameijeiras, 2009) while in Russia it can run anywhere between •3,000 and •35,000 (Klußmann, 2007). Yet, the largest and most accessible market remains the English language one. I contacted the first specialised company I found on Google and they offered to write for me a 200-page doctoral dissertation analysing Venezuela's relations with the US during and after President Chavez's tenure for only US$2,695, which I could pay in three installments (the price was also available in British Pounds). No more than ten days were needed to complete the high quality text.

Ph.D. plagiarism has become a huge business whose advantages, as Gaddafi's example shows, are not ignored by innovative politicians. At times, they come from the Global South. Like the Libyan strongman, the Iranian President, Hassan Rouhani, plagiarised parts of the doctoral dissertation he defended at the Glasgow Caledonian University in the 1990s (McElroy & Vahdat, 2013). Still, the idea of assessing such cases as a nefarious export of Middle Eastern political corruption to the immaculate Western academia has very little to do with reality. In recent decades, numerous Western politicians have been involved in known cases of Ph.D. plagiarism. Scandals ensued but, counter-intuitively, in certain cases public support for the faulty politician actually *increased* during the scandal. This chapter uses four case studies of high level European officials - two Presidents, one Prime Minister, and one Defense Minister - who plagiarised their Ph.D. dissertations in order to scrutinise this specific type of corruption and to assess its consequences for the host country. Plagiarism and the surprisingly large variation in the public reactions to it are analysed in relation to the general levels of corruption and democracy in the four European countries.

The chapter is structured as follows. The next section constructs the theoretical framework of the analysis. The following four sections present the case studies. Their findings are analysed in the final section.

2. PLAGIARISM AND CORRUPTION

In Ancient Rome, the *plagiarius* was a kidnapper. In fact, Martial did use the word to designate 'literary theft' (Marsh, 2007, 31). Yet, most Romans associated it with individuals who either stole slaves or stole and sold freemen into slavery, a crime repressed by a specific law, *Lex Fabia de plagiariis*. Similarly, ancient French law called *plagiat* (the present French word for plagiarism) the theft of children (Treppoz, 1894: 29). Around 1600, the latter's place was finally taken by 'children of the brain' and plagiarism acquired its present signification

(Weber-Wulff, 2014, 3). Charles Nodier defined it in 1812 as '*l'action de tirer d'un auteur (...) le fonds d'un ouvrage d'invention, le développement d'une notion nouvelle ou encore mal connue, le tour d'une ou de plusieurs pensées*' - in other words, misappropriating the essence, innovative notions, or thoughts of another author's work (Nodier, 1812, 17; for more recent but not necessarily different definitions and for their discussion see Marsh, 2007, 31-38). Plagiarism is a complex concept but, as suggested by the very title of Domenico Giuriati's 1903 *Il plagio. Furti letterari, artistici e musicali* (Giuriati, 1903), it has been frequently perceived as a form of theft and was associated with this phenomenon's negative moral, ethical, and legal connotations. Interestingly, certain scholars have adopted a different stance. Nick Groom has claimed that plagiarism, an 'aesthetic activity', can be used to subvert the 'dominant work ethic' he associated with creating value through the expenditure of labour and capital in production - a perspective reminiscent of Marx-inspired anti-capitalist activism. Similarly, Marilyn Randall identified plagiarism as a guerrilla tactic for feminist authorship (Marsh, 2007, 35). More relevant for this chapter, another atypical interpretation of plagiarism has to be mentioned that concerns a cultural dimension. Ranamukalage Chandrasoma, Celia M. Thompson, and Alistair Pennycook have analysed plagiarism as an act of resistance to the dominant forms of rhetoric that contradict non-Western students' epistemological traditions. Alistair Pennycook has further developed this idea, speaking of plagiarism as resistance against the more general imposition of alien rules (Bloch, 2008, 220, 221). China, with its tradition of collectivism, is frequently used as an example of a culture that devalues the Western concept of authorship while placing a greater value on imitation, which is encouraged and valued in the creation of new intellectual property. This results in a different system of values concerning plagiarism. Accordingly, it was claimed that 'Chinese students neither understand Western concepts nor feel that such plagiarism is an unacceptable practice' (*Ibid.*, 219-220). During the mid-2000s, a debate opposed one of the supporters of this view, Colin Sowden, to Dilin Liu and Le Ha Phan who rejected 'culturally stereotyped views of plagiarism' and claimed that in fact plagiarism is perceived as immoral in the Chinese and Vietnamese cultures. Yet, the latter authors' views seem to be contradicted by a growing body of empirical research (for details see Lei & Hu, 2014, 41-42). A somehow similar situation might concern parts of sub-Saharan Africa. Calixthe Beyala, a Cameroon-born French novelist, was convicted of plagiarism in 1996 and later faced a number of similar accusations. In her defence, she vigorously invoked the African 'oral tradition which falls outside of Western literary practice, thereby placing herself, like an outlaw, outside of, and thus unanswerable to, the law' (Angelo, 2013, 193). This is an important aspect that was instrumental in the selection of this chapter's case studies. In order to avoid distortions due to Chinese-type major cultural differences, the four case studies are European. Differences of perception clearly exist among Germans, Hungarians, Romanians, and Russians, and they are scrutinised in this chapter. However, at least at the level of principle, nobody in the four countries rejects the Western negative perception of plagiarism.

All this concerns plagiarism in general. This chapter preoccupies itself with academic plagiarism, which 'is a crime against academy. It deceives readers, hurts plagiarised authors, and gets the plagiarist undeserved benefits' (Bouville, 2008, 311). Academic plagiarism has been variously defined as reflecting the plagiarist's failure to meet academic standards; as an infringement of academic informal practices that undermines trust between teacher and student; as a practice that breaches ethical standards; and as a violation of intellectual property (Rosamond, 2002, 168). However, it is obvious that there is a significant difference between an undergraduate student who cheats when submitting a term paper and a Prime Minister that uses a plagiarised Ph.D. to enhance his personal prestige and electoral support. The former commits a 'crime against academy'. The latter discredits academia but also shatters the citizens' confidence in and respect for political class, state institutions, and rule of law. Moreover, it is likely that it was his position and influence that contributed decisively to his dissertation not being appropriately scrutinised by the jury. Consequently, this chapter is based on the idea that the specific case of high level politicians who plagiarised their Ph.D. dissertations is best analysed as a case of corruption.

The latter has variously been defined from public office-centred, public interest-centred, and market perspectives (Philp, 1997: 440). Within the first approach, Joseph S. Nye identified corruption as

> behaviour which deviates from the normal duties of a public role because of private-regarding (family, close private clique), pecuniary or status gains; or violates rules against the exercise of certain types of private-regarding influence (quoted in Gardiner, 2007, 26).

This includes bribery, nepotism, and misappropriation. Critically, it represents a deviation from the Weberian legal-rational type of authority that the state apparatus of a modern democracy is supposed to incarnate. Officials are expected to serve the state and subordinate their personal relationships with citizens to legal mechanisms centred on the office, not the incumbent (Lovell, 2005, 71). This is clearly incompatible with any type of private gain. Consequently, the office-based approach is a useful instrument for the study of corruption in executive agencies, which includes the cases of corrupt high-level officials. In a democracy, executive functions are associated with the idea of a collective agent that people can trust to execute collective decisions. Therefore, such functions imply public trust: the government is the trustee and executor of collective purposes. Corruption - and especially corruption of individuals at the top of the executive - involves violating that trust. This undermines democracy, leads to inefficient and ineffective government, and creates an atmosphere marked by differential treatment and arbitrary actions (Warren, 2015: 49). These effects have been emphasised in the case of more traditional forms of corruption, but they also are present when Ph.D. plagiarism of high-level officials is concerned. The case studies presented in the four next sections will show how serious the consequences of this phenomenon are especially in the case of weak, unconsolidated democracies.

3. GERMANY'S MINISTER OF DEFENCE: BARON CUT-AND-PASTE

3.1. Being a Doktor in Germany

In Germany, earning a doctoral degree is perceived as reaching a higher social status. The title is displayed on passports and identity cards (something also done only in Austria and the Czech Republic) (Wolf, 2013, 178) and is engraved on a brass plate on the door at home and in office. At work, new doctors normally get promoted to higher levels of responsibility (Weber-Wulff, 2014, 23), which on average implies a •20,000 increase of the annual salary. Consequently, the number of Ph.D. degrees rose from 15,500 in 1986 to 27,000 in 2011 (Müller, 2013), one of the highest in Europe. In 2010, doctoral degrees represented no less than 7% of all university degrees awarded in Germany (Wolf, 2013, 178). One of the negative consequences was the increasing temptation of taking advantage of fast track 'copy-and-paste' methods.

3.2. The 'German Kennedy'

In February 2011 it was revealed that the 2007 doctoral dissertation on the stages of development of constitutions in the US and the European Union defended at the University of Bayreuth (and published as a book in 2009) by the German Minister of Defence contained plagiarism on 94% of the pages. Almost two-thirds of the lines of the text were plagiarised, using mainly Internet sources. In only two weeks, the university withdrew the doctoral degree (Weber-Wulff, 2014, 29-30).

The Minister was the 39-year-old Baron Karl-Theodor Maria Nikolaus Johann Jacob Philipp Franz Sylvester Joseph von und zu Guttenberg (soon nicknamed Baron Cut-and-Paste, Zu Copyberg or Zu Googleberg by German media). Owner of a family castle in Bavaria and married to a stylish TV presenter, Countess Stephanie von Bismarck, he was voted 'Germany's most popular politician' in 2009. They were frequently referred to as the 'German Kennedy' and his 'Jackie O'. Described as the 'shooting star' of conservatism in Germany, the charismatic baron was a member of the Christian Social Union, the Bavarian sister party of the chancellor's Christian Democrats, and was viewed by some as the future German leader (Pidd, 2011; *BBC*, 6 May 2011). Good-looking, with a 'charming personality', he succeeded in achieving a rock-star status. His party even played an AC/DC track when he took to the stage. He became known during his brief tenure as Minister of Economy and especially after 2009 as Defence Minister. He 'fearlessly' visited German troops in Afghanistan, wearing a flight suit and desert boots. His pictures were published by all gossip magazines (Pidd, 2011; Weber-Wulff, 2014: 31).

When the plagiarism was revealed, zu Guttenberg first described the allegations as 'absurd'. He then stated he would only stop using the Ph.D. title during the investigation. Then he admitted having 'made serious errors', but not plagiarising (Pidd, 2011). However, after two weeks of daily attacks by media and outraged intellectuals (51,500 German academics signed a letter objecting to his continued role in the government) and the Parliament's Speaker describing his actions as 'a nail in the coffin for confidence in democracy', he finally decided to resign (*BBC*, 1 March 2011).

Out of the four case studies, this was by far the quickest resignation. However, it surprisingly was accompanied by ethically doubtful statements and developments within the German political system and society at large. During the entire crisis, Chancellor Angela Merkel supported zu Guttenberg, stating that she had 'appointed him as defence minister, not as an academic assistant' (Pidd, 2011). After the resignation, she told reporters she was confident that she 'would have the opportunity to work with Guttenberg again in the future' (*BBC*, 1 March 2011; Pidd, 2011). The Christian Social Union party also was willing to see a return of the former minister to frontline politics (*BBC*, 6 May 2011). Among the citizens, many supporters of the charming baron were angry that 'such a trivial offense' led to scandal: 'Surely everyone had cheated in school?' (Weber-Wulff, 2014, 30). Astonishingly, opinion polls showed that support for zu Guttenberg actually *increased* from 68% to 73% during the crisis, when he was accused of being 'a liar and an impostor' (*Le Monde*, 23 February 2011).

3.3. German Politicians' Favourite Sport

Ironically, Norbert Lammert, the Parliament's Speaker who harshly criticised zu Guttenberg, became himself the object of a Ph.D. plagiarism scandal in 2013 (Müller, 2013). He thus joined a rather numerous group of high level copy-and-paste German politicians who had their doctoral degrees questioned. Education Minister Annette Schavan, Vice-President of the European Parliament Silvana Koch-Mehrin, European Parliament member Jorgo Chatzimarkakis, Member of the Parliament of Baden-Wuerttemberg Matthias Pröfrock, as well as Member of the Parliament of Berlin and chair of the CDU parliamentary group Florian Graf lost their Ph.D. degrees because of plagiarism. Former Minister of Education and Cultural Affairs of Saxony Roland Wöller and the Minister of Education and Cultural Affairs of Lower Saxony Bernd Althusmann were in a somewhat similar situation, but they were able to keep their doctoral degrees despite having 'violated principles of good academic practice' (Wolf, 2013, 181; *BBC*, 5 February 2013). The Minister of Cooperation and Development Gerd Müller has also been accused of Ph.D. plagiarism (Müller, 2014). One only can be shocked by such a situation in a country well known for the quality of its academic system and for its lack of corruption.

3.4. Corruption in Germany

In fact, the latter aspect is associated more with the Cold War Western Germany than with the present country. The tradition of Prussian correctness dominant until the early 1980s has been increasingly challenged. Leaving aside corruption in the construction industry, Germany mainly has been affected by high-level corruption that involves a small number of senior figures. Typically, they do not take profit personally from corruption acts. In most cases, these concern the illegal financing of political parties (McKay, 2003, 54-55). Yet, this phenomenon has been so important and visible that today Germany is placed in the category of 'somewhat corrupt' countries (Bull & Newell, 2003, 51). Transparency International still ranks it 12th out of 174 states (Transparency International, 2014), but 65% of Germans feel that their political parties are corrupt or extremely corrupt; 48% believe the same thing about the Parliament (Transparency

International, 2013). Consequently, the public image of the German political system and political class has been seriously damaged (McKay, 2003, 63).

The German education system is better perceived: only 19% of the citizens believe that it is corrupt or extremely corrupt (Transparency International, 2013). However, zu Guttenberg and his fellow plagiarists have succeeded in constructing a corruption bridge between this sector and the already damaged image of German politicians. The plagiarism scandals affected both education and politics in a deeply negative way because they questioned the behaviour in public office and the moral status of key representatives of the German democracy. Even more disturbing are the hopes of both his party and the Chancellor that the former Defence Minister would eventually return to politics; and the shocking fact that public support for him actually increased during the scandal. This goes far beyond the human weakness of some isolated individuals. Indeed, it seems to be indicative of what a prominent political commentator described as 'the degeneration of political culture' in Germany (McKay, 2003, 63).

4. HUNGARY'S PRESIDENT: THE PLAGIARIST OLYMPIC CHAMPION

In January 2012, the Hungarian business weekly HVG revealed that the country's President, Pàl Schmitt, had plagiarised the 1992 doctoral dissertation on the modern Olympic Games he had defended in 1992 at the University of Physical Education, now part of Semmelweis University in Budapest (Facsar, 2012). Out of 215 pages, 16 were carbon copied from the translation of a 1991 German text by Klaus Heinemann while other 180 contained text as well as tables and charts taken from a 1987 book by a Bulgarian author, Nikolay Gueorguiev (Karasz, 2012). Only 18 pages were written by Schmitt himself (*Corriere della Sera*, 2 April 2012).

Schmitt won gold medals for fencing at the Olympic Games of 1968 and 1972. During the 1980s, he became a communist State Secretary for Sports (Beliczay, 2012) and since 1983 he has been a member of the International Olympic Committee. Showing 'a chameleon-like ability to adapt to changing circumstances', after the fall of communism he made a swift turn right (*The Economist*, 7 April 2012). He became the head of the Hungarian Olympic Committee in 1990, was vice president of the International Olympic Committee between 1995 and 1999 (Beliczay, 2012), served as a Member of the European Parliament for the ruling right-wing Fidesz party, and was elected President in the summer of 2010 by the Hungarian Parliament due to the support of the Fidesz Prime Minister, Viktor Orbán, whose coalition holds a two-thirds majority (Karasz, 2012). The presidency is mainly ceremonial, but allows the incumbent to challenge legislative acts. Schmitt did not, despite the fact that some of the 365 laws fast-tracked by Fidesz in its first 18 months in office were criticised by the European Commission and the Council of Europe (*The Economist*, 7 April 2012).

The news of plagiarism provoked outrage in social media. The President spoke of 'unfounded allegations' (Karasz, 2012) and claimed that texts were identical because he had worked with Gueorguiev and Heinemann, something the former's daughter and the latter strongly denied. A Semmelweis University commission investigated the case and concluded that there was no plagiarism, but that university's Senate decided otherwise and on 29 March withdrew

Schmitt's doctoral degree. The President stated on public radio that the decision was illegal (*Corriere della Sera*, 2 April 2012). He would nevertheless accept it, 'but this has got nothing to do with me being a president' (Facsar, 2012). He also declared that he was willing to rewrite the dissertation. In Parliament, opposition Socialists and Greens had initiated an impeachment procedure but it was rejected by Orban's two-thirds majority (*La Repubblica*, 2 April 2012). Yet, the growing scandal resulted in 'Hungary's most polarising political drama since riots in the autumn of 2006' (*The Economist*, 7 April 2012). After days of political turmoil (Karasz, 2012), on 2 April 2012 a large demonstration was held in front of the President's official residence in Buda. Socialists, Greens, civil society activists, but also members of the extreme right Jobbik party and of Fidesz demanded Schmitt's resignation (*La Repubblica*, 2 April 2012). The President claimed once more that 'his conscience was clear' (Facsar, 2012) but, in order to avoid dividing 'his beloved nation', accepted to resign (Karasz, 2012).

4.1. 'Una profonda crisi morale'

Very differently from the German case, the Schmitt plagiarism is singular among Hungary's high-level politicians. Unfortunately, something more is very different between the two countries. Since Viktor Orbán's conservative coalition came to power in 2010, its nationalist policies have initiated a 'U-turn and the systematic destruction of the fundamental institutions of democracy' (Kornai, 2015, 35). The clearly authoritarian trend was acknowledged by the Prime Minister himself, who in a July 2014 speech stated overtly that he was constructing an 'illiberal state' (Freedom House, 2015b). Hungary still is a semi-consolidated democracy (Freedom House, 2015b), but one of the consequences of the present evolution is that, due to the 'pyramid-like hierarchy' headed by Orban, most investigations of corruption cases involving people close to Fidesz are never completed (Kornai, 2015, 35-36). Political corruption scandals not resulting in retribution have contributed to raising the percentage of citizens feeling that institutions are corrupt or extremely corrupt to 68% in the case of political parties and to 56% in that of the Parliament. For the education system the figure is identical with that of Germany, 19% (Transparency International, 2013), but as many as 49% of young people aged 15 to 29 believe that corruption exists in educational institutions (Burai, 2013, 375). However, their main concern is closer to politics: like the rest of the population, they are acutely aware of the fact that one of the most corrupted areas of Hungarian public life is party and campaign financing, and this results in 'a loss of faith in the country's democratic values and processes' (*Ibid.*, 374).

The reaction to the President's Ph.D. plagiarism is part of this larger context. The Fidesz-controlled parliamentary majority had no ethical problem in openly supporting the plagiarist by voting against the impeachment motion. When asked about Schmitt's possible resignation, Orban stated that 'nobody except him can decide' (Facsar, 2012), as if this were a purely private matter. This is illustrative, as an Italian newspaper put it, of Hungary's 'profound moral crisis' (*La Repubblica*, 2 April 2012) and of the serious perils threatening its democracy.

5. ROMANIA'S PRIME MINISTER: THE NON-RESIGNING PLAGIARIST

Undoubtedly, the Romanian Prime Minister Victor Ponta provides the most colourful - and outrageous - case study. In June 2012, *Nature* revealed that more than half of his 2003 University of Bucharest dissertation on the functioning of the International Criminal Court (also published as a book in 2004) consisted of duplicated text. At that time, Ponta was Secretary of State in the government of Adrian Năstase, who also was his doctoral supervisor (Schiermeier, 2012a). Ironically, Năstase was eventually jailed twice for corruption. The university's ethics commission found plagiarised elements on 115 out of the 297 pages of the dissertation and confirmed charges. The state agency responsible for investigating Ph.D. plagiarism, the Romanian National Council for the Attestation of University Titles (NCAUT), concluded that 85 pages had been entirely copied and pasted. But Prime Minister Ponta *disbanded* NCAUT during its very meeting examining his own case. Instead, he decided that the National Ethics Council (NEC) be in charge of Ph.D. investigations, too (Schiermeier, 2012b). Incidentally, earlier that month all NEC members had been replaced with protégés of the Prime Minister one day before the Council examined the plagiarism charges against Ponta's Minister of Education, Ioan Mang, who was of course cleared of any wrongdoing with respect to the eight academic papers he had copy-and-pasted (Pantazi, 2014). Predictably, the NEC also cleared the Prime Minister, whose only minor mistake was found to be the omission of references in footnotes. Ponta claimed that all charges were part of a vicious political campaign launched against him by then Romanian President Traian Băsescu, and therefore there was no reason for him to resign (Schiermeier, 2012b). Because the entire society (but not Ponta's Social Democratic Party, the more or less reformed former Communist Party) was outraged, the Prime Minister stated, at first, that he would stop using the Ph.D. degree; and, later, that he would relinquish it. This was not legally possible, but in December 2014 he passed a Government Emergency Ordinance modifying the National Education Law to allow holders of academic degrees relinquish them without providing any explanation (Prisacariu, 2015). Yet, he also took the case to court in order to prove his innocence. The most recent episode of this still unfinished legal dispute is the July 2017 decision of the Court of Appeal in support of the plagiarism charges (Vulcan, 2017).

The Prime Minister was hardly the only high ranking Romanian politician in this situation. The Vice-Prime Minister and July 2015 Acting Prime Minster Gabriel Oprea also plagiarised his 2001 doctoral dissertation but when this was revealed in 2015 he was promptly cleared by the NEC. Moreover, as a professor at the Romanian Police Academy he supervised at least six plagiarised doctoral dissertations (Sercan, 2015). Ponta's Minister of Economy, Mihai Tudose, inserted in his 2010 Ph.D. dissertation about 50 pages from a dissertation defended one year earlier by a police superintendent. Interestingly, the latter told journalists that he was contacted by Tudose, to whom he simply 'sold the copyright as [he would have done with] any other merchandise' (Garaiman, 2015).

Overall, 33% of Romanians perceive their education system as corrupt or highly corrupt (Transparency International, 2013: 119), but it is believed that the most serious situation is precisely that of plagiarised doctoral dissertations. The Group for Social Dialogue, one of the most prestigious Romanian civic organisations, even held a highly publicised debate titled 'Plagiarism as State of the Nation' in September 2015 during which Andrei Ple'u, a university professor and former Minister of Culture, suggested that all holders of legitimate Ph.D. relinquish them until people like Ponta admit their fault and resign (Pantazi, 2015).

Of course, the latter scenario is highly unlikely because Ph.D. plagiarism is only one of the forms taken by the pervasive corruption of the Romanian political elite, a social group that Tom Gallagher characterised as 'cynical and amoral to an extent unusual even in the former Soviet satellites' (Gallagher, 2009, 6). A Stratfor report spoke of its 'culture of corruption' (Friedman, 2014). Accordingly, Transparency International's Corruption Perceptions Index ranks Romania 69th out of 174 countries (Transparency International, 2014) while 76% of its citizens believe that political parties are corrupt or extremely corrupt. In the case of the Parliament, the percentage is 68% (Transparency International, 2013). The lack of a clean political party led to large scale electoral apathy and further encouraged mass emigration to Western Europe. In turn, this allowed Ponta to lead in the opinion polls and to receive the largest number of votes at the first round of the November 2014 presidential election despite his plagiarism. Yet, on his orders, polling stations at embassies and consulates abroad prevented a large part of the four million Romanians outside the country from voting. This backfired, as live TV coverage of large queues, protests, and riots at consulates made first round abstentionists back home vote against Ponta at the second round. He lost the presidential election, but stated that there was no reason for him to resign from his position of Prime Minister (*BBC*, 17 November 2014). He repeated this statement when he was formally indicted for corruption in September 2015. However, in November 2015, 64 teenagers died in a nightclub fire ultimately due to corrupt practices resulting in the non-respect of anti-fire legislation. This triggered a 20,000-strong protest demonstration asking for Ponta's resignation and for the departure of corrupt politicians from public life. Finally, the plagiarist stepped down (Tran, 2015; *Pro TV*, 14 March 2016).

Overall, the Romanian Prime Minister's case is relevant for the way high level political corruption that includes an academic component compromises trust in politicians and politics, induces electoral apathy, and severely distorts democratic processes in a country whose semi-consolidated democracy (Freedom House, 2015c) remains weak and vulnerable.

6. RUSSIA'S PRESIDENT: THE PLAGIARIST TSAR

In March 2006, two fellows at the Brookings Institute in Washington DC, Clifford Gaddy and Igor Danchenko, discovered that more than 16 pages of the 20-page theoretical chapter of Vladimir Putin's 1997 dissertation entitled 'Strategic Planning of the Reproduction of the Mineral Resource Base of a Region under Conditions of the Formation of Market Relations' as well as six diagrams and tables had been taken almost word-for-word from the 1978 classic US management textbook *Strategic Planning and Policy* by William R. King and David I. Cleland that had been translated to Russian during the early 1990s by a KGB-related institute. There were no quotation marks and the source was not mentioned (Khvostunova, 2013; *The Washington*

Times, 24 March 2006; Shuster, 2013). The 218-page dissertation earned Putin a Candidate of Science degree, which is the lower stage of Russia's two-level Ph.D. structure (the higher one being that of Doctor of Science) (Knyazev, 2004, 155), from the St. Petersburg Mining Institute (*The Washington Times*, 24 March 2006).

Putin started his doctoral program after becoming an assistant to the rector of Leningrad State University responsible for international relations in 1990. Soon he also became an adviser and then the Chairman of the Committee for International Relations at the St. Petersburg City Hall. From 1994 he concurrently held the position of Deputy Chairman of the St. Petersburg City Government. In 1996, he moved to Moscow to become Deputy Chief of the Presidential Property Management Directorate and in March 1997 he was appointed Deputy Chief of Staff of the Presidential Executive Office and Chief of Main Control Directorate (Putin, 2015). Despite his busy timetable, he returned to St. Petersburg to defend his dissertation at the Mining Institute. The latter's rector, Vladimir Litvinenko, eventually became Putin's adviser on energy policy and a potential candidate for the position of head of the huge state-owned Gazprom energy company (*The Washington Times*, 24 March 2006).

There is a strong suspicion that the dissertation was in fact written by a ghostwriter. To quote a senior associate at the American Foreign Policy Council, E. Wayne Merry, 'it's probably an open question whether Putin even read his dissertation until shortly before he had to defend it' (*Ibid.*). In any case, it was extremely difficult to obtain a copy of the text, which suggests that the Russian President had tried to prevent a possible plagiarism scandal.

Yet, there was no scandal when plagiarism was revealed - and nobody has ever mentioned resignation. Putin himself 'never dignified the reports with any comment' (Khvostunova, 2013). State TV stations did not mention them. The independent *Kommersant Vlast* weekly did publish a cover story, but one that gave equal weight to plagiarism accusations and to pro-Putin statements by Vladimir Litvinenko. Except for some Russian bloggers, 'everybody knows about [the plagiarism], but nobody wants to bring it up' (Shuster, 2013). This is not different from what is happening in the case of other prominent Russian 'dubious doctorate-holders' such as Defence Minister Sergei Shoigu, Minister of Culture Vladimir Medinsky, former Defence Minister Boris Gryzlov, former Minister for Regional Development Vladimir Yakovlev, President of Chechnya Ramzan Kadyrov, and the nationalist party leader and Member of Parliament, Vladimir Zhirinovsky. All faced plagiarism accusations which have never been investigated (Osipian, 2010, 262; Shuster, 2013). Moreover, no less than 349 of the 612 members of the two chambers of the Russian Parliament hold doctoral degrees - normally in fields different from that of their first degree - despite the fact that only 76 are involved in research and teaching (Osipian, 2010, 268-271).

Some Western scholars claim that this situation should be perceived in the post-Soviet context that preserves the tradition of communist strongmen with doubtful academic credentials: 'it was really quite common for an up-and-coming apparatchik to get a ghostwritten work done to obtain a degree' (E. Wayne Merry quoted by *The Washington Times*, 24 March 2006). The problem, however, goes beyond the politicians. 72% of Russians believe that their education system is corrupt or extremely corrupt (Transparency International, 2013). Bribes are paid to school and university officials to have children admitted to the institution of their choice and to professors in order to get good grades (Raiklin, 2009, 413). At Ph.D. level, 'ready-made dissertations' are for sale for prices between •3,000 and •35,000 (Klußmann, 2007). A study identified no less than 169 legally registered, tax-paying firms offering doctoral ghostwriting (Osipian, 2010, 267). In fact, this is only one of the many dimensions of the corruption that permeates all aspects of the life of the Russian people 'from cradle to grave' (Raiklin, 2009, 412) and is believed to comprise no less than 20 percent of the country's GNP (Shlapentokh, 2013, 151). Unsurprisingly, Russia is ranked by Transparency International 136th out of 174 in its Corruption Perceptions Index (Transparency International, 2014).

Still, pervasive corruption including wide scale Ph.D. plagiarism is not the only reason that prevented the ignition of a scandal in Putin's case. The Russian plagiarist is also a dictator. He has succeeded in creating a consolidated authoritarian regime characterised by a 6.46 Freedom House Democracy Score (7 represents the worst possible level). Besides almost completely eliminating citizens' political rights and civil liberties, the President and his inner circle use their power to direct greater personal wealth to themselves and to loyal oligarchs. They only pursue corruption charges selectively against political rivals (Freedom House, 2015d). Accordingly, 83% of the citizens believe that the Putin-controlled Parliament is corrupt or extremely corrupt (Transparency International, 2013).

Consequently, the President's plagiarism, the surprising lack of an associated scandal, and the absolute absence of the idea of resignation illuminate two different but closely related aspects. On the one hand, as a dictator, Putin cannot be indicted because he is above the law; and cannot be criticised overtly because he controls mass media and the society at large. On the other hand, his act of academic-related corruption is legitimated by the culture of corruption his regime has helped develop. All this is proof of a distortion of ethical values totally incompatible not only with democracy but also with many of the key characteristics of a modern polity, be it democratic or not.

7. ANALYSIS AND CONCLUSION

In purely academic terms, it might be noted that the four case studies are associated with a somehow bizarre second-level plagiarism. All plagiarists seem to have paid ghostwriters to do their work; in turn, the ghostwriters plagiarised printed or Internet sources. At least in the case of zu Guttenberg, this was a total surprise for the customer, who certainly questioned ghostwriter's ethical position.

Less amusingly, the academic corruption of politicians perverts the educational purposes of research and scholarship and has a deeply negative influence on the processes of doctoral education and fundamental research (Osipian, 2010, 263). Negative consequences, however, go beyond these fields. It was found that there is a clear correlation between long term investment in education and decrease in corruption. These two elements tend to reinforce each other, thus creating a virtuous circle. One of the main causes is believed to reside in the fact that education builds self-reinforcing social trust, which helps curb corruption. Yet, if the expansion of high-quality public education is perceived as being implemented in corrupt ways - a situation greatly favoured by highly visible academic scandals such as those presented in previous sections - education ceases to be a generator of public trust and its anti-corruption effects dissipate (Transparency International, 2013, 6-7).

This suggests that, despite its incontestable importance, the academic dimension of the four case studies is dwarfed by the socio-political one. It is clear that this is public office corruption, with prominent members of the executive obtaining private gain by deviating from the normal duties of their public role: 'they convert their authority into personal assets'. Private gain is represented by enhanced reputation resulting in increased electoral support (Osipian, 2010, 265). The deviation from normal duties was present, first, within the act of plagiarism itself: members of the jury did not appropriately scrutinise the dissertations most likely because of candidates' positions and influence. At least in the case of Putin, the rector of the university eventually was rewarded with a political position. Second, political instruments at the disposal of the plagiarists were used abusively to prevent legal retribution. Ponta changed legislation to clear himself of charges, Schmitt used his allies' parliamentary majority to prevent impeachment, and Putin simply took advantage of his dictatorial immunity to legal investigation.

This raises serious ethical questions. One might be tempted to blame the four as individuals, but the numerous similar cases of slightly lower-level politicians suggest that this is not the right approach. In fact, 'choices about moral decisions and actions are not made solely by the individual'. Research indicates that ethical motivation and action depend on the continual creation of personal moral identity through social conditioning and socialisation (Hatcher, 2011, 148-149). This brings the discussion to the critical point represented by political culture and democratic practices. The survival of the Soviet tradition of communist officials using ghostwriters in order to acquire undeserved academic degrees (*The Washington Times*, 24 March 2006) as well as a background of generalised corruption turned Putin's plagiarism into something close to an uncanny 'normality'. Răzvan Theodorescu, a member of the Romanian Academy of Sciences and a former Minister of Culture in the government led by Ponta's corrupt doctoral supervisor, Adrian Năstase, provided an explicit acknowledgement of differences he perceived between Western and Eastern Europe:

> If Ponta is guilty [of plagiarism], he should apologise. In other parts of Europe, for something like this you resign. In Europe's borderlands, where we are located, you only apologise. You apologise and go on (Ruscior, 2012).

These differences are well illustrated by the large variation among the four case studies in what Martin Bull and James Newell called 'the degree of scandal', something determined mainly by different expectations amongst the national public (Bull and Newell, 2003, 235) which in turn relate to political culture and associated democratic practices. The overall repertoire of the four politicians' unethical acts included the plagiarism itself; rewarding of members of the Ph.D. jury with political positions; trying to make the dissertation unavailable to public scrutiny; lying in public statements; arbitrarily changing laws and modifying the membership of institutions involved in the investigation of academic fraud; using the protection of political allies to prevent impeachment; refusing to resign despite large scale public protest; and controlling mass media in order to prevent the ignition of a scandal. Yet, there were huge differences between what zu Guttenberg and Putin were willing and able to choose from this repertoire. As shown in Table 1, there is a clear parallel between the four politicians' attitude toward resignation (taken as the most relevant indicator of their behaviour), the public reaction to their plagiarism, and the levels of corruption and democracy in the four countries. More democracy is associated with a better civil society rating, less corruption, stronger outrage resulting in public protest, and quicker resignation of the plagiarist. Dictatorship and weak civil society mean more corruption, no scandal, and no talk about resignation. Each of the four case studies is representative for a different stage on the continuum between the two extremes.

Table 1. Democracy Indicators and Perception of Corruption for Germany, Hungary, Romania, and Russia; Public Reaction to and Behaviour of Case Study Ph.D. Plagiarist Officials

Country	Freedom House Regime Classification (2015)	Freedom House Democracy Score (2015) (1=best, 7=worst)	Freedom House Civil Society Rating (2015) (1=best, 7=worst)	Corruption Perceptions Index Score (2014) (100=least corrupt; 0=most corrupt)	Corruption Perceptions Index Country Rank (2014) (out of 174)	Political parties perceived as corrupt/ extremely corrupt (2013)	Parliament/ legislature perceived as corrupt/ extremely corrupt (2013)	Education systems perceived as corrupt/ extremely corrupt (2013)	Position of case study corrupt official	Public reaction to official's Ph.D. plagiarism	Delay before resignation
Germany	Consolidated Democracy	-	-	79	12	65%	48%	19%	Min. of Defence	public outrage; over 50,000 academics signed letter of protest; 5% increase in popularity	2 weeks
Hungary	Semi-Consolidated Democracy	3.18	2.50	54	47	68%	56%	19%	President	public outrage; large protest demonstration	3 months
Romania	Semi-Consolidated Democracy	3.46	2.50	43	69	76%	68%	33%	Prime-Minister	public outrage	refused to resign; changed legislation to clear himself of misconduct
Russia	Consolidated Authoritarian	6.46	6.00	27	136	77%	83%	72%	President	none	resignation never mentioned by anyone

Sources: Transparency International, 2013, 2014; Freedom House, 2015a, 2015b, 2015c, 2015d

It is hardly a new finding that 'the development of corrupt practices is more likely where cultural attitudes are not strongly supportive of a country's democratic institutions (...) or of democracy more generally', a situation that in Central and Eastern Europe has resulted in most corrupt countries being at the same time the least democratic ones (Bull & Newell, 2003, 236). Data presented in Table 1 can be used to support the idea that the less democracy-more corruption relationship is one of mutual enforcement. On the one hand, the corruption-related acts of the four plagiarists were more outrageous in countries where less democracy meant that they were less exposed to legal retribution. On the other hand, those corruption-related acts further weakened democracy. Indeed - and perhaps surprisingly - the key element emphasised by the four case studies is how perfectly academic plagiarism of high-ranking politicians intertwines with and enforces the most serious democratic failures in their respective countries. In the German consolidated democracy, zu Guttenberg's acts and attitude have been considered indicative of and contributing to that country's 'degeneration of political culture' (McKay, 2003, 63), something that support from his party and the Chancellor as well as the increase in his popularity after plagiarism was revealed seem to confirm. In Hungary, Schmitt could and did defy public outrage for three months because of the political support provided by his nationalist allies, whose authoritarian trends he had supported through his acts as a President. In Romania, Ponta mocked justice and democracy under the protection of a 'culture of corruption' he helped develop during his entire tenure and that made them ineffective if not irrelevant. In Russia, Putin did not even face a scandal because of the marriage between dictatorship and rampant corruption he had successfully promoted. This is to say that this specific type of plagiarism goes far beyond academia. It is a socio-political phenomenon that affects the entire polity and society. Because it combines with and significantly enhances other anti-democratic processes, it represents a direct, aggressive, and effective threat against democracy.

Consequences cannot be ignored even in the case of a consolidated democracy such as Germany. They are, however, much more destructive in the post-communist states, where they include the significant diminishing of citizens' confidence in and respect for political class, political parties, state institutions, and rule of law. This results in declining levels of public trust, electoral apathy, and disaffection with politics (Bull & Newell, 2003, 244). Support for democracy is deeply undermined and citizens might start to contemplate alternative, undemocratic forms of government. This is particularly dangerous in post-communist Central and Eastern Europe, where democratic consolidation is increasingly challenged by populist and authoritarian temptations, and in the Commonwealth of Independent States, where democratisation remains a remote and probably unrealistic prospect.

REFERENCES

Ameijeiras, Patricia. (2009). La venta de tesis doctorales, con precios en torno a los 50.000 euros, se convierte en un lucrativo negocio en Portugal. *El Periodico de Catalunya*, 28 May. http://www.elperiodico.com/es/noticias/mundo/venta-tesis-doctorales-con-precios-torno-los-50000-euros-convierte-lucrativo-negocio-portugal-96113

Angelo, Adrienne. (2013). Crime and Punishment: Calixthe Beyala's Manic Writing of Femme nue, femme noire. In Frédérique Chevillot and Colette Trout (eds.) *Rebelles et criminelles chez les écrivaines d'expression française*, Amsterdam. New York: Rodopi, 183-198.

Baram, Marcus. (2011). Gaddafi Son's Book Plans Dropped Amid Plagiarism Charges. *Huffington Post*, 2 March.

http://www.huffingtonpost.com/2011/03/02/gaddafi-son-book-plagiarism-charge_n_830540.html

BBC, 1 March 2011. German Defence Minister Guttenberg Resigns over Thesis. http://www.bbc.com/news/world-europe-12608083

BBC, 6 May 2011. Germany's Guttenberg "Deliberately" Plagiarised. http://www.bbc.co.uk/news/world-europe-13310042

BBC, 5 February 2013. German Minister Annette Schavan Stripped of Doctorate. http://www.bbc.co.uk/news/world-europe-21347510

BBC, 17 November 2014. Romania Election Surprise as Klaus Iohannis Wins Presidency. http://www.bbc.com/news/world-europe-30076716

Beliczay, Laszlo. (2012). Hungary President Pal Schmitt Quits in Plagiarism Scandal. *NBC*, 2 April. http://worldnews.nbcnews.com/_news/2012/04/02/10981451-hungary-president-pal-schmitt-quits-in-plagiarism-scandal?lite

Bloch, Joel. (2008). Plagiarism across Cultures: Is There a Difference?. In Caroline Eisner and Martha Vicinus (eds.) *Originality, Imitation, Plagiarism: Teaching Writing in the Digital Age*. Ann Arbor: The University of Michigan Press, 219-230.

Bouville, Mathieu. (2008). Plagiarism: Words and Ideas. *Science and Engineering Ethics*, 14(3), 311-322.

Bull, Martin J., and James L. Newell (eds.). (2003) *Corruption in Contemporary Politics*, New York: Palgrave Macmillan.

Burai, Petra. (2013). Youth, Integrity and Anti-Corruption Work in Hungary. In Transparency International (ed.) *Global Corruption Report: Education*. New York, N.Y.: Routledge, 372-376. http://www.transparency.org/whatwedo/publication/global_corruption_report_education.

Corriere della Sera, 2 April 2012. Il presidente Schmitt copia la tesi di dottorato. http://www.corriere.it/esteri/12_aprile_02/scandalo-tesi-copiata-ungheria_08e323ac-7cbc-11e1-b9fa-a64885bf1529.shtml

Facsar, Fanny. (2012). Hungary's President Quits over Alleged Plagiarism', *CNN*, 2 April. http://edition.cnn.com/2012/04/02/world/europe/hungary-president-resigns/index.html

Freedom House. (2015a). Freedom in the World 2015. https://freedomhouse.org/report/freedom-world/freedom-world-2015#.VivlwcuFMpw

Freedom House. (2015b). Nations in Transit 2015-Hungary. https://freedomhouse.org/report/nations-transit/2015/hungary

Freedom House. (2015b). Nations in Transit 2015-Hungary. https://freedomhouse.org/report/nations-transit/2015/hungary

Freedom House. (2015c). Nations in Transit 2015-Romania. https://freedomhouse.org/report/nations-transit/2015/romania

Freedom House. (2015d). Nations in Transit 2015-Russia. https://freedomhouse.org/report/nations-transit/2015/russia

Friedman, George. (2014). Borderlands: First Moves in Romania. *Stratfor*, 27 May. https://www.stratfor.com/weekly/borderlands-first-moves-romania

Gallagher, Tom. (2009). *Romania and the European Union. How the Weak Vanquished the Strong*. Manchester: Manchester University Press.

Garaiman, Roxana. (2015). Ministrul Economiei îngroaşă rândurile demnitarilor acuzaţi de plagiat. *Adevărul*, 19 August. http://adevarul.ro/news/eveniment/ministrul-economiei-ingroasa-randurile-demnitarilor-acuzati-plagiat-1_55d4b526f5eaafab2cba790e/index.html

Gardiner, John A. (2007). Defining Corruption. In Arnold J. Heidenheimer and Michael Johnston (eds.) *Political Corruption. Concepts and Contexts*, Third edition. New Brunswick, New Jersey: Transaction Publishers, 25-40.

Giuriati, Domenico. (1903). *Il plagio. Furti letterari, artistici e musicali*, Seconda edizione. Milano: Ulrico Hoepli.

Hatcher, Tim. (2011). Becoming an Ethical Scholarly Writer. *Journal of Scholarly Publishing*, 42(2), 142-159.

Karasz, Palko. (2012). Hungarian President Resigns amid Plagiarism Scandal. *The New York Times*, 2 April. http://www.nytimes.com/2012/04/03/world/europe/hungarian-president-pal-schmitt-resigns-amid-plagiarism-scandal.html

Khvostunova, Olga. (2013). Plagiarism-gate. Institute of Modern Russia, 8 May. http://imrussia.org/en/society/453-plagiarism-gate

Klußmann, Uwe. (2007). The Russian Parliament's Intellectual Giants. *Spiegel Online*, 21 November. http://www.spiegel.de/international/world/duma-s-dubious-degrees-the-russian-parliament-s-intellectual-giants-a-518754.html

Knyazev, Evgeny. (2004). The Russian Federation. In Jan Sadlak (ed.) *Doctoral Studies and Qualifications in Europe and the United States: Status and Prospects*. Bucharest: UNESCO, 153-188.

Kornai, János. (2015). Hungary's U-Turn: Retreating from Democracy. *Journal of Democracy*, 26(3), 34-48.

La Repubblica, 2 April 2012. Ungheria, si dimette il presidente Schmitt. http://www.repubblica.it/esteri/2012/04/02/news/ungheria_dimissioni_schmitt-32623351/

Le Monde, 23 February 2011. Le titre de docteur retiré au ministre allemand accusé de plagiat. http://www.lemonde.fr/europe/article/2011/02/23/le-titre-de-docteur-retire-au-ministre-allemand-accuse-de-plagiat_1484411_3214.html

Lei, Jun& Guangwei Hu. (2014). Chinese ESOL Lecturers' Stance on Plagiarism: Does Knowledge Matter?.*ELT Journal*, 68(1), 41-51.

Lovell, David W. (2005). Corruption as a Transitional Phenomenon: Understanding Endemic Corruption in Postcommunist States. In Dieter Haller and Cris Shore (eds.) *Corruption: Anthropological Perspectives*. London: Pluto Press, 65-82.

Marsh, Bill. (2007). *Plagiarism: Alchemy and Remedy in Higher Education*. Albany: State University of New York Press.

McElroy, Damien& Ahmad Vahdat. (2013). Iranian President Hassan Rouhani "Plagiarised Ph.D. Thesis at Scottish University". *The Telegraph*, 26 June. http://www.telegraph.co.uk/news/worldnews/middleeast/iran/10143799/Iranian-president-Hassan-Rouhani-plagiarised-Ph.D.-thesis-at-Scottish-university.html

McKay, Joanna. (2003). Political Corruption in Germany. In Martin J. Bull and James L. Newell (eds.) *Corruption in Contemporary Politics*. New York: Palgrave Macmillan, 53-65.

Müller, Enrique. (2013). Un nuevo escándalo por el plagio de una tesis salpica al presidente del Bundestag, *El País*, 31 July. http://internacional.elpais.com/internacional/2013/07/31/actualidad/1375296421_261293.html

Müller, Enrique. (2014). El ministro de Cooperación alemán, acusado de plagiar su tesis doctoral. *El País*, 10 April. http://internacional.elpais.com/internacional/2014/04/10/actualidad/1397141438_648808.html

Nodier, Charles. (1812). *Questions de littérature légale. Du plagiat, de la supposition d'auteurs, des supercheries qui ont rapport aux livres. Ouvrage qui peut servir de suite au Dictionnaire des anonymes et à toutes les bibliographies*. Paris: Barba.

Osipian, Ararat L. (2010). Le Bourgeois Gentilhomme: Political Corruption of Russian Doctorates. *Demokratizatsiya*, 18(3), 260-280.

Pantazi, Raluca. (2014). Mihnea Costoiu, la doi ani de la semnalarea cazului: Ioan Mang a plagiat. *HotNews.ro*, 19 December. http://www.hotnews.ro/stiri-esential-18873030-mihnea-costoiu-doi-ani-semnalarea-cazului-ioan-mang-plagiat.htm

Pantazi, Raluca. (2015). Dezbaterea Plagiatul ca stare a natiunii. *Hotnews.ro*, 8 September. http://m.hotnews.ro/stire/20408573

Philp, Mark. (1997). Defining Political Corruption. *Political Studies*, 45(3), 436-462.

Pidd, Helen. (2011). German Defence Minister Resigns in PhD Plagiarism Row. *The Guardian*, 1 March. http://www.theguardian.com/world/2011/mar/01/german-defence-minister-resigns-plagiarism

Prisacariu, Catalin. (2015). Ponta, încă doctor la opt luni de la ordonana de urgenă de renunare la doctorat. *România Liberă*, 18 August. http://www.romanialibera.ro/special/dezvaluiri/ponta—inca-doctor-la-opt-luni-de-la-ordonanta-de-urgenta-de-renuntare-la-doctorat-389646

Pro TV, 14 March 2016. Cine este Radu Sienerth, victima 64 a incendiului din Colectiv. https://stirileprotv.ro/stiri/incendiu-in-colectiv/bilantul-tragediei-din-colectiv-a-ajuns-la-64-de-morti-un-tanar-de-22-de-ani-care-nternat-la-spitalul-floreasca-a-murit.html

Putin, Vladimir. (2015). Biography. *Personal Website*. http://eng.putin.kremlin.ru/bio

Raiklin, Ernest. (2009). Continuity in Russian Corruption through Changing Societal Forms. *The Journal of Social, Political, and Economic Studies*, 34(4), 399-463.

Rosamond, Ben. (2002). Plagiarism, Academic Norms and the Governance of the Profession. *Politics*, 22(3), 167-174.

Ruscior, Cosmin. (2012). Răzvan Theodorescu: Dacă Ponta a plagiat, să-°i ceară scuze!.*Radio France Internationale-Romanian Service*, 29 June. http://m.rfi.ro/articol/stiri/politica/ac-razvan-theodorescu-rfi-dizolvarea-comisiei-ce-analizeaza-plagiatul-este

Schiermeier, Quirin. (2012a). Romanian Prime Minister Accused of Plagiarism. *Nature* 486, 18 June, 305. http://www.nature.com/news/romanian-prime-minister-accused-of-plagiarism-1.10845

Schiermeier, Quirin. (2012b). Conflicting Verdicts on Romanian Prime Minister's Plagiarism. *Nature News*, 20 July. http://www.nature.com/news/conflicting-verdicts-on-romanian-prime-minister-s-plagiarism-1.11047

Sercan, Emilia. (2015). A sasea lucrare de doctorat suspectata de plagiat, coordonata de Gabriel Oprea. Chestor-sef de politie Dumitru Parvu si-a obtinut doctoratul la Academia de Politie. *HotNews.ro*, 5 October. http://www.hotnews.ro/stiri-esential-20474669-exclusiv-sasea-lucrare-doctorat-plagiata-coordonata-gabriel-oprea-chestor-sef-politie-dumitru-parvu-obtinut-doctoratul-academia-politie.htm

Sherwin, Adam. (2011). Gaddafi Son 'Plagiarised his Degree Thesis' at LSE. *The Independent*, 2 March. http://www.independent.co.uk/news/education/education-news/gaddafi-son-plagiarised-his-degree-thesis-at-lse-2229620.html

Shlapentokh, Vladimir. (2013). Corruption, the Power of State and Big Business in Soviet and post-Soviet Regimes. *Communist and Post-Communist Studies*, 46(1), 147-158.

Shuster, Simon. (2013). Putin's Ph.D.: Can a Plagiarism Probe Upend Russian Politics?.*World Time*, 28 February. http://world.time.com/2013/02/28/putins-phd-can-a-plagiarism-probe-upend-russian-politics/

The Economist, 7 April 2012. Schmitt Quits. http://www.economist.com/node/21552258

The Washington Times, 24 March 2006. Researchers Peg Putin as a Plagiarist over Thesis. http://www.washingtontimes.com/news/2006/mar/24/20060324-104106-9971r/

Tran, Mark. (2015). Bucharest Nightclub Fire: PM and Government Resign after Protests. *The Guardian*, 4 November. http://www.theguardian.com/world/2015/nov/04/romanian-government-resigns-nightclub-fire-victor-ponta

Transparency International. (2013). National Results. *Global Corruption Barometer 2013*. http://www.transparency.org/gcb2013/results

Transparency International. (2014). *Corruption Perceptions Index 2014*. HTTP://files.transparency.org/content/download/1857/12438/file/CPI2014_DataBundle.zip

Treppoz, Lucien. (1894). *Droit romain: le Concept du vol dans le droit romain. Droit français: Étude théorique et pratique sur les condamnations conditionnelles (loi Bérenger)*. Paris: Chevalier-Marescq.

Vasagar, Jeevan& Mark Sweney. (2011). LSE Plans Libya Scholarship Fund with Gaddafi Donation. *The Guardian*,

1 March. http://www.theguardian.com/education/2011/mar/01/lse-libya-scholarship-fund

Vitzthum, Thomas. (2008). Gutes Geschäft mit gekauften Doktortiteln. *Die Welt*, 12 March. http://www.welt.de/politik/article1792387/Gutes_Geschaeft_mit_gekauften_Doktortiteln.html

Vulcan, Dora. (2017). Ponta a pierdut la Curtea de Apel anularea ordinului de retragere a titlului de doctor în drept. Revista 22, 7 February. https://revista22.ro/70260247/ponta-a-pierdut-la-curtea-de-apel-anularea-ordinuiui-de-retragere-a-titlului-de-doctor-în-drept-.html

Warren, Mark E. (2015). The Meaning of Corruption in Democracies. In Paul M. Heywood (ed.) *Routledge Handbook of Political Corruption*. New York: Routledge, 42-55.

Weber-Wulff, Debora. (2014). *False Feathers. A Perspective on Academic Plagiarism*. Berlin and Heidelberg: Springer.

Wolf, Sebastian. (2013). Bribe and Cheat to Get a Doctoral Degree in Germany?. In Transparency International (ed.) *Global Corruption Report: Education*. New York, N.Y.: Routledge, 178-184. http://www.transparency.org/whatwedo/publication/global_corruption_report_education.

4

Ethical Use of Information : The Contribution of the Academic Libraries in the Prevention of Plagiarism

Helena Isabel Pereira Leitão
Maria da Graça de Melo Simões
Patrícia de Almeida
Daniel Martínez-Ávila

1. INTRODUCTION

Generally speaking, plagiarism is understood as a conscious and deliberate appropriation of an intellectual work that belongs to someone else. It is a fraudulent behavior that not only goes against the ethical use of information but it couldeven be punishable by the law. Although it is accepted that plagiarism is something serious, the conceptual and ethical aspectssurrounding plagiarism aresometimes complex and subjective.In this sense, we believe it is important to understand the practicesand characteristics in which there is an actual infraction so libraries can establish effective strategies to prevent it.

The issue of plagiarism is very relevant and almost ubiquitous in today's society, in part because of the characteristics of the new information technologies that, as a side effectof all the benefits for information access, have alsofacilitated and increased the opportunities for the misappropriation of information. Although the problem of plagiarism affects everyone, it has become extremely relevant in the cases of higher education and scientific information, as plagiarism in the scientific production is a recurrent and relevant topic in the academia (Morais & Santos, 2017) and this affects the validity of the outcomes.

On the other hand, one of the main functions of the library is education, as it contributes to the integral education of citizens (Totterdell, 1978). For this reason, academic libraries are also responsible for information literacy programs, that include the promotion of an ethical use of information. In this sense, information services must consider the behavioral changes of their users as well as promote good practices for the study, research, and communication of science. This purpose allows the library to meet the educational and informational needs of its users and stakeholders, filling the gaps of students, faculty, and educators (Severino, 2017). In this regard, the library of a higher education institution is one of the most important assets in the prevention of plagiarism.

Provided this, the aim of our paper is to reinforce the contribution of the academic libraries in the prevention of plagiarism. More specifically, the objectives of our study are:

1. To understand the concept of plagiarism and the role of libraries in the promotion of an ethical use of information;
2. To collect a body of literature on the topic and to identify and analyze the reasons that lead academic libraries to establish guidelines in the prevention of plagiarism;
3. To summarize the diverse guidelines for academic libraries in the prevention of plagiarism in a single text in order to facilitate their dissemination.

To achieve our objectives, we conducted a literature review on the topic and a categorical analysis, paying attention on the general and terminological aspects, the possible reasons for its existence (intentionality and context), the aspects related to the ethical use of information, and the role and measures of the academic libraries for its prevention.

2. PLAGIARISM: GENERAL AND TERMINOLOGICAL REMARKS

Although the historical emergence of the term "plagiarism" is still unknown, its first mention dates back to the first century in referral to the unauthorized copy of a text (Diniz & Munhoz, 2011). According to these authors, in Latin, the term "plagiarist" originally meant an individual who robbed slaves or enslaved free people. The meaning was later extended to someone who copied poems, thus revealing the age of the term back to the *anno Domini*.

According to the Council of Writing Program Administrators (WPA, 2003, p. 1), plagiarism is when "a writer deliberately uses someone else's language, ideas, or other original (not common-knowledge) material without acknowledging its source." According to this institution, this definition refers to texts that are "published in print or on-line, to manuscripts, and to the work of other student writers." For the Office of Research Integrity (ORI, 1994), plagiarism comprehends "both the theft or misappropriation of intellectual property and the substantial unattributed textual copying of another's work."

Other definitions of plagiarism include the use of words, images, methods or ideas, that are authored by someone else and thus understood as fraudulent (Roig, 2002; Silva et al., 2018). The definitions of plagiarism that refer to the conscious and deliberate appropriation of something that belongs to someone else are in line with Pythan and Vidal (2013), who understand plagiarism primarily as an ethical question. In this regard, Pythan and Vidal, drawing on Booth et al.(2005), point out that it is essential to "condemn the practice of plagiarism" since the plagiarist, while being conscious of the act, does not misuse only the author's words, but rather a "much more valuable good in the collective consciousness of society which is trust in the scientific production." Roig (2002, p.2) stresses the important role of honesty in the context of science by stating that "scientific writing must be characterized by clear expression, conciseness, accuracy, and, perhaps most importantly, honesty."

Traditionally, plagiarism has referred to printed documents (Altbach & Vest, 2005; Eaton et al., 2017). Today, with access to the internet and the easiness of copying and pasting, the possibilities of plagiarism have also been increased (Almeida et al., 2016; Eaton et al., 2017; Ison, 2015; Silva, 2008). It can be considered that the internet facilitates plagiarism at three levels: the quantity and variety of sources; the effective access to information contents; and, at an operational level, the easiness of copying,as the transcription of information no longer requires a process of reading and writing,but in two mouse clicksany textcan be immediately transcribed regardless of its length. Provided this, Howard & Davies (2009, p.64) state that: "using sources with integrity is complex. The solution is teaching skills, not vilifying the Internet." The same authors also warn us about the increasing volume of information of dubious quality that populates the internet on a large scale. This aspect is even more relevant for our purpose if we accept that poor quality information is usually spread through plagiarism. In order to assessand question the quality of any kind of information, it is necessary, at least, to read it, and this is not always the case when automatically copying texts from the internet. At the same time, it should also be recognized that while the internet facilitates the practice of plagiarism, it also contributes to the development and applicationof technologies that are used in many systems of plagiarism detection (Almeida et al., 2016; Imran et al., 2018; İuraèík et al., 2018). In this sense, the internet and the new technologies are not the main factors to blame, but the context in which this problem appears as it is used both as a source and as a medium for the communication of information.

Regarding the reasons that lead people to plagiarize, it is arguedthat in most cases there is not an explicit intention to plagiarize, but ignorance about the concept, its rules, and consequences (Almeida et al., 2016; Carroll, 2016; Eaton et al., 2017; WPA, 2003). In this respect, Eaton et al. (2017) consider that there are a number of contextual reasons that contribute to plagiarism, such as peer pressure and the belief that there will be no consequences as reviewers do not detect, give importance or report this practice. In this vein, Helgesson and Eriksson (2014) state that it is not easy to define plagiarism and talk about "conditions of adequacy." For these authors, these conditions must "identify relevant restrictions on any suggested definition for the definition to be reasonably adequate for the intended purpose in the intended context." Thus, with respect to the conditions for plagiarism, they refer to "fitting language use," "precision," "reliability," "theoretical fruitfulness," "relevance for normative purposes," and "simplicity" (p.92). Kirsch and Bradley (2012) also point out that students often think they know what plagiarism is and the actions it encompasses, something that does not always correspond with the truth.

For the WPA (2003, p. 2) "students who are fully aware that their actions constitute plagiarism [...] are guilty of academic misconduct." Thus, it is important for instructors to be able to understand the reasons for the infractions in order to create strategies to minimize the opportunities for plagiarism. In this context, the WPA presents the following main reasons (WPA, 2003, p. 2):

- Students may fear failure or fear taking risks in their own work.
- Students may have poor time-management skills or they may plan poorly for the time andeffort required for research-based writing, and believe they have no choice but toplagiarize.
- Students may view the course, the assignment, the conventions of academicdocumentation, or the consequences of cheating as unimportant.
- Teachers may present students with assignments so generic or un particularized thatstudents may believe they are justified in looking for canned responses.
- Instructors and institutions may fail to report cheating when it does occur, or may notenforce appropriate penalties.

Provided this, we conclude that, even if there are technological mechanisms for detecting plagiarism, it is important to question the perceived capacity of the system to understand, *de facto*, what an infraction is and what is not (Helgesson & Eriksson, 2014), as the definition of plagiarism is a complex question that is somehow subjectiverelated to aspects such as intentionality and context.

3. ETHICAL USE OF INFORMATION: PREVENTION OF PLAGIARISM AND THE ROLE OF ACADEMIC LIBRARIES

Plagiarism is a prominent topic in the academic and research contexts (Almeida et al., 2016; Helgesson & Eriksson, 2014; ORI, 1994; Pythan & Vidal, 2013). In this regard, Almeida et al. (2016) consider that, as a manifestation of fraud in higher education and also a complex phenomenon, the university should have a fundamental educational role in this area and the creation of institutional policies should be encouraged.

Effective plagiarism management policies should follow a holistic approach (Carroll, 2016; Colella-Sandercock & Alahmadi, 2015). For Carroll (2016, 80-82), it is important "to give relevant information to students," "to promote the development of student skills," "to ensure that the evaluation is designed to promote genuine work," "to create management procedures that are not detrimental to the evaluator who detects plagiarism," "to promote coherent management," "to keep records," and "to let the link with the procedures for quality control clear."

Eaton et al. (2017) inquired on how *educators* can create efficient and proactive lines of action for the prevention of plagiarism based on three strategies: assessment design, formative feedback, and academic integrity education (30). Indeed, as Born (2003, 223) points out, "a proactive approach rather than a reactive approach needs to be used to reduce academic misconduct." This author, who also presents a set of recommendations, considers the first one ("treat a paper as a process not a product") the most important one. Colella-Sandercock and Alahmadi (2015) also point out that, in the case of higher education institutions, in spite of having institutional policies to fight plagiarism, students continuesubmittingwork with plagiarized information and poorly constructed references. These authors conclude that "misunderstandings of plagiarism" is one of the main reasons adduced by students when confronted with this issue. In this sense, they argue that the most efficient way to avoid plagiarism is to educate students on the topic in a clear way. They present a set of strategies, for example"Provide Students with Resources Regarding Plagiarism" (page 70), in which the library is one of the most important actors in the prevention of plagiarism.

The WPA (2003, 4-7) also presents a set of strategies that, although not guaranteeing the end of all cases of plagiarism, allow students to acquire tools that make plagiarism unnecessary, namely "Explain plagiarism and develop clear policies;" "Improve design and sequence of assignments;" "Attend to sources and the use of reading;" "Work on plagiarism responsibly;"and "Take appropriate disciplinar actions." Howard and Davies (2009, p.64) also propose strategies for the development of anti-plagiarism policies that include the awareness of concepts such as intellectual property, the evaluation of print-based and online information sources,and the importance for students tounderstand the content of the sources as a creation of a technically perfect bibliography is not enough. Thesestrategies stress the importance of the education of the use of sources over the consequences of the infraction.

Overall, although different aspects are emphasized in the literature, we conclude that the informative and educational aspects play central roles in the prevention of plagiarism, as they are common to all the strategies.

The key in these strategies is the education with positive reinforcement, in the sense that the focus should not be put on the predisposition of the researcher to infringe, but on the clarification and awareness of the advantages of an ethical use of information sources. This perspective is opposed to the negative reinforcement that assumes that as the researchers are prone to plagiarize, the clarification of the consequences (and punishment)must be the focus of the strategies. In the positive reinforcement, the clarification of the very definition of plagiarism and the difficulties in determining what an infraction is and what is not, its varying degrees of gravity, and the creation of practices to prevent plagiarism should be the priorities. It is argued that strategies focused on prevention are more effectivein the reduction of infractions and for not wasting resources in complex and costly procedures for detection and punishment.

An academic library, as its name implies, is an institution of higher education that is located in an academic context. Taking a prominent place in today's society (Nunes & Carvalho, 2016, 174), academic libraries are"spaces for the dissemination of knowledge par excellence" thathave evolved to meet not only "the information needs of the public, but also to follow the advances in the field of information and communication technologies, as well as the behavioral changes of users, who are increasingly connected."

For the American Library Association (ALA, 2016), "academic librarianship offers a great opportunity to utilize subject expertise", as well asacademic librarians play a relevant role in the development of academic and scientific activities by engaging in various challenges, such as the technological challenges and the training of the scientific community in digital contexts. The Integrated Library Service of the University of Coimbra (SIBUC 2018) states that "libraries - physical and virtual space of access to knowledge - are a fundamental support for the quality of the performance of academic institutions," because, as González Guitián and Molina Piñeiro put it (2008, p. 19),"Higher education establishes new educational paradigms and academic libraries must use all their capacities in order to adapt to these changes, aimed at achieving a higher quality in the training of their graduates."

Munarriz Zorzano (1977, 33) said: "The primary objective of the academic library and all its activities is eminently education, as well as of the university itself." Indeed, mainly using information literacy programs such as user training and the reference service, the library in higher education institutions is seen as an excellent space for the dissemination of information and good practices (González Guitián & Molina Piñeiro, 2008; Molina & Fernández Valdés, 2010; Stagg et al., 2013). It is in this context in which we frame the awareness of the ethical use of information, especially in relation to the fight against plagiarism. This educational function attributed to the library is aligned with the current trends of prevention of poor research habits that are focused, as mentioned before, on an educational, preventive, and informative paradigm, that ultimately integrates the user in the process of making science with the engine of human development –i.e., education in a broader sense.

4. METHODOLOGY

We followed a qualitative exploratory approach in order to frame the research question (Barbour, 2014) and to understand the phenomenon by the interpretation of the data (Bardin, 2016). In a first moment, we conducted a narrative literature review aimed to achieve the first objective and to define, characterize, problematize, and support the concepts theoretically (Bardin, 2016); and, in a second moment, we conducted a systematic literature review (Paré et al., 2015), using content analysis (Coutinho, 2015; Hart, 2009; Pickard, 2013), to achieve the second and third objectives, as it is based on the analysis of the corpus of collected articles following *a priori* criteria.

We consulted scientific documents, and more specifically articles and information from relevant institutions, that are directly related to the ethical use of information and plagiarism.

4.1. Corpus construction criteria

The data was collected from the B-on database[2] on May 22, 2018. We searched the terms "Plagiarism" and "Academic library" (using the Boolean operator AND) in the topic field of the advanced search feature. We filtered the results by document type to retrieve only peer-reviewed articles in order to collect a coherent corpus of validated scientific quality.

We selected the timespan 2003-2017 as 2002 was the year of the Budapest Open Access Initiative statement that marked the open access movement. This movement allowed a significant

---

2. Available at https://www.b-on.pt/. B-on is a comprehensive database that is widely used for academic research in Portugal. It includes a wide variety of sources, document types, access conditions, and publishers of high impact journals.

increase of information available for download, use, and sharing on the internet, that, although does not have a direct relation with the infringementof the copyright of the papers, is usually discussed in relation to the rise of plagiarism.

We retrieved a set of 56 articles that was narrowed using the filters title, abstract, and keywordslooking for references to: a) measures related to the prevention of plagiarism in academic libraries; b) empirical methodological approaches (i.e., presentation of concrete cases); c) reasons for libraries to create guidelines to prevent plagiarism.Based on these criteria, we constructed a corpus of 14 articles that are presented in Table 1.

Table 1. Articles that compose the corpus

	Author (Date)	Title	Publication
1.	Mansoor, Faiqa; Ameen Kanwal (2015)	Promoting Academic Integrity in South Asian Research Culture: The Case of Pakistani Academic Institutions	A Research Journal of South Asian Studies
2.	Fluk, Louise, R. (2015)	Foregrounding the Research Log in Information Literacy Instruction	The Journal of Academic Librarianship
3.	Strittmatter, Connie; Bratton, Virginia K. (2014)	Plagiarism Awareness among Students: Assessing Integration of Ethics Theory into Library Instruction	College & Research Libraries
4.	George, Sarah; Costigan, Anne; O'hara, Maria (2013)	Placing the Library at the Heart of Plagiarism Prevention: The University of Bradford Experience	New Review of Academic Librarianship
5.	Stagg, Adrian; Kimmins, Lindy; Pavlovski (2013)	Academic style with substance: A collaborative screencasting project to support referencing skills	The electronic library
6.	Greer, Katie; Swanberg, Stephanie; Hristova, Mariela; Switzer, Anne; Daniel, Dominique; Perdue, Sherry (2012)	Beyond the Web Tutorial: development and Implementation of an Online, Self-Directed Academic Integrity Course at Oakland University	The Journal of Academic Librarianship
7.	Domínguez-Aroca, María Isabel (2012)	Lucha contra el plagio desde las bibliotecas universitarias	El profesional de la información
8.	Kirsch, Breanne A.; Bradley, Lola (2012)	Distance Education and Plagiarism Prevention at the University of South Carolina Upstate	Journal of Library Administration
9.	Dadzie, Perpetua S. (201	Rethinking information ethics education in Ghana: Is it adequate?	The International Information & Library Review
10.	Ward, Randall; Harrison, Tiffany; Pace, Sean (2010)	Library Instruction from Scratch at a Career College	Community & Junior College Libraries
11.	Sciammarella, Susan (2009)	Making a Difference: Library and Teaching Faculty Working Together to Develop Strategies in Dealing with Student Plagiarism	Community & Junior College Libraries
12.	Germek, George P. (2009)	Imagine No Possessions: Librarians, the Net-Generation Student, and the Imminent Victory of Plagiarism	College & Undergraduate Libraries
13.	Drinan, Patrick, M.; Gallant, Tricia Bertram (2008)	Plagiarism and Academic Integrity Systems	Journal of Library Administration
14.	Lampert, Lynn (2004)	Integrating discipline-based anti-plagiarism instruction into the information literacy curriculum	Reference Services Review

4.2. Criteria for analysis

For the systematic literature review, we used a Bardinian content analysis (2016, p.145), based on the "categorization" method and the predetermination of criteria for analysis. Thus, three categories of analysis were defined: i) Definition of plagiarism, ii) Reasons for creating preventive measures, and iii) Preventive measures. The first criterion is justified by the complexity of the definition of the term plagiarism. We believe it is essential to clarify and understand the definitions presented in each article in order to contextualize and understand the recommendations they propose. The second category is justified by the importance of the reasons given by each institution in order to understand the measures proposed by the academic libraries, such as for instance the existence of a large number of cases of plagiarism in an institution, etc. In this sense, the concrete and specific reasons in which the recommendations are based upon are an important aspect that affect the functioning of the academic library in this regard. The third criterion is justified by the main objective of our paper as these guidelines are the basis of the set of recommendations on the prevention of plagiarism that we are proposing.

5. RESULTS AND DISCUSSION

The results of the analysis of the corpus based on the defined categories are presented in Table 2.

Table 2. Results of the analysis of the corpus

Article	Definition of plagiarism	Reasons for the development of preventive measures	Preventive measures
1	"(…) research misconduct, lack of academic integrity, misappropriation of intellectual property, and academic fabrication" (p.77)	-	"1. More IL instructions regarding fair use of information are need to be provide more by the universities. 2. The libraries should enhance the frequency of their anti plagiarism guidance activities to play an effective role in combating plagiarism with their universities." (p.88)
2	-	-	"Thus scaffolded by multiple learning theories, the information literacy instructor can use research logs for a wide variety of purposes…" (p.490) "assigning research logs is one of the best ways to combat plagiarism, whether the plagiarism is deliberate or, as is often the case, unintentional" (p.492)
3	-	-	"Library instruction sessions that combine the practical information related to plagiarism and a theoretical approach to ethics of plagiarism" (p.737)
4	-	"It was becoming clear that an increasing number of cases were due to ignorance of plagiarism and referencing rather than deliberate cheating and education rather than punishment was seen as the appropriate response" (p.144)	"Plagiarism Avoidance for New Students (PANS) course attempts to smooth the transition into Higher Education by introducing students to ideas of referencing and plagiarism in a timely and non-threatening manner. (…) method of delivery of the PANS was decided in negotiation with each School." (p.142)

5	-	"Students understand they should not copy words without referencing, but fail to grasp the reasons why; the reasons are not explicit and often cloaked in unfamiliar and impenetrable academic language." (p.453)	Support referencing skills
6	-	-	Using and Citing Sources Course"(…) course consisting of six distinct modules: (1) academicintegrity and plagiarism, (2) how and when to use sources, (3) paraphrasing, (4) direct quotes, (5) citation styles, and (6) putting it all together." (p.254)
7	"Above all, it implies violating the moral rights related to authorship, one of the most important parts of copyright. (...) an infringement of the copyright of any type of work, by presenting the copy as one's own, without the express authorization of the person who created it and owns it or holds the rights over it." (p.499, in translation)	"It is important that students acquire the information skills that allow them to take full advantage of both the information that is provided by the library, as well as the information that is accessible on the Internet, critically evaluating it and making an ethical use of it." (p.500, in translation)	"there are justified reasons for the university library to include information on plagiarism on its website. (p.502) It would be necessary to analyze how and where to place such information on the library's website. There are several possibilities:- with the information on intellectual property;- with the information on how to cite and citation styles;- in a comprehensive tutorial on information skills or in a specific one on "the ethical use of information";- in a specific section and with direct access from the main page of the library website;- it can include textual information or videos, tutorials, and attractive audiovisual materials- it can include news, articles, famous cases from the media or the institution itself, etc." (p. 501, in translation)
8	-	"plagiarism is part of the information literacy standards and it can be extrapolated that librarians can have a role to integrate the concept of plagiarism into library instruction sessions" (p.80)	"The workshops are intended to introduce students to the concepts related to plagiarism, such as types of plagiarism, academic integrity, paraphrasing, common knowledge, and citations (…) To take a more proactive approach against unintentional plagiarism, the authors proposed a plagiarism prevention workshop. (…) In addition, an online version of the workshop was created that could be offered to distance education courses using Blackboard." (p.79-80)
9	"borrowing words, sentences and even paragraphs from many sources without acknowledgement" (p.65)	"all universities should adopt concrete ways to implement their code of conduct on academic integrity and plagiarism.(…) Information ethics education is very important in Ghana"(p.68)	"Adequate sensitization programmes would guide members of the university community (both faculty and students) on the seriousness of plagiarism.(…) Some important aspects include copyright, referencing, plagiarism, research ethics, media ethics, information technology ethics as well as business ethics." (p.68)
10	-	"In order to enhance the students' educational experience and assist them in becoming lifelong learners, we in the library thought that some instruction on information literacy was needed" (p.192)	"Librarians at the Stevens-Henager Career College Salt Lake City Campus have developed a library-instruction program over the last year. The basic section consists of 40–45 minutes on primary, secondary, and tertiary literature, search techniques (…) APA-style

11	-	"Librarians are often confronted with the question about preventing plagiarism." (p.24)
12	-	"It is crucial that we reach Net-generation students" (p.341)
13	"use of others' work without acknowledgment" (p.126)	-

writing, and plagiarism. (…)We felt that a lecture was needed from library personnel who were versed in information literacy skills. (…)We felt a more-systematic approach was needed" (p.192)

"Collaboration between the library and classroom faculty is key to determining the students' research needs (…) The librarian provides a basic set of databases to students for exploration (…) provides faculty with Internet sites as to where students go to find information and provide a background as to what types of materials are available and what topics are covered (…) informs students of the necessity of obtaining the appropriate information to cite in a legal and ethical manner (…) reinforces the ideas that the process of accessing information and using it in a legal and ethical manner are different sides of the same coin (…)By developing research guides, librarians can help establish the necessary tools for student researchers (…) They also help students learn directly at reference desks, over the phone, by e-mail, and increasingly through "digital reference" (…) This one page [library website] contains a wealth of information available to faculty and students." (p.29-30)

"librarians must consciously pool their strengths and influential position and consider the following steps.Take Your Plan of Action to the Classroom(…) Form Partnerships(…) Prepare a Vision for the Future(…) Market Your Ideas in the Library and Across the Campus(…)Make Good Use of Technology(…)

"we examine three strategies institutions can take in building or maintaining an academic integrity system and the implications of each for librarian roles. (…) Rule Compliance Strategy (…)In this strategy, the focus is on defining and enforcing the citation and attribution rules that have been established to guide the presentation of written material (…)Integrity Strategy (…) which focuses first on education and student development and secondarily on discipline(…) Pedagogical Strategy (…) First, librarians as information experts may be able to help faculty and students understand the impact that the information explosion has on academic conduct (…) Second, librarians can partner with centers for learning and teaching, instructional development and/or writing centers" (p. 130-136)

| 14 | "plagiarism will be defined as it is in the 11th edition of Webster's Collegiate Dictionary (Merriam Webster, 2003) as: To steal and pass off (the ideas or words of another) as one's own or to use (a created production) without crediting the source." (p.349) | Plagiarism is an area where librarians and discipline faculty already agree there is a need for instruction. (p.347) | "Anti-plagiarism instruction, led by both librarians and faculty, primarily through process-based assignments, provides a nexus where disciplinary context and information literacy skill needs can be met through thoughtful collaboration." (p.348) |

Out of the 14 selected articles, only 5 articles (37.71%) include an explicit definition of plagiarism, 9 articles (64.28%) mentioned the reasons for creating preventive measures, and 14 articles (100%) presented preventive measures of plagiarism (see Table 3).

Table 3. Number and percentage (rounded to the hundredth) of articles according to the analysis criteria

	Definition	*Reasons*	*Measures*
Nº	5	9	14
%	35,71	64,28	100

Regarding the definition of plagiarism, based on the common aspects found in the literature, there is an aspect that is repeated in every case: someone using ideas or words by others as if they were his/her own. There are not many disagreements in the definitions. Based on them, we summarized the concept of plagiarism in the following ideas: it is a wrong research behavior; it negatively affects others in relation to their rights as authors; it is an action that puts in question the academic integrity of the individual; there is a subtraction of the credit of others; and it involves the use of a work without permission or reference to the author. In general, there are some inconsistencies in the rest of the articles that do not include an explicit definition of the term, as they refer to the emergence of the definition of the term and its context (George et al. 2013; Germek, 2012; Greer et al., 2012; Kirsch, 2014; Strittmatter & Bratton, 2014) without presenting a definition. This is awkward as it is often recognized in these articles that the lack of information about the concept is one of the main factors in the prevalence of plagiarism –as, in many situations, students plagiarize because they do not know what this act means (Greer et al., 2012; Sciammarella, 2009; Strittmatter & Bratton, 2014). George et al. (2013, p. 143), for example, understand that "the literature also finds much confusion as to what constitutes plagiarism," while in their information literacy program they answer the question "What is plagiarism?" (p.150) referring to the definition presented by Greer et al. (2012), yet they still do not present a definition of the term. Another example is Strittmatter & Bratton (2014), who mention the importance of defining plagiarism in information literacy programs, and yet they do not define the term either. Finally, although Germek (2009, 343) considers that a definition of plagiarism is fundamental, at the same time also wonders "can we ourselves be absolutely certain about providing a conceptual definition of plagiarism?" Thus, it seems that for this author the strategy to best inform about plagiarism should be based on showing examples rather than presenting a definition.

In relation to the reasons that lead to the creation of preventive measures, the literature does not reportprevious cases of plagiarism as a direct influence or cause of the creation of strategies. However, in more than half of the cases, there is a reference to a specific context that leads to the creation of measures. There is a clear link between the education on information skills and the reduction of plagiarism, as it is understood that most occurrences of plagiarism are caused by an unconscious ignorance on the subject (Drinan & Gallant, 2008; Germek, 2009; Greer et al., 2012; Kirsch & Bradley, 2012; Lampert, 2004; Sciammarella, 2009; Ward et al., 2010). An additional reason reported in the literature has to do with the lack of awareness and explanations of the reasons for not to plagiarize and with the way in which this information is presented by educators, that are supposedly difficult to understand (Domínguez Aroca, 2012). One of the most common reasonspresented in the literature is the consideration of the academic librarians as educators, as it is believed that one of their main competencies and responsibilities is educating on this lack of informationskills for the ethical use of information (Dadzie, 2011; Drinan & Gallant, 2008; Germek, 2012; Greer et al., 2012; Sciammarella, 2009). Thus, the education on information skills (Drinan & Gallant, 2008; Ward et al., 2010) and information ethics (Strittmatter & Bratton, 2014) are relevant reasons for academic libraries to take measures in relation to plagiarism.

Regarding the measures themselves, the most common one is the creation of information literacy programs (Drinan & Gallant, 2008; Fluk, 2015; Mansoor & Ameen, 2016; Ward et al., 2010), including theoretical and practical aspects (Strittmatter & Bratton, 2014), and ideally implemented in the classroom (Germek, 2009). Another proposed measure is the development of regular courses and workshops (Dadzie, 2011; George et al., 2013; Greer et al., 2012; B. A. Kirsch & Bradley, 2012) that raise awareness on the ethical use of information and copyright as well as the importance of the different citation and reference styles (Drinan & Gallant, 2008; Stagg et al., 2013). Other measures that are also considered in the literature are the creation of research tools such as research guides (Sciammarella, 2009) and research logs (Fluk, 2015). Finally, other important aspects that are also highlighted are the importance of providing relevant information on the topic on the library's website (Domínguez Aroca, 2012), as it is said that the good use of technology here is essential to reach the new generation (Germek, 2009).

6. CONCLUSION

In the prevention of plagiarism, we believe that it is important to inform and discuss the concept and context of plagiarism, something that is not an easy task. As Germek (2009, 343) pointed it: "The first pressing concern is based on the belief that librarians may inform student researchers what constitutes plagiarism without first offering a clear and sound definition (the ACRL provides none)." We concludethat the term plagiarism is generally understood as someone usingideas or words by someone else without giving proper credit. We found that the main drive in addressing this problem in libraries is linked to the educational role and the librarian's mission on the defense of the ethical use of information, while the most recurrent strategy is the implementation of information literacy programs. Based on the analysis of the corpus of study, we conclude that there are not concrete motives for plagiarists, but contexts of plagiarism, just as there are no absolute measures, but strategies. In this sense, it is important to create educational strategies that are not based on the idea of punishment. Thus, in the face of the ignorance of the rules and unintentionality in the crime, we advocate for the creation of information literacy programs based on awareness and the training on the ethical use of information, making use of practical examples and providing specific tools for research and writing. In this context, the role of the academic librarian is utmost relevant in the improvement of the quality of the scientific outcome. Another measure to be considered is the dialogue between the various actors that directly or indirectly act in the creation of policies to prevent plagiarism in an organization, including managers, instructors and researchers, students, and librarians, among others.

In our present study, we conclude that there are three fundamental areas for academic libraries to act in the prevention of plagiarism: raising awareness on the problem instead of hiding it; information about the structural aspects of plagiarism, such as its definition and legal framework; and training of users including the creation of educational programs with essential tools for researchers.

In this sense, the following recommendations for the prevention of plagiarism are proposed for academic libraries:

(a) To raise awareness of the importance on the issue. We need to bring the discussions on plagiarism to the public and not leaving them as a taboo as it is done in most cases. It is important to admit the ignorance and lack of knowledge on the subject because, as it is pointed out in the literature, in most cases plagiarism is not an intentional crime.

(b) To present the information in a simple and direct way. The scientific community should have a definition of plagiarism, the ways it works, and its legal aspects;

(c) To use technological resources to provide information. In addition to include information on the website, several resources and visuals should be used to overcome the geographical barriers.

(d) To create information literacy programs and bring them to the classroom. Libraries must collaborate with instructors and administrators to include contents on research, information access, and information organization in the courses and curricula.

(e) To diagnose each case and context of plagiarism. As it is necessary to understand the difficulties that users have in relation to plagiarism, new technologies can be very helpful for this purpose. Interactive strategies, such as games with questions and answers to know the contents that are unknown to the users, are essential to develop personalized training. Similarly, it is important to provide the users with the results of the diagnosis so they can manage their ignorance on the topic and select the training programs that are most useful to them.

(f) To create and promote further courses and workshops on different sub-topics. Providing too much information at once can be overwhelming and counterproductive for the users, as it can lead to misunderstandings and ambiguities. In this sense, we recommend a careful selection of the aspects to be covered in each course according to the characteristics and context of eachuser.

(g) To develop tools for facilitating research. The creation of guides for research, analysis, and writing can be a key factor for the prevention of plagiarism.

(h) To adapt the resources to the needs of the users. Each researcher, as every new student, is different and has different specificities, skills, and difficulties. In an age in which equity in the access to information is fundamental, adaptation must be seen as a key aspect of an efficient and effective education and training program.

(i) To show the advantages of citing and referencing the sources. Researchers and students must understand that the use and presentation of information by other authors, when proper credit is attributed, gives scientific authority and validity to their work in progress.

(j) To promote and publicize the library services. It is important for the community to know that the library has the potential to support the creation of strategies for research and the organization of information. This can avoid situations of plagiarism and other improper practices in relation to an ethical use of information.

(k) To use anti-plagiarism software as a preventive tool and not always to punish. This software can be used in a preventive way as it allowsstudents to check the percentage of similarity of a document before submitting it.

(l) To have all the administrative units or departments involved in the prevention of plagiarism. There are several units in an academic organization that can actively collaborate with the library in the prevention of plagiarism, such as policy makers.

In conclusion, we point out the need for a widespread implementation of anti-plagiarism policies in academic libraries, including measures reflecting the recommendations above. In our study we also came across the following questions: Should librarians assume that researchers and instructors, even the most experienced ones, effectively know what plagiarism is as well as its context and rules? Why the role of education is almost always assigned exclusively to the instructor ignoring the rest of the actors of an organization? As the academic library is one of the crucial foci in scientific development and sustainability of societies, is it not essential to create measures that include these aspects and value the educational potential of libraries? These open questions are presented here as lines of future research in the continuous prevention of plagiarism.

REFERENCES

ALA. (2016). Academic Libraries. Retrieved from http://www.ala.org/educationcareers/libcareers/type/academic

Almeida, F., Peixoto, P., Seixas, A., Esteves, D., & Gama, P. (2016). Uma cultura de integridade no ensino superior. In P. E. D. Almeida, Filipe; Seixas, Ana; Gama, Paulo; Peixoto (Ed.), *Fraude e Plágio na Universidade: a urgência de uma cultura de integridade no Ensino Superior* (pp. 11–30). Coimbra: Imprensa da Universidade de Coimbra.

Altbach, P. G., & Vest, C. M. (2005). Academic Corruption: The Continuing Challenge. *International Higher Education*, 38, 5–6.

Barbour, R. (2014). *Introducing qualitative research: A student's guide*. London: SAGE Publications Ltd.

Bardin, L. (2016). *Análise de conteúdo*. Lisboa: Edições 70.

Booth, W., Colomb, G., & Williams, J. M. (2005). *A arte da pesquisa* (2a ed.). São Paulo: Martins Fontes.

Born, A. (2003). How to reduce plagiarism. *Journal of Information Systems Education*, 14(3), 223–224. Retrieved from http://jise.org/Volume14/14-3/Pdf/14(3)-223.pdf

Carroll, J. (2016). Para que não se confunda a gestão do plágio estudantil com questões de ética, fraude e ludíbrio. In P. E. D. Almeida, Filipe; Seixas, Ana; Gama, Paulo; Peixoto (Ed.), *Fraude e Plágio na Universidade: a urgência de uma cultura de integridade no Ensino Superior* (pp. 59–98). Coimbra: Imprensa da Universidade de Coimbra.

Colella-Sandercock, J., & Alahmadi, H. (2015). Plagiarism Education: Strategies for Instructors. *International Journal of Learning, Teaching and Educational Research*, 13(1), 76–84.

Coutinho. (2015). *Metodologia de Investigação em Ciências Sociais*. Coimbra: Almedina.

Dadzie, P. S. (2011). Rethinking information ethics education in Ghana: Is it adequate? *International Information & Library Review*, 43(2), 63–69. https://doi.org/10.1080/10572317.2011.10762881

Diniz, D., & Munhoz, A. T. M. (2011). Cópia e pastiche: plágio na comunicação científica. *Argumentum*, 3(1), 11–28. https://doi.org/10.18315/ARGUMENTUM.V3I1.1430

Domínguez Aroca, M. I. (2012). Lucha contra el plagio desde las bibliotecas universitarias. *El Profesional de La Información*, 21(5), 498–503. https://doi.org/10.3145/epi.2012.sep.08

Drinan, P. M., & Gallant, T. B. (2008). Plagiarism and academic integrity systems. *Journal of Library Administration*, 47(3–4), 125–140. https://doi.org/10.1080/01930820802186472

Ďuračík, M., Kršák, E., & Hrkút P. (2018) Source Code Representations for Plagiarism Detection. In L. Uden, D. Liberona, J. Ristvej J. (eds) *Learning Technology for Education Challenges. LTEC 2018. Communications in Computer and Information Science*, vol 870. Springer, Cham

Eaton, S., Guglielmin, M., & Otoo, B. (2017). Plagiarism: Moving from punitive to proactive approaches. In A. Babb, L. Yeworiew, & S. Sabbaghan (Eds.), *Selected proceedings of the IDEAS Conference 2017: Leading educational change*. Calgary: Werklund School of Education, University of Calgary. https://doi.org/http://dx.doi.org/10.5072/PRISM/31643

Fluk, L. R. (2015). Foregrounding the Research Log in Information Literacy Instruction. *Journal of Academic Librarianship*, 41(4), 488–498. https://doi.org/10.1016/j.acalib.2015.06.010

George, S., Costigan, A., & O'hara, M. (2013). Placing the Library at the Heart of Plagiarism Prevention: The University of Bradford Experience. *New Review of Academic Librarianship*, 19(2), 141–160. https://doi.org/10.1080/13614533.2013.800756

Germek, G. (2012). The Lack of Assessment in the Academic Library Plagiarism Prevention Tutorial. *College and Undergraduate Libraries*, 19(1), 1–17. https://doi.org/10.1080/10691316.2012.652547

Germek, G. P. (2009). Imagine no possessions: Librarians, the net-generation student, and the imminent victory of plagiarism. *College and Undergraduate Libraries*, 16(4), 338–357. https://doi.org/10.1080/10691310903356000

Gil, A. C. (2002). *Como elaborar projetos de pesquisa*. São Paulo: Atlas.

González Guitián, M. V., & Molina Piñeiro, M. (2008). Las bibliotecas universitarias: breve aproximación a sus nuevos escenarios y retos. *Acimed*, 18(2), 1–23. Retrieved from http://scielo.sld.cu/scielo.php?script=sci_arttext&pid=S1024-94352008000800002

Greer, K., Swanberg, S., Hristova, M., Switzer, A. T., Daniel, D., & Perdue, S. W. (2012). Beyond the Web Tutorial:

Development and Implementation of an Online, Self-Directed Academic Integrity Course at Oakland University. *Journal of Academic Librarianship*, 38(5), 251–258. https://doi.org/10.1016/j.acalib.2012.06.010

Hart, C. (2009). *Doing a literature review: Releasing the social science research imagination.* London: SAGE Publications Ltd. https://doi.org/10.1080/01422419908228843

Helgesson, G., & Eriksson, S. (2014). Plagiarism in research. Medicine, *Health Care and Philosophy*, 18(1), 91–101. https://doi.org/10.1007/s11019-014-9583-8

Howard, R. M., & Davies, L. J. (2009). Plagiarism in the Internet Age. *Literacy 2.0*, 66(6), 64–67. Retrieved from http://people.kth.se/~ambe/KTH/Guidingstudents.pdf

Imran, S., Khan, M. U. G., Idrees, M., Muneer, I., & Iqbal, M. M. (2018). An Enhanced Framework for Extrinsic Plagiarism Avoidance for Research Articles. *Technical Journal*, 23(1).

Ison, D. C. (2015). The Influence of the Internet on Plagiarism Among Doctoral Dissertations: An Empirical Study. *Journal of Academic Ethics*, 13. https://doi.org/10.1007/s10805-015-9233-7

Kirsch, A. (2014). Technology Is Taking Over English Departments. *The New Republic*, 1–12. Retrieved from http://www.newrepublic.com/article/117428/limits-digital-humanities-adam-kirsch

Kirsch, B. A., & Bradley, L. (2012). Distance Education and Plagiarism Prevention at the University of South Carolina Upstate. *Journal of Library and Information Services in Distance Learning*, 6(2), 79–99. https://doi.org/10.1080/1533290X.2012.693903

Lampert, L. (2004). Integrating discipline- based anti-plagiarism instruction into the information literacy curriculum. *Reference Services Review*, 32(4), 347–355. https://doi.org/10.1108/00907320410569699

Mansoor, F., & Ameen, K. (2016). Promoting Academic Integrity in South Asian Research Culture: The Case of Pakistani Academic Institutions. *South Asian Studies*, 31(2), 77–90.

Molina, M. P., & Fernández Valdés, M. D. L. M. (2010). Alfabetización informacional, innovación evaluación como funciones de la biblioteca universitaria del siglo XXI: visión desde un enfoque cualitativo. *Ibersid*, 4, 81–91.

Morais, A. da L. C. de, & Santos, J. C. S. dos. (2017). O plágio em publicações científicas e a percepção dos graduandos em biblioteconomia e documentação do Instituto de Ciência da Informação da Universidade Federal da Bahia. *Ponto de Acesso*, 11(3), 57–72.

Munarriz Zorzano, M. T. (1977). Tendencias actuales en las bibliotecas universitarias. *Boletín de ANABA*, 27(4), 33–41.

Nunes, M. S. C., & Carvalho, K. de. (2016). As bibliotecas universitárias em perspectiva histórica: a caminho do desenvolvimento durável. *Perspectivas Em Ciência Da Informação*, 21(1), 173–193. https://doi.org/10.1590/1981-5344/2572

ORI. (1994). ORI Policy on Plagiarism. *ORI Newsletter*, 3(1). Retrieved from https://ori.hhs.gov/sites/default/files/vol3_no1.pdf

Paré, G., Trudel, M., Jaana, M., & Kitsiou, S. (2015). Information and Management Synthesizing information systems knowledge: A typology of literature reviews. *Information & Management*, 52, 183–199. https://doi.org/10.1016/j.im.2014.08.008

Pickard, A. J. (2013). *Research Methods in Information.* London: Facet Publ.

Pythan, L. H., & Vidal, T. R. A. (2013). O plágio acadêmico como um problema ético, jurídico e pedagógico. *Direito & Justiça*, 39(1), 77–82. Retrieved from http://revistaseletronicas.pucrs.br/ojs/index.php/fadir/article/viewFile/13676/9066

Roig, M. (2002). Avoiding plagiarism, self-plagiarism, and other questionable writing practices: A guide to ethical writing. *Office of Research Integrity (ORI)*, 1–63. https://doi.org/10.3109/0142159X.2011.579201

Sciammarella, S. (2009). Making a difference: Library and teaching faculty working together to develop strategies in dealing with student plagiarism. *Community and Junior College Libraries*, 15(1), 23–34. https://doi.org/10.1080/02763910802665086

Severino, A. J. (2017). Implicações éticas da construção do conhecimento: desafios para a prática da docência e da investigação científica. *Filosofia e Ensino*, 6(1). https://doi.org/http://dx.doi.org/10.5380/nesef.v6i1.59522

SIBUC. (2018). Sobre nós. Retrieved from https://www.uc.pt/sibuc/Sobrenos

Silva, O. S. F. (2008). Entre o plágio e a autoria: qual o papel da universidade? *Revista Brasileira de Educação*, 13(38), 357–414. https://doi.org/10.1590/S1517-86922007000100011

Silva, R., Silveira, S., Cruz Filho, A. M., & Sousa Neto, M. D. (2018). Plágio. In C. Estrela (Ed.), *Metodologia científica: ciência, ensino, pesquisa* (3a ed., pp. 281–292). Porto Alegre: Artes Médicas.

Stagg, A., Kimmins, L., & Pavlovski, N. (2013). Academic style with substance: A collaborative screencasting project to support referencing skills. *Electronic Library*, 31(4), 452–464. https://doi.org/10.1108/EL-01-2012-0005

Strittmatter, C., & Bratton, V. K. (2014). Plagiarism Awareness among Students: Assessing Integration of Ethics Theory into Library Instruction. *College & Research Libraries*, 75(5), 736–752. https://doi.org/10.5860/crl.75.5.736

Totterdell, Barry. (1978). *Public Library Purpose*. London: Clive Bingley.

Ward, R., Harrison, T., & Pace, S. (2010). Library instruction from scratch at a career college. *Community and Junior College Libraries*, 16(3), 192–196. https://doi.org/10.1080/02763915.2010.493100

WPA. (2003). Defining and Avoiding Plagiarism: The WPA Statement on Best Practices. Retrieved from http://wpacouncil.org/files/wpa-plagiarism-statement.pdf

5
Does Open Access Promote Plagiarism?

Prabhash N. Rath
Sanjaya Mishra

1. INTRODUCTION

The "Renaissance" that took place in Europe during 14th and 15th centuries, has given rise to numerous ideas and heralded the period of modernity in science. The scientific discoveries, which hitherto been product of instinct and sudden observations, emerged in a more structured way, taking note of past works on the subject of enquiry. The post Renaissance period saw the emergence of modern science, more popularly known as scientific revolution (Kuhn, 1970), saw the progress of knowledge in all areas of science leading to evolvement of scientific laws or principles, which became subject of further investigation and validation. The need to communicate results of research to large scientific community led to the establishment of formal channels of scholarly communication. The discovery of modern printing also facilitated in a great way the effective communication of scholarly writings across countries. Scholarly communication is "the system through which research and other scholarly writings are created, evaluated for quality, disseminated to the scholarly community, and preserved for future use. The system includes both formal means of communication, such as publication in peer-reviewed journals, and informal communication, such as electronic listservs" (ACRL, 2003). The 16th and 17th centuries witnessed establishment of learned societies in Europe typically named as "Royal Societies" because of patronage either from the Monarch or the State. These learned societies started communicating their research works through papers in different journals which heralded the role of journals as the prime vehicle for communicating scholarly communication. In 1665, two journals, viz. *Journal des Scavens* (the earliest research journal) and Journal of the Royal Society started publishing from France and England respectively. These two journals still continue to be published with modified titles. Soon they were followed by numerous other journals appearing from Europe. In India, The Asiatick Researches, or Transactions of the Society Instituted in Bengal, for Inquiring into the History and Antiquities, the Arts, Sciences, and Literature of Asia started in 1788 is the oldest scholarly journal published from Asia. In earlier times, the journals used to cover very broad subjects with titles such as *Transactions*, *Proceedings*, etc. However, gradually, with the proliferation of literature as a result of research in narrower areas, more journals covering specific subject areas emerged. Some academic journals are also of interdisciplinary nature covering papers from several distinct subject fields. Scholarly communication takes place in many other ways (such as conference proceedings, monographs, reports, patents, theses, working papers, etc.) than journal publications. However, the journal publication has emerged as the most popular and respected media for scientific communication because of their reliability, academic rigour, quality assurance and outreach. In social sciences and humanities, though, the books and book chapters from reputed publishers are still considered as communications of high credentials.

According to Guedon (2001) the journal is a social registry of scientific innovations, through which researchers seek recognition and establish 'ownership' (Mishra, 2012). As per one estimate (Jinha, 2010) by 2009, there were around 50 million journal articles that had been published since the first appearance of the *Philosophical Transactions*. One of the most important factors for acceptance of academic journals as chief vehicles of academic output has been the 'peer review' process, which refer to examination of a paper submitted for publication by one or more experts in the same subject field towards its suitability for publication.Peer review is a key component of the scholarly communication ecosystem that has four distinct sub-system: (i) the scholarly/academic environment mainly represented by universities and research institutions; (ii) the peer-review process, mainly supported by volunteer researchers; (iii) the editor-publisher relationship; and (iv) the publishing industry that disseminates the research information (Mishra, 2012).

The scholarly communication ecosystem, particularly, the academic publishing has undergone many changes since inception. One of the most significant transition is from print version to electronic version. This change not only made journal publishing easier, but also increased the possibility of 'access' along with the issue of 'ownership' and recognition of ideas. The learned societies, who have first initiated the process of academic publishing, gradually gave way to commercial publishers. Since 1960s and 1970s, many of the journal titles being published by learned societies have been taken over by commercial publishers. These journals are mostly subscribed by the university and research libraries, asthe acquisition of scholarly content through subscriptions has been primarily the duty of research libraries for many years. The journal market, seen from the point of view of the library, can be characterized by a high level of stability, due basically to two main factors: (a) the attachment of scholars to their favorite information sources, in a context where conservation is the main drive for publication and reading, and (b) the natural tendency not to break print collections within the library so that one can understand the library through its portfolio of "journals" (Romary, 2012). Taking advantage of the same, the journal publishers have successfully created a sort of 'inelastic demand' for academic publishing mainly academic journal publishing resulting in raising cost of journals. The emergence of electronic publishing in the 1990s allowed publishers to create journal bundles as 'big deals' and charged different pricing to different libraries. The average journal price increased significantly independent of the Consumer Price Index. A study found that prices jumped 51.9% from 1996 to 1999 and 32% from 1999 to 2002 (Schlimgen and Kronenfeld, 2004). The "journal crisis" of the 1990s along with ease of publishing online journals led to the emergence of Open Access.

2. OPEN ACCESS

Even though Open Access (OA) as a term was first mentioned by Dr. S.R. Ranganathan in 1931 (Mishra, 2012), the emergence of Open Access publishing as a revolutionary movement started at a meeting in 2001 organized by the Open Society Institute in Budapest, which later came to be known as Budapest Open Access Initiative (BOAI). Since then it has gathered considerable support in scholarly communication. The movement, which emerged as a challenge to the monopoly of commercial publishers over most of the prestigious journals and the corresponding rising cost of journals, has provided a ray of hope for the scholars who otherwise are not able to access a substantial portion of scholarly information.

The open access publishing is defined as as "free availability on the public Internet, permitting any users to read, download, copy, distribute, print, search, or link to the full texts of these articles, crawl them for indexing, pass them as data to software, or use them for any other lawful purpose, without financial, legal, or technical barriers other than those inseparable from gaining access to the Internet itself" (BOAI, 2002).

Broadly to be considered as an open access research communication, the following criteria can be applied:

1. Open access literature is freely available : Notwithstanding the differences about the other aspects of essential characteristics of open access literature, free availability is the first and foremost characteristic of open access literature. As Peter Suber puts it, free availability is the 'the element that catalyzed the open-access movement' (Suber, 2003);

2. Open access literature is online : The cost factor makes it almost mandatory for open access literature to be online as the cost of digital publication of literature and their distribution through Internet is minimal as compared to print versions;

3. Open access literature can be used with minimal restrictions : In addition to be made available free of cost to the readers, open access literature can also be used with minimal restrictions as long as there is correct attribution and the integrity of the work is maintained.

OA in practice can be seen in three different ways (Mishra, 2012): (i) Green route — archives/repositories through which authors provide access to their work as pre-print or post-print and with or without publisher's embargo; (ii) Gold route — journals that are available online for free access, and recently (iii) Platinum route – the social networking approach to sharing research work. The gold route to OA has resulted in new business models for publishers resulting in hybrid journals – that publish papers in toll access journals for a fee, normally called Article Processing Charges (APC). While the gold route mainly represents the open access journal publications, only about 30.3% journals listed in the Directory of Open Access Journals (DOAJ) charge APC (Crawford, 2018). While this model has resulted in some of the mega journals like PLOS ONE, Scientific Reports, SAGE Open, BMJ Open and PeerJ, some of OA journals that charge APC have contributed to the debate on quality of paid publications and increasing plagiarism in OA journals. This has also resulted in availability of more "predatory journals".

3. PREDATORY JOURNALS

There is a typical misconception that online journals, especially open access journals gave rise to predatory publishing. "Before the digital age, predatory publishing took the form of vanity monograph publishing" (Berger, 2017). However, the clear detection of predatory publishing is a discovery of electronic age. The 2013 "Bohannon Sting" published in *Science* highlighted the problem of predatory journals. John Bohannon, a science journalist, submitted a sham medical research paper to a broad list of OA journals from the well-regarded DOAJ and the predatory journal list maintained by Jeffery Beall (This list has been closed since 2017 (Beall, 2017) and maintained by an unknown doctoral scholar on a blog[3]). The 45% of journals listed in DOAJ accepted the article while 82% on Beall's list accepted it. Bohannon discussed this issue with a small group of scientists, who believed that the results would have been same with traditional subscription based journals (Bohannon, 2013). Interestingly, one third of the journals in the sting were from India. It may also be noted that bad or fraudulent peer review and other misconduct occur in all types of scholarly publication (Kulkarni, 2016). Another major academic misconduct that plague scholarly publishing is plagiarism and in the context of OA it is easy (Bailey, 2015).

4. PLAGIARISM

"Plagiarism is a deep-rooted, widespread and ever spreading malaise" (Satija, 2015). The most widely accepted definition of plagiarism is the act of stealing someone else's work and attempting to pass it off as your own. Plagiarism can apply to anything, from paintings, photographs, term papers, research papers, songs and even ideas. In academic circle plagiarism is considered as an unethical practice as it deprives the originator of the idea or papers his/ her due credit or in other words, credit is ascribed to somebody who actually doesn't deserve it. Ironically, lifting other's ideas and fine tuning the same to produce a new idea without giving due credit to the original work is nothing new and was actually not being considered as an unethical practice till the advent of printing in general and copyright issues in particular. The emergence of Internet, with its inherent quality of providing easy accessibility of literature and even more easier procedure to copy and use the same made plagiarism easier. The Committee on Publication Ethics (COPE) identified mainly three types of plagiarism (Wager, 2011):

i. Major plagiarism, i.e. when the author uses of large portion of text or data from some other author's work and passes off as his/ her own; or make use of 'online paper writing

---

3. https://beallslist.weebly.com/

services' or 'ghostwriting' (Singh and Ramenyi, 2016), or use readymade papers, dissertations etc. and submit the same (Janssens and Tummers, 2015);

ii. Minor plagiarism: Minor copying of short phrases only, typically less than 100 words; and

iii. Use of images without acknowledgement of source.

A new type of plagiarism is also reported in literature due to the advent of metrics based institutional assessment carried out by funding agencies and governments. This is termed as 'institutional plagiarism' that occurs when publication credit is given to currently affiliated institution while the original work was carried out in another institution (Berry, 2012).

Different studies suggest that common reasons for plagiarism are: poor academic skills, poor understanding of plagiarism, laziness/ convenience and lack of time/ facility, and publication pressure (Devlin and Gray, 2007). In a study amongst students within institutions of higher education in the UK, Park (2003) reported that reasons for plagiarism include lack of understanding, efficiency gain, time management issues, negative attitude towards teachers or task, social pressure and lack of deterrence. Another study from UJK also reported the reasons for plagiarism such as helping a friend, time pressure, extenuating circumstances, peer pressure, increasing workload, fear of failure and laziness (Franklyn-Stokes and Newstead, 1995). A study in Turkey revealed that students had a tendency to plagiarise using the Internet by copying material or using the same assignment in different courses. Time constraints, workload and difficulty of the assignments/projects were indicated as among the major reasons for tendencies towards Internet plagiarism (Eret & Ok, 2014). Irrespective of the reasons for plagiarism in the context of teaching and learning, we can categorise plagiarism as intentional and unintentional (Satija, 2015). There is always a rare possibility of similarity in expression of ideas that may amount to unintentional plagiarism. However, the bulk of the plagiarism that we encounter happen due to intentional cheating by the perpetrators. These do not give credit to the original creators of the ideas where it is due.

5. PLAGIARISM IN OPEN ACCESS JOURNALS

Plagiarism becomes easier with the ease of access and usability of web-based information resources that allows 'copy' and 'paste'. An author can simply lift lines after lines from another work available in electronic form without much effort. In our survey of literature, we did not find any empirical studies that indicated increase of plagiarism due to OA publications. However, Brandt, Gutbrody, Wellnitzy and Wolf, (2013) suggest that open access increases the possibility of detecting plagiarism as "nearly all recent examples of copyright violations in scientific, academic and scholarly areas, the original sources of the plagiarized passages can be found on Internet". They also indicated that nearly one third of all essays checked in the project were not free from plagiarism. A positive development of OA could be the discovery of cases of plagiarism which becomes much easier with online resources in general and open access resources in particular. We can rely on two specific studies that indicates there is no impact of online availability on increasing plagiarism.

1. Ison (2014) investigated the differences between plagiarism levels in doctoral dissertations submitted by students enrolled for face-to-face education and online education. The study revealed no significant difference between the originality indices of dissertations from face-to-face teaching institutions and those of dissertations from online institutions. Across both institution types, more than half of all dissertations contained some level of plagiarism.

2. In another study Ison (2015) analysed the potential influence of the Internet on doctoral dissertations written prior to widespread use of the Internet with those written in a period in ubiquitous Internet use. The study revealed mean similarity indices for pre-Internet and post-Internet eras were 14.5% and 12.3%, respectively and was statistically significant. However, when comparing plagiarized vs. non-plagiarized dissertations from both the era, there was no significant difference. This indicated that similarity decreased post Internet and free availability may not be having impact on plagiarism.

6. PLAGIARISM IN TOLL-ACCESS JOURNALS

Examples of plagiarism is not limited to open access journals only. The problem of plagiarism is increasing day by day with the easy availability of online resources. In India and elsewhere, there are increasing number of reports involving the problem of plagiarism in higher education (See, for example: Times of India, 2016; Singh, 2018; Ramya, 2012; DNA, 2014; Kausar, 2014; Ashwini, 2014; Prasad, 2014). Most of the cases of plagiarism as reported in Retraction Watch[4] involve books and subscription journals. Hence, the acts of plagiarism can't be attributed to either open access or toll-access journals. It depends on the attitude and academic temperament of the authors; their ability to communicate ideas clearly in English, and knowledge and skills of good academic writing and ethical practices. The authors, because of the reasons mentioned elsewhere in this paper, resort to plagiarism and would have continued to do so even if there is no open access literature. Thus, plagiarism is a behavioural issue and not something to do with ease of availability of information.

7. HOW TO PREVENT PLAGIARISM

Recognizing that plagiarism is a problem to genuine knowledge generation and research is the starting point. This recognition comes from establishment institutional policies for copyright, plagiarism and open access. The University Grants Commission in India has notified a comprehensive regulation to prevent plagiarism in Indian higher education institutions. The objective of such a regulation is to create awareness about the problems of plagiarism, create institutional mechanisms for education and training for academic integrity and establish a procedure to prevent and punish those involved in plagiarism. The regulation allows up to 10% similarly in non-core areas, where core areas are defined as "abstract, summary, hypothesis, observations, results, conclusions and recommendations" that fall under zero tolerance policy.

---

4. https://retractionwatch.com

The problem of plagiarism can be tackled by adopting 'plagiarism prevention' method or 'plagiarism detection' method (Lukashenko, Graudina and Grundspenkis, 2007). Plagiarism prevention involves a long term and broad-based approach, the results of which is likely to last longer, whereas plagiarism detection is a quick and easy approach and may not result in curtail plagiarism effectively. The following steps may be taken to prevent plagiarism:

(a) To consistently preach about the evils of plagiarism and educate students and faculty members about the steps may be taken to arrest the same;

(b) To report immediately about the instances of plagiarism. In fact, Fox and Beall (2011) have reported several positive results that may happen if plagiarism is reported.

(c) Library guides on how to avoid plagiarism may be made available on university websites to enable students and teachers follow instructions carefully (e.g. Gardner (1999); University of Malta (2007) etc.)

(d) Training on academic writing, copyrights, open access and plagiarism be part of the course work for research so that every student and teachers is skilled in scholarly communication and understand the academic and legal consequences of plagiarism.

(e) Using similarity checking software as part of academic writing works such as assignment submissions would also improve the ability of the students to improve their writing through practice. However, there is also an ethical question related to the use of similarity software that collect students work to build their database without consent (Lukashenko, Graudina and Grundspenkis, 2007).

8. CONCLUSION

Our review and analysis demonstrate that OA publications especially OA journals don't encourage plagiarism *per se*, rather they can be deterrent factors towards spread of plagiarism because of their accessibility for public scrutiny. Actually, plagiarism is more concerned with personal and professional ethics and of scientific credibility of researchers. Plagiarism is a phenomenon, which has affected creativity and knowledge generation from the very beginning and had appeared far earlier than OA. Open access journals also follow the same rigour and academic integrity in order to maintain the standard like good subscription based journals. The journals (mostly predatory journals) where more instances of plagiarism are reported, are actually taking advantage of the loopholes of a system especially in countries where careers in academic are strongly linked to quantification of publication output instead of quality. Open Access is about making publicly funded research available to all for use without double dipping the tax-payers, whereas plagiarism is a behavior of researchers that happen in all types of journals.

As researchers, we tried to look into the impact of open access on plagiarism from an interpretive critical discourse based on existing literature and inductive generalizations. However, a better way to answer the question – Does OA promote plagiarism? – would have to conduct an empirical study by comparing a set of open access and toll access publications over a period of time. We strongly believe that such a study would result no significant difference as plagiarism is more linked to personal and professional ethics of the individual researchers. Knowledge is generated with a purpose of getting transmitted easily so that the same can be used to generate more knowledge. It is a cycle and a necessity for advancement of knowledge itself. Hence, blaming Open Access publications for increased cases of plagiarism is rather an oversimplified and illogical conclusion. The focus should be more on initiating steps to reduce plagiarism by educating young scholars to avoid plagiarism and build strong ethical dimension to research rather than looking at open access publications as a cause of increase in plagiarism cases.

REFERENCES

ACRL Scholarly Communication Committee (2003). Principles and strategies for reforms of scholarly communication, Retrieved from http://www.ala.org/acrl/publications/whitepapers/principlesstrategies

Ashwini, Y.S. (2014, April 18). Clarification Sought from VC on Plagiarism Charges, *Deccan Herald*, Retrieved from https://www.deccanherald.com/content/400354/clarification-sought-vc-plagiarism-charges.html

Bailey, J. (2015). Open Access: Easy Access for Plagiarists, Retrieved from https://www.plagiarismtoday.com/2015/01/20/open-access-easy-access-for-plagiarists/

Beall, J. (2017). What I learned from predatory publishers. *Biochemia Medica*, 27(2), 273-9. Retrieved from https://web.archive.org/web/20170615124437/http://www.biochemia-medica.com/2017/2/273

Berger, M. (2017). Everything You Ever Wanted to Know About Predatory Publishing but Were Afraid to Ask, Retrieved from http://www.ala.org/acrl/sites/ala.org.acrl/files/content/conferences/confsandpreconfs/2017/EverythingYouEverWantedtoKnowAboutPredatoryPublishing.pdf

Berry, C. (2012). Metrics-Based Assessments of Research: Incentives for 'Institutional Plagiarism'? *Science and Engineering Ethics*, 19 (2), 337–340

BOAI (2002). Budapest Open Access Initiative, Retrieved from http://www.soros.org/openaccess/read

Bohannon, J. (2013). Who's afraid of peer-review? *Science*, 342 (6154), 60-65.

Brandt, J., Gutbrody, M., Wellnitzy, O., & Wolf, L. (2013).Plagiarism Detection in Open Access Publications, Retrieved from https://pdfs.semanticscholar.org/1382/85c040d2c03663909be94899add14b86022e.pdf

Crawford, W, (2018). *GOAJ3: Gold Open Access Journals 2012-2017*. Livermore, CA: Cites & Insights Books. Retrieved from https://waltcrawford.name/goaj3.pdf

Devlin, M., & Gray, K. (2007). In their Own Words: A Qualitative Study of the Reasons Australian University Students Plagiarize.*Higher Education Research & Development*, 26(2), 181-198

DNA (2014, March 4). Two PhD Guides Found Guilty of Plagiarism, Retrieved from http://www.dnaindia.com/pune/report-two-phd-guides-found-guilty-of-plagiarism-1966714

Eret, E., & Ok, Ahmet, (2014). Internet Plagiarism in Higher Education: Tendencies, Triggering Factors and Reasons among Teacher Candidates.*Assessment & Evaluation in Higher Education*, 39 (8), 1002–1016

Fox, M., & Beall, J. (2014). Advice for Plagiarism Whistleblowers. *Ethics & Behaviour*, 24(5), 341-349

Franklin-Stokes, A., & Newstead, S.E. (1995). Undergraduate Cheating: Who does What and Why? *Studies in Higher Education*, 20(2), 159-172

Gardner, D. (1999). Plagiarism and How to Avoid It, Retrieved from http://www4.caes.hku.hk/plagiarism/image/all_in_one.pdf

Guedon, Jean-Claude (2001). In Oldenburg's Long Shadow: Librarians, Research Scientists, Publishers and the Control of Scientific Publishing, Washington, D.C.: Association of Research Libraries, Retrieved from http://www.arl.org/storage/documents/publications/in-oldenburgs-long-shadow.pdf

https://timesofindia.indiatimes.com/city/chennai/Violations-bureaucracy-hit-research-at-158-year-old-University-of-Madras/articleshow/55360835.cms

Ison, D. C. (2014). Does the online environment promote plagiarism? A Comparative Study of Dissertations from Brick-and-Mortar versus Online institutions. *Journal of Online Learning and Teaching*, 10(2), 272-282, Retrieved from http://jolt.merlot.org/vol10no2/ison_0614.pdf

Ison, D. C. (2015). The influence of the Internet on Plagiarism among Doctoral Dissertations: An Empirical Study. *Journal of Academic Ethics*, 13(2), 151-166.

Janssens, K., & Tummers, J. (2015). A pilot study on students and lecturers' perspective on plagiarism in higher education in Flanders, In Plagiarism across Europe and beyond 2015: Conference Proceedings (pp.12-21). June 10–12, 2015, Brno, Czech Republic. Retrieved from https://plagiarism.pefka.mendelu.cz/files/proceedings_15.pdf

Jinha, A.E. (2010). Article 50 million: An Estimate of the Number of Scholarly Articles in Existence, *Learned Publishing*, 23(3), 258-263

Kausar, H. (2014, January 20). Jamia Millia Islamia Researchers hit by Plagiarism Slur, *India Today*, Retrieved from https://www.indiatoday.in/india/north/story/jamia-millia-islamia-researchers-plagiarism-slur-turnitin-software-177526-2014-01-20

Kuhn, T. S. (1070). *The Structure of Scientific Revolutions*, Ed2. Chicago: University of Chicago Press.

Kulkarni, S. (2016). What Causes Peer review Scams and how can They be Prevented? *Learned Publishing*, 29 (3), 211-213.

Lukashenko, R., Graudina, V., & Grundspenkis, J. (2007). Computer-based Plagiarism Detection Methods and Tools: An overview. *Proceedings of the 2007 International Conference on Computer Systems and Technologies, CompSysTech 2007*, Rousse, Bulgaria, June 14-15, 2007. Retrieved from https://www.researchgate.net/publication/220795593_Computer-based_plagiarism_detection_methods_and_tools_An_overview

Mishra, S. (2012). Scholarly Communication Reconsidered, *Library Herald*, 50(2), 105-126.

Park, C. (2003) In Other (People's) Words: Plagiarism by University Students-Literature and Lessons. *Assessment & Evaluation in Higher Education*, 28(5), 471-488

Prasad, R. (2014, July 16). IMTECH: CSIR Scientist Used Faked Data in Seven Papers, *The Hindu*, Retrieved from https://www.thehindu.com/sci-tech/science/imtech-csir-scientist-used-faked-data-in-seven-papers/article6218161.ece

Ramya, M. (2012, May 20). Madras University Bans Scholar for Plagiarism. *Times of India*, Retrieved from https://timesofindia.indiatimes.com/city/chennai/Madras-University-bans-scholar-for-plagiarism/articleshow/13309603.cms

Romary, L. (2012). Scholarly Communication. In Alexander Mehler and Laurent Romary, Eds. *Handbook of Technical Communication* (pp.379-402), Mouton: de Gruyter.

Satija, M.P. (2015). Preventing the Plague of Plagiarism, *Library Herald*, 53 (4), 363-378.

Schlimgen, J. B., & Kronenfeld, M. R. (2004). Update on inflation of journal prices: Brandon/Hill list journals and the scientific, technical, and medical publishing market. *Journal of the Medical Library Association*, 92(3), 307–314.

Singh, P.P. (2018, April 16). Plagiarism Row: Ex-scholar of JNU Moves Delhi High Court, Wants Nitin Kumar to be Summoned, *Indian Express*, Retrieved from https://indianexpress.com/article/india/plagiarism-row-ex-scholar-of-jnu-moves-delhi-high-court-wants-nitish-kumar-to-be-summoned-5138808

Singh, S., & Ramenyi, D. (2016). Plagiarism and Ghostwriting: The Rise in Academic Misconduct, *South African Journal of Science*, 112(5-6); 1-7

Suber, P. (2003) How Should We Define 'Open Access'? *SPARC Open Access Newsletter*, 64. Retrieved from https://dash.harvard.edu/bitstream/handle/1/4736589/suber_oadefine.htm?sequence=1

Times of India (2016, November 10). Violations, Bureaucracy hit Research at 158-year-old University of Madras. Retrieved from

https://timesofindia.indiatimes.com/city/chennai/Violations-bureaucracy-hit-research-at-158-year-old-University-of-Madras/articleshow/55360835.cms

University of Malta (2007). How to Avoid Plagiarism. Retrieved from https://www.um.edu.mt/__data/assets/pdf_file/0006/95568/how_to_avoid_plagiarism.pdf

Wager, L. (2011) How Should Editors Respond to Plagiarism? *COPE discussion paper.* Committee on Publication Ethics. Retrieved from *https://publicationethics.org/files/COPE_plagiarism_discussion_%20doc_26%20Apr%2011.pdf*

6

Plagiarism and the New Norm in Scholarly Communication: The New Information Professionals and Open Access Advocacy Groups' Perspective

Stavroula Sant-Geronikolou[5]

1. A SNEAK PEEK INTO THE STATE OF THE PROBLEM

Technological advancements and the new informational paradigm instigated by socio-economical circumstances has led to a new kind of scholarly communication where widespread network availability of background materials and their ease of reuse will eventually alter the way research articles are produced, making the research enterprise more efficient by reducing redundant effort (Citron & Ginsparg, 2015).

However, no development comes without a cost. Adaptation to the recent dramatic changes

---

5. **Acknowledgements:** The author would like to thank survey and email interview respondents for their valuable insights. She would also like to extend her appreciation to the Open Up Hub Competition for students and early career researchers as well as the organizing committee and presenters at the 1st OPERAS conference celebrated in Athens, June 2018 for their inspiration to engaging in present research endeavor. This paper builds upon a recent article posted in Open Up Hub Blog under the title '' Beyond training-the-trainers: Discussing New Information Professionals' capacity to addressing the OA challenge'' available at https://www.openuphub.eu/community/blog/item/beyond-training-the-trainers.

Software credits : Literature analyzed and coded withMAXQDA – Software for Qualitative and Mixed Methods Research, https://www.maxqda.com/

in scholarly communications' infrastructures is expected to have significant implications for how the next generation of researchers is trained and how their normative behavior evolves (Citron & Ginsparg, 2015). Despite the level of maturation of Open Access (OA) initiatives, there is still a lot of ambiguity surrounding the Open Access paradigm exacerbated by the lack of well-planned coordinated action which in its turn perpetuates OA stakeholder insecurity and apprehension.

These current scenario pain points combined with pressures the system exerts on scholars to 'publish or perish' has led to an increase in unethical and academic dishonesty practices among which cases of plagiarism, a transhistorical phenomenon that without been exclusively attributed to OA, has however lately become topic to a lot of controversial debates under the effect of new groundbreaking technologies and ethically dubious practices as in paraphrasing tools, plagiarism and predatory publishing (Rich, 2016).

But what exactly is plagiarism and how does it relate to the OA rise? Most surveys indicate that it constitutes a major issue that will never be adequately addressed if not through joint initiatives. Librarian insecurity to addressing the OA topic on one hand and OA advocacy or coordination group leaders' assumptions that it is a matter already tackled since the early stages on OA evolution continuum, complicate even more the situation that according to predictions is expected to escalate in years to come.

On one hand, according to valuable insights they shared in June 2018 as a response to our open call distributed through IWETEL and EDICIC listservs for participation in a survey seeking to investigate their capacity to addressing the OA challenge and identify factors hindering librarian successful involvement in OA advocacy campaigns, as we'll see later on in more detail, Ibero-American New Information Professionals (NIPs) and LIS undergraduates strongly repeated the need for institutional support to jointly, systematically and coordinately address the problem in close collaboration with professional associations, without however making explicit reference to OA advocacy organizations. On the other, OA advocacy support strategists don't seem to have either a clear picture of the extent of the problem or a library-oriented collaborative strategy established to address and help alleviate the issue.Thus, there seems to be a crosscutting or even intra-sectoral, given the OA advocacy entities institutional affiliations, collaboration and communication gap, which needs to be promptly addressed in a well-coordinated way, to raise awareness on OA risks, opportunities and threats andhelp tackle discrepancies and ambiguities from early researcher and librarian career stages.

2. THE OPPORTUNITIES AND THREATS SCENARIO

Contemporary science has brought about technological advances and an unprecedented understanding of the natural world (Casadevall & Fang, 2011) with development especially related to scientific publishing been warmly welcomed by the scholarly community as a solution to efficient communication and quality assurance issues ''in today's highly diverse and rapidly evolving world of science'' (Pöschl, 2010). And indeed the principle and intended benefits of open access publishing and archiving did and do increasingly receive a widespread support among the majority of academic authors (Stanton & Liew, 2011) with OA publications getting more and more popular in different research communities around the globe (Brandt et al., 2013) from east to west and north to south, from developed to developing countries such as Latin America, Africa and Brazil where much of the national research literature is distributed through Open Access Journal services (Jain, 2012).

It's a generally acknowledged fact that the OA movement has substantially grown in the last 20+ years with OA journals according to Ware and Mabe (In Padula et al., 2017) making up about 26-29% of all journals. (Also See Appendix 2). Similarly, a recent search we conducted in July 2018 in the Web of Science for the category ''INFORMATION SCIENCE LIBRARY SCIENCE'' within the last 5-year period in SSCI, returned 930 articles of which 253 were OA (232 Gold/Bronze OA) and 21 Green OA publications, which translates into a 27% of publications involving OA peer review while 2% self-archiving in repositories of either accepted or published versions.

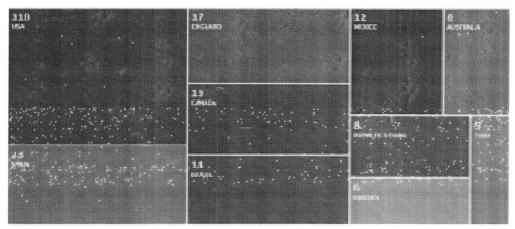

Fig. 1. Web of Science SSCI last 5-year period indexed OA publications visualization

Despite Budapest (2002), Bethesda and Berlin declarations' (2003) nuanced interpretation of the concept(Palmer et al., 2009; Machado, 2013), they all agree on the major characteristics of Open Access as "digital, online, free of charge and free of most copyright restrictions, allowing readers to download, print, distribute and even create derivative works as long as attribution is acknowledged" (Suber, 2007) that through all its different forms and types, from IRs to subject and disciplinary repositories and from multi-media to scholarly articles and preprints, has made significant inroads in a gradual rethinking and reforming of models of scholarly dissemination.

And although OA provides several benefits to all stakeholders involved - researchers, educators, journal publishers, funding agencies, government entities and academic institutions - by supporting research activities through the provision of information ''cost and time effectively at the right time in the right format'' (Jain, 2012), solving the pricing and permission crisis for scholarly journals, increasing researcher audience and impact, expanding and accelerating the research cycle, increasing the return on funding agencies' investment, giving authors a worldwide audience larger than that of any subscription-based journal, enhancing university visibility, providing reviewers with more information to work with (Pöschl, 2010; Brandt et al., 2013), providing researchers with (1) opportunities for professional networking and (2) the potential to receive feedback and commentary (Stanton & Liew, 2011), adding value thanks to the wide circulation possibilities to the published work as OA can benefit both the right to know and the right to be known (Willinsky, 2010), there seems to be a considerable gap separating (1) its widespread embedding as an objective in scientific policy making (Jariæ, 2016; Schimmer, 2016) and (2) academic library vested interest in supporting its growth and progress (Engeszer & Sarli, 2014) from its rate of adoption among the research community (Jariæ, 2016; Neugebauer & Murray, 2013; Stanton & Liew, 2011; Cullen & Chawner, 2009).

As the system is still very new, there are important issues ahead that need to be worked out for OA to establish itself as the predominant model of scholarly communication. Cultural and behavioral barriers (White, 2008), inertia, indifference and resistance to change (Pickton & McKnight, 2007), inadequate advocacy and misconceptions around status and benefits of OA publishing (Jain, 2012), the lack of coordinated professional discourse on the topic (Zhao, 2014), the lack of harmonization and the inexistence of a single route and ''voice'' for managing contentious issues related to Open Access (Tickell, 2016). Competing OA visions, nuanced definitions and OA impact diversified perspectives (Neugebauer & Murray, 2013) perpetuate the scholarly community's confusion and concerns over

- content misuse,
- OA publications quality and robustness checks,
- quality control and risks of copyright infringement and
- plagiarism, a highly recurring theme in the literature (Stanton & Liew, 2011; Neugebauer & Murray, 2013; Grandesso, 2018; Brandt et al., 2013; Ocholla & Ocholla, 2016)

3. THE UNDERSTATED PROBLEM OF PLAGIARISM

Incentives in the current system placing researchers under tremendous stress on one hand and easiness to publish and retrieve information on the other have created side effects among which increasing numbers in scientific misconduct that although not a new phenomenon, its implications have become dramatic in these times of expanding online databases and archiving scientific evidence (Gasparyan et al., 2017; Martin, 2013; Casadevall & Fang, 2011; Ercegovac & Richardson, 2004).

However, this dark side of the hypercompetitive environment of contemporary science (Casadevall & Fang, 2011; Martin, 2013) if seen under the pressure of the ''publish or perish'' syndrome (Zhao, 2014) and the scholarship McDonaldization in our highly corporatized audit society (Lorenz, 2012 in Callahan, 2018), cannot and should not be exclusively linked to the Open Access movement which after all, one might say that it is one of those infrastructural level disruptive innovations for the distribution of research, and not a mechanism that ensures quality (Neugebauer & Murray, 2013).

And yet, despite what cross-national studies suggest with regards to the potential effect of different academic cultures and contextual settings, namely academic infrastructures and mentoring, to stakeholder positive or negative stance toward plagiarism (Bohannon, 2014; Gasparyan et al., 2017; Akbar, 2018), misconduct is substantial, cross-national and growing (Martin, 2013; Carter & Blanford, 2016; Bohannon, 2013) with the quality and integrity of research not being very failsafe (Ercegovac & Richardson, 2004).

Recent rise in numbers of retracted publications reported by Jimenez & Garza (2017), Cokol et al., (2008), Casadevall & Fang (2011), Jariæ (2016), Martin (2013) and Gasparyan et al. (2017), is subject to dual interpretation and is already nurturing the polemic around OA association to plagiarism in all its forms and sizes, whether it is major or minor, facilitated and partial plagiarism, elicit, sham, close, direct, global or cyber paraphrasing, self-plagiarism or patchwriting.

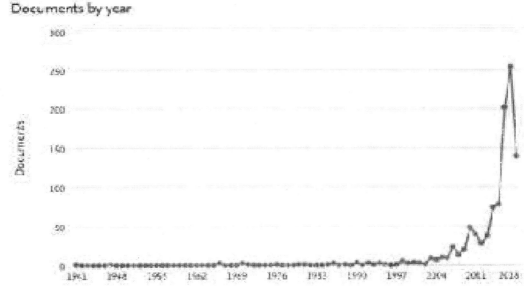

Fig. 2. Scopus 'Retracted' AND 'Publication' between 1941 and 2018 search results

Whether plagiarism is defined as the action of misappropriation of others' intellectual property including but not limited to scholarly texts, research methods, graphics and ideas (Gasparyan et al., 2017) or the intentional taking of the literary property of another without attribution and passing it off as one's own, having failed to add anything of value to the copied material and having reaped from its use an unearned benefit (Laurie Stearns in Ercegovac & Richardson, 2004) and according to Sutherland-Smith (2010, in Akbar, 2018) a matter of stealing the words and ideas, and ignorance for accrediting the original authors, it's widely understood as the unethical use of other people's publications, by claiming the content or parts thereof as one's own, without paying tribute to or recognizing the sources from which the information was obtained either at all or properly, and associated with among others stealing, appropriating, imitating, copying, cheating, paraphrasing, manipulating or alluding (Ocholla & Ocholla, 2016).

Along with fabrication and data falsification, it is classed as research misconduct (Gasparyan et al., 2017) with severe consequences on personal, professional, ethical or legal level (Saunders, 2009 in Gowri et al., 2014) destroying the purpose of research, curbing scientific improvements and advancements, undermining the entire scholarly enterprise (Hexham, 2005 in Callahan, 2018), increasing the review burden, diluting the quality of information available and discrediting journals' reputation as reliable curators of scientific knowledge (Carter & Blanford, 2016), and although it may lead to authorship disputes and occasionally copyright infringements with legal repercussions, it is widely viewed as a distinct ethical issue that even if committed unintentionally it cannot nevertheless be considered as less serious or less harmful.

The risk of plagiarism is among student top five concerns to depositing work in the Loughborough Repository (29,4%) (Pickton, 2005). According to Stanton & Liew (2011) use of work without permission and plagiarism are among two risks that cause the most concern to researchers, while Johnson (2007) highlights their consideration around the risk of ideas been copied. As for academics' perceptions of the problem, Ferguson's study (2011) reports Economists and Chemists moderate copyright and plagiarism expressed concerns while according to Neugebauer & Murray (2013) and Singeh, Abrizah & Karim's research in 2012 the fear that OA implies a loss of authorial control and plagiarism are major barriers for the faculty's willingness to participate in IRs. Finally, in regards to editor and learned publishers' concerns, Orton (2009) and Johnson (2007) identify a set of ethical problems such as duplicate publications, data fabrication, piracy and plagiarism worries that it will become rife and diminish the scholarly process somehow, while Roberts et al. reveal that 91,7% of college students reported having engaged in at least one type of academic misconduct during the surveyed year (Ercegovac & Richardson, 2004).

Also, similarities among Moylan & Kowalczuk (in Jimenez & Garza, 2017), Martin (2013), Jariæ (2016), Retraction Watch Database[6] and Scielo Electronic Library[7] catalogue findings support the argument that plagiarism is among most common retraction reasons and a most likely understated problem in mainstream publishing today (Misra et al., 2017) with its frequency increasing in parallel with the development of information and communication technologies (Mehiæ, 2013). However, this co-existence in time and space does not necessarily constitute or substantiate causality as it's thanks to the same technological and conceptual advances supporting OA that anti-plagiarism detection software and strategies are currently being deployed.

---

6. The retraction watch database (built with the generous support of the MacArthur and Arnold Foundations. Available at: http://retractiondatabase.org/RetractionSearch.aspx?) search on A WIDE INTERNATIONAL LEVEL RETRACTED PUBLICATIONS returned THE FOLLOWING TABLE WHICH IS INDICATIVE OF THE EXTENT OF THE PROBLEM (a median value of 30 and a median percentage of 9)

7. 19 retractions retrieved from Scielo between years 2007-2014 categorized as follows: Scielo search 'artículo retractado´returned 19 retractions. From the 10 retraction notes we were able to access, 5 involved plagiarism, 2 redundant publications, 2 co-author conflict and only 1 error.

Table 1. Retraction Watch database search

Country	Retractions or Other Notices	Plagiarism Cases	Percentage
Germany	624	38	6
Greece	75	30	40
Spain	226	28	12
Sweden	123	9	7
Russia	50	6	12
Australia	258	24	9
United Kingdom	581	50	9
United States	3067	215	7
Japan	843	35	4
South Korea	486	74	15
Brazil	142	14	10
Median		30	9

Existing ambiguity around OA meaning and repercussions, confusion around what constitutes scientific misconduct, the inefficiency of available tools and procedures to capture plagiarism, the lack of standardized policies and deviations from the Committee of Publication Ethics(COPE) guidelines, librarians not having yet fully assumed their Scholarly Publishing Literacy role and the oxymoron between their beliefs and behaviors toward OA, the lack of professional discourse and competing visions regarding the relationship or perhaps causality between OA and scientific immorality, the overrated power of industry self-regulation, self-correction or self-policing, the unwillingness of some editors to properly pursue cases of academic misconduct, slow down OA adoption rates, foster a sense of insecurity among librarians when researchers approach them with scholarly publishing queries (Hansson & Johannesson, 2013 in Zhao, 2014) and impede the development of the right partnerships across organizations.

4. IN SEARCH OF A NEW SET OF PROCESSES

Familiarizing researchers with open access publishing "the unknown unknowns" issue and associated challenges, opportunities and threats, requires delicate tactics, cultural change and a new set of processes including but not limited to establishing uniform misconduct policies and guidelines, the wide-scale adoption of plagiarism detection services, namely (1) semantic technologies that prove to be by far more powerful when it comes to capturing paraphrasing and article spinners' outputs, (2) citation-based plagiarism detection (Rogerson & McCarthy, 2017; Gasparyan et al., 2017) but most importantly

- reconsideration of advocacy and strategic directions where advocacy working groups and OA coordination entities will not only be serving directly the research/editorial communities but also collaborate in the co-development of train-the-trainers programs so that ambiguity, apprehension and competing views can be dealt with early in the process,

- revamping library research support services and rethinking of the way they engage with researchers and research processes (Zhao, 2014) as still their role is hotly debated with quite a few different stakeholder perceptions on the expertise and contribution they add to the field of scholarly publishing (Palmer et al., 2009; Zhao, 2014) and
- combined action from everyone in the research community if this scourge is to be eradicated (Martin, 2013).

Fundamental to the aforementionedtransformation of the current hypercompetitive scientific culture is above all serious reform achievable only through consistent methodologically rigorous and proactive action which focuses on the development of an information professional as competent ''researcher, planner, manager, assessor, teammember, problem-solver, electronic resources expert, and over all a versatile advocacy leader'' (Ghosh, 2011) that will effectively support the scholarly community to overcome unrealistic assumptions (1) on academic misuse context and factors (Fanelli, 2013), and (2) around the range and context of plagiarism that is not necessarily confined either to junior researchers or developing countries.

In line with professional associations', including the Association of College and Research Libraries, identification of OA as a main concern for the profession (Palmer et al., 2009) and as it is as yet unknown how NIPs and LIS undergraduates actually feel about OA and, specifically, about implications associated with their potential involvement in promoting Open Access,we addressed the Ibero-American university library closely affiliated community of LIS students and recent graduates a set of questions that sought to identify factors standing in the way of librarian success to addressing the OA challenge, hoping it would provide valuable feedback on student OA-specific knowledge gaps today and at the same time help better cater for the future (Sant-Geronikolou, 2018).

A substantial number of Ibero-American library school undergraduates and New Information Professionals responding to our open call for survey participation distributed through IWETELand EDICIClistservs, indicated the lack of training and continuing professional development around OA, research data, reutilization and scholarly communications, lack of institutional commitment, OA-oriented budgetary allocations, the lack of inter-departmental coordinated policies and actions and institutional OA advocacy activities among top five current OA scenario pain points while the Web along with scholarly literature and discussions with colleagues are their most frequent OA knowledge sources on the topic. Furthermore and above all, almost half of respondents share the same opinion on their low preparedness level to address community considerations around OA despite its gradual transformation to the new scholarly communication norm (See Appendix 1).

Their responses to the open ended last survey question (Q4) could substantially contribute to the greater OA advocacy conversation as they involve a variety of different perspectives, ranging from the need for a complete make-over of the study program to intensifying, enriching and generalizing CPD activities, placing a special focus on intra/inter-institutional collaboration and even greater importance on OA-associated entities' initiatives coordination with library schools and faculty, institutional commitment and even the establishment of an Open Access dedicated Chair. They also attribute fundamental value to librarian involvement in OA-related research and argue that only through instilling and promoting a holistic vision of science creation and dissemination practices among NIPs, librarians will be in the position to adequately respond to the new scholarly communication related community concerns.

What is worthwhile also highlighting is the fact that no specific mention to OA strategic coordination organizations' partnerships or contributions to raising future information professionals' awareness around OA benefits and implications was included in either their Q2 or Q4 responses.

Therefore, and according to their insightful comments, it all comes down to increasing LIS expert capabilities (KSAOs) to effectively support the OA community as it seems that the current model for disseminating reliable and authoritative information about OA is unsustainable and not effective on a large scale since its diverse, disperse, varied intensity nature can't adequately accommodate the needs of future research library staff.

5. LOOKING FORWARD TO THE OA ADVOCACY COMMUNITY PERSPECTIVE

OA strategic groups have been puzzled for quite some time now with the librarian OA skills' development case, without however providing them with any concrete large-scale cognitive and competential means to sustainably address the OA challenges.

And it's equally true that library schools are missing from the list of OA advocacy and networking activities aiming to raise awareness of OA, although networking with partner associations, joining research projects to providing further insights, innovative early-career researcher training programs, discussion fora and dedicated websites and collection of researcher testimonials are high on their agendas.

In an attempt to explore the OA strategic advocacy community perspective on the nexus between OA, plagiarism and librarian skills, we directed in June 2018 a number of e-mail interview invitations to an heterogenous pool of advocacy leaders within the European context, serving the OA cause either from learned societies, professional associations or university affiliated posts:

Q2.1. Have you been receiving any plagiarism related consultation requests?

Q2.2. Who are they coming from and what are they specifically about?

Q2.3. How does your advocacy group address plagiarism related librarian and / or researcher-expressed considerations?

Q2.4. Does your organization provide any specific white paper recommendations or guidance documentation dedicated to this issue?

Q2.5. How much attention does your group attribute to plagiarism concerns in comparison to other stakeholder OA expressed considerations?

Q2.6. To which extent do you believe these plagiarism considerations influence researcher decision to embracing OA?

Q2.7. Through your interaction with Information Professionals, what is the opinion you have formed on their adequacy to addressing the plagiarism-in-OA environments issue?

Q2.8. Does your organization propose any particular steps to supporting or better equipping librarians to cope with plagiarism within OA environments?

Q2.9 Do you consider OA averts all forms of plagiarism, including self-plagiarism?

Q2.10. Do you think there might be a fear of plagiarism or even self-plagiarism exposure involved in authors' decision not to adopt the OA paradigm and, if yes, to what degree?

In their majority, respondents indicated that they had not as yet received any plagiarism related requests. (5 out of 6 responses). According to their comments in Q2.2, scholarly community expressed considerations were basically revolving around preprints and the OJS.

As to their answers to our question on how their advocacy group addresses plagiarism related librarian and/or researcher expressed considerations, they strongly argued that plagiarism is not as much a problem where OA is concerned; anti-plagiarism tools and preprints as an authoritative stamp for research actually support and safeguard the OA cause and researchers' peace of mind where authorship and copyright infringement are concerned (Q2.3):

R1: "... anyway, plagiarism is more connected to the general research ethic than with Open Access; with online tools, plagiarism is even easier to detect...."

R2: "No concerns have been expressed so far."

R4: "It is not on our agenda, because we don't see any particular signs of such plagiarism."

R5: "By explaining to researchers that preprints are an authoritative stamp for research that in fact prevents scooping as it enables plagiarism detection and monitoring."

With regards to Q2.4, only two out of six interviewees acknowledged that their advocacy workgroups or organizations have developed training/support OA modules or documentation while one participant referred us to the specific statements in university OA journal code of ethics:

R6: "Regarding plagiarism, considerations for those wishing to practice OA, through training events we have been able to highlight that licenses protect authors and that OA means something more (and different) from simply putting your research outputs on a website."

It seems advocacy groups are currently more consumed by financial, infrastructural and technological issues as they strongly believe that plagiarism raises relatively little to no considerations as it was more of a "... problem some years ago, at the beginning of the Open Access movement..." (R1) (Q2.5, Q2.6):

> R2: "Very little [attention attributed to the plagiarism topic]. We do not have indications that plagiarism is one of the big issues for our researches right now"
>
> R3: "none"
>
> R4: "Relatively little compared to, for example, the cost of Open Access"
>
> R5: "Other than that, plagiarism has not been a key issue in related OA discussions with researchers".

As to the OA advocates 'opinion on Information Professionals' adequacy to addressing the plagiarism in OA environments issue, one of the OA advocacy leaders believes 'they are well-informed enough to deal with such issues. I think the main problem is more around fear and a lack of appropriate education, training, and guidance', two participants argued not having as yet formed a concrete idea on the matter while the remaining two respondents shared the conviction that plagiarism isn't or at least shouldn't be an issue where OA and librarians are concerned (Q2.7):

> R2: "I have not addressed the topic much with them"
>
> R3: "I'm not aware that plagiarism or the risk of plagiarism - as a consequence of OA! - is an issue for them"

Overall, their responses are mainly assumption-based as there is an obvious collaboration, communication gap, with OA advocacy groups undervaluing library role and apparently bypassing library staff to directly address the researcher community instead of jointly training the next trainers generation on how to tackle the rather unsurfaced nevertheless tenacious issue if judging from a long series of recent publications.

Four out of five participants confirmed the lack of librarian-oriented anti-plagiarism strategy. One more finding that is worthwhile mentioning is the fact that one respondent expressed ambivalent feelings as to whether offering them advice and consultation on this issue was among the groups responsibilities while a second OA advocacy strategist rhetorically asked whether there might be a chance the problem has been underestimated. (Q2.8)

As to the question of whether they consider OA averts all forms of plagiarism (Q2.9), the majority of responses were conditionally affirmative "provided people take the trouble of verifying academic output and checking for signs of (self-) plagiarism. As long as no-one checks existing literature or data, academic malpractice goes unnoticed." (R4)

With reference to the last structured interview question regarding the fear of plagiarism or self-plagiarism exposure involved in authors' decision not to adopt the OA paradigm, interviewees don't believe that it's true for the majority of the cases and especially not after 2013, as according to the last comment, it more relates to publishing as a whole rather than just OA:

> R1: "... there is no evidence whatsoever that after OA intake plagiarism grew. The more scared at the beginning were the elderly professors in the humanities, as they were used only to paper, and putting their work online was seen as a

potential "loss" of control on their work. But, I repeat, it was happening in 2013."

6. TECHNOLOGY, ADVOCACY AND LIBRARIANSHIP TRANSHISTORICAL VOCATION

Those who consider the availability of plagiarism detection software as a technological fix to the plagiarism or self-plagiarism problem are missing the point since plagiarism can take other forms that cannot be easily detected due to the use of a variety of strategies to circumvent detection (e.g. paraphrasing tricks to mask text-borrowing) not easily recognizable by non-experts. (Martin, 2013; Gasparyan et al., 2017; Carter & Blanford, 2016).

Indeed, according to Rogerson & McCarthy (2017), applying technology to identify where the paraphrasing tool has been used is difficult as detection moves beyond text summarization and matching. One more plagiarism issue this time specifically related to Open Access is the fact that there is a large volume of OA documents hidden from traditional search engine crawlers on the internet and only accessible through institutional intranets, a lack of openness, or better yet as Machado had very eloquently put it in 2013 ''half-restricted access'' giving room to much concern and contradictory, not to mention confusing to the spirit of OA (Ocholla & Ocholla, 2016).

Aiming to fill this gap, support the OA community and help strengthen the quality of OA publications (Brandt et al., 2013), the Open Access Plagiarism Search (OAPS) project was started in 2009 providing a plagiarism search service to OA data providers.

So it seems that the most obvious benefit that a plagiarism detection service could gain from the OA community, that is the free accessibility of OA documents, is often jeopardized by access restrictions, the lack of adoption of a common plagiarism detection system and above all the lack of understanding ''that detection is not the main objective in a campaign against plagiarism (Carter & Blanford, 2016; Jariæ, 2016; Ocholla & Ocholla, 2016) as among all anti-plagiarism strategies the preventive ones relying on human factor are probably the most reliable (Gasparyan et al., 2017). This understanding seems to be more in-tune with the transhistorical vocation of librarianship promoting a holistic approach to plagiarism prevention involving both pedagogical practices and raising awareness on related policies and procedures.

However, this leading role requires preparation and planning. In order for librarians to fulfil their fundamental mission to connect people with information (Engeszer & Sarli, 2014) and the OA goals, they have to become capable to confront the new challenges and capitalize on the promising opportunities that the new publication trends have introduced over the course of the past few years (Jain, 2012) and as no other than OA advocacy groups having the necessary resources, expertise, know-how and connections not only to help librarians build successful on-campus campaigns but also co-design with library school program developers the next generation of LIS courses and CPD programs that would equip NIPs with the cognitive and competental means to sustainably support the OA cause, remedy existing ambiguities and discrepancies, so as to "ensure a new cohort of information Professionals proficient in developing OA viable services, sustainable workflows, creative strategies and solutions in a full-service approach to effectively market OA benefits to academic and non-academic audiences" (Sant-Geronikolou, 2018), they should become librarian most valuable strategic partners in highlighting critical issues such as the drop in the level of morality among researchers that might have been ignored and submerged (Ghosh, 2011), influencing attitudes, enacting and implementing public policies so that visions of "what should be" become a reality.

7. IN NEED FOR A NEW STRATEGY - FUTURE PERSPECTIVES

With their role in OA and access to research not yet fully defined (Shaw, 2013) librarians uncertain about (1) its ultimate impact on their operations and their role in the OA process with under 46% of respondents agreeing that OA will "fail without their active involvement" (Palmer et al., 2009), (2) ways to handle openly available intellectual critical mass manifold consequences (Pöschl, 2010), internal scientific community threats (including scientist dissatisfaction with many of the business of science aspects as in peer review and publication pressures) and the corrosive impact of research errors and misconduct as reflected by the increasing number of retracted publications, neither can they creatively engage in meaningful partnerships to comprehensively promote OA benefits nor can they claim their proactive role in supporting Scholarly Publishing Literacy.

Additionally, and despite their high degree of understanding of Open Access, as attested by respondents in the EUA 2015/2016 (Morais et al., 2017) survey where librarians were indicated as the group with the highest knowledge on the OA topic (88,1% of participating universities considering it to be between good and very good while researchers were the group with a bad to very bad knowledge with almost 1/5 of institutions sharing this opinion), studies still show low levels of librarian involvement in

- education campaigns relating to OA where support is offered mostly ad hoc and failing to meet research community needs effectively (Palmer et al., 2009; Zhao, 2014)
- less formal means of education such as conversing with others about open access either non-library academic faculty (Palmer et al., 2009) or other librarians within their institutions (Lwoga & Questier, 2015)
- low librarian papers self-archiving rates (Palmer et al., 2009)

These statistics bring to surface ambivalent feelings regarding their level of preparedness to addressing the OA challenges and suggest that a new strategy is needed in terms of OA support methods and intensity involving rethinking the way they engage with stakeholders, capitalizing on OA-derived opportunities to increase their support services, reconceptualizing and reshaping their discourse and collaboration with OA advocacy organizations on both operational and professional development levels.

Until the day information professional OA training becomes extended beyond occasional workshops, ad hoc support and superficial awareness of OA (Zhao, 2014) to full-blown programs building on the momentum towards ensuring helping librarians develop the skills and expertise necessary to work in the new and evolving scholarly communication environment (ACRL

Libguides[8], 2018), and wide availability and uniform adoption of semantic anti-plagiarism tools, policy normalization, harmonization and internationalization become a reality, plagiarism will continue to be high up on the scholarly publishing community agenda.

REFERENCES

Akbar, A. (2018). Defining Plagiarism: A Literature Review. *Ethical Lingua: Journal of Language Teaching and Literature*, 5(1), 31-38. DOI : https://doi.org/10.30605/ethicallingua.v5i1.750

Bohannon, J. (2013). Who's Afraid of Peer Review? *Science*, 342(6154), 60-65 DOI: 10.1126/science.342.6154.60. Available at: https://pdfs.semanticscholar.org/f023/64efa2447498c552e6b2b5ffb05a442ce5ad.pdf

Bohannon, J. (2014). Study of massive preprint archive hints at the geography of plagiarism. Science *Insider*, [Online]. Available at: http://www.sciencemag.org/news/2014/12/study-massive-preprint-archive-hints-geography-plagiarism

Brandt, J., Gutbrod, M., Wellnitz, O., & Wolf, L. (2013, May). Plagiarism detection in open access publications. In *Proc. of the 4th Int. Plagiarism Conference*. Retrieved (Vol. 25). Available at: http://www.ibr.cs.tu-bs.de/papers/brandt-ipc10.pdf

Callahan, J. L. (2018). The retrospective (im) moralization of self plagiarism: Power interests in the social construction of new norms for publishing. *Organization*, 25(3), 305-319. Available at: http://journals.sagepub.com/doi/pdf/10.1177/1350508417734926

Carter, C.B. & Blanford, C.F. (2016). Plagiarism and Detection. *Journal of Material Science* (2016) 51: 7047. https://doi.org/10.1007/s10853-016-0004-7

Casadevall, A., & Fang, F. C. (2011). REFORMING SCIENCE I. METHODOLOGICAL AND CULTURAL REFORMS. Infection and immunity, IAI-06183. Available at: http://iai.asm.org/content/early/2011/12/12/IAI.06183-11.full.pdf

Citron, D. T., & Ginsparg, P. (2015). Patterns of text reuse in a scientific corpus. *Proceedings of the National Academy of Sciences*, 112(1), 25-30.

Cokol, M., Ozbay, F., & Rodriguez Esteban, R. (2008). Retraction rates are on the rise. *EMBO reports*, 9(1), 2-2. Available at: https://onlinelibrary.wiley.com/doi/full/10.1038/sj.embor.7401143

Cullen, R., & Chawner, B. (2009). Institutional repositories and the role of academic libraries in scholarly communication. In *Asia-Pacific conference on library & information education & practice* (pp. 268-277). Available at: https://core.ac.uk/download/pdf/41336223.pdf

Engeszer, R. J., & Sarli, C. C. (2014). Libraries and open access support: New roles in the digital publishing era. *Missouri medicine*, 111(5). Available at: https://digitalcommons.wustl.edu/cgi/viewcontent.cgi?article=1051&context=becker_pubs

Ercegovac, Z., & Richardson, J. (2004). Academic Dishonesty, Plagiarism Included, in the Digital Age: A Literature Review. *College & Research Libraries*, 65(4), 301-318. doi:https://doi.org/10.5860/crl.65.4.301

Fanelli, D. (2013). Why growing retractions are (mostly) a good sign. *PLoS medicine*, 10(12), e1001563.

Ferguson, N., Jennings, D., Schmoller, S. (2011). A further exploration of the views of chemists and economists on Open Access issues in the UK. Survey commissioned by the Research Communication Strategy project at the Centre for Research Communications at the University of Nottingham; funded by JISC. [Online]. Available at: http://crc.nottingham.ac.uk/projects/rcs/Chemists&EconomistsViews_on_OA.pdf

Gasparyan, A. Y., Nurmashev, B., Seksenbayev, B., Trukhachev, V. I., Kostyukova, E. I., & Kitas, G. D. (2017). Plagiarism in the context of education and evolving detection strategies. *Journal of Korean medical science*,

---

8. Scholarly Communication Toolkit: Take Action: Ways Librarians Can Engage in Scholarly Communication, https://acrl.libguides.com/scholcomm/toolkit/engagementideas

32(8), 1220-1227. Available at: https://doi.org/10.3346/jkms.2017.32.8.1220

Ghosh, M. (2011). Advocacy for open access: a selected review of the literature and resource list. *Library Hi Tech News*, 28(2), 19-23. Available at: https://doi.org/10.1108/07419051111135245

Gowri, S., Makkar, S., Singh, S. P., & Kaur, M. (2014). Plagiarism: A plaque to research. *Journal of Dental Research and Review*, 1(3), 164. DOI: 10.4103/2348-2915.146502

Grandesso, P. (2018). The Academic Publication Service AlmaDL Journals and the New Challenges of Open Access. *Conservation Science in Cultural Heritage*, 17(1), 193-202.

Jain, P. (2012). Promoting open access to research in academic libraries. *Library Philosophy and Practice*, 2012. Available at: http://www.webpages.uidaho.edu/~Mbolin/jain.pdf (Accessed 8 July 2018)

Jariæ, I. (2016). High time for a common plagiarism detection system. *Scientometrics*, 106(1), 457-459. Available at: https://doi.org/10.1007/s11192-015-1756-6

Jimenez, D. F., & Garza, D. N. (2017). Predatory publishing and academic integrity. *World neurosurgery*, 105, 990-992.

Johnson, G. (2007). SHERPA Plus Document-Hot Topics in Academic Libraries. Feedback from SHERPA OA Workshops -http://www.sherpa.ac.uk/documents/sherpaplusdocs/notts-emboc-writeup.pdf

Lwoga, E. T., & Questier, F. (2015). Open access behaviours and perceptions of health sciences faculty and roles of information professionals. *Health Information & Libraries Journal*, 32(1), 37-49. Available at: https://onlinelibrary.wiley.com/doi/pdf/10.1111/hir.12094

Machado, J. A. (2013). "Open" or "half-open" Access?: Re-thinking Open Access Initiative (OAI) Policies. *Observatorio (OBS*)*, 7(1). Available at: http://obs.obercom.pt/index.php/obs/article/viewFile/594/575

Marcus, A., & Oransky, I. (2012). Bring on the transparency index. [Online Article]. *The Scientist*. Available at: https://www.the-scientist.com/critic-at-large/bring-on-the-transparency-index-40672 (Accessed June 25, 2018)

Martin, B. R. (2013). Whither research integrity? Plagiarism, self-plagiarism and coercive citation in an age of research assessment. *Research Policy*, 42(5), 1005-1014. Available at: https://doi.org/10.1016/j.respol.2013.03.011

Mehiæ, B. (2013). Plagiarism and self-plagiarism. *Bosnian journal of basic medical sciences*, 13(3), 139. Available at: https://bjbms.org/ojs/index.php/bjbms/article/viewFile/2344/372

Misra, D. P., Ravindran, V., Wakhlu, A., Sharma, A., Agarwal, V., & Negi, V. S. (2017). Plagiarism: A viewpoint from India. *Journal of Korean medical science*, 32(11), 1734-1735. Available at: https://doi.org/10.3346/jkms.2017.32.11.1734

Morais, R, Bauer, J. & Borrell-Damian, L., (2017). Open Access 2015-2016 EUA Survey Results. European University Association. [Online]. Available at: http://www.eua.be/Libraries/publications-homepage-list/oa-survey-2015-2016-results

Moylan, E. C., & Kowalczuk, M. K. (2016). Why articles are retracted: a retrospective cross-sectional study of retraction notices at BioMed Central. *BMJ open*, 6(11), e012047.

Neugebauer, T., & Murray, A. (2013). The critical role of institutional services in open access advocacy. *International Journal of Digital Curation*, 8(1), 84-106. Available at: https://spectrum.library.concordia.ca/983116/1/238-1077-1-PB.pdf

Ocholla, D. N., & Ocholla, L. (2016). Does open access prevent plagiarism in Higher Education. *African Journal of Library, Archives and Information Science*, 26(2), 189-202.

Orton, C. G. (2009). Concerns of Editors and Publishers: Plagiarism, Rights of Authors, Open Access, etc. In *World Congress on Medical Physics and Biomedical Engineering*, September 7-12, 2009, Munich, Germany (pp. 5-7). Springer, Berlin, Heidelberg.

Padula, D., Brembs, B., Harnad, S., Herb, U., Missingham, R., Morgan, D., & Ortbal, J. (2017). Democratizing Academic Journals: Technology, Services, and Open Access. Available at: ttp://digitalcommons.unl.edu/scholcom/42

Palmer, K., Dill, E., & Christie, C. (2009). Where There's a Will There's a Way?: Survey of Academic Librarian Attitudes about Open Access. *College & Research Libraries*, 70(4), 315-335. doi:https://doi.org/10.5860/0700315

Pickton, M. J. (2005). Research students and the Loughborough institutional repository.[Dissertation] Loughborough University. Available at: https://dspace.lboro.ac.uk/2134/571

Pickton, M. J., & McKnight, C. (2007). Is there a role for research students in an institutional repository? Some repository managers' views. *Journal of Librarianship and Information Science*, 39(3), 153-161. Available at: https://dspace.lboro.ac.uk/dspace-jspui/bitstream/2134/999/4/Pickton%26McKnightJoLIS2006.pdf

Pöschl, U. (2010). Interactive open access publishing and public peer review: The effectiveness of transparency and self-regulation in scientific quality assurance. *IFLA journal*, 36(1), 40-46. Available at: http://origin-www.ifla.org/files/assets/hq/publications/ifla-journal/ifla-journal-36-1_2010.pdf#page=40

Rich, T. S. (2016). Predatory Publishing, Open Access, and the Costs to Academia. *PS: Political Science & Politics*, 49(2), 265-267. Available at: https://www.researchgate.net/profile/Timothy_Rich3/publication/301568864_Predatory_Publishing_Open_Access_and_the_Costs_to_Academia/links/5a46c68eaca272d2945ecdc2/Predatory-Publishing-Open-Access-and-the-Costs-to-Academia.pdf

Roberts, P., Anderson, J., & Yanish, P. (1997). Academic Misconduct: Where Do We Start?. Paper presented at the Annual Conference of the Northern Rocky Mountain Education Research Association, Jackson, WY, In Ercegovac & Richardson, 2004.

Rogerson, A. M., & McCarthy, G. (2017). Using Internet based paraphrasing tools: Original work, patchwriting or facilitated plagiarism?.*International Journal for Educational Integrity*, 13(1), 2. Available at: https://doi.org/10.1007/s40979-016-0013-y

Sant-Geronikolou, S. (2018). Beyond the training-the trainers challenge. Open Up Hub Blog. [Blogpost]. Available at: https://www.openuphub.eu/community/blog/item/beyond-training-the-trainers

Saunders J. A (2009). Guide to Plagiarism and Law. Oxford: Blake Lapthorn Tarlo Lyons; p. 1 13, In Gowri, S., Makkar, S., Singh, S. P., & Kaur, M. (2014)

Schimmer, R.(2016). Rebooting Open Access. Max Planck Research. [Online]. Available at: https://www.mpg.de/10856791/W001_Viewpoint_010-015.pdf

Shaw, C. (2013), How librarians can help widen access to research , live chatround-up: From access to data, resources to support, our panel's thoughts on how librarians are influencing the dissemination of research. [Online]. Available at: http://libblog.ucy.ac.cy/2013/02/how-librarians-can-help-widen-access-to.html

Singeh, F., Abrizah, A. & Karim, N. What inhibits authors to self-archive in open access repositories? a Malaysian case. *Information Development*, 2012, 29, 24–35 In Lwoga & Questier, 2015.

Stanton, K. V., & Liew, C. L. (2011). Open Access Theses in Institutional Repositories: An Exploratory Study of the Perceptions of Doctoral Students. *Information Research: An International Electronic Journal*, 16(4), n4. Available at: https://files.eric.ed.gov/fulltext/EJ971947.pdf

Suber, P. (2007). Open Access Overview. [Online]. Available at: http://legacy.earlham.edu/~peters/fos/overview.htm (Accessed June 20, 2018)

Tickell, A. (2016). Open access to research publications: independent advice. Available at: http://dera.ioe.ac.uk/25485/1/ind-16-3-open-access-report.pdf

Ware, M., & Mabe, M. (2015). The STM report: An overview of scientific and scholarly journal publishing.In Padula et al., 2017.

White, B. (2008). Minding our Ps and Qs: Issues of property, provenance, quantity and quality in institutional repositories. Paper presented at IATUL 2008: AUT University, Auckland, New Zealand, 21-24 April 2008. Available at: https://mro.massey.ac.nz/handle/10179/645 (Accessed June 27, 2018)

Willinsky, J. (2010). The access principle: The case for open access to research and scholarship. Available: http://

mitpress.mit.edu/catalog/item/default.asp?tid=10611&ttype=2

Zhao, L. (2014). Riding the wave of open access: providing library research support for scholarly publishing literacy. *Australian Academic & Research Libraries*, 45(1), 3-18. https://doi.org/10.1080/00048623.2014.882873

APPENDIX 1

Student survey questions:

Q1. Academic librarian OA advocacy impeding factors: lack of ...

Q2. NIP and library school undergraduate knowledge acquisition sources around OA strategies, initiatives and advances.

Q3. Do you feel your current competencies and familiarization with the OA topic can adequately help you educate, inform and advise on OA benefits, advantages and opportunities in the academic library context?

Q4. What steps and actions would you propose to remedy potential knowledge gaps in the area (whether library science curricula or librarian CPD programs)?

Fig. 3. Responses to Student survey Q1

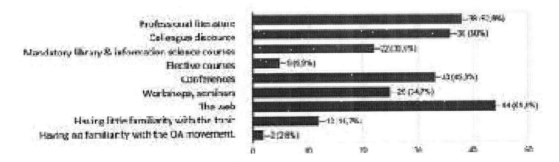

Fig. 4. Responses to student survey Q2

Fig. 5. Responses to survey Q3

APPENDIX 2.

11,723 Journals

8,489 searchable at Article level

128 Countries

3,156,104 Articles According to Doaj

According to OpenDOAR, the number of repositories has triple in a decade with 3723 available for authors to digitally deposit their work and counting.

Fig. 6. OA repository increase between 2005-2018

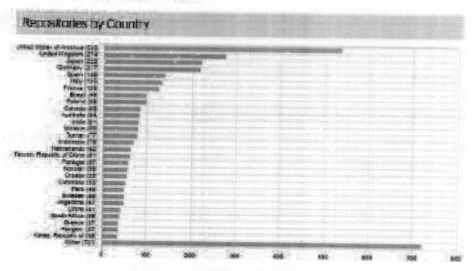

Fig. 7. OA repository distribution by country

7

Measuring Plagiarism Research Output: A Bibliometric Analysis

Suresh K Chauhan

1. INTRODUCTION

Plagiarism has become as one of the biggest evils in academic or scientific research. The advent of Information Communication Technology (ICT) and its applications in all spheres of life boosted ways of academic misconduct. Today the situation has become so grave that immediate measures need to be explored to deter it. Establishing and promoting academic integrity during first stage of education has become essential.

Historically dwelt, the plagiarism or literary theft is not a new impression. Wager (2014) stated that during Century AD 80 a Roman poet Martial claimed that his works were recited by another contemporary poet. Seo (2009) stated that during Martial literature the term 'Plagiarius', with a literary meaning of 'kidnapper' was used for illegal or improper enslavement. There were not much reports were found about plagiarism in the medieval period but its presence during this period could not be denied. Park (2003) considered the concept of plagiarism as old as writing itself but it started exposed frequently after the advent of printing. The existence of Internet and its availability had given impetus to the growth of plagiarism cases across the world. Now, plagiarism is known as academic or scientific misconduct, unethical writing, academic stealing, cheating etc. Satija (2011) defined plagiarism as a snake that had not spared even legendary Shakespeare who had also alleged for plagiarism. Initially, it was difficult to identify the real author during the ancient times, one of the common thoughts was 'the knowledge belongs to those who could memorise it or recite it'. The plagiarism related cases were increased with the use of printing technology and other means of expressions. Anderson and Steneck (2011) considered plagiarism as "a form of research misconduct and a serious violation of the norms of science". Cunha (1946) mockingly but very interestingly defined plagiarism as "if you steal from one author, it is plagiarism; if you steal from many, it is research". Through his statement, he advocated for using proper attribution while quoting or referring to others' works.

Around the globe, various publications have been written to highlight this grave issue of plagiarism, how it prevailed and how it can be prevented. Earlier it was difficult to identify the copied text from quantum of information available over the internet but presence of various tools, such as iThenticate, Turnitin, eTBlast, URKUND etc has, to some extent, reduced the human intervention while identifying the plagiarism. It can be assumed that the countries publishing quality research output on specific issue have considered its importance. The research publications on plagiarism are offering best practices and measures being adopted in various institutions or countries. Van and Workman (2012) reported that bibliometrics method is concern with the analysis research output and citations. Analytics in research play an important role in assessing the strength and weaknesses of a country with respect to research policy making. Bibliometrics is the only technique available to measure research output of an author, institute, country and research in a specific subject area (Chauhan, 2018). In this study, an effort is made to quantify research output on plagiarism that has taken place during 1998 -2017 across the world. The study also highlighted publication growth, authorship pattern and degree of collaboration etc.

2. LITERATURE REVIEW

Plagiarism as scientific misconduct has been growing rapidly among researchers, science policymakers and society (Garcia-Romero and Estrada-Lorenzo, 2014). Devlin (2006) also showed his concern over various issues of plagiarism and indicated that most of the Australian universities have been grappling plagiarism issues. He further stated that Australian universities are finding it difficult to determine the ways to tackle plagiarism and related issues.The knowledge industry accommodates information and ideas from different sources that certainly offered a great scope of plagiarism. Therefore, students, knowingly or unknowingly, get attracted towards easy ways of plagiarism.Park (2003) analysed the need for institutional plagiarism policy and practice in higher academic institutions of UK. He stated that student plagiarism has become more common and widespread. Qui (2010) highlighted concern about academic frauds taken place in China. He tried to point out the policy of Chinese universities on offering various benefits (promotion, increments, cash prize etc.) for publishing in high-profile journals has put pressure on the academic community that encouraged academic misconduct. China's science ministry conducted a survey of more than 6000 researchers of the top six universities of the country. The final report was not exposed to the public, however, some sources revealed that over one-third of those surveyed admitted to plagiarism. Yimin (2001) shared various examples of China in which researchers or scientists received many fold boosts in pay on writing quality publications there were also examples of researchers who lost their jobs or promotions or increments for not writing anything constructive. That inevitably put pressure on academic misconduct. In a general opinion, plagiarism cases are more frequent in Asian countries. International trainees who were charged with plagiarism at universities of USA often admitted that they followed practices common in their home countries. Most of these international trainees were from Asia. The various cases of plagiarism against senior academics in Asian countries like Korea, China, India, Peru and Iran offered speculations that plagiarism is more prevalent in these countries (Heitman and Litewka, 2011). Butler (2009) highlighted a few cases of plagiarism in Iran where government ministers and senior officials were the authors or co-authors. Vasconcelos and others (2009) stated that although the issue of plagiarism is very sensitive but the concept of plagiarism itself is not clear and not yet appropriately addressed in Latin America. They further stated that countries, especially in Western Europe and the USA have been paying serious attention to address plagiarism. The US Office of Research Integrity (ORI) was established in 1992, similarly, the UK Research Integrity Office (RIO) created in 2006 were some of the initiatives taken place to deter plagiarism at the national level.

Neelakantan (2009) shared example of an Indian leading scientist who alleged for plagiarism, later the scientist enforced to resign from the positions he was holding. During one of the sessions of Indian parliament, Minister of Science and Technology highlighted that China contributed 8.6 per cent of world's scientific papers while India published merely 2.4 per cent. That indicated India's worry of low research output. Subsequently, Indian government came up with revised rules for promotions and pay-increase of teachers enveloping the requisite number of research papers for promotions. This revision on rules offered a push to academic misconduct and triggered the frequency of plagiarism cases. Aggarwal and others (2016) shared that the Medical Council of India (MCI) issued some guidelines for appointments and promotions in medical institutions in India. Producing research publications was put as a mandatory requirement. They felt that these guidelines (writing papers) might take teachers away from teaching or clinical duties, the quality of papers might not be good and finally need a number of publications for the promotion that somewhere lead to plagiarism.

He (2013) discussed retraction of publications which generally takes place because of errors, ethical reasons and scientific frauds. He placed India at fifth place for more number of retractions after the USA, China, Germany and Japan. Steen (2011) evaluated 788 papers retracted from the PubMed database during 2000 - 2010. He reported that 53 per cent of fraudulent papers were written by repeat offenders. He further revealed that India and Italy ranked at first and second positions respectively for the highest rate of retractions based on fraud. It offered some confirmation on a claim about prevailing of plagiarism in Asian countries. Poultney (1996) argued that proliferation of scientific research needs to be measured but should not only on the basis of citations receive. He indicated the fear of computing citations as many controversial publications do also attract number of citations. He also put forward his greater fear of plagiarism especially in biology at the pre-publication stage. Chauhan (2018) measured plagiarism related Indian publications by extracting data from Scopus database for the period from 2002 to 2016. He anlaysed 385 records of Indian authors and found that Indian authors have published publications on plagiarism with the annual growth rate of 38.12 per cent and single authorship pattern was more prevalent. The degree of author collaboration was computed to 0.48 by deriving mean value. The journal Current Science has published a highest number of publications but Lung India, another Indian journal obtained the first rank while calculated 'Source Title Impact Ratio'. Velmurugan and Radhkrishnan (2015) conducted a bibliometric study on plagiarism related publications. They used Web of Science citation database for extracting needed data for the period from 2010 to 2014. They found that the USA had contributed 200 publications which accommodated 25.3 per cent share of total publications of the world. India's share was merely 2.07 per cent (16 publications) of total plagiarism research output and held the 9th position for producing plagiarism related publications.

In the last few decades, publications on plagiarism or academic-misconduct or ethical writing have mushroomed with a moderate growth rate.In the race of producing more share in scientific writing and accommodating a considerable place in the research output brought all the countries in the realm of scientific misconduct. Various studies have been conducted to assess the degree of plagiarism at existence, policy, practice and execution levels.

3. METHODOLOGY

The study aims to quantitatively measure the research output on plagiarism, published across the world. The data were extracted from Scopus database which is one of the largest citation and abstracting databases of peer-reviewed literature. The word 'Plagiarism' was taken and searched only in Title, Abstract and Keyword indexes. The data were extracted by executing the following query:

(TITLE-ABS-KEY (plagiarism)ANDPUBYEAR>1998ANDPUBYEAR<2018)

The data for 20 years, covering a period from 2002 to 2017 were taken into consideration and computation. In total 4907 records were extracted. These records were brought into an excel file and analysed by using bibliometric techniques. For easy representation of data the whole period was segregated into four block periods, i.e. 1998 – 2002, 2003 – 2007, 2008 – 2012 and 2013 – 2017, covering five years in each block.

4. DATA ANALYSIS

A total of 4907 publications on 'Plagiarism' were indexed by the Scopus. All these records were referred as publications throughout the study. The document type distribution of these publications accommodated 39.47 per cent (1937) research articles, 23.05 per cent (1131) conference papers, 10.21 per cent (501) editorials, 4.75 per cent (233) book chapters. The remaining document types were books, reviews and editorials.

The study analysed plagiarism related publications of 20 years (1998-2017) in four block periods, covering five years in each block. The table 1, presented Total Publications published during each block period.

Table 1. Publications during 1998 - 2017

Block Period	Total Publications
1998-2002	254
2003-2007	805
2008-2012	1676
2013-2017	2172
Total	4907

4.1. Citation Per publication and cited rate

The citations received by any publication broadly highlight the quality of the publication. In this study, an effort was made to identify the number of publications attracted at least one or more than one citations. Table 2 highlights Average Citations of Per Publication (ACPP) computed for each block period. It shows that all publications (4907) received 35699 citations with an average of 7.28 citations per publication. In the block period of 1998-2002, the ACPP was 12.42 which got improved to 13.46 in the block period of 2003-2007. The ACPP for 2008-2012 was reported lower (9.75) than the previous blocks. The last block period of study, i.e. 2013-2017 obtained merely 2.48 ACPP that expected to improve in next couple of years as publications published in the second half of this block period may start attracting citations within a year one or two.

Table 2. Citations per publications and cited rate

Block Period	TP	TC	ACPP	CR (%)
1998-2002	254	3154	12.42	70.47
2003-2007	805	10835	13.46	76.27
2008-2012	1676	16333	9.75	70.05
2013-2017	2172	5377	2.48	54.42
Total	4907	35699	7.28	64.17

TP – Total Publications
TC – Total Citations
ACPP – Average Citations Per Publications (TC/TP)
CR – Cited Rate (% of articles having one or more number of citations)

Identifying Cited Rate (CR) is another key aspect of analyzing research output of any country, institute, individual or subject area. In CR the proportion of publications that achieved at least one or more than one citation is derived from the total number of publications. The Table 2 indicates that the overall Cited Rate of publications published during the last 20 years, i.e. 1998-2017 was 64.17 per cent. It also indicates that about 36 per cent of total publications on plagiarism were not yet cited even once. The CR was 54.42 per cent was reported during 2013-2017 which was lowest among all block periods of the study. That is because the new publications start attracting citations after one or two years. Therefore, the publications published during 2016 and 2017 may yet to get cited.

4.2. Annual Growth Rate

An attempt to analyse Average Annual Growth Rate of plagiarism related publications was also made. It helped in assessing the year by year production flow of publications in terms of numbers. The Annual Growth Rate was computed on the basis of the following formula.

$$\text{Annual Growth Rate (GR)} = \left(\frac{\text{Present Publications}}{\text{Past Publications}}\right)^{\wedge}\left(\frac{1}{\text{Number of Years}}\right) - 1$$

The world has published 4907 publications on plagiarism from 1998 to 2017. In the first block period, i.e. 1998-2002 published 254 publications with the annual growth rate of 15.42 per cent. In the second block period (2003-2007) the annual growth rate improved to 21.98 per cent, wherein it was dipped to 8.10 per cent during the block period 2008-2012 that further slipped to its lowest level of 0.61per cent during fourth block period (2013-2017) of the study. The lowest growth rate during 2013-2017 appeared because some of the publications published in the second half of 2017 may yet to be indexed by the Scopus.

Figure 1 shows an average annual growth rate of each block periods covered under the study. The overall annual growth rate of 12.50 per cent was observed while calculating it for 1998 to 2017 period.

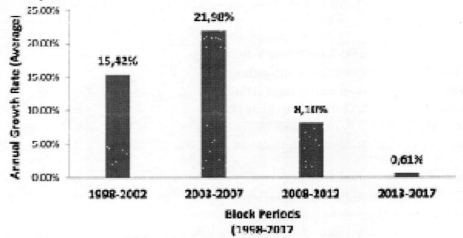

Fig. 1. Annual Growth rate of publications

4.3. Authorship pattern

The authorship pattern of publications on plagiarism published across the world was also assessed. About 228 publications were recorded without the name of the author, hence, the authorship pattern was analysed for 4679 publications only. As indicated in Figure 2, the 2031(43.41%) publications were written in single authorship. These single-authored publications attracted Cited Rate of 60.56, that means about 60 per cent of total publications written in single authorship were cited at least once. The multi-authored (publications written by two or more authors) publications (2648, i.e. 56.59%) were achieved 71.34 Cited Rate. It shows the dominance of multi-authored pattern of plagiarism related publications. The publications written by two authors accommodated 24.68 per cent (1155) of total publications which attained 71.95 Cited Rate. The publications written by three authors contributed to 16.18 per cent (757) share of total publications on plagiarism and achieved 70.94 Cited Rate. Publications written by four authors contributed 7.59 per cent (355) with Cited Rate of 70.14 and five or more authors put in 8.14 per cent (381) share of total plagiarism related publications with 71.39 Cited Rate.

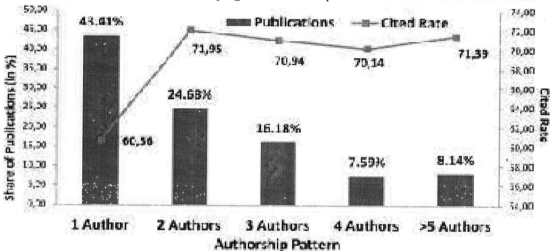

Fig. 2. Authorship pattern of plagiarism publications

The analysis revealed that multi-authorship is more prevalent than the single authorship pattern in plagiarism related publications at the global level. It was also derived from the analysis that multi-authorship publications have higher Cited Rate than the single authorship publications. It indicates that publications written by multiple authors attracted number of citations as compared to publications written in single authorship.

4.4. Degree of author collaboration

The degree of author collaboration was also assessed by using the following mathematical formula offered by Subramanyam in 1983.

$$\text{Degree of author collaboration (C)} = \frac{Nm}{Nm + Ns}$$

In this mathematical formula, C reflects the degree of author collaboration, Nm is the number of publications under multiple-authorship and Ns indicates the number of publications in single-authorship. On basis of this expression, the block-wise degree of author collaboration was presented in Table 3.

Table 3. The degree of Author collaboration

Block Period	Nm+Ns	Ns	Nm	C
1998-2002	236	147	89	0.38
2003-2007	769	436	333	0.43
2008-2012	1600	717	883	0.55
2013-2017	2075	732	1343	0.65
	4680	2032	2648	0.57 (0.50 Mean)

The degree of author collaboration was merely 0.38 (i.e., 38%) during the block period of 1998-2002. It reflects that plagiarism publications written under single authorship were more common and percentage of publications written in joint authorship was only 38 per cent. The degree of collaboration was gradually improved in the second block period (2003-2007) to 0.43 (i.e., 43%), 0.55 (55%) in third block period and in fourth block period (2013-2017) the degree of author collaboration was 0.65 (65%). The overall degree of author collaboration was recorded 0.57 (57%) with the mean value of 0.50 for the publications published during 1998-2017. The table 3 reflects that collaborative studies on plagiarism were not common during first block period (1998-2002) of the study but improved gradually in all next block periods.

4.5. Most Prolific Authors

Table 4. Prolific authors

Author	Affiliation	Country	TP	TC	ACPP
Stein, B.	Web Technology and Information Systems Group, Bauhaus-Universitat, Weimar, Germany	Germany	30	1091	36.37
Potthast, M.	Web Technology and Information Systems Group, Bauhaus-Universitat, Weimar, Germany	Germany	21	757	36.05
Rosso, P.	Natural Language Engineering Lab, ELiRF, Universidad Politécnica, Valencia, Spain	Spain	49	1010	20.61
Roig, M.	St. John's University, Department of Psychology, United States	USA	21	318	15.14
Salim, N.	Faculty of CS and Info. Sys., Universiti Teknologi Malaysia, Johor, Malaysia	Malaysia	21	222	10.57
Wiwanitkit, V.	Wiwanitkit House, Bangkhae, Bangkok, Thailand	Thailand	43	73	1.70

The analysis was also made to find out the most prolific authors, who have published higher number of publications on plagiarism around the globe. Table 4 highlights the authors who published 20 or above publications on plagiarism. It was found that only 6 authors have contributed more than 20 publications. Dr. Paolo Rosso has written 49 publications which is the highest number of publications in the area of plagiarism by any author. His publications attracted 1010 citations with the rate of 20.61 citations per publications. Prof. V. Wiwanitkit has 43 plagiarism related publications which attracted only 73 citations with 1.70 average citations per publication. Although, publications of Prof. Wiwanitkit made people aware of plagiarism and related issues but his publications received minimum citations. Prof. Benno Stein's publications (30) received more number of citations that reflect the quality of his work as his publications achieved 1091 citations with 36.37 average citations per publications. Authors, like Martin Potthast achieved 36.05 ACPP on his 21 publications, M Roig 15.14 for 21 publications and N Salim got 10.57 ACPP over the same number of publications.

4.6. Source Title Impact Ratio

The 4907 publications appeared in nearly 400 sources (source titles). An assessment was done to identify the sources preferred by authors to publish plagiarism related publications. Ten source titles were identified in which most of the publications on plagiarism were published. For determining Source Title Impact Ratio (STIR), the total number of publications in a respective source (TP), Cited Rate (CR) and Average Citations per Publication (ACPP) were computed and incorporated. The following metrics was used to know the Source Title Impact Ratio (STIR).

$$\text{Source Title Impace Ratio (STIR)} = \frac{TP + CR + ACPP}{100}$$

In this, TP is total publications accommodated by the source title that offers weight-age on a number of publications. CR is cited rate which is to accommodate the quality impact of the source with respect to publications cited. Similarly, ACPP representing the quality of publications through the citations these sources received.

Table 5. Source Title Impact Ratio (Top 10 sources by number of publications)

Source	TP	TC	CR	ACPP	STIR	Rank
Lecture Notes In Computer Science (Germany)	131	877	67.18	6.69	2.05	2
CEUR Workshop Proceedings (Germany)	134	710	73.88	5.30	2.13	1
Nature (United Kingdom)	62	425	82.26	6.85	1.51	4
Science and Engineering Ethics (United Kingdom)	45	352	93.33	7.82	1.46	5
ACM International Conference Proceeding Series (United States)	43	115	37.21	2.67	0.83	8
Journal of Academic Ethics (Netherlands)	42	307	85.71	7.31	1.35	6
Communications In Computer And Information Science (Germany)	42	27	38.10	0.64	0.81	9
Assessment And Evaluation In Higher Education (United Kingdom)	36	1006	94.44	27.94	1.58	3
Science (United States)	20	148	85.00	7.40	1.12	7
Ethics And Behavior (United States)	22	480	13.64	21.82	0.57	10

4.7. Most productive countries

The computation was also executed to know the share of total publications on plagiarism by some most prolific countries during period of the study. It was found that the United States of America has published 23.70 per cent (1163) publications and attained the top position among most productive countries who have been publishing on plagiarism. United Kingdom captured the second spot by contributing 9.33 per cent (458) of total publications of the world, followed by India, who held third most productive country by producing 5.60 per cent (275) of the total research output on plagiarism. Australia with 4.65 per cent (228) of contribution attained the fourth place, followed by China 4.46 per cent (219) and Germany 4.14 per cent (203) captured fifth and sixth positions respectively.

An assessment was also done to highlight quality of publications on plagiarism produced by these countries. Table 6, shows the Average Citations per Publications computed for top six highly productive countries.

Table 6. Top Six Most productive countries

Country	Total publications	Total Citations	Average Citations per Publication
USA	1163	12319	10.59
UK	458	6532	14.26
India	275	516	1.88
Australia	228	4906	21.52
China	219	753	3.44
Germany	203	2141	10.55

The table depicts that on an average research output of Australia, the country that produced 228 publications on plagiarism and received 4906 citations with an average of 21.52 citations per publication. It shows the high standard quality of research output Australia has been generating. United Kingdom (UK) also produced quality publications that received on an average 14.26 citations per publication. The research output of United States of America and Germany were also obtained moderate average citations per publications of 10.59 and 10.55 respectively. The concern is with production of India who produced 275 publications with the average citations rate of 1.88 only. That means, the quality of Indian publications on plagiarism is considerably poor than the countries listed in the table. China has achieved slightly higher rate of citations per publications than India. However, both these countries need to adopt substantial measures for bringing quality instead of quantity.

5. CONCLUSION

Plagiarism has become one of the most critical issues of academic and scientific research. Its existence has spread all across the world. A majority of research on plagiarism provided awareness on the issue and provided best practices to address this critical issue. Some of the experts have insisted for stricter rules and laws for combating with plagiarism at higher education system and some suggested bringing academic ethics in the elementary level education system. However, publishing best practices and policies through various research publications also worked as boon. It has offered a platform to discuss this grave issue globally to find out some quality measures as deterrent. In this study, it was found that United Stated of America has produced (23.70 per cent share) higher number of publications. The publications produced by

Australia are being highly referred and research output of UK, USA, and Germany found to be of moderate quality, whereas Asian research output, especially in India, assessed as of poor quality while analysed on basis of citations. The degree of author collaboration was only 37 per cent initial period of research but it improved gradually in subsequent block periods.

REFERENCES

Aggarwal, R., Gogtay, N., Kumar, R, and Sahni, P. (2016). The revised guidelines of the Medical Council of India for academic promotions: Need for a rethink. *Indian Journal of Gastroenterol*, 35(1), 3-6.

Anderson, M. S. and Steneck, N. H. (2011). The problem of plagiarism. In Urologic Oncology: *Seminars and Original Investigations*, 29(1), 90-94.

Butler, D. (2009). Plagiarism scandal grows in Iran. *Nature*, 462, 704-705. doi:10.1038/462704a

Chauhan, S. K. (2018). Research on Plagiarism in India during 2002-2016: A Bibliometric Analysis. *DESIDOC Journal of Library & Information Technology*, 38(2), 69

Cunha, F. (1946). Gastrostomy: its inception and evolution. *The American Journal of Surgery*, 1946, 72(4), 610-634.

Devlin, M. (2006). Policy, preparation, and prevention: Proactive minimization of student plagiarism. *Journal of Higher Education Policy and Management*, 28(1), 45-58.

García-Romero, A. and Estrada-Lorenzo, J. M. (2014). A bibliometric analysis of plagiarism and self-plagiarism through Déjà vu. *Scientometrics*, 101(1), 381-396.

He, T. (2013). Retraction of global scientific publications from 2001 to 2010. *Scientometrics*, 96(2), 555-561.

Heitman, E. and Litewka, S. (2011). International perspectives on plagiarism and considerations for teaching international trainees. In Urologic Oncology: *Seminars and Original Investigations*, 29(1), 104-108.

Neelakantan, S. (2009). In India, plagiarism is on the rise. *Global Post*. 2009.https://www.pri.org/stories/2009-10-18/india-plagiarism-rise (Accessed on 21 August 2018).

Park, C. (2003). In other (people's) words: Plagiarism by university students—literature and lessons. *Assessment & Evaluation in Higher Education*, 28(5), 471-488.

Poultney, R. W. (1996). Front-ends are the way to go. *Europhysics News*, 27(1), 24-25.

Qiu, J. (2010). Publish or perish in China. *Nature*, 467, 142-143. doi:10.1038/463142a

Satija, M. P. (2011). Plagiarism: a tempting snake. *University News*, 49(21), 4-8.

Seo, J. M. (2009). Plagiarism and poetic identity in Martial. *American Journal of Philology*, 567-593

Steen, R. G. (2011). Retractions in the scientific literature: do authors deliberately commit research fraud?. *Journal of medical ethics*, 37(2), 113-117.

Subramanyam, K. (1983). Bibliometric studies of research collaboration: a review. *Journal of Information Science*, 6(1), 33-38.

Van Harmelen, M. and Workman, D. (2012). Analytics for understanding research. *CETIS Analytics Series*, 1(4).

Vasconcelos, S., Leta, J., Costa, L., Pinto, A. and Sorenson, M. M. (2009). Discussing plagiarism in Latin American science: Brazilian researchers begin to address an ethical issue. *EMBO reports*, 10(7), 677-682

Velmurugan, C. and Radhakrishnan, N. (2015). Literature output of Plagiarism: a Scientometric approach through Web of Science. In *Combating Plagiarism: a new role for Librarian*, edited by M. Patra & S. K. Jena, SK Book Agency, New Delhi, pp.78-88.

Wager, E. Defining and responding to plagiarism. *Learned publishing*, 2014, 27(1), 33-42.

Yimin, D. (2001). In China, publish or perish is becoming the new reality. *Science*, 291(5508), 1477-1479.

8
Plagiarism : A Growing Menace Across Academia

Ramesh Pandita
Shivendra Singh

1. INTRODUCTION

Information and Communication Technology has revolutionized human life in many ways and so has it helped in the production and reproduction of information in both print and electronic form. The production and reproduction of information in both electronic and print form, if on one hand has unfolded as a blessing in the human evolution, on the other this exponential growth of information somewhere also seeks its roots through undesirable practices.The biggest advantage of production and reproduction of information is that information seekers are in a position to quench their cognitive appetite for knowledge. While as, one of the common abuses involved with the easy production and reproduction of the information is the intellectual theft, the problem with which the modern society in general and the academia in particular is battling with for quite a while now. There are many ugly faces of the intellectual theft and plagiarism is just one such ugly face of this multi headed hydra, which demeans the real value of information, for the want of authenticity, reliability and exactness of information produced. The other common terms, used as equivalent to plagiarism by various researchers are copyright violations, infringement, copying, stealing, piracy, theft, cribbing, chiseling poaching and many more.

In a survey conducted by iThenticate over 60% respondents viewed that the instances of plagiarism are on increase and so do every third editor encounters the act of plagiarism (iThenticate, 2012). Given the fact, University Grants Commission (UGC) in India in 2009 issued a notification, whereby it has been made mandatory to all the UGC recognized institutes to check M.Phill and Ph.D theses for plagiarism before submitting the soft copy of the same to the INFLIBNET for uploading on Shodhganga (INFLIBNET, 2009).

Plagiarism is a practice, whereby researchers steal the research ideas, concepts and even the technical writings from different sources through fraudulent means and reproduce those ideas, concepts and research results as their own. As per Webster's Dictionary, plagiarism is "to steal and pass off the ideas or words of another as one's own or to commit literacy theft". As per Collins Dictionary of English Language 'plagiarism is the act of plagiarizing, ideas and passages, etc., from other work without attributions' (Hanks & Wilkes, 1979), while as, the Association of American Historians defined plagiarism as "the misuse of the writings of another author, including limited borrowings" (Fialkoff, 1993). If we look at the etymology of the word plagiarism, then the word seeks its roots to the early 17th century Latin word plagium, which means to kidnap. However, the word plagium is believed to have been itself derived from the Greek word 'plagion' and over the period of time the word came to be known as plagiarism. However, it is believed that in 1601 the plagiarus was introduced by Ben Jonson, an English playwright, poet, actor and literary critic (Valpy, 2005), while its derived form, plagiarism was introduced in English around 1620 (Harper, 2018).

The undergoing discussion is about the concept of plagiarism, different forms of plagiarism, some of the primary reasons which have inflated the practice of plagiarism across the scientific and research community. These and many other concepts related to plagiarism have been discussed for the better and broader understanding of the common masses in general and academia, scientific & research community in particular.

2. WHAT IS PLAGIARISM

Although there are varying views about the concept of plagiarism, and each researcher views the concepts through the spectrum of his/her own prism. But, while going broadly and for the understanding of a layman, then the definition of plagiarism can be summed up as an 'intellectual theft'. The definition of plagiarism presented by the Department of English, University of Middle Georgia State University reads "plagiarism occurs whenever we incorporate the intellectual property of others into our own work without proper acknowledgment of whose words, ideas, or other original material" (Middle Georgia State University, 2018). Similarly, as per the Oxford English Dictionary, plagiarism is "the practice of taking someone else's work or ideas and passing them off as one's own". This clearly indicates that intellectual theft is not only about stealing the others work directly, but also borrowing an idea from some other source or person during a discussion, debate or even while exchanging the words with another person and presenting that idea in one's own words amounts to plagiarism.To this affect a clear and simple definition of plagiarism is given by the Cambridge English Dictionary, which reads plagiarism as "to use another person's ideas and pretend that it is your own".

Apart from these, there are various other definitions of plagiarism stated at the institutional level, like Stanford University defines plagiarism as "use without giving reasonable and appropriate credit to or acknowledging the author or source, of another person's original work, whether such work is made up of code, formulas, ideas, language, research, strategies, writing or other form (Stanford University, 2012). As per the Princeton University, plagiarism is "deliberate use of someone else's language, ideas, or other original material without acknowledging its source"(Council of Writing Program Administrators, 2014) and so did Yale University defined it as "use of another's work, words, or ideas without attribution" (Yale University, 2018). 'The appropriation of another person's ideas, processes, results, or words without giving appropriate credit' (OSTP, 2000).

Writing is simply a medium whereby one gives expression to his/her thoughts through words. So one has to be very careful and selective with his/her words while expressing his/her ideas or thoughts and one is not at the liberty to integrate others expressive words in his/her works. Any attempt whereby one tries to integrate other's expressions in his/her works without acknowledgment and tries to present those expressions as his/her own amounts to a willful plagiarism.

Although, each one of us can produce intellectual ideas to a lesser or a greater extent, but those minds which are fertile enough to create new knowledge and new ideas at will and contribute significantly to the society at large are known as intellectuals.The harsh reality about this intellectual growth and development is that each one of us learns things from others, each one of us get ideas and inspiration from other sources one way or the other, but this is something which gets hardly acknowledged. The fact remains, that it is the reward in the form of appreciations and acknowledgements which one receives for the work done, actually breeds the new intellectual ideas. Critically the concept of plagiarism has been stated as "if you steal from one author, it is plagiarism; if you steal from many, it is research" (Cunha, 1946). People read so many authors, so many books, experience a variety of encounters, exchange ideas, share thoughts with each other, including classroom teaching and many more other similar activities helps one to groom intellectually.Now the question arises, does getting ideas or inspirations from all such activities amounts to plagiarism and the answer will be perhaps a big no. The fact remains that all such activities are intentionally undertaken to promote the intellectual growth, to help upcoming researchers or writers to hone their skills by correcting their fundamentals by getting ideas from the work done by the well established authors, researchers, scientists etc.

3. PREVALENCE OF PLAGIARISM

It is not that the menace of plagiarism came into being with the advent of the printing press, but was prevalent in the society much earlier. However, this surely has spread its tentacles with the advent of the printing press and still more the menace became more visible in the present day society with the unfolding of the digital age. The mass production of books made the published information widely available to the public and in a way also served as a reason towards the increased use of stolen work by others, which was termed as 'textual misappropriations' (Thomas, 2000).

It is a known fact that, in absence of printing technology or the printing press, literary contributions used to be recorded in the form of manuscripts and any production or reproduction of that content in that era meant, writing and rewriting the same manuscript again and again. So in a way this slow and steady production and reproduction of handwritten content, which used to have a limited audience in a limited territory and used to be circulated in a very closed and limited expanse for reading, had very lesser chances to be stolen and reproduced by another author as his/her own work. This does not mean that there was no moral corruption in the past. There are recorded instances around A.D 80, whereby a Roman poet Martial reported about the theft of his work, which was recited by another person as his own (Wager, 2014). Similarly, a study on plagiarism discussed about the prevalence of practice of plagiarism in the society around 2000 years ago (Fox, 1946).

4. WHAT AMOUNTS TO PLAGIARISM

Plagiarism has become a buzz word these days across the academic circles all over the world, especially after the application of softwares to detect if there is any text similar to other documents. This reflects how far the academia has become aware of this prevailing menace, which hitherto remained unnoticed to a larger extent and so did a good number of researchers across the world played mischief with their research activities. There are some misconceptions, as what amounts to plagiarism and what not. Generally there is a notion among the researchers, especially among the budding researchers that to copy content from other sources and to acknowledge properly with references, does not amount to plagiarism, the fundamental mistake which a large research community makes. However, the fact of the matter is any content which matches with other sources, except those portions of text which may be in verbatim, amounts to plagiarism, even if properly cited. Secondly, it is needless to mention that borrowing text from other sources without citing it properly amounts to plagiarism.

To have a better understanding of plagiarism, Fishman pointed it out in the simplest terms, that plagiarism occurs when someone uses words, ideas or other work products, which though being attributable, but are not attributed to the original authors with the sole aim to benefit from the work, but not necessarily monetary (Fishman, 2009).

5. INTELLECTUAL PROPERTY AND COPYRIGHT ISSUES

Knowledge creation is an intellectual activity, which requires a steady, continuous and rigorous effort on the part of an individual/researcher etc., to evolve new concepts and facts. These newly established facts are supposed to withstand the test of times, whereby the findings or the results may be subjected to repeated verifiability by the subject experts from time to time. Some of the common creativities of an individual are in the areas of library works, music, film production, artistic works, patents, architectural or any other type or form of a design etc. In short, anything creative in any area of activity is intellectual property. What demeans this intellectual property is, when there is intellectual theft, whereby people try to discredit the original author or creator by claiming the creativity as their own, what is commonly known as plagiarism across the academia.

In the earlier times, use, misuse and abuse of intellectual property was common, but with the passage of time, the need was felt that like any physical property, intellectual property needs to be protected by well defined ownership rights of an individual. Given the fact, the need was felt to put in place the system, whereby intellectual property rights of individuals may be protected and so was the issue for the first time discussed during the Paris convention for the *Protection of Industrial Property in 1883* (WIPO, 1883). Subsequently, it was the Berne convention where voice for the *Protection of Literary and Artistic Works in 1886* (WIPO, 1883) was raised. *World Intellectual Property Organization* (WIPO) administers and ensures that intellectual property in all its forms is protected globally (WIPO, 1883). The article 27 of the *Universal Declaration of Human Rights* highlights the rights towards the protection of authorship of scientific, literary or artistic production (United Nations, 1948). Experts are of the view that legal protection of the intellectual property encourages the budding researchers, as it also ensures that all the benefits of patents, trademarks, art work etc. reach to its original creator and discourages the counterfeiting and piracy etc.

Copyright can be termed as a sub-form of intellectual property, which covers intellectual creativity of all forms, including industrial property, but copyright is seen in relation to the literary and artistic works and the rights to copy the content are vested with the original authors. The fundamental difference between the plagiarism and the copyright is that in the case of the former, one makes use of research findings of other researcher in his/her study without attributions hence amounts to plagiarism, but in the case of lateral, the content is protected under the copyright law and can be produced or reproduced only with the permission of the copyright holder, which can be the original author or the publisher etc. Any violation in the production or reproduction of content without the permission of the copyright holder is referred as copyright infringement. The term copyright has a dual meaning, which means right to copy and right not to copy. Authors who want their creative works to get published through formal publishing channels are supposed to transfer the necessary copyrights to the publisher and any production or reproduction of the work requires obtaining necessary copyright permission from the copyright holder, which again can be a publisher or an author. Keeping in view the growing instances of plagiarism in the society, whereby at one point of time it becomes increasingly difficult to know the original author, especially due to the internet and the easy accessibility it has given the users to access the sources of information, so were the copyright laws formulated in the 18th century following the change in the perception of public attitude towards the intellectual property and its protection (Bowden, 1996).

6. OFFICE OF THE RESEARCH INTEGRITY (ORI)

The growing instances of research misconduct in the United States ultimately resulted into the establishment of the Office of Research Integrity (ORI) in the 1992, with the sole purpose to deal with the case of research misconduct reported in the United States from time to time (ORI, 1994). The ORI is basically a merger of the institutions like Office of Scientific Integrity (OSI) and the Office of the Scientific Integrity Review (OSIR) as both the offices were consolidated into ORI in 1992. Some of the key responsibilities of the ORI are to detect, investigate, prevent research misconduct and to promote research integrity. The ORI also recommends the instances of research misconduct to the Department of Health and Human Services, United States and provides all technical support to the institutions with reported research misconduct.

There is always need to have a national policy over the issues related to academic and research misconduct. India too is struggling with issues of plagiarism, whereby the issues related to academic and research misconduct across the academic and scientific community has become somewhat endemic. It is always advisable to nip the problem in the bud, before it assumes the shape of uncontrollable hydra. Although, the University Grants Commission (UGC), New Delhi, India has already come up with draft to prevent the growing instances of plagiarism across the academia, but there is a far greater need to strengthen such draft-proposals by coming up with laws (UGC, 2017).

The researchers also correlate the growing instances of academic misconduct to the moral education, which more or less are missing these days across the school syllabi. Young school going children are being pushed to perform beyond their true capacity both by their parents and teachers. Nobody is ready to accept academic scores below 100%, all this ultimately results into academic misconduct among the students and the parents and teachers least bother as long as their wards/students attain higher grades.

7. SOME EARLIER RELATED STUDIES

The concept of plagiarism has been discussed and studied threadbare by the researchers all across the world and so do we find a very wide range of opinions about the subject. Almost each individual researcher has given his/her own definition of the concept based on his/her individual understanding of the subject.

Ethics are followed by people in almost each walk of life. These ethics can be sometimes termed as the guiding force as well, which not just helps a person to regulate his/her behaviour, but also helps one to confine his/her activities within the acceptable parameters and the same holds true about undertaking a research activity. A researcher is always supposed to follow the necessary research ethics, these research ethics help a researcher to build his/her work around solid and firm quality parameters. A researcher turns out to be unethical in his/her research activity, if he/she does not give due credit to the person, who may have helped him during his/her research activity in whatever manner (Shamoo & Resnik, 2015). Another common and widely prevailing aspect of plagiarism is, when the content as it is copied from the others work and is published without any attributions to the original authors. With the view to avoid such unethical practice and to avoid any disrepute to their journal, publishers generally use similarity detection software's to assess in the first place, if the document suffers with any similarity or not (M. S. Anderson & Steneck, 2011).

Research integrity is one more facet of the research ethics, whereby collaborative researchers are supposed to uphold research ethics. Collaborative researchers should give due credit to their research associates working on the same project (ORI, 1994). It should not be like that on one hand researcher is collaborating at work, but at the same discredit his/her fellow collaborators, by not acknowledging them, while publishing research results. McCabe in his study found that nearly 40% students admitted of plagiarizing content from other sources (McCabe, 2005).The acts of plagiarism were also found in the past, as pointed out in a list of prominent writers who were accused of plagiarism (Mallon, 1989; Shaw, 1982). Mallon showed more concerns towards the electronic documents, which he believes that ownership of such documents is more or less evanescent, which he believes is just a click away to change the whole authorship and identity of the document.Similarly, White viewed that Renaissance period was full of imitations, when the Romans imitated the Greek art (White, 1935). Keyes discussed about quotations and misquotations, whereby borrowings are simply kept in the quotes to overcome the problems of plagiarism (Keyes, 1992). Keyes also discussed about how actually even the quotes of famous personalities like Kennedy, Roosevelt, and Reagan etc., were found to borrow their lines from different sources.In fact borrowing content from other sources is a tradition in the literature and arts (Angelil-Carter, 2000).

Plagiarism has been equated as reuse of text (Clough, 2001).Clough believes it is about reusing the existing text for the creation of new text. The author also discusses about the reuse of text in the areas of literature, historical text, translation etc. Hannabus termed plagiarism as the 'close imitation of the others ideas and language and representing the work as own' (Hannabuss, 2001). Martin listed out six main forms of plagiarism, which include, word for word plagiarism, paraphrasing plagiarism, plagiarism of secondary sources, plagiarism of the form of a source, plagiarism of ideas, plagiarism of authorship (Martin, 1994).

The acts of plagiarism have become very common among the student community all across the world (Paldy, 1996) and keeping in view the growing instances of widespread acts of plagiarism among students, (Alschuler & Blimling, 1995) termed it as 'epidemic cheating' as there is hardly any country in the world which is not suffering on this account.Researchers have weighed plagiarism differently, be it the sin against originally, an attack on basic human rights and even some termed it as a cancer that erodes the rich legacy of scholarship (Freedman, 1994; Miller, 1993; Zangrando, 1991).And so do have been given different names to the plagiarists or the people, who intentionally get involved in the acts of plagiarism like thought thief, intellectual shoplifter (Stebelman, 1998; Whiteneck, 2002) which is termed as a disease of inarticulateness' (Bowers, 1994).

The practice of plagiarism is not only prevalent in the academia, but is faced by people in other areas and professions as well and the showbiz industry is one such big arena where directors, producers, writers face such criticisms on day to day basis. Copying the concept and plot from one movie and remaking a movie around the same concept is a very common practice, but what makes such practices more noticeable and worrisome is when picturization resembles as it is in two or more movies.Some of the prominent faces from the showbiz industry, which faced plagiarism charges include, Michael Jackson, Steve Spielberg and many more (Dezzani, 1999; Kessler, 1998).

From the various studies conducted all across the world around the concept of student plagiarism, it appears that it is the lack of information among the student community which breads more plagiarism at the student level. Cheating is one of the most common forms of plagiarism among the students at all levels, be they undergraduates, graduates, Master's students, or even research scholars (Ashworth, Bannister, Thorne, & on the Qualitative Research Methods Course Unit, 1997; Barnett & Dalton, 1981; Baty, 2001; Leming, 1980; Morgan & Thomson, 1997; Raffetto, 1985). The common forms of plagiary among students have been rated as academic misconduct, dishonesty, lacking academic integrity, unethical behaviour. Students cheat in class test, institutional internal exams, produce bogus data in surveys, discrediting others by using their data and other text material, manipulation of data and many more (Ferrell & Daniel, 1995; Saunders, 1993). The most common reasons for this widespread prevalence of plagiarism among the student community is the access to the internet and the easy access to different sources of information on the internet, which include, CD-documents, electronic journals, databases etc. (Ashworth et al., 1997).Given the rise in the incidence of internet based plagiarism practices, what researchers term differently, like cyber cheating, cyber plagiarism, mouse click plagiarism, cyber sloth, (G. L. Anderson, 1999; Auer & Krupar, 2001; Carnie, 2001; Stebelman, 1998). The universities in the UK have started taking measures to curb this growing menace among students(Baty, 2000). Students need to understand that whatever exists on the web is not open and free to use. The information available across different web servers on different web pages is the intellectual property, which is protected under copyright law and those who make use of such an information have to properly acknowledge the original author/s (Young, 2001).

Some other authors who have contributed in the area of plagiarism are LaFollette; Bull et al.; Culwin and Lancaster; Joy and Luck (Bull, Colins, Coughlin, & Sharp, 2000; Culwin & Lancaster, 2000; Joy & Luck, 1999; LaFollette, 1994).

8. SELF PLAGIARISM

Self-plagiarism is one more ugly face of the plagiarism, whereby an author steals his/her own work without acknowledging it (Roig, 2010). Although, it may appear quite absurd that an author may steal his/her own work, but the fact of the matter is this practice is prevalent across academia to a far greater extent than the practice of simple plagiarism, whereby an author steals others work and presents it as his/her own. In fact, it won't be inappropriate to say that majority of the researchers are unaware of the fact that they are not at the liberty to produce and reproduce their own work. Most of such authors are of the view that since this is their own work as such, they can easily reproduce any portion or part of their work in their upcoming work. This is simply one form of self-plagiarism; another form of self plagiarism is whereby the authors or researchers reproduce a sizable portion of their earlier work by properly acknowledging it. The lateral form of self-plagiarism serves two purposes of the researcher; one the researcher tries to show his/her research prowess by increasing the number of research papers by putting in minimum effort, as bulk or major portion of his work comes from his/her earlier work, secondly, by properly acknowledging his early work by self-citing the sources, increases citations count to improve his/her h-index or impact factor. What is more interesting about this practice of self-plagiarism is that majority of such researchers' project themselves as ignorant about the concept of self-plagiarism.

Researchers argued about the use of the word self-plagiarism, which (Bird, 2002) termed as a misnomer for the fact that plagiarism amounts to theft, by using others material. However, Resnik termed that self-plagiarism by no means can be termed as an intellectual theft, but involves dishonesty, whereby a researcher befools by reproducing his own work through a different channel (Resnik, 1998).

The worst form of self-plagiarism is, when a researcher reproduces his/her work almost as it is in another journal by making slight changes here and there, especially with the title and in other key headings and publish the same paper in another journal. Of late, a good number of softwares are available, which help the researchers and the publishers to scan the document to see if there is any content similar to other sources.

Researchers have also put forth arguments whereby they justify the use or rather reuse any portion or portions of their previous work. The common argument, which supports any such use of the previous work, is simply justified, as the researcher wants to extend his previous research or want to further explore the already worked out concept. And to have the acceptance of the concept, there is always need to seek basis for it, which can be sought only from his/her previous work. Samuelson, outlined the excuse to reuse the previously published findings for laying groundwork for the upcoming work, to deal with new evidence and to reach out to a different audience (Samuelson & Pamela, 1994). Roig outlined four main forms of self-plagiarism, which include, publishing an article in more than one journal with slight changes here and there, Salami-Slicing, text recycling, and copyright infringement (Roig, 2005).

9. GHOST WRITING

When we talk about the intellectual property, it means the creation of a particular mind, even if this creative work is undertaken for money and is sold out to any person by no means can abrade the fact that a particular work is an intellectual property of a particular person.Ghost writing is one such area which deserves mention, while talking about plagiarism. As aware, ghost writing is generally related to writing public speeches, whereby public figures, especially political personalities appoint good writers to write their public address, speeches, messages even up to updating and taking care of their web pages, blogs, social media accounts etc.

There is no denial of the fact that most of the public addresses, speeches etc., cover the policies and programmes of the government and a ghost writer simply gives shape to the draft by incorporating all such ideas and policies, which one is supposed to highlight in the public address. But, apart from these there are many other works which involve total independence of such ghost writers, who write for a particular person and is suitably paid for the services. Now the question arises, how far such ghost writings amounts to plagiarism, which being the intellectual property of the ghost writer is made to public as someone else's work.Ghost writing is such a form of plagiarism, which takes place with the mutual consent of both the original intellectual property holder or the original author and the person who steals it or uses such writing as his own with the consent of the original author.

10. UNAUTHORIZED TRANSLATION AND TRANSLITERATION WORKS

To overcome the barriers of language, good translators were always pressed it to service all across the world. Translation work is important for many reasons and the foremost being that people not well versed with a particular language are able to read others works in their preferred or favoured language. But there is always need to understand that translation work cannot be undertaken without the prior permission of original author. If a translator intends to undertake the translation work of a particular document authored by a particular person is required to seek the prior permission of the original author before going ahead with the translation work and if the translation work is undertaken without the prior permission of the original author, the translated work amounts to plagiarism.

Ideally, any individual interested to translate the work of any other author should seek the written permission of the original author, clearly mentioning that a particular person is hereby authorized to undertake the translation of a particular work. Before, giving the necessary permission to the translators, it is the responsibility of the original author to verify the necessary credentials of the person, as whether the interested translator is enough qualified to do the justice to his work without demeaning and losing the original essence of the work. Still more, it should be made mandatory on the part of translators to publish the authority letter itself in the translated work, issued to him/her by the original author. Nevertheless, scientific agencies across the globe are involved with the translation work of the scientific research published in regional and other cryptic languages. Most of the translation work is undertaken without the prior permission of the original authors, as the purpose of all such translation works is secretive in nature and are aimed to boost the scientific investigation in their own country. All such unauthorized translations of scientific works amounts to plagiarism.

11. SOME PRIME REASONS FOR PLAGIARISM

There cannot be one or two specific reasons for the growing instances of plagiarism among the academia and research community across the world. But still, there are some compelling reasons which in a way push researchers to opt for dishonest means to prove their worth.

1. Researchers and academicians are known by their research strength and if a researcher is not able to maintain a good momentum of his/her research work, he/she is bound to face criticism from many quarters, hence to maintain the much needed charm, a research at times in the attempt to push beyond limits, seeks solace through deceit or dishonest means.

2. Budding researcher always look for the much needed opportunity, whereby they may show their research prowess in terms of number of research papers one has published, a quantitative approach often preferred over the qualitative approach, hence in the race to

increase the numbers, these researchers do not hesitate in treading the undesirable road.

3. Career advancement, promotions, annual increments, annual appraisals etc., are some of the key areas, which are evaluated on the basis of the overall performance of an individual during a particular period of time and research contribution is one of the foremost aspects associated with performance evaluation of researchers and other academicians. Academicians or the researchers, who are so more by chance than by choice are somewhat forced to opt for deceitful means to show that they do exist and having a few articles by stealing work from here and there is an easy way, rather taking serious pains in undertaking a quality research.

4. Easy access to information resources, especially those available in the digital form is turning out to be one of the prime reasons for the increased indulgence of researches in the acts of plagiarism. Researchers find it easy to copy and paste the content from different sources. Sometimes the researcher give due attributions to the original authors, while as at others, attributions are missed out intentionally, to get the credit for the work done by others.

5. Apart from some voluntary reasons, there are also some involuntary reasons, which contribute to the growing instances of plagiarism across academia, especially among the budding researchers. The young researchers for the want of proper knowledge, and due to lack of research experience do not know what attribution means and how they can properly acknowledge the original researcher, who needs to be credited for his/her, work.

6. Excessive use and growing dependence on the internet and its sources of information has altogether changed the information seeking behaviour of the scholarly community, which has been correctly pointed out as "Skimming, navigation, browsing, squirreling, cross-checking" (Rowlands & Fieldhouse, 2007). More so, it is the behaviour which is about piling the loads of information for another day, which at times results into plagiarism.

7. Lack of awareness among students and scholars about the research ethics, and abstaining from unauthorized copying results in to the acts of plagiarism (Power, 2009). The growing instances of plagiarism across academia warrants for the need to have a mass awareness among the student community about this menace, and there cannot be any means better than including topics like plagiarism in their course content.

12. INTERNET AS A SOURCE OF PLAGIARISM

Internet has become one of the prime reasons for the growing instances of plagiarism across the research and academic community all across the world. There is no denial in it that each day internet is penetrating deeper and deeper in all sections of society across the world and so have people grown addicted to use of the internet. The World Wide Web is laced with both open access and propriety (subscription based) sources of information. Researchers who are immune to mischief find it easier to copy and paste the content from different sources and project it as their own work. Stealing content from other sources so openly may be very less prevalent among the researcher, but one can find people sharing lots of content on their walls across social networking sites, blogs, web pages, newspaper stories and many more. Since, people can find information of their interest easily available on the net, hence and without wasting much of their time they prefer to copy and paste it there, where it is required.

13. DIGITAL DOCUMENTS

Apart from the internet, there are also some other easy means whereby researchers or for that matter other information seeker can get the information in digital form.Digital documents, in the form of CD's/DVD's are easily available in the market. In fact, publishers have started a trend whereby they have started publishing documents both in the print as well as in digital form, which is generally referred as hybrid publishing.Most of the publishers are these days making CDs itself available with the book, which is the soft copy of the printed document, which can be accessed/read by using the electronic device like laptop, desktop, palmtop etc. An individual can easily copy the content from the CD and paste it in the desired location.Since the content made available by the publishers through CD documents is not available on the net, as such the softwares which are used for similarity check can't get hold of such content; hence such content easily escapes from the clutches of similarity detection software's.

14. PREDATORY JOURNALS

Research loses its relevance, when quantity is preferred over quality and this quantitative explosion of research publications breeds predatory journals. Although it is not that difficult to check the market of predatory journals and predatory publishers, what is required to do so, is to have will to curb all such means of publishing. It was Jeffery Beall, who first coined the term 'predatory journals' with the release of the first list of predatory publishers in 2010 (Beall, 2017). Jeffrey Beall, a librarian by profession, at the University of Colorado Denver with his vast work experience found that how actually the journal publishing business is flourishing all across the world with lesser to no attention paid to the maintenance of quality parameters. The Beall's list of predatory journals, serves a good purpose to the researchers, whereby they come to know about the journals they should avoid publishing with.

These predatory journals are simply aimed to earn money and earn more, which they mostly earn in the name of manuscript handling charges. The fact remains that researcher all across the world excel in their career given their research contribution, but while doing so, unfortunately it is the quantity which is preferred over quality. Given the fact, the majority of researchers are in a hurry to increase the number of their research articles, no matter if these numbers come at the cost of poor and stolen research.All this ultimately gave space of bogus publishers, who without reviewing the papers publish them after charging hefty publication charges, in the name of manuscript handling charges.

When research publications in terms of quantity start finding weightage, so do researchers get involved in the undesirable practices, whereby quality parameter remains a last priority, while as increasing the number of research articles becomes first priority. In this process, it is the predatory journals which come to the rescue of all such researchers who are hell bent to increase the number of their research articles.Some of the common reasons, which somewhat impel the researcher to chose predatory journals over the well recognized and prominent research journals is to avoid the rigorous peer review process they follow, and still more, it takes almost anything from six months to over a year to publish a research paper in any mainstream journal. While as, in the case of predatory journals the articles are published within the days of their submission, without any criticism or peer review process, with no anti-plagiarism policy.

Researchers who are well aware of their research weakness or the poor quality of their research, know it very well, that it would be difficult for them to publish any such substandard research article through a mainstream recognized journal. With the results all such researchers prefer these predatory journals, which most of the time accommodate most of the interests of the researcher, including compromising with the research quality and the plagiarism aspects. In fact, it is these journals, which offer the breeding ground for plagiarism, as a good number of researchers know it very well that those predatory journals don't pay heed to such things.

The researchers are not able to make it out, as which journal is predatory and which is genuine. These predatory journals mostly target the budding researchers, who for the want of strengthening their research profile are generally in a hurry to publish their research results without any delay. Apart from Bealls list, researchers can also look into different aspects, whereby they can themselves ascertain whether they should publish with a particular journal or not.Journal website, editorial board members, volume and issue details, indexing of journal with some good indexing services like Scopus, web of science, Ulrich's Periodical Directory, DOAJ, ISSN no, manuscript handling charges, author guidelines, review process,etc., clearly indicate about the true nature of a research journal, which a researcher should evaluate before submitting a manuscript for publication.

15. SIMILARITY VS PLAGIARISM

With the introduction of plagiarism detection softwares, a sort of controversy has generated around plagiarism and similarity. The common masses use both interchangeably, but subject experts suggest that there is a considerable difference between the two and both cannot be used interchangeably. Fundamentally, there is a need to understand that software service providers want to play safe as such the automated reports generated after scanning the documents on the internet reflect that this particular document has some percentage of content similar to various other sources. Since the use of word plagiarism may offend the person, as such, the use of 'plagiarism' has been substituted with a more acceptable and better term 'similarity'. But the fact remains that the text reflected as similar in the report may or may not amount to plagiarism, is something which can be decided by the involvement of human judgment. One has to understand that when we talk about the softwares, it means we are talking about artificial intelligence, so, how so smart and intelligently the technology may operate, ultimately it has to rely on the human intelligence for the final decision and so holds true about deciding whether the content reflected as similar in machine generated report amounts to plagiarism or not. The fact remains that artificial intelligence is itself a creation of human mind, hence by no means can replace the rational thinking ability of the human mind. Similarly, when it comes to assess the level and amount of plagiarism a document suffers with, the similarity reports generated by the softwares give us simply an idea about the sources with which it matches, but not the exact rational view whether it amounts to plagiarism or not, which can only be assessed by the application of mind.

Technically, what makes similarity different from the plagiarism is that in the former case, the researcher may quote text as it is from the other sources with proper attributions to the original authors, but in the case of lateral, the attributions remain missing hence amounts to plagiarism. Budding researchers need to understand that even if the text is taken from the other sources is properly attributed also amounts to plagiarism unless the text taken as it is from other sources is not kept in verbatim along with proper references.

16. SIMILARITY DETECTION SOFTWARES

With the advancement in Information and Communication Technology, IT professionals have developed softwares whereby one can scan a document across the web to detect if the content or the text of that particular document matches with any other document or not. These similarity detection softwares are also often referred as plagiarism detection tools, as the ultimate purpose of any such similarity detection is to assess if the document suffers with plagiarism or not.Since, the softwares cannot corroborate that the text detected as similar to other matching sources amounts to plagiarism or not, but it is only the human factor or the human intervention which can judge the actual credibility of any such text to be plagiarism or not, as such it is always appropriate to refer all such tools as similarity detection tools or softwares instead of plagiarism detection tools.

Some of the common and popularly used similarity detection softwares by the researcher and other scientific community including publishers are

- Turnitin.com http://turnitin.com/
- iThenticatehttp://www.ithenticate.com/
- Urkund http://www.urkund.com

All the listed softwares are propriety softwares, apart from these there are other numerous softwares both open source, free and propriety as well, which are being widely used by the researcher all across the world. Keeping in view the growing number of instances paper retraction at the international level, the publishers no more want to take the chances to publish the papers without scanning them. In fact, it won't be inappropriate to say that before initiating the review process of a research article, it must be scanned for similarity check and only after ensuring that the paper is free from any such similarity, which may potentially end up in plagiarism, should only then enter into the peer review process.

In India, with the view to draw awareness among researchers both budding and seasoned, the University Grants Commission, New Delhi has arranged a similarity detection software (Urkund) for all Indian universities recognized by UGC under sections 2(f) and 12 (b), whereby these institutions have been granted access through their inter university centre INFLIBNET Ahmadabad to check similarity of the research articles. Still more, to promote the academic integrity, UGC, has come up with the Promotion of Academic Integrity and Prevention of Plagiarism in Higher Education Institutions Regulations, 2017 (UGC, 2017).The draft resolution clearly emphasizes over the role of individual institutions to promote academic integrity, providing necessary training and guidance to faculty, students and other staff about the proper attributions to the original authors by conducting seminars, workshops etc., over the research ethics.

17. LIMITATIONS OF PLAGIARISM DETECTION TOOLS

Softwares used for the plagiarism detection have their own limitations, whereby one cannot say that we have a foolproof mechanism or the system whereby the practice of plagiarism can be checked to its entirety. One must accept this fact that those who are committed and sincere researchers always desist from any such practice (plagiarism) which may bring shame or defame them. So it is only those researchers who are addicted/prone to such practices (plagiarism) look out for different means whereby they can steal the content and still escape from the clutches of plagiarism detection tools. Besides, the limitations of the softwares or the plagiarism detection tools itself serve as a breeding ground for all those researchers who always look for ways and means to give a slip to an artificial eye.

Some of the common limitations of the plagiarism detections softwares are:

1. The fundamental limitation of all the plagiarism detection softwares is that a document can be scanned for similarity only against the limited digital documents and with zero effectiveness against print documents. This means if the content is copied from any printed source, can't be detected with the help of plagiarism detection tools.

2. The softwares can effectively scan a document against almost the freely available digital documents, which can be web pages, open access content available through different channels on the internet. Open access journals, web pages, online newspapers, open access institutional repositories and the numerous other forms of open access content. This means that if the software does not have access to the closed access content, cannot scan a document against such sources, despite their availability on the internet. So all the documents or the text available on the internet is not accessed by the plagiarism detection tools like softwares etc.

3. When we talk about the software's limitations to scan limited digital documents, it is aimed to point out that digital documents which are published by publishers and made available in CD's and DVD's or through other means are inaccessible to the plagiarism detection software to the same degree as that of the print documents. A dubious researcher can easily copy and paste content from the all such offline digital documents and can still evade the detection.

4. In order to scan a document against both the open and closed access documents, the service providers have to get the necessary access to scan all such closed content from

their owners. All such content generally includes the propriety databases of popular journal publishers. And when we talk about the academic fraud or academic misconduct, it is these research journals which are mostly consulted by the researchers. So it is always imperative that a plagiarism detection service provider should have necessary access to all such major databases and other databases as well, so that these softwares may scan a particular document almost against all the sources available on the internet.

5. Language acts as a barrier for similarity detection tools, as these softwares generally fail to detect the content which is similar but is written in different scripts. Even though it is quite difficult to put in place the similarity detection system, whereby language may no more act as a barrier.

If on one hand, these plagiarism detection tools or softwares have a range of limitations, on the other hand, these tools are proving instrumental in checking the practice of plagiarism.

18. SOME MYTHS AND REALITY ABOUT PLAGIARISM

With the growing instances of plagiarism across academia, which have come to the fore with the use of similarity detection softwares has also breaded some misconception about plagiarism and the percentage similarity reflected by these softwares. Even though some debate is going across the academic circles that a certain percentage of similarity should be allowed and even UGC in India also issued a notification in this regard.

The simple argument, which one can make in this regard is that theft cannot be allowed even to a single percentage, because theft is theft be it of one percent or more. But, there is something more which people in general and academia in particular should understand is that the content reflected as similar after scan by a software may not necessarily amount to plagiarism and this is something, which can be ascertained by the subject expert or by the research supervisor. And the fact of the matter is even one percent content reflected as similar may amount to plagiarism, while as on the other hand a much higher percentage of content reflected as similar may not necessarily amount to plagiarism.

References are quite often shown in the similarity match and constitute a larger percentage of similarity, which by no means amounts to plagiarism, even if reflected. Similarly, text in verbatim, use of common or proper nouns, mathematical expression, equations, formulas, etc., are very often reflected in the similarity index. Author name, author information, author affiliations, etc., are also reflected in the similarity index, which again does not amount to plagiarism, thereon, if there is a proper attribution to the original authors the exception can be granted. Accordingly, there are other areas in the text itself, which may be reflected as similar, but may not necessarily amount to plagiarism, something which can be assessed only by the subject expert, as how the outcome of the present study will benefit or suffer in the presence or absence of the text similar to other sources if found in a study.

19. CONCLUSION

Keeping in view the growing instances of plagiarism across all walks of academic and research community, there is an urgent need to draw awareness among the scholarly community to desist from all such practices which may not only bring disrepute to them, their institutions, but may also ruin their careers. There is a need to lay stress on the research ethics and to maintain research integrity across the scientific community of the country, as researchers by no means can afford to steal the content from other's work and project it as their own. Still more, there are many misconceptions about the plagiarism and the scholars having rich research experience are the worst sufferers on this account. If a researcher is totally unaware of what amounts to plagiarism and what not, is bound to invite trouble for self.

More often young researchers talk about the percentage plagiarism permissible in research writing, who are quite often backed by their supervisors, senior academicians and other, which is quite pathetic. This also means that any supportive argument in this regard is about allowing theft to a certain percentage, which is totally unacceptable. There is a need to understand that a theft is theft, be it one percent or beyond, which cannot be allowed by any means. Still more, the whole story gets confused by the similarity detection tests, whereby people fail to differentiate that the content detected as similar by the softwares may not necessarily amount to plagiarism, whereby a lower percentage of content reflected as similar may amount to plagiarism, while as, a higher percentage of content reflected as similar may not necessarily amount to plagiarism. These fundamental differences need to be cleared along with some misconceptions, myths & reality and wisdom needs to be given vent to pour in.

The government and its agencies have got a role to play, whereby some tough measures need to be taken up to discourage the practice of plagiarism in research. Similarly, the academic community of the country is feeling overburdened for being pushed to publish. Career advancement of the academicians has been put at stake whereby their promotions have been directly linked to their research performance. All this has given rise to many undesirable practices, like those academicians having no interest in the research activities are forced to undertake the research activity. This has promoted ghost writing, predatory journal culture, fondling with research ethics, plagiarism, copyright violations, intellectual theft, money laundering, bogus data, bogus studies, bogus findings and many more. If all this unsolicited research practice is to be stopped and research integrity is to be promoted, the need is to establish a regulatory body, which will act as a watchdog on the similar lines to that of the ORI United states.There is no point in forcing academicians to undertake research, which lack the scientific temper, with no research acumen at all.

REFERENCES

Alschuler, A. S., & Blimling, G. S. (1995). Curbing Epidemic Cheating Through Systemic Change. *College Teaching*, 43(4), 123–125. http://doi.org/10.1080/87567555.1995.9925531

Anderson, G. L. (1999). Cyberplagiarism: A look at the web term paper sites. *College & Research Libraries News*, 60(5), 371–373.

Anderson, M. S., & Steneck, N. H. (2011). The problem of plagiarism. *Urologic Oncology: Seminars and Original Investigations*, 29(1), 90–94. http://doi.org/10.1016/j.urolonc.2010.09.013

Angelil-Carter, S. (2000). Stolen language?: plagiarism in writing (2nd ed.). Boston: Longman.

Ashworth, P., Bannister, P., Thorne, P., &Students on the Qualitative Research Methods Course Unit(1997). Guilty in whose eyes? University students' perceptions of cheating and plagiarism in academic work and assessment. *Studies in Higher Education*, 22(2), 187–203.

Auer, N. J., & Krupar, E. M. (2001). Mouse click plagiarism: The role of technology in plagiarism and the librarian's role in combating it. *Library Trends*, 49(3), 415–433.

Barnett, D. C., & Dalton, J. C. (1981). Why College Students Cheat. *Journal of College Student Personnel*, 22(6), 545–51. Retrieved from https://eric.ed.gov/?id=EJ253567

Baty, P. (2000). Copycats roam in an era of the new. *Times Higher Education Supplement*, 14 July, p 4.

Baty, P. (2001). Cambridge postgrad fights to clear his name. *Times Higher Education Supplement*, 9, 8.

Beall, J. (2017). Beall's List of Predatory Publishers.

Bird, S. J. (2002). Self-plagiarism and dual and redundant publications: What is the problem? *Science and Engineering Ethics*, 8(4), 543–544. http://doi.org/10.1007/s11948-002-0007-4

Bowden, D. (1996). Plagiarism (Coming to Terms). *English Journal*, 85(4), 82–84. Retrieved from https://eric.ed.gov/?id=EJ525761

Bowers, N. (1994). A Loss for Words: Plagiarism and Silence. *The American Scholar*. The Phi Beta Kappa Society. http://doi.org/10.2307/41212121

Bull, J., Colins, C., Coughlin, E., & Sharp, D. (2000). *Technical review of plagiarism detection software report*. University of Luton.

Carnie, A. (2001). How to handle cyber-sloth in academe. *Chronicle of Higher Education*, 47(17), B14.

Clough, P. D. (2001). *Measuring Text Reuse and Document Derivation: Postgraduate Transfer Report*. University of Sheffield, Sheffield. Retrieved from https://ir.shef.ac.uk/cloughie/papers/transfer.pdf

Council of Writing Program Administrators. (2014). Defining and Avoiding Plagiarism: The WPA Statement on Best Practices | Council of Writing Program Administrators. Retrieved June 18, 2018, from http://wpacouncil.org/positions/WPAplagiarism.pdf

Culwin, F., & Lancaster, T. (2000). A review of electronic services for plagiarism detection in student submissions. In *Proceedings of 8th Annual Conference on the Teaching of Computing*. Edinburgh. Retrieved from http://www.scism.sbu.ac.uk/~fintan

Cunha, F. (1946). Gastrostomy: Its inception and evolution. *The American Journal of Surgery*, 72(4), 610–634. http://doi.org/10.1016/0002-9610(46)90402-3

Dezzani, M. (1999). Michael Jackson found guilty in Italy of plagiarising song. *Billboard*, 111(22), 46.

Ferrell, C. M., & Daniel, L. G. (1995). A frame of reference for understanding behaviors related to the academic misconduct of undergraduate teacher education students. *Research in Higher Education*, 36(3), 345–375. http://doi.org/10.1007/BF02208315

Fialkoff, F. (1993). There's no excuse for plagiarism. *Library Journal*, 118(17), 56.

Fishman, T. (2009). "We know it when we see it" is not good enough: toward a standard definition of plagiarism that transcends theft, fraud, and copyright. In *4th Asia Pacific Conference on Educational Integrity* (4APCEI) (pp. 1–5). Retrieved from http://ro.uow.edu.au/apcei/09/papers/37

Fox, H. G. (1946). Evidence of Plagiarism in the Law of Copyright. *The University of Toronto Law Journal*, 6(2), 414. http://doi.org/10.2307/824106

Freedman, M. (1994). The persistence of plagiarism, the riddle of originality. *The Virginia Quarterly Review*, 70(3), 504.

Hanks, P., & Wilkes, G. A. (1979). *Collins dictionary of the English language: an extensive coverage of contemporary international and Australian English* / Patrick Hanks, editor...[et al.]. - Version details - Trove. Sydney: Collins.

Hannabuss, S. (2001). Contested texts: issues of plagiarism. *Library Management*, 22(6/7), 311–318. http://doi.org/10.1108/EUM0000000005595

Harper, D. (2018). plagiarism | Origin and meaning of plagiarism. Retrieved June 18, 2018, from https://www.etymonline.com/word/plagiarism

INFLIBNET. (2009). Shodhganga/ : a reservoir of Indian theses @ INFLIBNET. Retrieved June 18, 2018, from http://shodhganga.inflibnet.ac.in/

iThenticate. (2012). 2012 Survey Highlights: Scholarly Plagiarism. Retrieved June 18, 2018, from https://www.ithenticate.com/hs-fs/hub/92785/file-16017086-pdf/docs/plagiarism-survey-results-120412.pdf

Joy, M., & Luck, M. (1999). Plagiarism in programming assignments. *IEEE Transactions on Education*, 42(2), 129–133. http://doi.org/10.1109/13.762946

Kessler, S. (1998). Steven Spielberg wins plagiarism case. *New York Times*, 29, A20.

Keyes, R. (1992). *"Nice guys finish seventh": False phrases, spurious sayings, and familiar misquotations*. New York: HarperCollinsPublishers.

LaFollette, M. C. (1994). Stealing into Print: Fraud, Plagiarism, and Misconduct in Scientific Publishing. *The Library Quarterly*, 64(2), 221–223. http://doi.org/10.1086/602692

Leming, J. S. (1980). Cheating Behavior, Subject Variables, and Components of the Internal-External Scale under High and Low Risk Conditions. *The Journal of Educational Research*, 74(2), 83–87. http://doi.org/10.1080/00220671.1980.10885288

Mallon, T. (1989). *Stolen words: forays into the origins and ravages of plagiarism*. New York: Ticknor & Fields.

Martin, B. (1994). Plagiarism: a misplaced emphasis. *Journal of Information Ethics*, 3(2), 36–47,96. Retrieved from https://search.proquest.com/openview/fcc70ae750421809429c1f0aaac7bd58/1?pq-origsite=gscholar&cbl=2035668

McCabe, D. (2005). CIA Research: The Center for Academic Integrity. Retrieved June 19, 2018, from http://www.waunakee.k12.wi.us/hs/departments/lmtc/Assignments/McConnellScenarios/AcadHonesty_5Article.pdf

Middle Georgia State University. (2018). The MGA English Department's Definition of Plagiarism. Retrieved June 18, 2018, from https://www.mga.edu/arts-sciences/english/docs/Plagiarism_Definition.pdf

Miller, K. D. (1993). Redefining plagiarism: Martin Luther King's use of an oral tradition. *Chronicle of Higher Education*, 39(20), A60.

Morgan, B., & Thomson, A. (1997). Keele to probe standard of PhDs. *Times Higher Education Supplement*, 7, 1.

ORI. (1994). ORI Provides working Definition of Plagiarism. *ORI Newsletter (Office of Research Integrity, U.S. Public Health Service)*, 3(1), 5–6. Retrieved from https://ori.hhs.gov/sites/default/files/vol3_no1.pdf

OSTP. (2000). Federal Research Misconduct Policy | ORI - The Office of Research Integrity. *Federal Register*, 65(235), 76260–76264. Retrieved from https://ori.hhs.gov/federal-research-misconduct-policy

Paldy, L. G. (1996). The Problem That Won't Go Away: Addressing the Causes of Cheating. *Journal of College Science Teaching*, 26(1), 4–6. Retrieved from https://eric.ed.gov/?id=EJ533204

Power, L. G. (2009). University Students' Perceptions of Plagiarism. *The Journal of Higher Education*, 80(6), 643–662. http://doi.org/10.1080/00221546.2009.11779038

Raffetto, W. G. (1985). The Cheat. *Community and Junior College Journal*, 56(2), 26–27.

Resnik, D. B. (1998). *The ethics of science: An introduction*. London: Routledge.

Roig, M. (2005). Re-Using Text from One's Own Previously Published Papers: An Exploratory Study of Potential Self-Plagiarism. *Psychological Reports*, 97(1), 43–49. http://doi.org/10.2466/pr0.97.1.43-49

Roig, M. (2010). Plagiarism and self-plagiarism: What every author should know. *Biochemia Medica: Biochemia Medica*, 20(3), 295–300.

Rowlands, I., & Fieldhouse, M. (2007). Information behaviour of the researcher of the future- Work Package I, *Trends in Scholarly Behavior*. Retrieved from http://www.jisc.ac.uk/media/documents/programmes/reppres/ggworkpackagei.pdf

Samuelson, P., & Pamela. (1994). Self-plagiarism or fair use. *Communications of the ACM*, 37(8), 21–25. http://doi.org/10.1145/179606.179731

Saunders, E. J. (1993). Confronting Academic Dishonesty. *Journal of Social Work Education*, 29(2), 224–231. http://doi.org/10.1080/10437797.1993.10778817

Shamoo, A. E., & Resnik, D. B. (2015). *Responsible Conduct of Research* (3rd ed.). Oxford University Press. Retrieved from http://www.oxfordscholarship.com/view/10.1093/acprof:oso/9780195368246.001.0001/acprof-9780195368246

Shaw, P. (1982). Plagiary. *The American Scholar*, 51(3), 325–337. http://doi.org/10.2307/41211158

Stanford University. (2012). What Is Plagiarism? Retrieved from https://web.archive.org/web/20121026061453/http://studentaffairs.stanford.edu/judicialaffairs/integrity/plagiarism

Stebelman, S. (1998). Cybercheating: Dishonesty goes digital. *American Libraries*, 29(8), 48–50.

Thomas, M. W. (2000). Eschewing Credit: Heywood, Shakespeare, and Plagiarism before Copyright. *New Literary History*, 31(2), 277–293. http://doi.org/10.2307/20057603

UGC. (2017). Promotion of Academic Integrity and Prevention of Plagiarism in Higher Educational Institutions Regulations. Retrieved from https://www.ugc.ac.in/pdfnews/8864815_UGC-Public-Notice-on-Draft-UGC-Regulations,-2017.pdf

United Nations. (1948). Universal Declaration of Human Rights | United Nations. Retrieved June 19, 2018, from http://www.un.org/en/universal-declaration-human-rights/

Valpy, F. E. J. (2005). The crime of kidnapping. In *Etymological dictionary of the Latin language* (p. 345). Adamant Media Corporation.

Wager, E. (2014). Defining and responding to plagiarism. *Learned Publishing*, 27(1), 33–42. http://doi.org/10.1087/20140105

White, H. O. (1935). *Plagiarism and imitation during the English renaissance: a study in critical distinctions*. London: Harvard University Press.

Whiteneck, P. (2002). What to Do with a Thought Thief. *Community College Week*, 14(24), 4–6.

WIPO. (1883). Paris Convention for the Protection of Industrial Property. Retrieved June 19, 2018, from http://www.wipo.int/treaties/en/ip/paris/

Yale University. (2018). What Is Plagiarism?: Center for Teaching and Learning. Retrieved June 18, 2018, from https://ctl.yale.edu/writing/using-sources/understanding-and-avoiding-plagiarism/what-plagiarism

Young, J. R. (2001). The Cat-and-Mouse Game of Plagiarism Detection. *Chronicle of Higher Education*, 47(43).

Zangrando, R. L. (1991). Historians' procedures for handling plagiarism. *Publishing Research Quarterly*, 7(4), 57–63.

9

Beleaguered and Tousled Research: Murky Waters of Plagiarism and Retractions

Sumeer Gul
Taufat Hussain

1. INTRODUCTION

"Scientific enterprise is not just a quest for knowledge and truth; it is also a fairly good reflection of the whole spectrum of human behaviour: from genius, passion, and jealousy, to mistakes and misconduct" (Cokol, Ozbay & Rodriguez-Esteban, 2008). The negative behaviour adopted in the scientific enterprise leads to a collapsive phenomenon, i.e. retraction. Retraction is the phenomenon of withdrawal of a research manuscript from the published literature if its validity is questionable and eventually proved anyway. It is one of the most severe penalties employed against authors in case a scientific misconduct is identified. "Publication retraction is a mechanism to preserve the scientific literature against publications that contain seriously flawed or erroneous data, redundant publication, plagiarism, unethical research, and other features that compromise the integrity of science" (Nogueira, Gonçalves, Leles, Batista & Costa, 2017). It may lead to an irreparable loss to the honour and the calling of an individual. So, retractions must be controlled prudently, and journals must have mechanisms for ascertaining the validity of research articles to decide whether an article needs to be retracted or not (Wager & Williams, 2011). In 2009, the Committee on Publication Ethics (COPE) produced procedures wherein it was specified that causes of retractions must be evidently identified in retraction notices (Wager et al, 2009). Retractions usually represent inaccuracies that are of sufficient degree to totally nullify the findings of a research manuscript. They signify a danger to the reliability of both the scientific literature as well as any future investigation grounded on invalid findings and conclusions established previously (Nath, Marcus & Druss, 2006). The replicability of findings stated in a research article is an important assurance of the legitimacy of knowledge. If the similar method is adopted as explained in the research article, it might be anticipated that the findings in the original manuscript be replicated to a large magnitude. Nevertheless, if several efforts made by researchers fail to reproduce the findings as reported in the original manuscript, the legitimacy of the manuscript may become suspicious (Chen, Hu, Milbank & Shultz, 2012). Retraction rates of research articles have shown a steep growing trend over a couple of decades (Cokol, Ozbay & Rodriguez-Esteban, 2008; Corbyn, 2009; Grieneisen and Zhang, 2012). In the time span of 1990-2008, the retractions show a 20-fold escalation in the "Science Citation Index Expanded" (Corbyn, 2009). "The number of retracted articles has increased dramatically over the past 20 years and now comprises about .02% of the 2 million articles published each year" (Kuroki & Ukawa, 2018). The latest research reveals that misconduct is responsible for most of the retractions in prolific databases like PubMed (Fang, Grant & Casadevall, 2012). A number of reasons have been theorized to elucidate the trend like consciousness about the issue among publishers, precise detection systems and guidelines for handling misconduct accusations (Steen, 2011). Assuming the enigmatic and mostly disgraceful nature of research misconduct, a comprehensive understanding of its occurrence appears to be doubtful. It is hard to advocate that growth in a number of retractions is directly proportional to the real growth of research misconduct. But, it seems that escalation of retractions is the result of amplified vigilance mechanisms established by publishers, editors, and peer-reviewers (Fanelli, 2013).

As far as the misconduct is concerned, numerous elements may be expected to provoke researchers to disrespect ethical obligations and face a retraction (Davis, Riske-Morris & Diaz, 2007). One of the elements is the impact of the publish or perish tradition that has been implemented over the time (Colquhoun, 2011). So far, different reasons have been found to be responsible for retraction of research articles like a scientific error, duplication of content, plagiarism, falsification, fabrication, authorship conflicts, intellectual property right violation or ethical or legal misconduct (Steen, Casadevall & Fang, 2013). So, the occurrences of misconduct range from data fabrication and deficiency of informed consensus to duplicate manuscript and self-plagiarism. However, the scientific misconducts that are lethal to patient's lives or have consequences of flawed scientific information are of utmost concern (DeMaria, 2012). Plagiarism being one of the causes has received a huge attention from the global scholarly community in the context of retraction philosophy.

2. RETRACTIONS AND PLAGIARISM

Etymologically speaking, the term plagiarism, which means literary piracy, has been derived from Latin words- plagiarius (kidnapper) and plaga (huntingnet). Historically speaking, plagiarism has been witnessed since humans have been involved in creating and recording knowledge (Maurer, Kappe & Zaka, 2006). It is a multifaceted problem as it is founded upon a modern theory of intellectual property as old as the 18th century (Buranen & Roy, 1999) but in a lighter vein Cunha (1946) lays a satirical comment on plagiarism through the following statement:"if you steal from one author, it is plagiarism; if you steal from many, it is research".

It is a misuse of someone else's work enclosing scientific literature, research methods, images and ideas (Roig, 2012) without acknowledging the actual source. The main ingredient of misuse is an inability to have an authorization for replicating the work published hitherto and cite primary scientific literature (Council of Science Editors: US, 2012). The misuse may result in authorship conflicts and copyright violation with lawful penalties. The magnitude of the penalty would be in compliance with the nature of the purpose of plagiarism (deliberate, indeliberate or accidental), the knowledge about associated ethical codes, the language skill and the degree of duplication (Chaddah, 2014; Resnik & Dinse, 2013; Roig, 2009; Wittmaack, 2005).Plagiarism, as a way of intellectual property right violation, symbolizes a grave and increasing concern in science and is regarded as one of the most destructive instances of scientific malpractice which twists the basis on which further research is grounded (Amos, 2014). Self-plagiarism is a particular form of plagiarism. The American Psychological Association (2010) defines it as, "The process of referring to the practice of presenting one's own previously published work as though it were new". The issues of plagiarism and powerful detection tools have attracted an increasing attention from the public (Jaric, 2015).The restriction of plagiarism only by digital tools seems to be an inadequate resolution to the problem. A dynamic and proactive approach needs to be exhibited by Journal editors by communicating with readers, authors, and reviewers before and after the publication of research manuscripts.Since electronic access and open access platforms have exponentially increased the visibility of research, therefore, readers may play an important part in addressing scientific misbehaviour by identifying it and demanding corrections or retractions (Gasparyan, Ayvazyan, Akazhanov & Kitas, 2014). For instance, a Russian author, Olga D. Baydik, reported the plagiarism of her article published in 2011 in Russian language in a subscription journal to the Chief Editor of Pakistan Journal of Medical Sciences in which Chinese authors (Lin Feng, Hua Li, Ling-Ling E, Chuan-Jie Li, Yan Ding) had published the same content in English translated version under the title Pathological changes in the maxillary sinus mucosae of patients with recurrent odontogenic maxillary sinusitis (Baydik & Gasparyan, 2016).

Let us now focus on retractions attributed to plagiarism. It is difficult to search for retractions for plagiarism as numerous journals employ ambiguous language in retraction notices by avoiding the terms "plagiarised" and "plagiarism". This practice is observed when retraction notices are matched with notices on Retraction Watch (RW) and other sources (Fang, Grant & Casadevall, 2012). It may be due to deficiency of consent about the definition of plagiarism (Ribeiro & Vasconcelos, 2018). Retractions as a result of plagiarism have mushroomed extensively in the contemporary times. Plagiarism and duplicate research may signify as much as 4% of the published manuscripts and stand for one-third of all the withdrawn research articles (Jaric, 2015). Retractions on account of plagiarism and duplication are expected more from the journals having low impact factors as those journals may be comparatively incapable of identifying plagiarism (Madlock-Brown & Eichmann, 2014). In a study by (Grieneisen &

Zhang 2012), it was found that 46% of the retractions were because of plagiarism and duplicate publication. Ribeiro and Vasconcelos (2018) found that India and Iran account for 36% and 39% of their total retractions accredited to plagiarism respectively. But, Citron and Ginsparg (2015) find that less number of retractions were credited to plagiarism for India and China. In a study by Amos (2014) using PubMed, it is reported that among 53 countries understudy for the time period between 2008-2012, 34 faced retractions due to plagiarism. From the retractions, 16.6% of the retractions were attributed to plagiarism. Among the countries with 5 or more number of retractions, Italy accounted for 66.7 % of retractions for plagiarism, followed by Turkey (61.5 %), Iran & Tunisia (42.9 % each) and France (38.5 %). Wager and Williams (2011) found that 16% of all the retractions identified in Medline database from 2005-2008 with respect to research articles occur for plagiarism. They also found that most of the withdrawn reviews, case reports and abstracts were retracted on account of plagiarism (40%) or redundancy (20%). Huh, Kim and Cho (2016) also report that plagiarism accounts for 2nd highest percentage (8.8%) of retractions issued for the period between 1990-Jan 2016 indexed in KoreaMed database. A promising percentage of articles (ranking 2nd) retracted in the field of Dentistry due to plagiarism is also reported by Nogueira, Gonçalves, Leles, Batista and Costa (2017). Almeida, de, Catelani, Fontes-Pereira, and Vasconcelos (2016) report plagiarism as the main cause of retractions in major Latin American/Caribbean databases. The results suggest that the correction of the literature is becoming global and is not limited to mainstream international publications. Resnik & Dinse (2013) have streamlined plagiarism as a cause of scientific retractions. A systematic and retrospective study conducted by Stretton et al., (2012) affirm plagiarism as that of the retracted misconduct publications, the majority were retracted for plagiarism. The findings have implications for developing appropriate evidence-based strategies and allocation of resources to help mitigate plagiarism misconduct. Cassão, Herbella, Schlottmann and Patti (2018) owe plagiarism to the retracted articles in the surgery journals. Shamim (2018) aims to audit the articles retracted from PubMed indexed dental journals from India and he also reveals that plagiarism is one of the causes of article retractions. Aspura, Noorhidawati and Abrizah (2018); Liao et al., (2018) also reveal plagiarism among the main causes of article retractions. The aim of this prospective study was to understand the perceptions of Chinese biomedical researchers towards academic misconduct and the trend from 2010 to 2015. However, Wang, Xing, Wang and Chen (2018) label plagiarism at the 2nd place among the reasons tagged for retraction of research articles.

However, as and when a case of possible plagiarism is brought to the surface, timely action or withdrawal of the research article is hampered by the delayed official enquiry of the scientific malpractice (Jaric, 2015). Cox, Craig and Tourish (2018) find that the research manuscript with the highest citation count (81) was retracted in 2014 for plagiarism from Economic Modelling after seven years after its publication. Arda (2012); Park (2003) report that undergraduates of business studies and engineering, and scholars from non-Anglophone countries often disobey the publication ethics. In certain Asian Countries, plagiarism is regarded as a social phenomenon embedded in the rigid system of education, discouraging creative thinking and emergence of unestablished ideas (Chaurasia, 2016). In order to address the issue of plagiarism, a collective endeavour is needed on behalf of academic publishers and editors. Currently, insufficient communication and data exchange amongst the editorial offices of peer-reviewed journals are among the serious hurdles to timely exposure of plagiarism. A standard plagiarism detection mechanism- a unified database of all publications, adopted by all peer-reviewed systems and publishers can be a viable solution to the issue. Such mechanism can effectively discover the occurrences of plagiarism of unpublished literature, which, however, would be impossible and can reduce the retraction problem in the research world. The mechanism would not be effective in recognizing the plagiarism of ideas or data manipulation, but a considerable number of scientific malpractice instances may be solved prior to their publication. So, the general image of science in general public would be comparatively better and prevent the reputation of the scientific community from further damage (Jaric, 2015).

3. CONCLUSION

Plagiarism, if managed at a proper time can save the research circles from the collapsive retracted phenomenon. It will surely try to bring the positive research behaviour saving the author and scholar community from the shame the retracted articles bring. Though these days managing plagiarism is a norm but online availability of research makes it more prone to the menace of plagiarism. So, the strict, vigilant and ethical guidelines need to be adopted so that there will be a no to plagiarism and this, in turn, will manage the menace of retractions.

REFERENCES

Almeida, R. M. V. R., de, A. R. K., Catelani, F., Fontes-Pereira, A. J., & Vasconcelos, S. M. R. (2016). Plagiarism Allegations Account for Most Retractions in Major Latin American/Caribbean Databases. *Science and Engineering Ethics*, 22 (5), 1447-1456. DOI: 10.1007/s11948-015-9714-5

American Psychological Association. (2010). The Publication Manual of the American Psychological Association (6th ed.). Washington, DC: American Psychological Association

Amos, K. A. (2014). The ethics of scholarly publishing: Exploring differences in plagiarism and duplicate publication across nations. *Journal of the Medical Library Association*, 102(2), 87–91. DOI: 10.3163%2F1536-5050.102.2.005

Arda B. (2012). Publication ethics from the perspective of PhD students of health sciences: a limited experience. *Science and Engineering Ethics*, 18(2): 213-22. DOI: 10.1007/s11948-011-9256-4

Aspura, M. K. Y. I., Noorhidawati, A., & Abrizah, A. (2018). An analysis of Malaysian retracted papers: Misconduct or mistakes? *Scientometrics*, 1–14. DOI: 10.1007/s11192-018-2720-z

Baydik, O.D., & Gasparyan, A.Y. (2016). How to Act When Research Misconduct Is Not Detected by Software but Revealed by the Author of the Plagiarized Article. *Journal of Korean medical science*, 31(10), 1508-1510. DOI: 10.3346/jkms.2016.31.10.1508

Buranen, L., and A. M. Roy (Eds.). (1999). *Perspectives on plagiarism and intellectual property in a postmodern world.* Albany, NY: SUNY Press.

Cassão, B. D. A., Herbella, F. A. M., Schlottmann, F., & Patti, M. G. (2018). Retracted articles in surgery journals. What are surgeons doing wrong? *Surgery (United States)*, 163(6), 1201–1206. DOI: 10.1016/j.surg.2018.01.015

Colquhoun, D. (2011). Publish or perish: Peer review and the corruption of science. *The Guardian*. Retrieved fromhttps://www.theguardian.com/science/2011/sep/05/publish-perish-peer-review-science

Chaddah, P. (2014). Not all plagiarism requires a retraction. *Nature*, 511(7508), 127. DOI: 10.1038/511127a

Chaurasia, A. (2016). Stop teaching Indians to copy and paste. *Nature*, 534(7609), 591. DOI:10.1038/534591a

Chen, C., Hu, Z., Milbank, J., & Shultz, T. (2012). A Visual analytic study of retracted articles in scientific literature. *Journal of the American Society for Information Science and Technology.* 64 (2), 234–253. DOI:10.1002/asi.22755

Citron, D. T., & Ginsparg, P. (2015). Patterns of text reuse in a scientific corpus. *Proceedings of the National Academy of Sciences*, 112(1), 25–30. DOI: 10.1073/pnas.1415135111

Cokol, M., Ozbay, F., & Rodriguez-Esteban, R. (2008). Retraction rates are on the rise. *EMBO Reports*, 9(1), 2. DOI: 10.1038/sj.embor.7401143

Corbyn, Z. (2009). Retractions up tenfold. *Higher Education: Times*. Retrieved fromhttp://www.timeshighereducation.co.uk/407838.article.

Cox, A., Craig, R., & Tourish, D. (2018). Retraction statements and research malpractice in economics. *Research Policy*, 47(5), 924-935. DOI: 10.1016/j.respol.2018.02.016

Council of Science Editors (US). (2012). CSE's white paper on promoting integrity in scientific journal publications. Retrieved fromhttp://cseditors.wpengine.com/wp-content/uploads/entire_whitepaper.pdf [accessed on 31 March 2017]

Cunha, H. (1946). Gastrostomy. Its inception and evolution. *The American Journal of Surgery*, 72(4), 610–634. DOI: 10.1016/0002-9610(46)90402-3

Davis, M.S., Riske-Morris, M., & Diaz, S. R. (2007). Causal factors implicated in research misconduct: Evidence from ORI case files. *Science and Engineering Ethics*, 13(4), 395–414. DOI: 10.1007%2Fs11948-007-9045-2

DeMaria, A.N. (2012). Scientific misconduct, retractions, and errata. *Journal of the American College of Cardiology*, 59(16), 1488-9. DOI: 10.1016/j.jacc.2012.03.005

Fanelli, D. (2013). Why growing retractions are (mostly) a good sign. *PLoS Medicine*, 10 (12), 1-6. DOI: 10.1371/journal.pmed.1001563

Fang, F., Grant, S.C.R., & Casadevall, A. (2012). Misconduct accounts for the majority of retractedscientific publications. *Proceedings of the National Academy of Sciences.* 109(42), 17028–17033: DOI: 10.1073/pnas.1212247109

Gasparyan, A.Y., Ayvazyan, L., Akazhanov, N.A., Kitas, G.D. (2014). Self-correction in biomedical publications and the scientific impact. *Croatian Medical Journal*; 55(1), 61-72. DOI:10.3325/cmj.2014.55.61

Grieneisen, M. L., & Zhang, M. (2012). A comprehensive survey of retracted articles from the scholarly literature. *PLoSOne*, 7(10). DOI: 10.1371/journal.pone.0044118

Huh, S., Kim, S.Y., & Cho, H.M. (2016). Characteristics of Retractions from Korean Medical Journals in the KoreaMed Database: A Bibliometric Analysis. *PLOS ONE*, 11(10). DOI:10.1371/journal.pone.0163588

Kuroki, T. M. D., & Ukawa, A. P. D. (2018). Repeating probability of authors with retracted scientific publications. *Accountability in Research: Policies and Quality Assurance*, 25(4), 212-219. DOI: 10.1080/08989621.2018.1449651

Liao, Q.-J., Zhang, Y.-Y., Fan, Y.-C., Zheng, M.-H., Bai, Y., Eslick, G. D., He, X.-X., ... He, H. (2018). Perceptions of Chinese Biomedical Researchers Towards Academic Misconduct: A Comparison Between 2015 and 2010. *Science and Engineering Ethics*, 24(2), 629-645. DOI: 10.1007/s1194

Nogueira, T. E., Gonçalves, A. S., Leles, C. R., Batista, A. C., & Costa, L. R. (2017). A survey of retracted articles in dentistry. *BMC Research Notes*, 10(1), 253. DOI: 10.1186/s13104-017-2576-y

Resnik, D.B., & Dinse, G.E. (2013). Scientific retractions and corrections related to misconduct findings. *Journal of Medical Ethics*, 39(1), 46–50. DOI:10.1136/medethics-2012-100766

Ribeiro, M.D., & Vasconcelos, S.M.R. (2018). Retractions covered by Retraction Watch in the 2013–2015 period: prevalence for the most productive countries. *Scientometrics*, 114(2), 719-734. DOI: 10.1007/s11192-017-2621-6

Roig, M. (2009). Plagiarism: Consider the Context. *Science*, 325, 5942, 813-814. DOI: 10.1126/science.325_813c

Roig, M. (2012). Avoiding unethical writing practices. *Food and Chemical Toxicology*, 50(10), 3385–3387. doi.10.1016/j.fct.2012.06.043.

Jaric, I. (2015). High time for a common plagiarism detection system. *Scientometrics*, 106(1), 457-459. DOI:10.1007/s11192-015-1756-6

Madlock-Brown, C.R., & Eichmann, D. (2014). The (lack of) Impact of Retraction on Citation Networks. *Science and Engineering Ethics*, 21(1), 127–137. DOI: 10.1007/s11948-014-9532-1

Maurer, H., Kappe, F., & Zaka, B. (2006). Plagiarism - a survey. *Journal of Universal Computer Science*, 12(8), 1050–1084. doi.10.3217jucs-012-08-1050

Nath, S., Marcus, S., & Druss, B. (2006). Retractions in the research literature: misconduct or mistakes?. *The Medical Journal of Australia*. 185(3), 152-154. DOI: 10.3174/ajnr.A0775

Park, C. (2003). In other (people's) words: plagiarism by university students—literature and lessons. *Assessment and Evaluation in Higher Education*, 28(5), 471-88. doi.10.1080/02602930301677

Shamim, T. (2018). Data regarding articles retracted from PubMed indexed dental journals from India. *Data in Brief*, 18, 1069-1072. DOI: 10.1016/j.dib.2018.03.133

Steen, R. G., Casadevall, A., & Fang, F. C. (2013). Why has the number of scientific retractions increased?. *PLoS ONE*, 8(7), e68397. doi:10.1371/journal.pone.0068397

Steen, R. G. (2011). Retractions in the scientific literature: Is the incidence of research fraud increasing?. *Journal of Medical Ethics*, 37(3), 249–253. DOI:10.1136/jme.2010.040923

Stretton, S., Bramich, N. J., Keys, J. R., Monk, J. A., Ely, J. A., Haley, C., ... Woolley, K. L. (2012). Publication misconduct and plagiarism retractions: a systematic, retrospective study. *Current Medical Research and Opinion*, 28(10), 1575–1583. DOI: 10.1185/03007995.2012.728131

Wager, E., & Williams, P. (2011). Why and how do journals retract articles? An analysis of Medline retractions 1988-2008. *Journal of Medical Ethics*, 37(9), 567-570. doi.10.1136/jme.2010.040964

Wager, E., Barbour, V., Yentis, S., Kleinert, S., et al. (2009). Retractions: Guidance from the Committee on Publication Ethics (COPE). *Maturitas*, 64(4), 201–203. doi.10.1016/j.maturitas.2009.09.018

Wang, T., Xing, Q.-R., Wang, H., & Chen, W. (2018). Retracted Publications in the Biomedical Literature from Open Access Journals. *Science and Engineering Ethics*, 1-14. DOI: 10.1007/s1194

Wittmaack, K. (2005). Penalties plus high-quality review to fight plagiarism. *Nature*, 436(24), 258–259. doi.org/10.1038/436024d

10

Plagiarism in Research Publications and Violation of Law and Ethics

R Saha[9]

1. INTRODUCTION

Plagiarism in scientific research papers has, in the recent time, become a topic of discussion and concern in India. Plagiarism in other fields of knowledge has also been reported. The core level of discussion in India has largely been driven by ethical considerations without any reference to violation of the existing laws in the country such as the Copyright Act. Ethics can mean different things to different people and, therefore issues related to legitimacy of one point of view as against another point of view will always remain debatable. Punitive actions purely based on ethics may not be acceptable to all and may be difficult to implement unless supported by law. It is therefore necessary to address the issue both from legal and ethical angles.

2. INTELLECTUAL PROPERTY RIGHTS (IPR) AND PLAGIARISM

Plagiarism is violation / infringement of the intellectual property rights (IPR) of the original author in the form of authorship rights, sometimes also called the paternity right. A plagiarist attempts to pass off the copied work as his/ her own. The right of authorship in India is derived from the Indian Copyright Act. Copyrights, an important form of IPR. protects original literary, dramatic, musical and artistic works.

3. RIGHTS AND PENALTY UNDER COPYRIGHT

The Copyright Act gives the following rights to an author: to reproduce the work in any

---

9. The content of this paper has been majorly taken from the author's article "Plagiarism, research publications and law" published in Current Science in its issue of June 25, 2017, Vol.112(12). Permission of Current Science was obtained vide their e mail of April 3, 2018.

material form, issue copies of work to the public not being copies already in circulation, perform the work in public or communicate the work to public, translate the work, make adaptation of the work and make cinematograph films or sound recording of the work. Infringement of copyright is a cognizable offence leading to fine in rupees and / or imprisonment. Specifically, an infringer shall be punishable with imprisonment for a term which shall not be less than six months but which may extend to three years and with fine which shall not be less than fifty thousand rupees but which may extend to two lakh rupees. In terms of civil remedies infringement can lead to injunction and damages. However, if the infringer can establish that on the date of infringement he / she was not aware and had no reasonable ground for believing that copyright subsisted in the work, the copyright holder shall be entitled only to an injunction and not any damages. The term of copyright is equal to author's life after creating the work plus sixty years. Copying of a work beyond the term of copyright is not an infringement of copyright of the original author. However, plagiarism will take place even beyond copyright term if the work is reproduced in the name of plagiarist. There is no law at present to punish the plagiarist beyond the term of the copyright. That signifies that the authorship of an original work cannot be misappropriated by any one at any point of time since the original work was authored.

4. AUTHORSHIP RIGHT

The Copyright Act provides protection to an expression or presentation of an idea and not to the idea itself; the presentation may be textual, visual or audio or a combination of these three forms of presentation. The authorship rights are derived from the author's special rights under Section 57 of the Indian Copyright Act. The Section stipulates " Independently of the author's copyright and even after assignment either wholly or partially of the said copyright, the author of a work shall have the right (a) to claim authorship of the work; and (b) to restrain or claim damages in respect of any distortion, mutilation, modification or other act in relation to the said work which is done before the expiration of the term of copyright if such distortion, mutilation, modification or other act would be prejudicial to his honour and reputation." In the context of plagiarism, point (a) is relevant. This right stipulates that an author's original work cannot be reproduced in someone else's name according to the Copyright Act. In other words, replacing the original author's name by some other name is the violation of authorship right of the original author and the law may take its own course in ensuring that the original authorship is retained. Plagiarism is also an act of copyright infringement if undertaken within the term of the copyright. In other words, one can say Plagiarism = infringement of copyright + infringement of authorship right. As stated, beyond the term of copyright, no copyright infringement would take place; therefore, plagiarism will then be the same as infringement of authorship right. Further, it may be noted that selling of a pirated / copied book is a copyright infringement but not a case of plagiarism. The infringer will also become a plagiarist if he/ she sells the copied or pirated work as an original created by him/ her.

5. DEFINITION OF PLAGIARISM

The Oxford Dictionary defines plagiarize as "take and use (the thoughts, writings, inventions etc. of another person) as one's own; pass off the thoughts etc. of (another person) as one's own". There are several other definitions of plagiarism. In order to keep the discussionsimple, we would accept the definition given in the Oxford Dictionary. In view of this definition it is necessary to examine how plagiarism is different from infringement of copyrights at the conceptual level. Firstly, thoughts and ideas cannot be copyrighted under the law and therefore, plagiarism has something more than the legal connotation of copyright. Secondly, raw data does not get protection in copyrights but the organization of data in the form of a database is protectable. Therefore, copying of an idea or a thought or data may not be copyright infringement but it may be a case of plagiarism. The point being made is that plagiarism needs to be viewed both from legal and non-legal angles at the same time, which makes the life a little more difficult. The non-legal angle could be linked to ethics, morality, consideration towards the original author, honesty and appropriation of credit not due etc. In fact, Section 57 provides special status to the author of a literary work and puts the authorship right on a higher pedestal than the normal objects of copyright. (Mannu Bhandari v. Kala Vikas Pvt. Ltd., AIR 1987 Del 13.)

6. SOME EXAMPLES AND ANALYSIS

Can I copy from my own original writings already published somewhere or reproduce the writings or adapt them in some other form? A common-sense answer would be that there is nothing wrong in doing so as I was the original author or creator of the work. This answer would be correct if I had not assigned the copyrights in my writings to a journal or a magazine for getting the writings published. Once I assign my copyright to a journal (assignment is like selling my house thus losing all rights in the house), then that journal becomes the new copyright owner and can prohibit me from copying my own work for another journal or even for a different article or paper in the same journal unless there is an agreement with the journal to do so. Therefore, copying my own work, for publishing it in another journal, may become a straight case of copyright violation. It may however, be noted that assignment of copyright does not snatch away the authorship right from the author meaning thereby, that the work cannot be shown to have been created by someone else.

Consider another situation. Two authors A and B write an article and get it published in a journal X by assigning their copyrights in the work to the publisher of X. An article written later by A is published in another journal Y. The article written by A happens to contain some portion of the earlier article written by A and B for the journal X without the permission of the publisher of X. A may feel that no plagiarism or copyright violation has taken place while publishing an article in Y. Firstly, the original authorship of A and B has been misappropriated by A and secondly, it is a straight case of copyright infringement. This point is often missed by authors. It can be seen that the complexity of rights will increase with multiplicity of authors.

It should be pointed that in the area of publishing research papers and books, the authors generally assign their copyrights to the publisher of the journal or the book. Most academicians and researchers in India (and perhaps in many other countries) sign the assignment forms without carefully reading the terms and conditions, especially those written in fine print because of the overwhelming desire to get the work published and to share it with peers.

7. EXTENT OF COPYING

There are some other dimensions to be kept in view. Copying has not been considered unethical in many cultures. Copying religious songs or texts was never and is still not considered an act of copyright infringement (although it may be illegal). Similarly, quoting proverbs such as "An apple a day keeps the doctor away" without acknowledging the author is also not considered infringement of copyright or authorship right.Consider another situation relating to use of common expressions by many. All of us use so many common expressions to describe a situation or an activity or a thought. Would repeating such common expressions be treated as plagiarism or violation of copyrights? Take, for example, an expression "I go to drop my son at his school every morning at 7 AM. I come back home and get ready for the office. I leave from my house at 9 A M and reach my office at 10 AM." It would be difficult to describe it as a case of plagiarism or copyright violation if such expressions (even if identical) are used by other persons because these are common usage expressions and the order of sentences reflect regular and common activities of a day for a father. However, if the above description is accompanied by some original thoughts or emotions or description of nature or the route followed while going to the school, then the chances of plagiarism and/ or copyright violations having taken place are high if you find another description identical to the one mentioned above with the accompaniments. Now consider yet another situation where the original description does not consist of only two or three sentences but say 15 to 20 sentences. If someone is found to publish 15 to 20 sentences identical to the earlier sentences, then the chances of a copyright infringement or plagiarism are very high. It is reported that in the publishing business copying and publishing of 300 words of text in continuation is considered copyright infringement.

Sometimes authors are so careless while copying that they copy commas, semi-colon and full stops, even grammatically wrong sentences and wrongly spelled words. I remember my days in school (early 1950s), the teacher gave a question for answering in English- "What is your name?" A boy named Kumar sitting next to one Ramesh copied from Ramesh's copy and wrote "My name is Ramesh" (of course the names are changed). Such incidents would be more common when one relies on cut and paste. Such mistakes are a strong proof of copying

8. ECONOMIC DIMENSION OF PLAGIARISM

Intellectual property rights play a central role in the knowledge economy. Plagiarism in this context has become a point of concern and is no longer purely driven by ethics. Does plagiarism have any associated benefits for the plagiarist other than the authorship? An act of plagiarism should not be considered as a trivial happening. A plagiarist's scholarly article may raise the recognition of the plagiarist in many ways especially in the eyes of those who have not read the original work. This may also undermine the reputation of the original writer whose work may sometimes be considered by new readers as plagiarized. Pecuniary benefits may not accrue immediately to the plagiarist but in the long run the possibility of benefits, due to his enhanced reputation, cannot be ruled out. The enhanced reputation may lead to pecuniary benefits such as getting further assignments to write. It would therefore appear that plagiarism may also get linked to economic benefits, hence plagiarism is not an ethical issue alone.

9. EASE OF DETECTING COPYING AND PLAGIARISM

Prima facie, it would appear that plagiarism is not a new phenomenon but used to take place in the past as well; but detection of plagiarised work in earlier days was difficult. Even now, it is not easy to detect plagiarism in respect of non-digitized works. Many computer programmes (software), paid or free, are available to check if a work claimed to be original is a case of copyright violation or plagiarism. It has now become much simpler to find out instances of plagiarism and copyright violations with the help of such software. The underlying concept is that the original writing and the documents published earlier should be available in digital form. The current debate is both about copyright violation and plagiarism indicating that some published research papers contain already published work mostly in parts and there are also instances of appropriating authorship.

In the Indian context, the writings in vernacular languages are not digitized barring a few exceptions. Detecting plagiarism in these languages is not easy mainly because of time consuming efforts involved in the process. However, plagiarism was detected in the past as well when there was no digitization and works were available only in the form of hard copy and hence, the number of cases of plagiarism reported was relatively low. Scientific research papers by Indian scientists are predominantly published in English therefore, they can be easily digitized and checked for copying and plagiarism. That may not be the case in respect of research papers in non-science areas such as literature, philosophy, history etc. which will also be in vernacular languages and therefore, may not be easily digitized.

10. LARGER NEGATIVE DIMENSIONS OF PLAGIARISING

Negative effects of plagiarism are well known and are described in the rule books of many universities and institutions such as disqualification of students from further studies, non-acceptance of papers by journals and magazines and in some cases pecuniary penalty / other legal action. These are the practices in many developed countries. Such rule books are not common in India; one reason would be that most universities and institutions do not have written down policies for IPR.

A copied work certainly points towards lack of originality in the work. It would follow that questioning the originality of several research papers may not be illogical and unreasonable. Researchers interested majorly in increasing the count of their publications may give a go-by to originality in content and expression while submitting their papers to journals. However, it has become exceedingly difficult to get such works published in reputed journals to start with. If we were to apply the strict criterion of copyright law to the research papers published in the past, several of them may not pass the tests of copyright law and plagiarism. If so, the quality of our research would be subject to scrutiny and may call for review especially when the research was funded by government. At the time time it my be reckoned that plagiarism may be found not only in research papers emanating from academic institutions but also those from government research laboratories, R&D institutions and so on.

Plagiarism certainly points towards lack of originality and novelty in any writing whether scientific or otherwise. Plagiarism in scientific research, which also leads to research publications, is a serious matter because it creates doubts about the quality of research in terms of novelty. Obviously, the return on investment in research can be improved / enhanced if the research yields novel and original results. In the Indian context, we have more reasons to be concerned as majority of research papers emanate from publicly funded institutions. If there is perceptible reliance, even in few case, on copying of others' works, it becomes a case of inefficient use of public funds. In other words, it may be necessary to review research funding to promote novelty and originality in research. In this backdrop it is urgently required that young students and researchers including faculty members and senior scientists are trained to focus on originality and novelty in their research.

The above arguments are applicable to publications in all other areas of knowledge such as philosophy, economics, history, sociology and other areas in social sciences.

11. POSSIBLE REMEDIES

We need to create extensive awareness about plagiarism among Indian students, researchers, academicians, policy makers and research managers. It must be understood that it is a legal and ethical matter and cannot be handled by common sense. Most academic and research institutions do not have policies for protecting their intellectual property rights and, hence there is lack of awareness about this subject 0f plagiarism. It is essential to remember that issues of plagiarism and copyrights violations cannot be neglected. This decade has been declared as the "Decade of Innovation" and, both governmental and non-governmental systems have shown their noble intention to create an ecosystem for innovations. Therefore, setting up of institutional IPR policy / guidelines is the need of the hour to establish a healthy ecosystem How do we expect to establish a healthy ecosystem for innovations if the creators of works and innovations are not careful about honouring someone else's intellectual property rights such as copyrights? The mind set of copying others' work shows our weakness or inability to create and invent. Innovations without due attention to IPR would have little meaning as you lose the strength to avoid and stop competition. In this context we should give due weightage to avoiding plagiarism in research and development as that would encourage and nurture originality and novelty.

Some people have suggested that a separate a body may be set up for checking plagiarism in Indian research. Any idea of setting up a central agency should be rejected as it may end up becoming counter-productive as such a body may become a hurdle in creation and publication of original work. The system for checking plagiarism should be decentralized to the level of each institution and self-regulating as far as possible.

It is possible for each institution to determine whether a research paper from the institution violates copyright of someone or is a case of plagiarism. Let us remember that a plagiarized work brings disrepute to an institution if a member of the faculty/ student engages in the act of plagiarism. While creating awareness is the primary need and challenge, it is essential to create enabling systems in parallel for stakeholders to check IPR violations. Measures such as installing suitable software for this purpose in the college library or individual's computer would go a long way in creating anti-plagiarism culture. Some software are also available free of cost which can be used without any financial burden.

Eliminating copying and plagiarism in publications in vernacular languages remains a big challenge because most of the literature, scientific or otherwise, is not available in digital format. Awareness creation at regular interval among researchers would be useful in the interim period. There should be positive and definite efforts to digitize the literature in vernacular languages.

In schools and junior colleges, where increasingly, students are required to write term papers or reports to train them in independent thinking and expression, cases of cut and paste must be minimized or totally removed. A very brief and concise course on plagiarism and copyright violations in all universities and academic institutions may be introduced. The best and never-failing step would be to exercise self-discipline and stop copying and plagiarizing. This initiative would pay rich dividends in future.

There is already an existing law. What is required is educating researchers, especially the young ones such PhD scholars, research associates and assistants in the basics of copyright principles, and guidelines for "Dos and Donts" in this regard. Even senior researchers will benefit greatly by learning about such principles and laws. Teachers who have the prime role in strengthening the anti-plagiarism culture may be trained in Academic Staff Colleges under the University Grants Commission.

In several universities abroad, strict punishments are prescribed for students engaging in plagiarism. It is understood that some institutions in India have come out with their policy on plagiarism. However, majority of institutions and universities do not have such policies and hence, the awareness about copyrights and plagiarism is extremely low. It is essential thatuniversities, colleges and institutions should undertake awareness programmes and also establish facilities to be used by researchers to determine if their research papers violate someone else's copyright or authorship right.

There has been a call for a new law on plagiarism to curb plagiarism. First of all, we must not make new laws when the existing laws can take care of it in majority of cases. Taking plagiarism as a moral or unethical offence may demand different type of censorship or punishment. The Copyright Act does not prescribe any punishment for indulging in plagiarism or violating authorship rights. Can you imprison or fine a person purely on the charge of plagiarism if there is no law? The answer is perhaps no. One has to identify the elements which are not covered by the Copyright Act such as raw data and ideas and plagiarising a work after the term of the copyright while formulating a legal framework to penalize plagiarism.

Although the present article focusses on research publications, it must be appreciated that plagiarism can also take place in visual and audio manifestations. The issue of plagiarism needs to be handled at a much higher level of academic, legal, political and social debate as both legal, non-legal and ethical issues are involved. Quality of research papers, so closely related to originality and novelty of work, places a country's R&D in a prominent position on the global platform. India has earned global prestige because of its efforts and achievements in science and technology, especially in the areas of space and atomic energy. Let us not allow it to be diluted and belittled by not exercising adequate care for protecting IPR and discouraging violations of others' IPR. Science and technology in the country needs to be nurtured through research and development and therefore some amount of hand holding of researchers and research institutions is called for. While adopting a new paradigm driven by both legal and non-legal principles and practices, we should clearly understand the existing IPR laws of the country including the Copyright Act.

11

Plagiarism : An Academic Dishonesty. A Bibliometric Insight into the Spread of Problem

V.J. Suseela
V. Uma

1. INTRODUCTION

Plagiarism, the unethical activity of stealing other's work and projecting as their own has been spreading in all the sectors associated to creativity and originality i.e., literature, arts, scientific experiments and academic writings. The activity has become threat to the originality, hardship and endeavours of the creators, thus has been widely discussed and condemned by the entire scholarly research community irrespective of the nation, period, discipline.

Plagiarism in the context of academic/research writing, can be perceived as using other's writings - publications in full or in parts without acknowledging the source as well claiming as their own. The Council of Writing Program Administrators - WPA (2003), the national association of college/university faculty holding the professional responsibilities for directing the writing programs ranging from undergraduate level to research in USA stated that "plagiarism occurs when a writer deliberately uses someone else's language, ideas, or other original (not common-knowledge) material without acknowledging its source", in the context of higher academic institutions, where teaching, advanced studies and research contributes to the development of country. The council applied the statement to the published documents in print or on-line, manuscripts, student's papers or submissions to various repositories etc.

The technological advancements in information industry such as - scholarly communication, and the proliferation of e-resources coupled with open access initiatives of publishers, research funding agencies as well as the emergence of institutional repositories, are facilitating the easy (even free) access of scholarly articles full text, images, models etc. to researchers helping them in onward progress of their research.Unfortunately, the hidden and rare form plagiarism trend, turned into a copy paste activity that has been increasing with the easy availability of scholarly literature over networks. Though there are several factors contributing to the unethical activity of plagiarism, primarily in higher education it occurs unintentionally - due to negligence; carelessness, ignorance, arrogance, lack of awareness, proper use of information resources for teaching, learning and research; and lack of English knowledge; lack of policy and apathy within academic institutions and academia, etc. The situation undoubtedly demotivates many students to work independently and to put efforts to learning in case of impunity of plagiarism. (Ocholla, & Ocholla, 2016, Satija, 2011, Suseela, 2014, Lukashenko, Anohina and Grundspenkis, 2007).

2. RESEARCH PROBLEM

This plagiarism, the dishonest activity in academics appears to be a global phenomenon pervading in almost every discipline in sciences, technology, arts, social sciences, humanities, etc. and in every demographic region and has become threat to the original research writings and the intellectual property of the researchers all over the world.

When e-resources were not prominent among academic circles, the scientific societies or intellectual organizations were settling the plagiarized issues legally based on complaint or report of the creator of work. The realization of the problem among the academic circles has been growing over the years and the researchers in various disciplines, scientific & academic publishers, academic administrators and librarians have been looking at the problem in different perspectives and communicate their research results, experiences, experiments, opinions, perceptions in books, journals, and various other media suggesting suitable measures to control such an unethical activity like plagiarism. Proper assessment of the problem and the extent of awareness spread helps to institute controlling as well as remedial measures such as - formulating plagiarism policy at national as well as institutional levels, for increasing the awareness programs, implementing the policy, screening of similarity of text of academic documents – theses, dissertations, project reports, assignments etc.

3. REVIEW OF RELATED LITERATURE

Research relating to the topic of plagiarism is vast and diversified. The literature on plagiarism and related issues is published in huge quantities in all the principle languages including forms of plagiarism, policies, academic integrity, anti-plagiarism initiatives, text similarity measuring tools, discussing about the cases of academic dishonesty, applying qualitative or quantitative analytical methods. The literature not only covers journal articles, books, conference proceedings, notes, book chapters, editorials, notes, letters, web pages, email messages, interviews, news items, artworks or any other audio & visual media. Few studies are reviewed hereunder.

A retrospective study was conducted by Wooley, KL et al. (2011) to find the quantum of publications were taken out due to misconduct, involving whether declared medical writers or declared pharmaceutical industry associations and also to find the issues related to misconduct retractions. PubMed database was searched limiting to 'English language' and 'human values' for the period Jan 1966 - Feb 2008, to retrieve publications data on misconduct. The results were tested applying statistical methods. It was found that retraction due to misconduct hardly involved declared medical writers or declared pharmaceutical industry association. Retraction due to misconduct than by mistake was significantly associated with the absence of declared medical writers and absence of declared pharmaceutical declared industry involvement. The first author was from low/middle-income country. Publications retracted because of misconduct rarely involved declared medical writers or declared pharmaceutical industry support. Stretton, Serina et al (2012) conducted a systematic, retrospective study to find out whether plagiarism is more predominant in publications drawn from the medical literature and the first authors of retracted publications were affiliated with lower-income countries or higher-income countries. Further they investigated other issues related to plagiarism like the national language of the first author's country affiliation, type of publication, the ranking of the journal etc. The withdrawn publications were classified according to the first author's country affiliation, country's income level, and country's national language, publication type, and ranking of the publishing journal. The data were analysed (odds ratio [OR], 95% confidence limits [CL], chi-squared tests) by the academic statistician. It was proved by the chi-square test that the publications drawn for plagiarism were significantly associated with the first authors from lower-income countries than higher income countries and with lower ranked journals to highly ranked journals. The findings have stronger implications for emerging right evidence-based policies and distribution of resources to help minimize academic dishonesty or plagiarism.DeLong (2012) examined the impact of culturally embedded individual differences such as plagiarism, knowledge, beliefs, anxiety, social values, learning style preferences, culture etc. on unintentional plagiarism to measure and compare the relative influence of cognitive, emotional and cultural factors on students' propensity toward plagiarism. The study sample was consisting of 116 first-year undergraduate students (90 "Western Heritage" -WEST: American nationality and 26 "Confucian Heritage") enrolled in a small liberal arts university in the eastern US. They received 2-hour standard information literacy-training module that reviews rules for properly citing quotations, information, and ideas borrowed from secondary sources and the data was collected from 20-minute survey in paper-and-pencil format applying the above criteria. The findings revealed that plagiarized material is positively associated with evaluative beliefs about the plagiarizer, a preference for a reflective learning, and weaker information literacy knowledge. On the whole, the study suggested that rates of unintentional plagiarism might be corrected by condemning erroneous beliefs about the superficial quality of the plagiarizer's writing and the training modules should provide an opportunity for in-depth understanding of acknowledging the sources instead of narrating rules and procedures. Garcia-Romero and Estrada-Lorenzo (2012) made a bibliometric study on plagiarism.Déjà vu is the largest database of duplicate records and comprises 79,383 cases of extremely similar Medline citations containing instances of duplicate publication and probable plagiarism. It works through an eTBLAST algorithm and the similarity score is established based on the text included in the author, title, affiliation and abstract. Additional information stated that the document cited original study and the percentage of references common to both documents are provided by the curators. Out of 79393 document pairs, 840 pairs containing full text have been examined by the curators. The authors used the classification which could pair similar documents into two groups. The first group of pairs had at least one shared author (SA) from earlier and later documents. The second group had pairs of documents with no shared authors between two documents. (NSA). To search citations from SCOPUS database the sample was reduced to 450 documents from 1997 to 2006 due to coverage problem. The authors were intended to observe a minimum of a 2-year window in SCOPUS for both the earlier and later documents in each year. After searching in SCOPUS some pairs were excluded as there were no citations for either earlier or later documents. So the sample was with fewer cases of only 247 document pairs of which 172 related to plagiarism (NSA) and 75 to self-plagiarism (SA). They had to create a second data set containing all the pairs of shared authors (SA) labelled them as examines, whenever they were published which increased the number of SA pairs to 149. Bibliometric analysis was carried out by the authors to a set of similar documents sharing one or more authors to know original documents co-exist with fraudulent (self- plagiarized) documents and compared pairs of documents sharing authors in cases in which the later document cited the earlier document against the later documents that did not cite earlier documents. Results revealed that plagiarized cases were published in low visibility journal and received a number of citations. On an average, the time between the publication of original article and duplicate article was around 12 months. For shared similar documents (such as self-plagiarism) in shared authorship, a higher level of self-citation rate existed than among earlier non shared author documents (NSA). Further, it was observed that later shared author documents not citing original article had an average a higher FTS than an earlier document. Authors suggest that bibliometric study of plagiarism cannot be based only on bibliometric indicators. So, they recommend that journals should support cross check to detect possible cases of plagiarism and felt that self-plagiarism for the reuse of their texts should not be considered as plagiarism as there may be issues or topic to argue under discussion by readers or editors. Foo and Tan (2014) analysed the implications of retraction period and co-authorship of fraudulent publications. They have taken 5 researchers for study having 15 fraudulent publications. A total of 113 retracted publications from the 5 studied researchers were extracted from the PubMed database. The study revealed that the number and frequency of fraudulent publications have not come down even with much awareness of such occurrences in the recent years. For the 113 retracted publications, they had a total of 6,127 citation count generated from the Google Scholar database. The number of co-authors afûliated to each of the retracted publications was also taken. Using month and the year of publication as the base, the mean, and standard deviation (SD) of the retraction period (in months) were computed for each of the 5 researchers under study. The linear regression analysis showed that only limited correlation ($R(2) = .008$) between citation counts and retraction period existed. The p-value for several F-tests (carried out to compare two populations having same variations or Standard deviation) to know the number of co-authors to fraudulent publications on an inter researcher basis was found to be ranging from <.001 to .458. It was observed that a good amount of correlation (R(2) =.592 existed between the possibility of a researcher to include different individuals for isolated fraudulent publications at the same time selecting only a small number to be the co-authors of their ill-behaved acts. It is known that the co-authors approach was used for publishing fraudulent work. The authors suggested for putting the names of the fraudulent work "shame list" on the website of organizations on publication ethics such as COPE to control misconduct. Such matters would be discussed by the committee and its members consisting of major publishers like Elsevier, Wiley-Blackwell, Springer, Taylor & Francis, Palgrave Macmillan, and Wolters Kluwer. Presently the ethical issues of COPE (Committee on Publication Ethics) are handled in anonymity. The main limitation of the study is less sample i.e. 5 researchers cannot represent all researchers who had their publications retracted in the PubMed database. Harkanwal Preet Singh et al. (2014) attempted to assess various aspects associated with withdrawal of scientific articles from 2004 to 2013. Data was taken from PubMed and Medline using the keywords - retraction of articles, retraction notice, and withdrawal of article in April 2014 to detect articles retracted from 2004 to 2013. Analysis of data and statistical testing was done using t-test and Karl Pearson's correlation coefficient. Results showed that a total of 2343 articles were retracted during the period 2004 – 2013, including case reports, but editors of some journals were not willing to withdraw the articles because the research has been processed through the peer-review in most of the highly ranked journals in science and medicine and such occurrences would defame the image of the journal and its ethical standards. To cite an example, authors quoted an article by Bezouka et al (1994) published in Nature was withdrawn after 19 years in (2003), but surprisingly it has been cited 255 times as per Thompson's Web of Knowledge. Further it was also noticed that the retracted articles continued to receive citations even after the withdrawal notices were served, thereby ascertaining that retractions did not make changes to the citation behaviour. Since the study is limited to retractions indexed in Medline database and so it has the biomedical bias, concluded that retractions only occupy a small portion/ or fraction of a percentage among the total publication in any given area in any year. Authors recommended that editors should follow COPE guidelines to minimize misconduct as it has an adverse impact not only on the scientific community but also the general public. Original articles should be available freely mentioning about the retraction on the journal website, in the beginning, and at the end of the article as a note. Velmurugan and Radhakrishnan (2015) made a scientometric study on plagiarism literature output globally. They attempted to evaluate the research articles of plagiarism in Universal level in terms of document and year wise, author wise, institution wise, country wise, journal wise and keyword wise during the period of recent five years from 2010 to 2014. Data was taken from Web of Science (WOS) and found that there was a constant growth of literature output in Plagiarism in the world during the period of study. It is further noticed that the Indian share of publications for the period is 16 articles i.e. 2.07% of 776 papers published by authors from all over the world in different journals. A Total number of 7641 keywords found in the plagiarism literature output during the period of study. Out of 7641 keywords and again amongthe top 15 the keyword "PLAGIARISM" occupied first position with 466, 58.8 %, and the TLCS (Total Local Citation Score) is 374 and

TGCS (Total Global Citation Score) is 762, followed by "SCIENTIFIC" 62 (7.8%), "STUDENTS" 59 (7.45%), "ACADEMIC" 52 (6.6%), "DETECTION" 48 (6.1%) respectively. The study reveals that the highest number of contributions was published in the year 2013. Many of the articles have been contributed by multiple authors.However, Indian authors have produced very least articles of plagiarism compared to foreign authors. It is noticed that awareness of plagiarism is a basic requirement for researchers, scientists, and LIS Professionals to enhance the quality of education.Leonard et al. (2015) examined the perceptions of University of Florida graduate students in science, technology, engineering, and mathematics (STEM) regarding the misconduct and integrity issues by conducting survey with 188 respondents in connection with Gaming against Plagiarism (GAP) project, to find the strong need for instructors, advisers, and mentors to incorporate aspects of academic integrity into graduate students' activities. The survey results revealed that over half of our student respondents were "not sure" about the level of academic dishonesty at university and one-third indicated that this was a serious problem, with the remainder viewing it as a minor or non-existent concern. Further, the open-ended comments indicated that the honor code is weak, poorly understood, and not detailed and lack of awareness of the full Code (Only 15.1 % reported learning "a lot" about the Honor Code in the Graduate Orientation program fewer (7.7 %) report learning from fellow students. Another study of retractions in medical journals published in Korea and indexed through the KoreaMed database from January 1990 to January 2016, by Huh, Kim, Cho (2016) explored the characteristics of retractions such as – content related, issuer, reason, adherence to guidelines, and appropriateness.Out of 217,839 publications and 114 papers addressing the retraction showed that 58.8% were issued by the authors, 17.5% jointly issued by author, editor, and publisher, 15.8% came from editors, and 4.4% were dispatched by institutions; in 5.3% of the instances, the issuer was unstated. It was found that the 8.8% articles were retracted due to plagiarism reasons. The degree of adherence to COPE's retraction guidelines varied (79.8%±100%), and some retractions were inappropriate by COPE standards. Suseela and Uma (2017) attempted to examine University of Hyderabad users' perceptions regarding plagiarism, plagiarism detection tools, similarity verification process and their feedback on implementation and the role of the library in executing the plagiarism screening operation, by posting an online questionnaire to all the students/research scholars who got their work screened in the Library for plagiarism. The survey results reported that around 80% of respondents were aware of these practices, and were satisfied with the information received and screening services provided by the Library. Respondents also mentioned their constraints in handling repeated terms, own publications etc. Based on user's expectations and results, it was suggested that institutions should be proactive in promoting ethical values/code among students by inculcating the best practices in writing, depositing their thesis/dissertations, articles in institutional repository, promoting the use of online plagiarism screening tools and conducting orientation or training classes in language writing, citation styles, research methodology, ethical values etc.

4. OBJECTIVES OF THE STUDY

The literature indicates that the plagiarized practices, whether intentional or unintentional are prevailing in all most all the disciplines, despite the application of mechanical detection measures, imposition of severe penalties on those caught such as - retraction of the publications, getting defamed, loosing career etc. The present paper attempts to examine the awareness of 'plagiarism' as an academic dishonest and unethical activity' among the researchers in different disciplines over the period, applying bibliometric method, under the assumption that 'plagiarism' activity' has been growing over the period in each discipline. The bibliometric study helps to understand the relationships or patterns within the literature involving authors, different types of documents such as books, monographs, journals in several languages, subjects and all forms of written communications. Rousseau (2014) defined the term as "the measurement of all aspects related to the publication and reading of books and documents."

5. DATA COLLECTION & DESCRIPTION

For the study, it is attempted to retrieve bibliographic data pertaining to the topic 'plagiarism the academic dishonesty' 'from the following 6 multi-disciplinary bibliographic search databases with 3 keywords. The records were retrieved from 6 databases on the above topic, using 3 keywords i.e., 'plagiarism'; 'anti-plagiarism'; and 'academic dishonesty', since the database publishers are organizing the literature published by many publishing companies/societies/organizations on various topics. The details of the records retrieved from 6 databases on the above topic, using 3 keywords are presented in table 1.

Table 1. Number of Bibliographic Records Retrieved from Databases

Coverage	KW1 (Plagiarism)	KW2 (Anti-plagiarism)	KW3 (Academic Dishonesty)	Total of Records
SCOPUS	11004	324	3106	14434
Web of Science	2361	23	540	2924
EBSCO	7337	90	580	8007
J-Gate Plus	4127	93	658	4878
ERIC	1238	20	367	1625
Google Scholar	413000	6360	64300	483660

The SCOPUS database is selected for the study, as the records count is 14434 is moderately higher covering peer-reviewed journals and other types of scholarly resources. Out of the total records retrieved from SCOPUS database with 3 keywords i.e., 'plagiarism'; 'anti-plagiarism'; and 'academic dishonesty', 12789 records were ultimately selected excluding the overlapping retrieval (same records) of bibliographic records 1645.

The SCOPUS is published by the popular publisher Elsevier. This is subscriptions based multidisciplinary bibliographic database of peer-reviewed literature containing the records of scientific journals, books and conference proceedings, etc. with citations from 5000 publishers all over the world. The database covers over 64 million records of 21,500 + peer-reviewed journals, 131,000 plus books, book series, including monographs, edited volumes, major reference works and graduate level text books. It is focussing on science, technology & medicine (STM), social sciences literature and arts & humanities. The database includes more than 39.5 million records from the period 1995 to current, whereas 24+ million records from pre-1996 are also available from the year 1823. It provides citations-based analytics to authors, institutions, publishers and publications such as - citations overview, h-index, journal performance/ comparison etc. well integrating with sophisticated tools like - Source Normalized Impact per Paper (SNIP), SCImago Journal Rank (SJR), CiteScore metrics, etc.

The bibliographic data pertaining to documents (publications) on plagiarism and related topics was comprehensively collected (in the year 2017) from Scopus database for each category in 'counts', irrespective of the type of document or source, discipline, original language of the publication, publication year, whether cited or not. The data operations and computation work was done with MS Excel.From the retrieved records, theimportant data elements such as – authors, titles of the documents as well as sources, year of publication, type of document, citations received were considered for the bibliometric study, assigning the subject element to each record (document) according the title of the source.

The findings related to publications and the citations pattern, applying the different criteria are mentioned in separate sections.

6. PUBLICATION PATTERN - BIBLIOMETRIC FINDINGS

The bibliometric findings applying the following parameters are presented in tables and charts.

- Type of Documents
- Authorship pattern
- Year-wise distribution of Documents
- Documents against 'Sources'
- Discipline-wise distribution of Documents

6.1. Type of Documents

The data on plagiarism comprises of articles, books, book chapters, conference papers, and other types of documents such as letters, notes, editorials, surveys etc. as presented in table 2. It is noticed that journal articles (49%, 6221) are more in retrieved documents, followed by conference papers (18%, 2234), whereas books (5%, 686) are very less. Interestingly other miscellaneous works occupied major portion of the retrieval (22 %, 2854) after journal articles, indicating that the discussions, exchange of opinions, surveys took place on the topic to considerable extent among the academic circles.

Plagiarism : An Academic Dishonesty ...   151

Table 2. Type of Documents

Type of Document	Documents Count	Type of Documents (%)
Articles	6221	49
Books	686	5
Book Chapters	794	6
Conference Papers	2234	18
Other Type of Documents	2854	22
• Conference Review	81	
• Editorial	772	
• Erratum	95	
• Letter	424	
• Note	328	
• Review	1062	
• Short Survey	92	
Grand Total	**12789**	**100**

6.2. Authorship Pattern

To observe the authorship pattern of the retrieved documents, all the document records were categorised marking each one with - single author, 2 authors, 3 authors and 'more authors' for 4 authors and onwards.

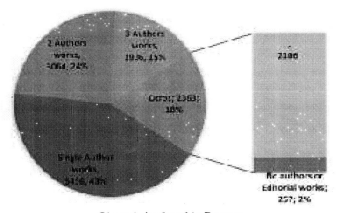

Chart 1. Authorship Pattern

From the chart 1, it is observed that documents with single author (43%, 5456) are almost double than 2 authors works, and 2 times more than 3 author's works and multiple authors works. However, there only 2% of editorial or no author works are found in the retrieval. Though single author works are more prominently seen compared to other author categories, joint authorship (more than one author) pattern is found to be predominant with 57% of documents on plagiarism issues, indicating the collaborative efforts in this direction.

6.3. Year-wise Distribution of Documents

The 12789 retrieved documents are grouped as – initially 'pre-1980' and further per each decade and illustrated vide chart 2. The pre-1980 period is representing older publications, 1981-90 period can be marked for the predominance of print only type of publications. From 1991-2000 decade e-resources are included since the ICT advancements were leading in developed countries. However, further 2 decades 2001-2010 and 2011 to 2017 can be identified for the spread of ICT advancements and electronic publications all over the world including developing countries.

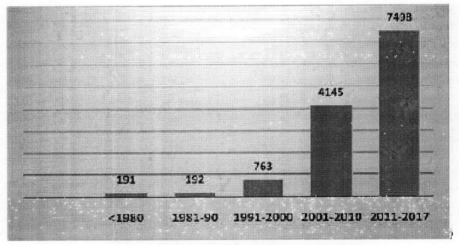

Chart 2. Year-wise distribution of Documents

The data indicates less number of document publications during pre-1980 period and also in 1981-1990 decade, where print publications were major source of information. Therefore it can be interpreted that the awareness about the plagiarism problem is very less in these periods than during 1991-2000. The steep increase in publications on plagiarism noticed in further decades of 2001-2010 can be associated with the gradually increasing awareness about the unethical issue, which could be due to ICT developments, proliferation of electronic resources, and their easy access through internet.

6.4. Publication Pattern (Sources vs. Published Documents)

It is noticed from the retrieved records that 5846 publication sources have generated entire 12789 documents on plagiarism and related issues. The data of published sources was sorted according to descending order of documents and presented in table 3. It shows that the single sources published multiple documents were ranging from 230 to 22 and 2 sources together produced publications ranging from 180 to 60. Interestingly, it is observed that each one of the 4059 documents were produced by single source, while 872 sources published 2 documents each.

Table 3. Publication Pattern (Documents vs. Sources)

Documents by Sources	Sources	Total Documents	Documents by Sources	Sources	Total Documents	Documents by Sources	Sources	Total Documents
230	1	230	39	2	78	16	4	64
200	1	200	36	1	36	15	9	135
135	1	135	32	1	32	14	8	112
109	1	109	31	4	124	13	7	91
106	1	106	30	2	60	12	11	132
95	1	95	28	1	28	11	14	154
90	2	180	26	1	26	10	22	220
85	1	85	25	3	75	9	21	189
60	1	60	24	3	72	8	30	240
58	2	116	23	4	92	7	48	336
51	1	51	22	1	22	6	62	372
49	1	49	21	5	105	5	118	590
48	1	48	20	9	180	4	148	592
45	1	45	19	3	57	3	347	1041
43	1	43	18	3	54	2	872	1744
40	1	40	17	5	85	1	4059	4059
					Total Sources and Total Documents		5846	12789

The above data once again establishes the Bradford Law of Scattering – creating a zone for core category of sources and so on.

6.5. Documents Distribution in Subject Categories

All the retrieved documents on plagiarism and related topics were found published in different sources pertaining to a wide range of subjects. They were grouped and regrouped into 12 prominent subject categories and the data is presented in table 4.

From the data, it is noticed that large portion of documents were published in Computer & Information Science (19.46%, 2489) sources, occupying the 1st position. It is followed by Medical Sciences (17.84%, 2282), Education (16.95%, 2168) subject categories in 2nd and 3 positions, whereas less number of publications are found in engineering (1.87%, 239) and physical sciences (1.72%, 220) in 11th and 12th positions.

The data clearly illustrates that the plagiarism issue is affecting almost all the domains of knowledge and authors from various disciplines are making significant contributions by writing about it. However, the effect is found less in engineering, physical sciences, but higher in social sciences, language related literature. It is interesting to note that library & information science sources are showing considerable contribution in this area.

Table 4. Documents Published in Different Subject Sources

Broad Subject Category	Subjects grouped	Documents	% of Documents in each Category (Position)
Computer & Information Sciences		2489	19.46 (1)
Medical Sciences	Medicine, Nursing, Pharmacy	2282	17.84 (2)
Education		2168	16.95 (3)
Social Sciences	Economics, History, Archeology, Law, Sociology, Psychology	1895	14.82 (4)
Languages, Literature & Linguistics	Languages, Literature, Writing, Linguistics, Communication	1313	10.27 (5)
Management & Business Administration		637	4.98 (6)
Library & Information Sciences	Libraries, Information Science, Resources, Scholarly, Publishing	476	3.72 (7)
General Sciences		475	3.71 (8)
Humanities	Humanities, Philosophy, Religion, Arts	317	2.48 (9)
Biological Sciences	Agriculture, Veterinary, Biology, Plants, Animals, Food Science	278	2.17 (10)
Engineering	Civil, Mechanical, Electronic, ComputerEngineering, Architecture	239	1.87 (11)
Physical Sciences	Physics, Chemistry, Mathematics, Geosciences	220	1.72 (12)
Grand Total		**12789**	

The impact of documents published on plagiarism and related issues through different sources covering varied subject categories, is further studied applying citations criteriai.e. citations received against each of the publications as per types of documents, broad subject categories and over the period.

7. CITATIONS PATTERN - BIBLIOMETRIC FINDINGS

References are commonly called 'citations' (Weinstock, 1971). Wikipedia describes a bibliographic citation as – "a reference to a published or unpublished source i.e. reference to a book, article, web page, or other published item". Citation is an important bibliographic indicator that establishes credibility to the creator/author, article, published source (journal or book or conference proceedings etc.) and denotes to the continuation and spread of research work. The above documents retrieved on plagiarism and related issues are further studied applying the additional parameters 'Cited Documents Count' (along with corresponding percentage of 'Published Documents Count') and 'Citations Count'.

From the data of citations and cited documents it is noticed that out of 12789 documents retrieved, 7936 (62.05%) documents received 112400 citations i.e. approximately in the ratio of 1:15.

These citations were categorized as per their number against the cited documents count in below mentioned distinct ranges, to analyse the citation pattern of published as well as cited documents as per the 'Type', 'Period' and 'Broad Subject Categories'.

- Above 1000 Citations
- 500 to 1000 Citations
- 101 to 500 Citations
- 51 to 100 Citations
- 31 to 50 Citations
- 11 to 30 Citations
- 1-10 Citations

As the citations range decreases from 'above 1000' to '1-10' it is noticed that number of citations has been increasing together with cited documents, e.g. the 1-10 ranged category has 19509 citations from 5842 documents. As a result the average counts of citations (per cited document) is found decreasing from 1347 in >1000 category to 3.34 in 1-10 as illustrated in chart 3.

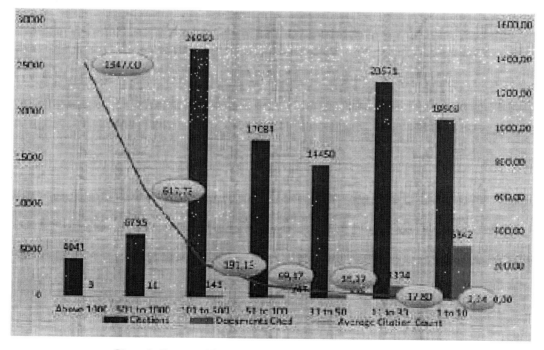

Chart 3. Counts of Published, Cited Documents and Citations

The data is presented in tables 5-10 to study the citation pattern as per the type of document, over the period and broad subject categories.

7.1. Citations as per the Type of Document

The data pertains to the citation pattern as per the type of document is presented in tables 5. Among document types, 70.89%, (4410) of the journal articles received 74995 citations and then 58.15% (1299) of conference papers got 11189 citations. Though 59.18% (406) of books attracted citations, its count is lesser in number. In these matters of plagiarism communications, other peripheral types of documents 53.71% (1533) found received significant attention and response by way of 20959 citations. Book chapters are the least as per the cited documents count (%) and also citations

Table 5. Citations as per the Type of Document (* % of Published Documents)

Document Type	Published Documents Count	Cited Documents Count*(%)	Citations Count
Articles	6221	4410 (70.89)	74995
Books	686	406 (59.18)	4247
Book Chapters	794	288 (36.27)	1010
Conference Papers	2234	1299 (58.15)	11189
Other Types	2854	1533 (53.71)	20959
Grand Total	**12789**	**7936**	**112400**

For each document type, the citations received within the stipulated range were computed against the cited documents and the data is presented in table 6.

Table 6. Citations Count Range vs. Type of Document

Document Type/ Citations Range	Citations Count (Cited Documents Count)						
	> 1000 (above)	501 - 1000	101 - 500	51 - 100	31 - 50	11 - 30	1 - 10
Articles	2396 (2)	5590 (9)	18091 (98)	12595 (180)	9968 (252)	15366 (853)	10989 (3016)
Books	0	0	817 (3)	867 (13)	719 (18)	867 (49)	977 (323)
Book Chapters	0	0	0	62 (1)	0	263 (16)	685 (271)
Conference Papers	0	0	2079 (11)	1302 (19)	1307 (33)	3263 (189)	3238 (1047)
Other Types	1645 (1)	1205 (2)	5963 (29)	2258 (34)	2456 (65)	3812 (217)	3620 (1185)
Total	**4041 (3)**	**6795 (11)**	**26950 (141)**	**17087 (247)**	**14450 (368)**	**23571 (1324)**	**19509 (5842)**

Among types of documents under study, articles received major portion of citations, followed by conference papers and other peripheral documents in all citation categories. It is observed from the data in more than 1000 category that, total 4041 citations received for 2 articles (2396) + other types 1645). The next 501-100 category has 11 articles collectively provided 6795 citations, whereas 1-10 category received 19509 citations from 5842 documents, but its average citations count is as low as 3.34.

7.2. Year-wise Citations

Table 6 contains period-wise citations data against the cited documents and table 7 presents the citations data against the cited documents computed for each specific range for each period.

Similar to the counts of year – wise distribution of documents illustrated vide chart 2, the counts of cited documents have been increasing over the period from 50 (26.18%) documents in early years prior to 1980 to the current decade 4017 (53.57%). In the same way, the citation count has been rising from 1175 to 60674 in the 2001-2010. The lesser counts of cited documents (53.57%) and citations (27504) accrued during the current decade of 2011-2017 can be attributed to the fact that the data was collected during the 7th year of the decade.

Table 7. Citations as per the Period of Publication (* % of Published Documents)

Year	Published Documents Count	Cited Documents Count *(%)	Citations Count
Pre 1980	191	50 (26.18)	1175
1981-1990	192	130 (67.71)	2545
1991-2000	763	571 (74.84)	20412
2001-2010	4145	3168 (76.43)	60764
2011-2017	7498	4017 (53.57)	27504
Total	**12789**	**7936**	**112400**

The data pertaining to citations range as per the period of publication reveal that above 1000 category is traced only during periods 1991-2000 and 2001-10, whereas during pre-1980 period only 1 document elicited 704 citations and the remaining citations from 49 documents are placed in 51 -1 ranges. All the above citation categories, higher counts of cited documents and citations are found during the periods of 2001-10 and 2011-17.

Table 8. Citations Range as per the Period of Publication

Period/Citation Range	Citations Count (Cited Documents Count)						
	Above 1000	501 - 1000	101 - 500	51 - 100	31 - 50	11 - 30	1 - 10
PRE 1980	0	704(1)	0	136(2)	123(3)	107(6)	105(38)
1981 to 1990	0	513(1)	471(2)	321(5)	380(9)	602(31)	258(82)
1991 to 2000	1029(1)	2049(3)	7703(41)	4231(58)	1976(49)	2303(124)	1121(295)
2001 to 2010	3012(2)	3003(5)	14860(74)	9964(146)	9123(234)	13351(735)	7451(1972)
2011 to 2017	0	526(1)	3916(24)	2432(36)	2848(73)	7208(428)	10574(3455)
Grand Total	**4041(3)**	**6795(11)**	**26950(141)**	**17084(247)**	**14450(368)**	**23571(1324)**	**19509(5842)**

7.3. Disciplines-wise Citations

It is found from the data of cited documents and citations presented in table 9 as per the broad subject category that the cited documents counts followed almost the similar order to published documents counts for each subject category except in 'Medical Sciences' (1368) and 'Humanities' (165). According to the cited documents counts 'Computer & Information Science' subject had more documents (1538) cited, which is followed by 'Education' (1382), 'Medical Sciences' (1368) and 'Social Sciences' (1338).

Further, it is noticed that the percentage of documents cited is seen in different order, wherein the 'Management & Business Administration' subject category received maximum percentage of documents (71.11%, 453) citations, followed by Social sciences (70.61%, 1338). The 'Engineering' subject category received citations for the least number of documents (49.79%, 119).

In view of citation counts pertaining to different subject categories, some variation is observed in the order of published documents counts and cited documents counts. For example 'Social Sciences' subject category received the highest number of citations, whereas the subject in 4th position as per the documents published and 4th according to cited. Similarly, another subject category 'Humanities' is in the least position vide citations (856), but 9th according to documents published and 10th as per cited documents.

Table 9. Citations as per the Broad Subject Category (*% of Published Documents)

S. No.	Subject	Published Documents Count	Cited Documents Count (* %)	CitationsCount
1	Computer & Information Sciences	2489	1538(61.79)	18828
2	Medical Sciences	2282	1368(59.95)	15719
3	Education	2168	1382 (63.75)	18606
4	Social Sciences	1895	1338(70.61)	31141
5	Languages, Literature & Linguistics	1313	680(51.79)	7034
6	Management & Business Administration	637	453(71.11)	8682
7	Library & Information Sciences	476	302(63.45)	3091
8	General Sciences	475	301(63.37)	2753
9	Humanities	317	165(52.05)	856
10	Biological Sciences	278	175(62.95)	2609
11	Engineering	239	119(49.79)	1472
12	Physical Sciences	220	115(52.27)	1609
	Grand Total	**12789**	**7936**	**112400**

For each broad subject category, the citations received within the stipulated range were computed and presented in table 10.

From the data of 12 subject categories it is observed that only Medical sciences (1645 per 1 document) and social sciences (2396 per 2 documents) received citations in more than 1000 category. Further, in 501 to 1000 group, 5 subjects received citations including medical sciences (2435 per 4 documents) and social sciences (2010 per 3 documents), Computer & Information sciences (545 per 1 document), education (2435 per 4 documents) and physical sciences (702 per 1 document). It is noticed that all the subject categories received citations in remaining ranges 101 – 500 to 1-10 and cited documents as well as citations more or less followed similar numerical order of published documents. The subjects Computer & Information sciences, medical sciences and education indicated more citations and cited documents in all the categories than others.

Table 10. Citations Count Range vs. Broad Subject Category

Subject/Citation Range	> 1000 (above)	501–1000	101 – 500	51 –100	31 –50	11 –30	1 –10
			Citations Count (Cited Documents Count)				
Computer & Information Sciences	0	545 (1)	5345 (26)	2115 (31)	2969 (75)	4060 (236)	3794 (1168)
Medical Sciences	1645 (1)	2435 (4)	3639 (19)	1924 (29)	1535 (39)	3690 (209)	3464 (1067)
Education	0	1103 (2)	4384 (23)	3143 (45)	2523 (66)	4127 (231)	3326 (1015)
Social Sciences	2396 (2)	2010 (3)	7712 (39)	4786 (67)	3514 (89)	4878 (266)	3232 (872)
Languages, Literature & Linguistics	0	0	525 (4)	1978 (29)	1188 (30)	1778 (100)	1565 (517)
Management & Business Administration	0	0	2857 (15)	1435 (20)	1330 (34)	2003 (108)	1057 (276)
Library & Information Sciences	0	0	457 (3)	343 (5)	598 (15)	868 (51)	825 (228)
General Sciences	0	0	466 (3)	431 (6)	313 (8)	756 (44)	787 (240)
Humanities	0	0	0	142 (2)	0	273 (14)	441 (149)
Biological Sciences	0	0	774 (4)	597 (9)	286 (7)	547 (31)	405 (126)
Engineering	0	0	791 (5)	117 (2)	70 (2)	182 (11)	312 (99)
Physical Sciences	0	702 (1)	0	73 (1)	124 (3)	409 (23)	301 (87)
Grand Total	4041 (3)	6795 (11)	26950 (141)	17084 (247)	14450 (368)	23571 (1324)	19509 (5842)

8. DISCUSSION & SUMMARY

The bibliometric study of the literature published on plagiarism and related topics reveals that abundant research, collaborative efforts have been going on to highlight the problem and improve the situation. It appears true from the enormous literature retrieved from different multidisciplinary databases such as – Scopus (14434 records), Web of Science (2924 records), EBSCO (8007), ERIC (1625), Google Scholar (483660) etc. in all the written forms of communication. The study indicates that the researchers in almost all the disciplines have been experiencing the issue, and the research activity has been rising over the period to handle it in right way.

From the quantum of literature retrieved addressing the plagiarism issue and the following bibliometric study results based on SCOPUS data, it is ascertained that the awareness of the plagiarism problem is very high on the whole, growing over the period and persisting in all the disciplines.

- Out of 12 forms of literature retrieved, conventionally the journal articles (49%) and conference papers (22%) occupied the major portion than the books (5%) and book chapters (6%). In this specific subject area even other types of documents (22%) such as conference reviews, editorials, letters, notes, surveys together found important place in written communications. Significantly 70.89% of journal articles, 58.15% (4247) of conference papers received citations about 74995 and 11189. Though the book publications count is very less, 59.18% books were referred. Other miscellaneous form of literature 53.71% (1533) also attracted citations about 20959. On the whole (out of 12789 documents retrieved) more than 7936 (62.05%) documents received 112400 citations, i.e. approximately in the ratio of 1:15. The 2 journal articles + 1 other type of document together produced 4041 citations in above 1000 category, whereas 11 articles collectively provided 6795 citations in 501-100 category.

- Though single authorship (43%) is numerically high in the literature published on plagiarism issues, the joint author (2, 3 and more authors, editors) works are found higher about 57%. The authorship pattern, depicts the stronger collaborative motives in handling the plagiarism related issues.

- It is an established fact that ICT advancements during the recent two decades resulted in the radical production of publications including electronic, which is also witnessed true by the steep increase of counts of published documents from 763 to 4145 during 2001 - 2010 and 7498 for further period of 7 years. Moreover, above 91% of retrieved documents are published during recent decades. The percentage of cited documents have been increasing from 26.18% (pre-1980 period) to 76.43% (2001-2010) and citations from 1175 to 60764 along with publications. These findings related to the steep increase of publications as well as citations on plagiarism issues portray the increasing awareness of this unethical problem that has been underlying in scholarly academic publishing since pre-1980 period. The higher range of citations i.e. above 1000 category is found during periods 1991-2000 and 2001-10, while all other citation categories, higher counts of cited documents and citations are found during the periods of 2001-10 and 2011-17.

- The effect of plagiarism the dishonest activity and the awareness of the problem has beenpersistent in all most all the academic disciplines, which has reflected in the sources of literature published inwide range of subjects, on the topic. From the literature published under the broad subject categories, Computer & Information Sciences has larger share (19.46%, 2489) of publication occupying the 1st position, followed by Medical Sciences (17.84%, 2282), Education (16.95%, 2168) subjects in 2nd and 3 positions. Though cited documents as per counts follow more or less similar order, it is varied in the computations of percentages of cited documents as well as citation counts. The subject category occupied 6th position according to (637) publications as well as citations counts (8682), and first (71.11%) by the percentage of documents cited. The literature related to medical and social science subject categories received citations in higher ranges i.e. above 1000 and 501 to 1000, whereas 3 more subjects joined in 501-100 category and from 101– 500 onwards all subject documents began getting citations.

In the present age of ICT advancements, spread of electronic / digital documents over the easily accessible networks and openly available scholarly literature, it is much essential for students, research scholars, project personnel to be thoroughly aware of the academic values, copyright provisions to creators/authors, publishers, stipulated practices for the fair-use of e-resources, ethical, as well as legal implications of plagiarising the scholarly content, to prevent the possible penalties in their career and also unforeseen damage to their personal as well as professional profile. This is a fact, especially in academic and research institutions, where originality is the prime concern and considered as virtue while plagiarism wherever suspected deemed to be condemnable and the students/faculty concerned need to face dire consequences. (Lathrop, 2000). There can be several factors including cultural, psychological, and emotional, literacy motivating the students towards these dishonest activities in academics/research, but many studies are specifying that most of the plagiarized activities are unintentional and occurring due to lack of awareness of students, research scholars. (DeLang, 2012, Satija, 2011). They were primarily suggesting to impart orientation, training courses regarding the fair use of scholarly resources specifically the internet resources, explaining the importance of originality in academic or research writings.

9. SUGGESTIONS

In view of the above discussion based on the study results and research problem, the following suggestions are put forth for the consideration of plagiarism free academic/research environment in developing nations like India.

These awareness building programs should be instituted from the early stages of academics to each student by employing mechanical tools for screening of assignments and the plagiarism screening of documents should be made part of evaluation in the curriculum as being done in developed nations by awarding credits. Creating such an academic environment may be a herculean task in the current scenario of relying on electronic information for each and every work, especially the trend being more in academics.However, the task may not be impossible, when parents, teachers, students, institutional authorities and government education departments, social organization such as COPE (Committee on Publication Ethics, UK), SSV (Society for Scientific Values, India) coordinate with each other while executing the following tasks for the betterment of students, institutions, society and nation in –

- Framing plagiarism policies
- Inducting ethical values motivating for original research work and writings,explaining its importance in the development ofnations
- Planning for information literacy programmes, imparting orientation/training courses concerning the fair-use of scholarly resources emphasising more on e-resources, search techniques, research methodologies, citation styles, technical writing methods in English language, and etc.
- Standardizing the evaluation procedures integrating with plagiarism screening task of student's submissions.

Sometimes the journal publishers are too modest to withdraw their peer-reviewed published articles, though found plagiarized, in the fear of losing their reputation, causing damage to image of the journal or even the profile of a researcher or a renowned top graded scientist.Such sensitive cases need to be handled with utmost care, as many research projects often run in collaboration, though working under the supervision of a senior scientist or a faculty member. The scientists or faculty members who are guiding the research projects and researchers should also ensure that their assistants or students screen their documents through plagiarism verification tools before submitting for peer review process and their research work should be shared over the intranet to avoid duplication of research work.

Due to the plagiarized activities or unethical practices of stealing original research content, the intellectual property rights of the researchers are under threat and their entire efforts, creativity remain unacknowledged and the same will be credited to those undeserved.Thus, the plagiarism practises should be condemned, whether they are unintentional or intentional. In case of unintentionally plagiarised cases, the ways and means can be explored to educate them with information literacy programs. The institutions also should be able to support the student's learning process by providing opportunities to practice skills with trained staff available to provide timely and constructive feedback (Anyanwu 2004; Leask 2006).

Though it is harsh to mention, the cases of intentionally plagiarised incidents should not be tolerated, moreover they should be well publicized within the institution, among the research circles, apart from tagging the retracted articles on the journal websites. The COPE (Committee on Publication ethics) who have major publishers in their editorial board should display the names of the plagiarized work so that there is much awareness and fear of being listed in the "shame list".

The higher educational institutions like universities and research organizations, should put more focus on the prevention than punishing the individuals to achieve better performance and results in academics and research. In this connection, it is worth mentioning the words of Pecorari (2003) 'the focus of preventing plagiarism should be shifted from post facto punishment to proactive teaching.'

REFERENCES

Anyanwu, R. (2004). Lessons on Plagiarism: Issues for Teachers and Learners. *International Education Journal*, 4(4), 178-187. (Source: DeLong, 2012)

Chandran, V. and Natarajan, R. (2015). Literature Output of Plagiarism: a Scientometric Approach through Web of Science. In M. Patra and S. K. Jena (Eds.), *Combating Plagiarism: A New Role for Librarian* (pp 78-88). New Delhi: S.K. Book Agency.

COPE – Committee on Publication Ethics.https://publicationethics.org/

DeLong, D. (2012). Propensity toward Unintentional Plagiarism. *Global Education Journal*, (4), 136-154.

Foo, J.Y. and Tan X.J. (2014). Analysis and Implications of Retraction Period and Co-Authorship of Fraudulent Publications. *Accountability in Research Policies and Quality Assurance*, 21(3), 198-210. DOI: 10.1080/08989621.2013.848799.

García-Romero, A. & Estrada-Lorenzo, J. M. (2014). A Bibliometric Analysis of Plagiarism and Self-Plagiarism through Déjà vu. *Scientometrics*, 101(1), 381-396.

Huh, S., Kim, S. Y. & Cho, H-M. (2016). Characteristics of Retractions from Korean Medical Journals in the KoreaMed Database: A Bibliometric Analysis. *Plos One*, 1-7.DOI:10.1371/journal.pone.0163588

Lathrop, A. and Foss, K. (2000). *Student Cheating and Plagiarism in the Internet Era: A Wake-Up Call*. Englewood, CO: Libraries Unlimited.

Leask, B. (2006). Plagiarism, Cultural Diversity and Metaphor—Implications for Academic Staff Development. *Assessment and Evaluation in Higher Education*, 31(2), 183-199.

Leonard, M. et.al. (2015). Perceptions of Plagiarism by STEM Graduate Students: A Case Study. *Science and Engineering Ethics*, (21), 1587-1608.

Lukashenko, R., Anohina, A. & Grundspenkis, J. (2007). "A Conception of a Plagiarism Detection Tool for processing Template-Based Documents". *Annual Proceedings of Vidzeme University College "ICTE in Regional Development"*, 2007.

Ocholla, D. N. & Ocholla, L. (2016). Does Open Access Prevent Plagiarism in Higher Education? African Journal of Library, *Archives & Information science*, (26), 187-200.

Rousseau, R (2014), Library Science: Forgotten Founder of Bibliometrics. *Nature*, (510- 218).

Satija, M.P. (2011). Plagiarism: A Tempting Snake. *Library Progress*, 31(1), 99-106.

Singh H. P. et al. (2014). A Comprehensive Analysis of Articles Retracted Between 2004 and 2013 From Biomedical Literature - A Call For Reforms. *Journal of Traditional and Complementary Medicine*, 4(3) 136 139. Accessed from https://www.ncbi.nlm.nih.gov/pmc/articles/PMC4142449/

Singh, J.N. (2014). Literature Review on Copyright Infringement and Protection. *Library Herald*, (52/ 2) (158-181).DOI: 10.5958/0976-2469.2014.00505.3

Stretton, S. et al (2012). Publication Misconduct and Plagiarism Retractions: A Systematic, Retrospective Study. *Current Medical Research and Opinion*, 28(10) 1575-83. DOI: 10.1185/03007995.2012.728131.

Suseela,V. J. &Uma, V. (2017) Plagiarism and Academic Dishonesty: Study of Users' Perceptions in the University of Hyderabad. *SRELS Journal of Information Management*, 54(6) 293-301

Weinstock, N. (1971). Citation Indexes. In *Encyclopedia of Library and Information Science* (pp. 16–41). New York: Marcel Dekker.

Wooley, K.L. et al. (2011). Lack of Involvement of Medical Writers and the Pharmaceutical Industry in Publications Retracted for Misconduct: A Systematic, Controlled, Retrospective Study. *Current Medical Research and Opinion*, 27(6) 1175-82.DOI: 10.1185/03007995.2011.573546.

Writing Program Administrators (2003). *Defining and Avoiding Plagiarism: the WPA Statement on Best Practices*. www.wpacouncil.org/positions/WPAplagigiarism.pdf

12
Reflections about Research Ethics in Contemporary Society

Marta Ligia Pomim Valentim

> "Science without conscience is the soul's perdition"
> *François Rabelais (1494–1553)*[10]

1. INTRODUCTION

Discussing ethics in research today involves multiple perspectives related to the attitudes of the researcher interrelated to the construction of scientific knowledge. The first perspective refers to the understanding of what Classical Science and Post-Modern Science are, as the distinction is significant in knowledge construction, in case the researcher opts for one paradigm or another.

In Classical Science, subject and object must not interact, it is even recommended that the researcher does not *interfere* with the researched reality. Another aspect in Classical Science refers to the use of specific methods and techniques recognized by the scientific community of the field or discipline for data collection and analysis. These aspects are questioned in the context of Post-Modern Science, as under this paradigm, it is understood that the researchers, by defining the object or phenomena to be researched, have already interacted with them in some way since researchers are the ones who have chosen them. In the same line, by defining the method(s) and technique(s), researchers subliminally express their ideological position and the conduction of the investigative process. Moreover, in selecting the authors with whom they will dialogue, aiming at the elaboration of the theoretical framework that, in turn, supports

---

10. Powell, J. (2009). Biography Rabelais. Instituto Ordem Livre, April 10. François Rabelais (Chinon, 1494-Paris, 1553). Writer, priest and French doctor of the Renaissance. Author of the works Pantagruel (1532) and Gargantua (1534). Retrieved on June 2, 2018, from <http://ordemlivre.org/posts/biografia-rabelais>.

their reflection and debate, their epistemological position is indicated in front of the object and investigated phenomena.

From the considerations above, it is worth highlighting that currently, we are still building scientific knowledge based on the paradigm of Classical Science, with exceptions. Thus contemporary researchers and the scientific community of a given field or discipline need to expand the possibilities of knowing. Change is necessary, but it is difficult to implement.

Knowledge construction in the context of Post-Modern Science demands attitude determined behavior from the researchers: first to perceive the multiple possibilities of knowing, secondly to realize the fallibility of knowing, there is no absolute truth; third, to perceive the complexity of the investigated object or phenomena; fourthly, to prepare to interact with other fields or disciplines – through multidisciplinary, interdisciplinary or transdisciplinary investigations – to complement what was not sufficiently understood and explained. In this perspective, perception is amplified, reflection is denser, debate is dialogic, propitiating more representative knowledge construction, closer to the real.

For Elgin (2011) in Modern Science, researchers do not start their investigations 'from scratch', instead, they are based on previously established findings, they use methods that others have designed and tested, and they analyze data using validated techniques. It is also worth noting that investigations are carried out by teams, rather than individually, as investigations are based on epistemic interdependence, that is, building knowledge is a collaborative/cooperative effort.

In order to reflect on some elements related to research ethics, this chapter will focus on the following aspects: social system; educational system; and political system.

2. ETHICS IN RESEARCH AND SOCIETY

Etymologically, the term 'ethics originates from the Greek 'ethos', which means 'character', 'custom' or 'way of being', i.e., it concerns a historical and social reality, built from the collective relations of beings in the societies in which they are born and live (Dictionary, 2008). In the context of scientific knowledge construction, ethics constitutes a determinant element for researchers to guide their conduct in the investigative process and, thus, must permeate all aspects involving the investigated object and phenomena. The term 'research' whose etymological origin comes from the Latin '*perquirere*', which means 'to search diligently', 'to inquire' or 'seek, search, problem' (Origin, [n.d.]). Thus, research ethics is directly related to the investigator's conduct during the process as a whole.

The first aspect related to this conduct concerns the researcher's responsibility in relation to the process of scientific knowledge construction. Padilha, Ramos, Borenstein & Martins (2005) explain that the investigator's responsibility can be understood from two axes, the first one related to intellectual honesty, the defense of the truth – even though it is clear that this is fallible –, the criticism to fallibility; and the second one refers to the social use of constructed knowledge, becoming responsible for the creation, use and reuse of their knowledge, including the social consequences from this knowledge.

In the contemporary society, from the advance of the scientific activity, initiating the discussions and regulating the ethical conduct in research became necessary and, for that, declarations and codes were elaborated to inform and support actions and the practice in this context. Kottow (2008) highlights the Nuremberg Code[11] as an ethical but legalistic document; on the other hand, the author considers the Declaration of Helsinki[12] a broader document. In addition, the author mentions the Belmont Report[13] which, according to Kottow (2008, pp.12), "intentionally introduces the language of ethical principles by requiring that all research be respectful to people, beneficial to society and fair in its balance between risks and benefits".

By understanding the non-neutrality of science, the researcher notes the "easiness to obtain funding to investigate some subjects and the difficulty of obtaining it to investigate others. His/her performance is deeply marked by this viewpoint and by the scientific community to which he/she belongs. Therefore, the produced knowledge is never neutral" (Guerriero, 2013, pp.475). This is a crucial issue which often prompts researchers to choose recurrent themes or themes considered important by the scientific community, which are linked to the development of their scientific research, forming a vicious cycle of the researched topics within a field or discipline.

Another aspect that must be considered refers to the subordination of the researcher to a particular economic group, serving capitalist interests and not to scientific interests. Spink (2012, pp.40) understands that there is a "growing subordination of certain scientific areas to powerful private economic groups", significantly influencing the direction of research activities, as well as their achieved results.

Researchers must understand their social responsibility regarding the performed investigations, how they affect and will affect society, i.e., how their results will be used and reused in the medium and long term.

3. ETHICS IN RESEARCH AND EDUCATION

Research ethics in the academic-scientific context has taken on staggering proportions: undergraduate and graduate students plagiarize papers, the elaboration of final papers, monographs, dissertations and theses. These are delicate issues, as on the one hand it is necessary

---

11. Nuremberg Code refers to a set of ethical principles governing human research, considered as one of the consequences of the Nuremberg War Processes, which occurred at the end of World War II. Retrieved on June 2, 2018, from <https://en.wikipedia.org/wiki/Needberg_Category>.

12. The Helsinki Declaration refers to a set of ethical principles governing human research, written by the World Medical Association (WMA) in 1964. It has been revised seven times, the last one in 2013, during the WMA General Assembly in Fortaleza (Brazil). The Declaration is an important document in the history of ethics in research and appears as the first significant effort of the medical community to regulate research itself. Retrieved on June 2, 2018, from <https://en.wikipedia.org/wiki/Declara_de_Helsinque>.

13. Belmont Report. Report of the National Commission for the Protection of Human Subjects of Biomedical and Behavioral Research. Michigan: University of Michigan, 2005. 11p. Retrieved on June 2, 2018, from <https://www.fhi360.org/sites/default/files/webpages/po/RETC-CR/nr/rdonlyres/eoadxuvvlkl3j6tmluuaa6ymdhqes33v6bhwjg6pxscq4nqiblht5xmsdtrqvkkh5xojh3ba3rhnan/BelmontEng.pdf>.

to verify and sometimes punish, and on the other hand, these students are often completely unaware of the country's institutional norms and regulations on research ethics.

The contemporary ethical issues may involve broader understandings. Severino (2014 pp.203) considers that the problem must be evaluated from three perspectives: "its macro-social interface, when initiatives involving societies and states are on the agenda [...] internal situations to more restricted groups, when people's behaviors, individually or collectively, hurt rights and dignity of other people or groups [...] when, through personal actions, one may be violating the rights of third parties, defrauding, certain ethical principles in the microcosm of his practice". In this sense, the educators/researchers must be concerned with training students in the ethical aspects that involve their conduct in the academic-scientific milieu, promoting the essential ethical values, as well as becoming a model to be followed by their advisees and scientific aggregates.

In the academic-scientific world, ethical conduct is essential to the researcher, as a high-pressure situation [publish or perish] is experienced, demanding from journal editors and from the scientific community actions aimed at verifying the consistency and veracity of the research data presented in scientific texts. Neill (2008) explains that in the academic-scientific context, those with high scientific production in qualified publications are rewarded. Under pressure to generate bulky, quality production, researchers use unethical practices such as duplicate publication, self-plagiarism, and even plagiarism.

In addition, there are disputes among the researchers of a particular scientific community, both in the search for resources, and in relation to obtaining prominent academic positions; universities and research institutes also compete, currently too preoccupied with their national and international rankings, as Spink (2012) explains.

In this perspective, universities, governmental funding agencies and scientific journals have been developing codes, declarations and documents on good practices in research, focusing on essential ethical aspects for conducting academic-scientific research.

The Coordination of Improvement of Higher Education Personnel (CAPES) emphasizes that higher education and research institutions should adopt information policies aimed at raising the awareness of professors and students of the country's graduate programs on intellectual property rights, "adopting specific procedures aimed at curbing the practice of plagiarism in theses, monographs, articles and other papers by students and other members of their communities" (CAPES, 2011, pp.1).

In the same line, the National Council for Scientific and Technological Development (CNPq) published the 'Report of the Commission of Research Integrity' prepared by a Commission established for this purpose, which emphasizes:

> The need for good conduct in scientific and technological research has been a growing concern of the international community and in Brazil, it is not different. Misconduct is not a recent phenomenon, given the various examples that history has given us of fraud and falsification of results. Publications presuppose

truthfulness and trustworthiness of what the authors report in their articles, since there is no a priori verification of this veracity. Science has correction mechanisms, because everything that is published is subject to verification by others, regardless of the authority of the publisher (CNPq, 2011, pp.1).

The aforementioned document considers as ethical misconduct in research:

(a) Fabrication or invention of data - consists in the presentation of data or untrue results.

(b) Falsification: consists of the fraudulent manipulation of obtained results to change their meaning, their interpretation or even their reliability. This definition also comprises the presentation of real results as if they had been obtained under conditions different from those actually used.

(c) Plagiarism: consists of the presentation, as if of own authorship, of results or conclusions previously obtained by another author, as well as of integral texts or of a substantial part of other texts without the care detailed in the Guidelines. It is also plagiarism who uses ideas or data obtained in analyzes of projects or unpublished manuscripts to which one had access as a consultant, reviewer, editor or the like.

(d) Self-plagiarism: consists of the total or partial presentation of texts already published by the same author, without due references to previous works (CNPq, 2011, pp.4-5).

São Paulo Research Foundation (FAPESP) provides the 'Code of good scientific practices' on its website, and designates as ethical misconduct in research:

(a) The fabrication or assertion that data, procedures or results were obtained or conducted, when actually they were not;

(b) The falsification or presentation of data, procedures or research results in a significantly modified, imprecise or incomplete way, to the point of interfering in the evaluation of the scientific weight that they actually confer to the conclusions drawn from them;

(c) The plagiarism or the use of verbal, oral or written ideas or formulations of others without expressly and clearly giving them the due credit, so as to reasonably generate the perception that they are ideas or formulations of self-authorship (FAPESP, 2014, pp.31).

Ethics in the context of scientific production needs to be based on human values, namely:

Honesty: the researcher must be honest regarding data, results and other actions involved in the research;

Trust: must be established among research team members, between the researcher and research participants regarding information confidentiality and the relationship between the scientific community and society;

Justice: must ensure that the recognition of a difference does not result in discriminatory behavior of the researchers in relation to the research participants;

Respect: based on the justice value, should be evidenced by the adoption of a proper attitude of the researcher toward all those involved in the research;

Responsibility : of all research members, involving their actions and mainly the lead researcher who accounts for this value throughout the research (Torres & Alves, 2017, pp.30)

Therefore, research ethics in the academic-scientific context should be discussed and reflected by the whole community, to foster ethical values that lead both professors and students during the investigative process, as well as in what concerns the dissemination of the results obtained in this scope.

4. ETHICS IN RESEARCH AND POLICY

In Brazil, several initiatives aim to regulate the ethical conduct in research of professors/ researchers and students, either in relation to verifications and legal punishments, or in relation to verifications and institutional punishments [governmental funding agencies, universities and research institutes].

The Brazilian Bar Association published in 'Justice Diary' (2010) the 'Proposition 2010.19.07379-01', regarding the adoption of measures to prevent plagiarism and illegal trade of monographs, to curb unethical practices in research in the context of the Brazilian educational system and recommending the country's higher education institutions to use software to search for similarities, and to adopt intellectual property awareness policies in their communities.

Brazilian national policies related to ethical conduct in research emerged from the needs of researchers from the area of Health. As a result, the regulatory framework was established through Resolution 466/2012 (Brazil, 2012), which addresses ethics in research in the context of the Human and Social Sciences (HSS), however, without considering the significant differences between the areas of Health and HSS. In this context, different scientific entities from HSS showed the "unifying character of the resolution in force" (Duarte, 2014). The dissatisfaction with the content of the aforementioned resolution led to the Forum, which established seven basic principles for the elaboration of a new resolution:

> which includes all the investigations in HSS, understood as those based on the epistemologies and methodologies of these sciences, regardless of its thematic area or of the involved empirical issues;

1. which is limited to the implications and consequences of the research practice for the researched subjects (or participants), without intrusion on the epistemological and methodological questions of the projects, subject to the evaluation by the conventional academic spheres;
2. which recognizes the procedural and dialogical nature of the research relationship in the HSS, without undue formal requirements for a priori confirmation of good procedures;
3. which recognizes the different levels of "risk", with different implications for the authorization processes of the submitted projects;
4. which runs briefly and quickly for "risk-free" or "minimal risk" research, with increasing scaling of attention only at the more complex or questionable levels, to prevent the system from becoming a bureaucratic deterrent for conducting research in HSS;

5. which recognizes that HSS representatives must participate in the evaluation of HSS research at its various levels; which is more educational than supervising and controlling (Duarte, 2014, pp.13).

The National Commission for Research Ethics (CONEP), based on Resolution 466/2012, approved, in 2014, a Resolution Minutes on "Ethical specificities of research in the Humanities and Social Sciences and others that use specific methodologies to these areas" (Brazil, 2016), highlighting some specificities of the investigations conducted in the scientific context of these Sciences, as follows:

> Considering that the Human and Social Sciences have specificities in their conceptions and research practices, in as much as they prevail in a pluralistic sense of science from which the adoption of multiple theoretical-methodological perspectives takes place, as well as dealing with attributions of meaning, practices and representations, without direct intervention in the human body, with specific nature and degree of risk;
>
> Considering that scientific production should imply current or potential benefits for the human being, the community in which they are inserted and for society, enabling the promotion of a dignified quality of life based on respect for civil, social and cultural rights and ecologically balanced environment;

It is noteworthy that the public policies focused on research ethics, as mentioned above, do not contemplate specific aspects of the research conducted in the field of HSS. Guerriero & Bosi (2015, pp.2622) argue that in the context of HSS "transdisciplinarity breaks the walls across disciplines and articulates different knowledge and concepts for the compression of complex objects. There is no hierarchical relationship among disciplines, which articulate and construct the object of study during the process of research".

5. FINAL CONSIDERATIONS

Reflecting on research ethics in contemporary society is not an easy task, as a result of the dual and sometimes paradoxical situations experienced by professors/researchers and graduate students. Morin (2003) explains that the ethical problem refers to a conflict of values, since it arises when there is a plurality of contradictory imperatives. However, the researcher, aware of the complexity of the objects and phenomena present in a given reality, and conscious of his/her own limits related to knowing, will be able to conduct himself/herself ethically in the investigative process and in the construction of scientific knowledge.

Morin (2003, pp.289) explains that "the question of science and action can be modified by a vision that gives meaning to the notions of actor, autonomy, freedom, subject, which were pulverized by the simplifying conception of 'classical' science". In this perspective, the researcher is the protagonist of the investigative process and, as such, must position himself/herself clearly on his/her epistemological and methodological choices.

Ethics must underpin every stage of scientific research, for "knowledge is not a pure thing, independent of its instruments and not only of its material tools, but also of its mental tools, which are concepts; scientific theory is an organizing activity of the mind, which implements observations, and which also implements dialogue with the world of phenomena" (Morin, 2003, pp.45).

Research ethics in contemporary society requires a change of understanding from the researcher, that is, his/her responsibility towards knowledge construction, that is, "it is more than professional awareness inherent in any professionalization; than ethics of knowledge that animates every researcher who does not consider himself a simple employee" (Morin, 2003, pp.211).

In this perspective, Morin (2003) highlights some essential aspects for the researcher to conduct himself/herself within research ethics: a) responsibility, which implies the reform of the structures of knowledge itself; b) resist the powers that know no limits and, to a large extent, gag and control knowledge, except the scientific knowledge used by them.

The results obtained from the research developed in all fields of knowledge are essential for the advancement of society. However, there is growing distrust over who controls them and what motivates them to do so. Thus, the relationship between science and society is at least difficult (European, 2010).

In this context, it is worth highlighting the responsibility of the education and research institution in the ethical investigative process, since the institution will also be responsible for the results obtained and disseminated to the scientific community and, ultimately, society itself, once the researcher is bound to an institution, whose reputation will be interwoven with that of the researcher himself. Therefore, it is the institution's responsibility to establish policies and documents that raise awareness of the ethical conduct in research to its affiliates, as well as to provide norms to regulate and punish misconduct in research.

Last but not least, education and research institutions should be structured to meet the so-called open science, through institutional repositories that store and disseminate research data after publication of the results, revealing the data collected in the investigative process to the scientific community and society.

From these considerations, it is believed that research ethics may, in fact, be a reality in contemporary society, to meet scientific and technological advances for the benefit of society.

REFERENCES

Brasil. Ministério da Saúde. Conselho Nacional de Saúde (2012). *Resolução nº 466, de 12 de dezembro de 2012*. Brasília. 11p. Retrieved on June 2, 2018, from <http://bvsms.saude.gov.br/bvs/saudelegis/cns/2013/res0466_12_12_2012.html>.

Brasil. Conselho Nacional de Saúde. Comissão Nacional de Ética em Pesquisa (2016). *Minuta de Resolução sobre "Especificidades éticas das pesquisas nas Ciências Humanas e Sociais e de outras que se utilizam de metodologias próprias dessas áreas"*.Brasília. 11p. Retrieved on June 2, 2018, from <https://www.abrasco.org.br/site/wp-content/uploads/2016/04/Minuta-de-Resoluc%CC%A7a%CC%83o-CHS-06-abril-2016_-CNS_59%C2%AA-RO.pdf>.

CAPES - Coordenação de Aperfeiçoamento de Pessoal de Nível Superior (2011). *Orientações de combate ao plágio.* Brasília. 2p. Retrieved on June 2, 2018, from <http://www.capes.gov.br/images/stories/download/diversos/OrientacoesCapes_CombateAoPlagio.pdf>.

CNPq - Conselho Nacional de Desenvolvimento Científico e Tecnológico (2011). *Relatório da Comissão de Integridade de Pesquisa. Brasília.* 7p. Retrieved on June 2, 2018, from <http://www.cnpq.br/documents/10157/a8927840-2b8f-43b9-8962-5a2ccfa74dda>.

Dicionário Etimológico: etimologia e origem das palavras (2008). Matosinhos (Portugal): 7Graus. Retrieved on June 2, 2018, from <https://www.dicionarioetimologico.com.br>.

Duarte, L. F. D. (2014). Práticas de poder, política científica e as ciências humanas e sociais: o caso da regulação da ética em pesquisa no Brasil. *História Oral,* 17(2), 9-29, jul./dez. Retrieved on June 2, 2018, from <http://revista.historiaoral.org.br/index.php?journal=rho&page=article&op=view&path%5B%5D=401&path%5B%5D=pdf>.

Elgin, C. (2011). Science, ethics and education. *Theory and Research in Education,* 9(3), 251-263. Retrieved on June 2, 2018, from <http://elgin.harvard.edu/phied/sciedintegrityfinal.pdf>.

European Comission (2010). *European textbook on ethics in research.* Brussels. 203p. (KI-N1-24452-EN-C). Retrieved on June 2, 2018, from <https://ec.europa.eu/research/science-society/document_library/pdf_06/textbook-on-ethics-report_en.pdf>.

FAPESP - Fundação de Amparo à Pesquisa do Estado de São Paulo (2014). *Código de boas práticas científicas.* São Paulo. 46p. Retrieved on June 2, 2018, from <http://www.fapesp.br/boaspraticas/FAPESP-Codigo_de_Boas_Praticas_Cientificas_2014.pdf >.

Guerriero, I. C. Z. (2013). Aspectos éticos das pesquisas em Ciências Sociais e Humanas: o desafio de elaborar uma resolução específica. *Revista Brasileira de Educação Médica,* 37(4), 475-476. Retrieved on June 2, 2018, from <http://www.scielo.br/pdf/rbem/v37n4/a01v37n4.pdf>.

Guerriero, I. C. Z., & Bosi, M. L. M. (2015). Ética em pesquisa na dinâmica do campo científico: desafios na construção de diretrizes para ciências humanas e sociais. *Ciência & Saúde Coletiva,* 20(9), 2615-2624. Retrieved on June 2, 2018, from <https://www.scielosp.org/pdf/csc/2015.v20n9/2615-2624>.

Kottow, M. (2008). História da ética em pesquisa com seres humanos. RECIIS: Revista Eletrônica de Comunicação, *Informação e Inovação em Saúde,* 2(Sup.1), 7-18, dez. Retrieved on June 2, 2018, from <https://www.arca.fiocruz.br/bitstream/icict/17570/2/2.pdf>.

Morin, E. (2003). *Ciência com consciência.* 7.ed. Rio de Janeiro: Bertrand Brasil. 350p.

Neill, U. S. (2008). Publish or perish, but at what cost? *The Journal of Clinical Investigation,* 118(7), Jul. Retrieved on June 2, 2018, from <https://www.ncbi.nlm.nih.gov/pmc/articles/PMC2439458/pdf/JCI0836371.pdf>.

OEA - Ordem dos Advogados do Brasil (2010). Proposição 2010.19.07379-01 - Proposta de adoção de medidas para prevenção do plágio nas instituições de ensino e do comércio ilegal de monografias. *Diário da Justiça,* (222), 22 nov. Retrieved on June 2, 2018, from <http://w3.ufsm.br/ppgcsociais/images/Secretariaonline/CombatePlagioDocumentoOAB.pdf>.

Origem da Palavra (n.d.). [s.n.t.]. Retrieved on June 2, 2018, from <http://origemdapalavra.com.br>.

Padilha, M. I. C. de, Ramos, F. R. S., Borenstein, M. S., & Martins, C. R. (2005). A responsabilidade do pesquisador ou sobre o que dizemos acerca da ética em pesquisa. *Texto & Contexto Enfermagem,* 14(1), 96-105.

Severino, A. J. (2014). Dimensão ética da investigação científica. *Práxis Educativa,* 9(1), 199-208, jan./jun. Retrieved on June 2, 2018, from <http://www.revistas2.uepg.br/index.php/praxiseducativa/article/view/5927/3809>.

Spink, P. K. (2012). Ética na pesquisa científica. *GV Executivo,* 11(1), 38-41.

Torres, V. G. A., & Alves, L. R. G. (2017). A responsabilidade ética na pesquisa nas Ciências Humanas e Sociais: uma reflexão sob a perspectiva da integridade na comunidade científica. *Revista EDaPEC,* 17(2), 30-45.

13
Role of Information Literacy in Curbing Plagiarism

Helen de Castro S. Casarin

1. INTRODUCTION

The purpose of the Information Literacy is to prepare individuals to know the informational universe and to deal with information more effectively, both at work and in everyday situations. This includes ethical use of information and prevention of plagiarism. However, throughout history, Information Literacy has not always included this issue.

Information Literacy was first proposed by the American librarian, and then the president of the Information Industry Association (IIA), Paul Zurkowski (1974). He described the changes that were occurring in the market of companies related to the production of information, the relationship of these companies with the libraries and, consequently, the impact on people's daily lives, particularly in the work situation. For Zurkowski (1974, 6):

> People trained in the application of information resources to their work can be called information literates. They have learned techniques and skills for utilizing the wide range of information tools as well as primary sources in molding information solutions to their problems.

The author pointed to the need for massive US government investments "[..] to train all citizens in the use or the information tools now available as well as those in the development and testing states"(p. 27). It is noticed that the emphasis of the proposal is on the available information resources that would be further developed, demonstrating that the author had a clear vision of the changes that would occur in his field. Zurkowski's proposal presupposes knowledge about the various types of sources of information, forms of access and retrieval of information. The ethical use of information was not yet contemplated, at least explicitly.

In the late 1970s, Information Literacy began to be regarded as a necessity outside the context of work and associated with librarians (Behenrs, 1994,310).

Information Literacy gained momentum from a report published by ALA Presidential Committee which defined that "[...] to be information literate, a person must be able to recognize when information is needed and have the ability to locate and use information effectively." (Behenrs, 1994, 330). However, it has maintained the character of capacity building for the use of information sources and not on the appropriation and use of the selected and recovered information. Since then, other entities and associations, such as the Association of College and Research Libraries (ACRL), Council of Australian University Libraries, and Society of College, National and University Libraries (SCONUL) have formulated new definitions and guiding documents for information literacy. According to Virkus (2003), definitions of IL in this period are very broad and combine several skills and competencies related to information handling and use, including:identifying, locating, gathering, selecting, storing, recording, retrieving and processing information from a variety of sources and media; developing successful information seeking and retrieval strategies; mastering complex and multiple information systems; organizing, analyzing, interpreting, evaluating, synthesizing, and using information; and, presenting and communicating information clearly, logically, concisely and accurately".

It is noted that the ethical use of information remains absent, although it may be implied in communicating information concisely and accurately.

In the late 1980s, librarians, influenced by the ACRL documents and the work of C. K. Kuhlthau, engaged in the defense of Information Literacy, mainly in the Educational context. Such a proposal included the integration of library and informational skills into the curriculum at different levels of education, research and research training, and broad access to information resources. The discourse of learning to learn has gained prominence. It is also in this period that information ethics became part of the discourse of librarianship (Bielby, 2014).

Information Literacy, although not focused on the library, but rather on informational resources, or as Behens (1994) states, Information Literacy - not library literacy, has been incorporated into the work of librarians because it has a close proximity to some of its more traditional activities, such as library instruction, bibliographic instruction and user / reader education (Bruce, 2000).

In mid-1994, Australian researcher Cristine Bruce drew attention to - seven facets of information literacy - IL (conceptions of: based on information technologies, sources of information, information as process, information control, knowledge, in the extension of knowledge and based on knowledge.

In this period, there is the experimental phase of informational competence, in which libraries invest in information literacy programs in higher education institutions and there are reports in the literature about the difficulty of teaching ethical and wise use of information (Tuominen, Savolainen& Talja, 2005,332). In the academic context, where the concern with plagiarism and ethical use of information goes back to the very development of science and the emergence of the notion of author (Boden and Holloway, 2006), this content was addressed in IL programs, although the use of information was not included in the IL definitions of the time. However, it is noted that the approach was more concerned with the application of documentation standards.

Since 2000, different institutions of the Information Science area have been dedicated to the elaboration of documents that guide librarians and other actors involved in activities related to IL. One of the most influential was the Information Literacy Competency Standards for Higher Education proposed by ACRL (2000), which contains five major standards, twenty-two performance indicators, and eighty-six outcomes of IL behavior (ACRL, 2000). It has been translated into several languages and has given rise to Standards for different domains and educational levels. This document explicitly cites the ethical aspect of the use of information: The individual considered competent in information determines the extent of their informational need; accesses the information you need effectively and efficiently; evaluates information and its sources critically; incorporates the information selected in your knowledge base; uses information effectively to fulfill a specific purpose; understands the economic, legal and social issues and issues that relate to the use of information (ACRL, 2000).

The definition of Webber & Johnston (2003), contemporary to the publication of the Standards by the ACRL, also contemplates the ethical use of information: "[...] Information literacy is the adoption of appropriate information behaviour to identify, through whatever channel or medium, information well fitted to information needs, leading to wise and ethical use of information in society."

The standards served as a parameter for both the choice of contents of the programs of informational competence and for the development of IL evaluation tools (Webber & Johnston, 2007; Neely, 2006).

The study of the content of some of these instruments for evaluating the information literacy (Santos&Casarin, 2014), among them: Bay Area Community Colleges Information Competency Assessment Project, Beile Test of Information Literacy for Education (B-TILED), Information Literacy: Study (FYILLAA) and the First Year Information Literacy in the Liberal Arts Assessment (FYILLAA), revealed that the parameters were not approached in a proportional way in the instruments. Parameter 5, which "[...] understands many of the economic, legal, and social issues surrounding the use of information and accesses and uses information ethically and legally", was addressed in 12% of the total sum of questions of the four instruments analyzed. The indicator that specifically mentions plagiarism has been addressed in three of these instruments. The number of questions devoted to the theme per instrument also varied greatly, with Bay Area having eight issues, B-TILED having five, FYILLAA having two issues, and CREPUQ having one issue. This finding demonstrates that the more traditional the librarian content related to information literacy, such as: characterization and evaluation of sources, elaboration of search strategy, application of documentation standards, the easier it is to incorporate into IL programs and evaluations in academic settings.

In other educational levels, Thomas (2004) cites the work of Nancy Everhart (2003), who analyzed the impact of technologies on the behavior of search and use of information by students and emphasized the need to develop specific actions on the ethical use of information and the role of the school and teachers not only in punishment but in the prevention of plagiarism.

Other international documents have also raised the issue of the ethical use of information. The Australian and New Zealand Information Literacy Framework: Principles, Standards and Practice (Bundy, 2004), for example, establishes six core standards which underpin information literacy acquisition, understanding and application by an individual, to develop lifelong learners through undergraduate studies. Among the expected standards is: the information literate person uses information with understanding and acknowledges cultural, *ethical, legal, and social issues surrounding the use of information* (Terra, 2014).

The SCONUL Seven Pillars of Information Literacy: Core Model For Higher Education (2011) included: identify (ability to identify a personal need for information); scope (can assess current knowledge and identify gaps); plan (can construct strategies for locating information and data); gather (can locate and access the information and data they need); evaluate (can review the research process and compare and evaluate information and data); manage (can organize information professionally and *ethically*); and present (can apply the knowledge gained).

The impact of information society on people's daily lives was addressed by UNESCO (2009), in particular broadband internet and mobile technology. With this, the role of individuals as a producer and consumer of information was highlighted. Another aspect to be highlighted is that not only adults, but children from different parts of the world (Asia, America, Africa and Europe) began to seek, use, produce and share information. With this change of posture of individuals, the ethical use of information gained greater prominence.

After 15 years of its publication, the Information Literacy Competency Standards for Higher Education were revised due to "the rapidly changing higher education environment, along with the dynamic and often uncertain information ecosystem in which all of us work and live, require new attention to be focused on foundational ideas about that ecosystem. Students have a greater role and responsibility in creating new knowledge, in understanding the contours and the changing dynamics of the world of information, and in using information, data, and scholarship ethically" (ACRL, 2015). The most recent document is no longer called Standards and has come to be called Frameworks because it presents a set of interconnected core concepts that can be flexibly implemented. The document also broadens IL's concept for Metaliteracy.

The *Framework* (ACRL, 2015) is organized into six frames: Authority Is Constructed and Contextual; Information Creation as a Process; Information Has Value; Research as Inquiry; Scholarship as Conversation, and Searching as Strategic Exploration.

The frame 'Information Has Value' says that: "Information possesses several dimensions of value, including as a commodity, as a means of education, as a means to influence, and as a means of negotiating and understanding the world. Legal and socioeconomic interests influence information production and dissemination." The users of information are also referred to as information creators, highlighting the growing role of people in the production of information that has been leveraged with information technologies. Between the Knowledge Practices, "which are demonstrations of ways in which learners can increase their understanding of these information literacy concepts", it is planned:

- give credit to the original ideas of others through proper attribution and citation;
- understand that intellectual property is a legal and social construct that varies by culture;
- articulate the purpose and distinguishing characteristics of copyright, fair use, open access, and the public domain;
- understand how and why some individuals or groups of individuals may be underrepresented or systematically marginalized within the systems that produce and disseminate information;

Dispositions, "which describe ways in which to address the affective, attitudinal, or valuing dimension of learning" (ACRL, 2015), predict that learners who are developing their information literate abilities

- respect the original ideas of others;
- value the skills, time, and effort needed to produce knowledge;
- see themselves as contributors to the information marketplace rather than only consumers of it;

In addition to the academic context, the school library has also carried out actions of informational competence and in particular prevention of plagiarism.

In the school context, for example, there is the AASL Standards framework. The Standards is anchored by six core educational concepts or Shared Foundation: Inquire, Include, Collaborate, Curate, Explore, and Engage. Each Shared Foundation is elaborated by three to five Competencies for each learning category or Domain: Think (cognitive), create (psychomotor), share (affective), grow (developmental).

The ethical use of information is addressed in the Engage item of Shared foundation:

VI. ENGAGE : Demonstrate safe, legal, and ethical creating and sharing of knowledge products independently while engaging in a community of practice and an interconnected world.

Think : Learners follow ethical and legal guidelines for gathering and using information by: 1. Responsibly applying information, technology, and media to learning. 2. Understanding the ethical use of information, technology, and media. 3. Evaluating information for accuracy, validity, social and cultural context, and appropriateness for need.

Create : Learners use valid information and reasoned conclusions to make ethical decisions in the creation of knowledge by: 1. Ethically using and reproducing others' work. 2. Acknowledging authorship and demonstrating respect for the intellectual property of others. 3. Including elements in personal-knowledge products that allow others to credit content appropriately

Share : Learners responsibly, ethically, and legally share new information with a global community by: 1. Sharing information resources in accordance with modification, reuse, and remix policies. 2. Disseminating new knowledge through appropriate means for the intended audience.

Grow : Learners engage with information to extend personal learning by: 1. Personalizing their use of information and information technologies. 2. Reflecting on the process of ethical generation of knowledge. 3. Inspiring others to engage in safe, responsible, ethical, and legal information behaviors.

The Information Literacy Standards for Teacher Education (ACRL, 2011) aims to approximate the Standards (ACRL, 2000) of the school context. The document provides for six standards, the latter encompassing several aspects of the ethical use of information, including: "Demonstrating an understanding what constitutes plagiarism; Giving proper credit to others' ideas."

Another source in which IL's contribution to plagiarism can be observed is through the annals of the European Conference on Information Literacy, which is a traditional Information Literacy event held every two years in a country. Docents, professionals and PhD students participate in the event. Between 2014 and 2017 it has been verified that the number of works on plagiarism has been increasing, as seen in the table below:

Table 1. Number of works about plagiarism in ECIL proceedings (2014-2017)

Year	Frequency
2014	03
2015	00
2016	05
2017	12
Total	20

Regarding the context of application of the studies, it is perceived that the university is still the most contemplated context by the studies and experiences. Even though there is one of the events with the theme: workplace, the academic is still predominant. It is also noticed that school and daily life are also being contemplated in the studies.

Table 2. Context types focused on ECIL works (2014-2017)

Groups	Frequency
academic/scientific	14
Everyday life	02
School	03
Work place	1
Total	20

As Table 2 demonstrates, the academic and scientific context has more publications and possibly has received more attention from researchers and practitioners. The works relate to reports of experience of user training programs to combat plagiarism, to the knowledge of research subjects (university students and teachers) regarding the concept of plagiarism.

2. FINAL CONSIDERATIONS

Information literacy emerged in a work context and aimed at optimizing the use of diversified and constantly changing information resources. Over the years, the librarian class has incorporated IL's proposal that, in several aspects, approaches the work of user education traditionally carried out by libraries.

The academic and scientific context is that they have focused more on the training of their users to combat plagiarism, as the scientific production on the subject points out, as well as on the documents edited by professional entities in the area and which inspire the production of guiding documents for different domains of knowledge and educational levels.

Due to the fact that information literacy addresses the knowledge of the sources of information and the whole process of search and use of information, it has a more adequate approach to the prevention of plagiarism, since it is not restricted to the application of documentation standards (citation, references, for example). By addressing training activities in understanding the search process and the informational universe, and even synthesizing and producing knowledge, with accompanying librarians and other actors as teachers, informational competence has great potential for curbing plagiarism, especially if it started in the initial series.

REFERENCES

Association of College and Research Libraries. (2000). Information Competency Standards for Higher Education. January 18, 2000, at the Midwinter Meeting of the American Library Association, San Antonio, Texas. Available at http://www.ala.org/acrl/ilcomstan.html-

Association of College & Research Libraries. (2015). *Information Literacy Framework for Higher Education.* Available at http://www.ala.org/acrl/standards/ilframework.

Bielby, J. (2014). *Information Ethics I: Origins and Evolutions, Academia.* June 01, 2014. Available at https://ualberta.academia.edu/JaredBielby.

Boden, D.& Holloway, S. (2004). Learning about plagiarism through information literacy: a fusion of subject and information management teaching at Imperial College London. Plagiarism: Prevention, Practice and Policies 2004 Conference. Available at https://www.plagiarism.org/paper/learning-about-plagiarism-through-information-literacy

Bruce, C. (2000). Information Literacy research: Dimensions of the emerging collective consciousness. *Australian Academic & Research Libraries*, 31(2), 91-109, DOI: 10.1080/00048623.2000.10755119

Bundy, A., ed. (2004) *Australian and New Zealand Information Literacy Framework: Principles, standards and practice.* Adelaide: Australian and New Zealand Institute for Information Literacy

Association of College & Research Libraries. (2011). Information Literacy Standards for Teacher Education (2011). EBSS Instruction for Educators Committee 2006 2007 – 2010 2011. Approved by the ACRL Board of Directors at the Spring Executive Committee Meeting May 11, 2011.

Kurbanoðlu, S. et al. (Eds.) (2014). *Information Literacy: Lifelong Learning and Digital Citizenship in the 21st Century.* 2 th ECIL. Spring.

Kurbanoðlu, S. et al. (Eds.). (2015). *Information Literacy: Moving Toward Sustainability:* 3 th ECIL 2015. Spring.

Kurbanoðlu, S. et al. (Eds.). (2016). *Information Literacy: Key to an Inclusive Society.* 4 th ECIL 2016. Spring.

Kurbanoðlu, S. et al. (Eds.) (2018). *Information Literacy in the Workplace:* 5 th ECIL 2017. Spring. DOI 10.1007/978-3-319-74334-9

Everhart, N. (2003). Studants & plagiarism. *Knowledge Quest,* 31(4), 43-45

Neely, T. Y. (2006). *Information literacy assessment: standards-based tools and assignments.* Chicago: American Library Association. 6-18.

Santos, C. A. dos & Casarin, H. de C. S. (2014). Habilidades informacionais abordadas em instrumentos de avaliação de Competência Informacional. *Informação & Sociedade,* 24(3), 135-144.

SCONUL Working Group on Information Literacy (2011). Seven Pillars of Information Literacy: Core Model. Available at http://www.sconul.ac.uk/groups/information_literacy/seven_pillars.html

Terra, A. Information Literacy Skills of Portuguese LIS Students: Some Topics on Evaluation of Resources Credibility. In: S. Kurbanoðlu et al. (Ed.). *Information Literacy: Lifelong Learning and Digital Citizenship in the 21st Century.* 2 th ECIL. Spring. pp.752-762 DOI: 10.1007/978-3-319-14136-7_78

Thomas, N. P. (2004). *Information literacy and information skills instruction.* Westport, Conn.: Libraries Unlimited, 2004.

Tuominen, K., Savolainen, R. & Talja, S. (2005). Information Literacy as a Sociotechnical Practice. *The Library Quarterly: Information, Community, Policy,* 75(3), 329-345.

UNESCO. (2009). Information society policies. Annual world report. Available at http://portal.unesco.org/ci/en/files/29547/12668551003ifap_world_report_2009.pdf/

Virkus, S. (2003). Information Literacy in Europe: A Literature Review. *Information Research* 8 (July). Available at http://informationr.net/ir/84/paper159.html

Zurkowski, P. G. (1974). The Information Service Environment Relationships and Priorities. Washington, D.C.: National Commission on Libraries and Information Sciences. Related Paper No. 5.

Johnston, B. & Webber, S. (2003). Information literacy in higher education: a review and case study. *Studies in higher education,* 28(3), 335-352.

14
Policies and Guidelines for Academic Conduct in Universities: A Survey of the International Landscape

Manorama Tripathi
Gayatri Dwivedi
Parveen Babbar

1. INTRODUCTION

Governments worldwide spend colossal amount of money in extending and maintaining higher education and research programmes. For instance, there were 36.6 million students enrolled in higher education, the Gross Enrolment Ratio (GER) was 25.8% in 2016-2017; 34,400 were awarded PhD degree in 2017 in the country (MHRD, 2018).

Universities and Research institutions are supposed to undertake seminal research projects and generate new knowledge by adhering to the highest standards of the scholarship. Honesty and hard work are the pillars which hold the edifice of education and research. But it has been observed that the rules of education and research are often blatantly violated (The Times of India, 2016). There are many reasons behind this rampant phenomenon of infraction in higher education and research. The Internet technology facilitates easy access to information and "cut and paste" culture". The students and researchers may lack adequate writing and referencing skills and may become victims of inadvertent plagiarism. At times, the students and researchers have a misconception that there is no harm in resorting to shortcuts or unethical ways or misconduct as others do the same. Another important reason is that there are lapsed morals-loss of values in the younger generations. Universities worldwide have taken concerted efforts to stem the rising tide of misconduct in education and research. In this context, the present chapter has highlighted what the best universities of the world have done to educate their students and researchers with regard to conduct in education and research. It has spot lighted the polices which UGC, India has framed and implemented.

2. MISCONDUCT IN EDUCATION AND RESEARCH

Research misconduct is fabricating, falsifying or plagiarizing data in proposing, performing, reviewing and reporting findings of research. It also includes manipulation of images. It does not include honest errors or difference of opinion in analyzing and interpreting research results (ORI, 2016). There are others forms of misconduct too like,

- Manipulating authorship (ghost or gift authorship)
- Self plagiarizing-republishing substantial parts of one's own earlier publications without citing the source.
- Citing selectively to enhance one's research findings.
- Selectively reporting or withholding research results
- Accusing researchers of infractions and misconduct.
- Adding inflated bibliography to the theses and dissertations.
- Hampering the work of other researchers
- Using influence or seniority to encourage misconduct.
- Publishing and promoting predatory journals.

3. REASONS BEHIND MISCONDUCT

Plagiarism is the name given to stealing of ideas and dishonesty in scholarly works and then putting them across to the community as your original thought process without acknowledging the original author or source.

A closer study reveals complicated reasons and challenges - not so exclusive to misconducting researchers and scholars alone. Rote learning and orthodoxy in thought process are also the culprits and share the blame, equally. An analytical mindset has to be encouraged, right from the beginning. It doesn't happen overnight. It starts with the early education and depends on the conditioning the children receive in their formative years. Besides, professional and personal ethics also play a vital role.

The practice mirrors human love for ease, shirking efforts- intellectual and otherwise and of course preference for anonymous deceit if it goes unnoticed and gets you what you want. The phosphorescent lure of the fame a good research publication gets is too irresistible.

The checks which come as punitive measures when misconduct is detected can act as deterrence but for honesty in the context to be ingrained in scholarly behaviour and attitude, we need to do much more. Academic integrity preferably should come from within. No change can be affected sustainably, otherwise. Punitive measures are the second best alternative and can be surpassed by shrewd scholars easily who can dress up facts as their original pieces or next best -subjects of critique.

Too much formalization or obfuscation of ideas to give them a requisite level of presentability at elite research and publication forums takes away the directedness, impact, influence and the penetrative simplicity of those moves. Moreover, if an idea is good enough, why the need to gild the lily? But for getting published in coveted and high impact factor journals, one does need good content and a requisite level of linguistic proficiency and style of expression. That is where many good thoughts lose their steam and drive as the authors plagiarise for proper language and linguistic sheen.

The researchers in the sciences use a lot of images to explain and substantiate their laboratory experiments and findings. It has been observed that they manipulate scientific images by using online tools. Ever since Photoshop arrived in 1988, the cases of manipulated images have gone up. The researchers manipulate images as per their convenience. They also know that their manipulation will not be caught. Even if it is found, it will not harm them. Automated programs should be used to detect image manipulation in the biomedical literature (Bucci, 2018).

Gunsalus and Robinson (2018) have coined the acronym, "TRAGEDIES" to summarize the factors which lead to misconduct in research. These factors are "temptation, rationalization, ambition, group and authority pressure, entitlement, deception, incrementalism, embarrassment and stupid systems". They say these are major pitfalls of misconduct and suggest that authorities must audit the departments to find strength and weaknesses and suggest solutions for proper conduct and practices for researchers.

4. IMPACT OF MISCONDUCT IN EDUCATION AND RESEARCH

Research for all practical purpose is to create new knowledge, which may be further used to build upon new derivations, solutions to the existing challenges. But if it is itself based on the shoplifted content, then it ceases to be genuine, and anything further built upon on the same would not be as useful. It becomes a jerry-built piece of knowledge that does good to no one. Research cannot be just a general representation of the good works of others.

The genuine research comes out only after a telling analysis of the existing facts, situations and existing knowledge put together and studied holistically in a particular context. Furthermore, the researcher arrives at the specific conclusion what these indicate, how they could be deciphered. There are times when months of research fail to reach a desirable outcome.

The excellent research asks for a lot of hard work put together by a decent calibre and scholarly temperament. It needs to be respected and acknowledged with due references to the authors whose works have been an integral part of one's research.

The young researchers are the ones who later go on to become professors heading some of the very prestigious educational institutions, commanding a sway and influence over countless heads and the thought process therein. Hence if it is expected from them to have exceptional levels of caliber and analytical skills and clairvoyance to connect the dots, trends and decipher them to predict a certain unfolding trend, there is nothing wrong in it. They should be the best brains of the times, and hence any kind of misconduct which leads to compromising on integrity in research and education should be considered sinful. So if the high standards of scholarly integrity are expected, that is fine and should be the prevalent norm.

When the students or researchers don't read, they plagiarize in the long run; they internalize the habit of copying. As a result, their faculty of analyzing and evaluating to form judgment is stunted. They lack subject knowledge and skills to articulate and convey their thoughts and ideas. The capabilities of critical thinking and academic writing are considered as characteristic of scholarship.

Plagiarism also causes negative externalities on others. The students who do not plagiarize may score fewer marks. The researchers who do not indulge in any misconduct may not get published, or grants or promotions as all these are linked to the number of publications the researchers have to their credit.

The researchers may be reluctant to undertake fieldwork to collect data, as they may feel it is not feasible, or they may not get enough data or information, in spite of investing time and money. Further, they know that the integrity of the data they use (or fabricate) in their research work will not be checked.

When misconduct is caught, journals issue retraction notices and articles are withdrawn. The retractions occur with high frequency these days. It has been observed that the retracted articles are either based on falsified or fabricated data or have plagiarised content (Williams & Wager, 2013). Retractions cause wastage of funds of funding agencies and damage to careers of researchers and disrepute for the organisation. Misconduct in medical and veterinary sciences can cause massive damage to the livestock and human lives. Steen (2011) has observed that the human beings are endangered because they are administered treatment based on fraudulent research.

The obliquities in research and education are growing. The publishers, funding bodies and universities are taking concerted efforts to curb them by framing policies and guiding the researchers about the importance of ethics and integrity in research.

5. METHODOLOGY

The best 85 universities of the world were selected from the following website for the present study:https://www.timeshighereducation.com/world-university-rankings/2018.

Considering the fact, that they must be following rigorous standards of integrity in education and research, if the link or tab of plagiarism or research integrity or ethics was found on the website, it was considered that the university provided the information and services about integrity and ethics to the students and researchers. It is assumed that providing information on the websites is also like extending services to the students, researchers and faculty members. The websites of the universities were visited to find out if these had provided information for the students and researchers. When the direct tab of plagiarism or research integrity or ethics was not found, the websites were searched through the search box provided on the websites.

The table given below shows the countries of 85 best universities of the world.

Table 1. Number of universities

Country	Number of universities
Australia	05
Belgium	01
Canada	04
China	02
France	01
Germany	06
Hongkong	03
Japan	02
Netherland	06
Singapore	03
South Korea	01
Sweden	01
Switzerland	02
UK	10
USA	38

These universities were spread across 15 countries. The authors found information pertaining to academic integrity on 77 websites only. As a result the content of 77 websites was analyzed for further study.

Voyant-Tool Website was used, available at https://voyant-tools.org/ for reading, analyzing and visualizing the content of 77 websites. This tool is available through open source project and code is available through GitHub and GPL3 License under a Creative Common Attribution License.

A corpus was created by pasting each website relevant links relating to Academic Integrity. The corpus has been established in the following three ways:

1. For each University 'Academic Integrity Policy' web pages were analyzed individually
2. The first main relevant page of all the Universities was examined together as a single corpus
3. All the relevant (to academic conduct) pages of 77 Universities were analysed together as a corpus

The Voyant Website provides the corpus for viewing the frequency of the terms. The cirrus has been created through the website to give a word cloud that visualizes the top frequency words of a corpus.

Fig. 1. Word cloud of high frequency words of guidance and policies of academic and research conduct.

The data was collected in the month of June, 2018.

The information of the websites was categorized in to the following heads:

- Availability of Information about Academic integrity
- Policies of research conduct or integrity
- Education and training
- Providing guides to avoid plagiarism and out linking to online resources for helping students and researchers.

6. INITIATIVES AT THE INTERNATIONAL LEVEL TO PROMOTE ACADEMIC INTEGRITY

The Office of Research Integrity UK established in 2006 to promote the good governance, management of academic, scientific and medical research. It extends guidance on how to overcome malpractices, misconduct and unethical behavior. It also provides confidential and independent expert advice on specific research projects cases, problems and issues (UK Research Integrity Office, n.d.)

The Office of Research Integrity (ORI), USA oversees and directs public health services and research integrity activities on behalf of the Secretariat of Health and Human Services. It develops policies procedures and regulations for detecting, investigating, preventing research misconduct. It reviews and monitors research misconduct perpetrated by applicants and their institutions (ORI, 2016).

The Singapore Statement on Research Integrity (World Conferences on Research Integrity, 2010), which was developed as part of the 2nd World Conference on Research Integrity, held in Singapore in July 2010, mentions that the value and benefits of research are dependent on the integrity of research. It reiterates that there may be national or disciplinary differences in the way research is conducted but some cardinal principles and basic values like honesty, accountability, professional courtesy and fairness good stewardship are universally applicable in research and education.

The Montreal Statement on Research Integrity in Cross-Boundary Research Collaborations (2013), was developed as part of 3rd world conference on research integrity held in Montreal, in May 2013.It highlighted the principles which need to be followed in collaborative research which is undertaken across the institutions from different countries.

The IAC/IAP has launched a report which describes the basic values which govern the conduct of research and its communication through scholarly publications. The report provides the basic principles-honesty, fairness, objectivity, reliability, accountability, openness and guidelines which students, researchers, universities, research organizations funding agencies, journals policy makers, publishers should follow to ensure integrity in research endeavors. It has advocated that the authors should follow all the seven principles on which science and research is based. The funding bodies should stress the quality of publications instead of the quantity of the publications. The journal editors must prescreen the manuscripts for originality by passing them through plagiarism detection software tools. The publishers should take extra efforts to ensure that the retracted articles are publicized, more visible and cease to be cited. The reviewers involve in reviewing the manuscripts must communicate to the editors if they have conflicting interest, lack of background knowledge in a particular field to give their opinion. The institutions, head of the departments, editors should not downplay the instances of plagiarism. The perpetrators should be exposed and penalized. The institutions should also accord maximum protection to the whistleblowers against reprisal or retaliation of any kind.

The European Code of Conduct for Research Integrity was set up at the second world conference on research integrity. It guides researchers across all subject areas for conduct. It does not intend to replace existing national or academic guidelines. The code represents the continent wise consensus on fundamental principles and conduct which must be followed to ensure research integrity in education and research (ALLEA, 2017).

In Canada, Tri-Agency Research Integrity policy has been introduced. It is a joint policy of the Canadian Institutes of Health Research(CIHR), the Natural sciences and Engineering Research Council(NSERC) and the Social Sciences and Humanities Research Council(SSHRC).The purpose of the policy is to support the agencies in discharging their respective mandates to promote and assist research, foster a positive research environment and resolve cases of infraction of Tri-agency policies of research integrity (Government of Canada, 2018).

Committee on Publication Ethics (COPE) was established in 1997 by a small group of medical journal editors in the UK but now has over 9000 members worldwide from all academic fields. It provides advice to editors and publishers on all aspects of publication ethics and, in particular, how to handle cases of research and publication misconduct. It also provides a forum for its members to discuss individual cases. The committee does not investigate individual cases but encourages editors to ensure that cases are investigated by the appropriate authorities (Committee on Publication Ethics, 2018).

The Council of Science Editors (CSE) is an international membership organization for editorial professionals publishing in the sciences. It is an authoritative resource on current and emerging issues in the communication of scientific information. It serves editorial professionals in the sciences by creating a supportive network for career development, providing educational opportunities, and developing resources for identifying and implementing high-quality editorial practices. It aims at ensuring responsible and effective communication in science(Council of Science Editors, 2018).

International Centre for Academic Integrity is a virtual organisation, set up in 1992 to eliminate misconduct from higher education. It extends assessment services, resources and consultation to its members. It also facilitates discussion on the crucial issue of academic honesty by holding an annual conference. Academic integrity is an obligation or accountability on the part of students and researchers to strictly adhere to the six core values of honesty, truth, fairness, respect, responsibility and courage. The students, researchers by adhering to these values and the university authorities by ensuring implementation and compliance with these values may contribute to the execution of seminal research and generation of real knowledge (International Centre for Academic Integrity, 2017).

UGC, India has introduced Promotion of Academic Integrity and Prevention of Plagiarism in Higher Education Institutions Regulations, 2018 (University Grants Commission, 2018). These shall apply to all students, researchers, faculty members and staff of higher educational institutions in India. According to it, it is obligatory for the higher educational institutions to spread awareness about the responsible conduct of research, promote a culture of academic integrity and prevent plagiarism. The higher educational institutions will include cardinal principles of academic integrity as required coursework at undergraduate, postgraduate and doctoral levels. The regulations also mention that the higher educational institutions must conduct awareness programmes for all stakeholders. It mandates the use of anti-plagiarism software to ensure originality of content in the theses and dissertations submitted for the award of the degree. There should be a Departmental Academic Integrity Panel(DAIP) and Institutional Integrity Panel (IAIP) to handle the cases of plagiarism. The UGC regulations have prescribed graded punishment for the researchers and faculty members who are found to have plagiarised in their theses and dissertations (Stanford University, n.d.).These regulations are silent on other forms of misconduct like falsification, fabrication of data, manipulation of images, collusion, gift and ghost authorship and other questionable research practices.

7. DATA COLLECTION AND INTERPRETATION

There were 291,686 words on the webpages pertaining to academic and research conduct. Out of the total 291,686, there were 11,219 unique words and the average number of words per sentence was 34.2. The vocabulary density was 0.038. The information has been presented in a consolidated manner.

8. AVAILABILITY OF INFORMATION

All the 77 universities have provided information on plagiarism, academic misconduct etc. The websites have explained the concept of academic misconduct which includes the following:

9. PLAGIARISM

It is caused when a student or researcher has a sinister motive to deceive; he copies the content from previously published sources and passes it off as his own. In other words, he does not acknowledge or give credit to the original source.

10. USE OF UNAUTHORIZED MATERIAL OR FALSE INFORMATION

If the students use unauthorized material or help in completing their assignment or help others in completing their assignments it tantamount to cheating which is unacceptable in education and research. Taking recourse to falsehood for gaining academic or employment advantage by submitting wrong information on their resumes is equivalent to lying.

11. CHEATING

If students submit a chemical product by purchasing and not conducting the assigned activity in the laboratory or if they purchase term papers from websites or market, these are instances of extreme flagrance. Contract cheating occurs when one person completes academic work for another, who then submit it for academic credit. This kind of conduct threatens the quality and integrity of the degree and weakens the entire educational system. It undermines standards in universities but devalues the hard earned qualification of the one who plays by the book. There should be strong policies and sanctions to address this issue.

12. COLLABORATION WORK

Collaboration in writing activities is unethical and prohibited until and unless permission is sought from the teachers. The students should not cooperate in the analyzing and reporting the datasets which their teachers give to them. The unauthorized collaboration on work or activities which are to be graded or evaluated is known as collusion and it is not permissible. The computer science students should not use online solution for programming assignments. They should not share their solution code or algorithmic strategies with other students.

13. FALSIFICATION OF DATA

It means representing imaginary or fictional data as genuine data, without conducting experiment or field surveys. It is also known as dry-labbing. It occurs when students provide fictional readings or observational data without conducting the assigned experiments. They should not use or present data which are not collected in accordance with the standard guidelines of the universities for collecting and generating data. The students and researchers should make careful notes in diaries and log books to avoid the occurrence of misconduct.

14. MANIPULATION OF IMAGES

The students and researchers use online technologies and tools to change and manipulate images; for example they change one part of the image and use filters to enhance the quality of the images. This is highly unethical and unacceptable in education and research.

15. AIDING AND ABETTING ACADEMIC DISHONESTY

The actions of stealing, reproducing, gaining access to examination material before the due time permitted by the university authorities, destroying, defacing or concealing reading materials of libraries and forging signatures are unacceptable. The actions of supporting others in academic dishonesty are highly unethical. The students should not provide material or information to others, which may be used in in the violation of norms of academic honesty, as aiding and abetting academic dishonesty is unacceptable.

16. COMMON KNOWLEDGE

Generally, there is no need to cite the common knowledge. The common knowledge includes the historical facts, universal truths, scientific facts and standards which are known and intelligible to more number of people. The common knowledge is subject, group and country-specific and may not be common to people from another subject, group and country.

It is hard to decide how far the common knowledge is common. It may depend on many variables like the readers or audience or subject of the article in which the common knowledge has been described. The students should cite the source of common knowledge, if they are in doubt

17. POLICIES OF RESEARCH CONDUCT OR RESEARCH INTEGRITY

All the universities have framed policies for the students and researchers to ensure compliance with the rules of academic honesty and integrity. The policies are known by different names like honor code or charter, code of conduct, code of conduct on academic matters, code of behavior on academic matters, Advanced Academic Programme(AAP) code of conduct, academic conduct code. For instance, the University of Pennsylvania has "Code of Academic Integrity" and charter of the University of Pennsylvania student disciplinary system". For example, in the Stanford University, the Honor Code is the university statement on academic integrity and was written by the students in 1921.It conveys the expectations of the university from the students and teachers in promoting and maintaining quality in academic work. The Stanford University has also in place the Fundamental Standard which specifies the conduct which the students should follow. It was written by the first president of the university in 1896.It states that the students of Stanford University must follow rules of honesty, order, morality, respect each other inside and outside the university. The violation of Fundamental Standard may invite penalties from warning to expulsion, for defaulters.

These incorporate rules of academic and research conduct. The written policies and charters specify the behavior expected of the students and researchers and the results of failing to meet the norms. The policies mention that if students are caught in the actions of plagiarism, they will be subject to disciplinary or corrective procedures like written reprimands, probation, suspension, expulsion or even degree may be revoked. The policies spell special instructions for international students to follow and adhere to academic integrity otherwise they may endanger their immigration status as students. The honor codes or policies have clearly delineated the different acts of misconduct. The policies have specified that if any student or researcher or teacher feels that an act of misconduct has been perpetrated, he may inform the same to the department with which the perpetrator is associated. The universities conduct a speedy investigation of all charges of non-compliance with honesty and integrity by maintaining the confidentiality of the identity of the alleged student or researcher. The accused is given the opportunity to explain his stand. In case the accused is found guilty by the investigating committee, which offers initial adverse decision, he may appeal to the higher authorities. The universities impose sanctions for the proved incidents of misconduct and the same is recorded in the official record of the students and researchers. The guilty may be failed or declared invalid or ineligible for certain honors and awards of the universities.

The universities have departments and offices for implementing integrity policies and investigating allegations and imposing sanctions. For example the University of Edinburgh UK has Research Policy group (RPG) for monitoring matters pertaining to integrity and ethics in research at the various departments of the universities. The University of California, San Diego has academic Integrity office to promote and foster a culture of academic integrity in order to strengthen quality teaching and learning in the university(University of California, San Diego, 2018).

18. EDUCATION AND TRAINING

The libraries conduct workshops and orientation sessions to disseminate information among the students and researchers about the damaging effect of academic misconduct on universities and society as a whole. Libraries also educate and train students on different aspects of scholarly writing, how to cite the references which one has used; they train the students and researchers in the use of reference management tools like Mendeley, Endnote and Zotero. Libraries have provided online tutorials on their websites for the users. They have also provided style manuals and guidelines for researchers across different disciplines. Many libraries have provided online tutorials.For example the University of Pennsylvania has provided PORT: Penn Online Research Tutorial https://web.archive.org/web/20170614012241/http://gethelp.library.upenn.edu:80/PORT to help the students and researchers.

The Duke University has made it compulsory for post graduate and PhD students to undergo 4 and 12-18 hours of training on Responsible conduct of Research https://gradschool.duke.edu/professional-development/programs/responsible-conduct-research. It offers a plagiarism tutorial and self-test, which is password enabled, for students and researchers. The University of California, San Diego has introduced a mandatory Academic Integrity Training for the students. It has also introduced Integrity Mentorship Programme (IMP), under which the students are entrusted to educators to understand strategies and techniques to achieve academic excellence by adhering to the fundamental value of integrity. The programme runs for ten weeks.

The Karolinska Institue (KI), Sweden has subscribed to an online course Called, "Avoid Plagiarism" https://ki.se/en/staff/web-course-avoiding-plagiarism-available-for-all-doctoral-students.

KI undertook a pilot project in 2014-2015 for six months. Under this project, every tenth thesis was randomly selected for checking. The pilot project checked 24 theses and it was found out that, there was extensive lifting of content which was certainly not in keeping with the guidelines of writing theses at KI. It has specified that the text of the summary chapter must be the student's own original work without extensive reproduction from other sources.

The University of Edinburgh, UK maintains a comprehensive list of resources to ensure that the highest standards of research ethics and integrity are followed. It provides guidance, factsheets and tips on good academic practices, how to avoid plagiarism by citing and referencing.

Most of the universities use plagiarism detection software like Turnitin.com, IThenticate for detecting possible cases of plagiarism. The University of Edinburgh has integrated the use of Turnitin in Moodle. It also provides guidance to the teachers and students in the use of the software. The University of Stanford, computer science department uses MOSS (measure of Software Similarity) for detecting plagiarism.

In 2012, in the UK a document, "The Concordat to support research integrity" was published by Government of UK, Research Councils UK, NIHR, Welcome Trust and other key holders. The concordat specifies five commitments which the researchers must take to ensure that the highest standards of rigour and integrity are followed and maintained. All stakeholders are supposed to support the commitments laid out in the Concordat. All the ten UK universities under the study are members of Universities UK and are a signatory to the concordat. They rigorously follow the five commitments of the Concordat. All the ten universities provide an Annual Statement on Research Integrity on their websites. The universities specify the measures which they take to support and maintain the highest standards in research. The universities also report the instances of misconduct on their premises and the corrective actions which they chose to handle the cases of misconduct.

19. PROVIDING GUIDES TO AVOID PLAGIARISM AND OUT LINKING TO ONLINE RESOURCES FOR HELPING STUDENTS AND RESEARCHERS

The universities out link to various resources and websites to disseminate the knowledge about academic conduct. For instance UCL, UK has provided links to the following:

- Singapore Statement on Research Integrity 2010
- Montreal Statement on Research Integrity in Cross-Boundary Research Collaboration 2014
- UK Research Integrity office.

The University of Stanford has provided links to resources which may be useful and relevant for the students and researchers. Some of the resources are listed below:
- Dartmouth College :Sources: Their Use and Acknowledgment
- Georgetown University :How to Avoid Plagiarism
- Purdue University Online Writing Website :Avoiding Plagiarism
- University of California, Davis, Avoiding Plagiarism, Mastering the Art of Scholarship.

There are Libguides provided on how to cite references and referencing styles for students and researchers.

20. BEST PRACTICES FOR ALL STAKEHOLDERS.

1. The universities must have an Academic Integrity Policy in place and they must ensure their strict compliance. The Academic Integrity Policy should be clearly stated on the website and in the prospectus of the university.

2. The deans and chairpersons should widely disseminate and publicize the academic integrity policy of the university in order to ensure that the students and research scholars are well aware of the issue and the university's stand on it. It should be clearly conveyed that in case, some irregularity in the form of academic misconduct is noticed or observed, any assertions of ignorance will not be accepted or considered by the university.

3. Libraries should impart academic integrity education to the students and researchers through the workshops and discussions.

4. The faculty members are should provide discipline specific guidance on good academic and research practices. Libraries should provide information about correct citation techniques, plagiarism avoidance and how to draw line between collaboration and collusion. Libraries should provide libguides, online tutorials on various aspects of scholarly writing and reporting, how to cite references and acknowledge the intellectual work of others. The computer science students should acknowledge the source if they copy a snippet or the whole module of code. If then students and researchers use code from an open source project, they must cite the source and ensure compliance with the terms of open source license which applies to the code which they use in their work.

5. The libraries should provide links to useful resources and websites to educate the researchers on different aspects of research integrity and use and presentation of images in scholarly writing and reporting. For instance, they may provide link to the website https://ori.hhs.gov/research-misconduct;https://ori.hhs.gov/education/products/RIandImages/default.html.This site explains how the images should be used and presented.

6. Libraries should have a cell-like Academic Integrity Cell to promote and foster a culture of academic integrity and support and strengthen quality education and research in the universities.

7. Libraries should also have adequate resources to extend Research Data Management

(RDM) to the students and researchers. RDM refers to all the activities and procedures which are followed for describing, documenting, organizing, archiving, preserving the datasets which are generated during research projects, for sharing and reuse in the future by others. The researchers should be taught about the basics of data lifecycle. This would also help in ensuring compliance to integrity in research. The Research Integrity Training Framework created at university College London (UCL) mentions that RDM is essential for ensuring that any research activity is based on integrity.

21. CONCLUSION

The present chapter has dealt with the vital issue of misconduct in education and research. It has analyzed the content of websites of the best universities of the globe to find out what steps they have initiated to guide students and researchers about adhering to integrity and ethics in education and research. The universities have written policies for ensuring compliance with integrity and ethics. The universities have guided the students about how to write and undertake research as per the norms and standards of the discipline. They have also provided links to many learning resources and policies of the research councils for researchers. The essence of the guidance and policies of the universities' websites is that no matter, how adverse the conditions are, the universities advocate that the academic and research work should be done with honesty and integrity, failing which, the authorities will impose sanctions on the perpetrators.

The chapter has also suggested best practices for all stakeholders. It underlines that the students, researchers, supervisors, administrators must follow the fundamental principle of honesty in their work, research, education, training, guidance and functioning which will benefit one and all.

REFERENCES

MHRD (2018) AISHE Presentation Retrieved on 26 August 2018 fromhttp://mhrd.gov.in/sites/upload_files/mhrd/files/New%20AISHE%202017-18%20Launch_Final.pdf

The Times of India (2016) 2,500 BU PhDs under scanner for plagiarism Retrieved on 26 August 2018 fromhttps://timesofindia.indiatimes.com/city/bhopal/2500-BU-PhDs-under-scanner-for-plagiarism/articleshow/51761795.cms

ORI(2016) Frequently Asked Questions Retrieved on15August 2018 fromhttps://ori.hhs.gov/frequently-asked-questions#5

Bucci, E. M. (2018). Automatic detection of image manipulations in the biomedical literature. Cell death & disease, 9(3), 400.

International Centre for Academic Integrity (2017) Cultivating Integrity Worldwide. Retrieved on 26 August 2018 from https://academicintegrity.org/about/

Gunsalus, C. K., & Robinson, A. D. (2018). Nine pitfalls of research misconduct. Retrieved on 26 August 2018 fromhttps://www.nature.com/articles/d41586-018-05145-6

Williams, P., & Wager, E. (2013). Exploring why and how journal editors retract articles: findings from a qualitative study. Science and engineering ethics, 19(1), 1-11.

Steen, R. G. (2011). Retractions in the scientific literature: is the incidence of research fraud increasing?. Journal of medical ethics, 37(4), 249-253.

UK Research Integrity Office(n.d.) Research Integrity Retrieved on15August 2018 fromhttps://www.research-integrity.admin.cam.ac.uk/research-integrity/uk-research-integrity-office

World conferences on Research Integrity(2010) Singapore statement on Research Integrity Retrieved on15August 2018 from https://wcrif.org/guidance/singapore-statement

Montreal Statement on Research Integrity in Cross-Boundary Research Collaborations(2013) Retrieved on15August 2018 from https://www.etikkom.no/en/library/practical-information/legal-statutes-and-guidelines/montreal-statement-on-research-integrity-in-cross-boundary-research-collaborations/

ALLEA(2017) The European code of Conduct for Research Integrity Retrieved on15August 2018 from https://www.allea.org/wp-content/uploads/2017/05/ALLEA-European-Code-of-Conduct-for-Research-Integrity-2017.pdf

Government of Canada (2018) Panel of Responsible Conduct o of Research. Promoting a positive research environment. Retrieved on15August 2018 from http://www.rcr.ethics.gc.ca/eng/index/

Committee on Publication Ethics (2018) About COPE Retrieved on15August 2018 fromhttps://publicationethics.org/about Council of Science Editors(2018) Council of Science editors Retrieved on 26 August 2018 from https://www.councilscienceeditors.org/

International Centre for Academic Integrity(2017) Cultivating Integrity Worldwide Retrieved on 15August 2018 fromhttps://academicintegrity.org/about/

University Grants Commission (2018) Promotion of Academic Integrity and Prevention of Plagiarism in Higher Educational Institutions) Regulations, 2018 Retrieved on15August 2018 fromhttps://www.ugc.ac.in/pdfnews/7771545_academic-integrity-Regulation2018.pdf

Stanford University(n.d.) Policies Retrieved on15August 2018 fromhttps://communitystandards.stanford.edu/policies

University of California, San Diego (2018) Academic Integrity Retrieved on15August 2018 from http://academicintegrity.ucsd.edu/

APPENDIX : LIST OF UNIVERSITIES COVERED IN THE STUDY

Name of University	URL	Country
University of Oxford	https://www.ox.ac.uk/students/academic/guidance/skills/plagiarism?wssl=1	UK
University of Cambridge	https://www.plagiarism.admin.cam.ac.uk/	UK
Stanford University	https://communitystandards.stanford.edu/student-conduct-process/honor-code-and-fundamental-standard/additional-resources/what-plagiarism	USA
Massachusetts Institute of Technology	https://integrity.mit.edu/handbook/what-plagiarism	USA
Harvard University	https://projects.iq.harvard.edu/student-handbook/book/academic-integrity#two	USA
Princeton University	http://www.princeton.edu/pr/pub/integrity/pages/intro/index.htm	USA
Imperial College London	http://www.imperial.ac.uk/student-records-and-data/for-current-students/undergraduate-and-taught-postgraduate/exams-assessments-and-regulations/plagiarism-academic-integrity	UK
University of Chicago	https://college.uchicago.edu/advising/academic-integrity-student-conduct	USA
ETH Zurich – Swiss Federal Institute of Technology Zurich	https://www.ethz.ch/students/en/studies/performance-assessments/plagiarism.html	Switzerland

University of Pennsylvania	University of Pennsylvania	USA
Yale University	http://catalog.yale.edu/undergraduate-regulations/policies/definitions-plagiarism-cheating/	USA
Johns Hopkins University	http://advanced.jhu.edu/current-students/policies/notice-on-plagiarism-2/	USA
Columbia University	https://www.arch.columbia.edu/plagiarism-policy	USA
University of California, Los Angeles	https://www.registrar.ucla.edu/Registration-Classes/Enrollment-Policies/Class-Policies/Plagiarism-and-Student-Copyright	USA
UCL	https://www.ucl.ac.uk/students/exams-and-assessments/plagiarism	UK
Duke University	https://studentaffairs.duke.edu/conduct/z-policies/academic-dishonesty	USA
University of California, Berkeley	http://gsi.berkeley.edu/gsi-guide-contents/academic-misconduct-intro/	USA
Cornell University	https://cuinfo.cornell.edu/aic.cfm	USA
Northwestern University	https://www.northwestern.edu/provost/policies/academic-integrity/	USA
University of Michigan	https://internationalcenter.umich.edu/students/academic-integrity	USA
National University of Singapore	http://www.nus.edu.sg/celc/programmes/plagiarism.html	Singapore
University of Toronto	http://www.artsci.utoronto.ca/newstudents/transition/academic/plagiarism	Canada
Carnegie Mellon University	https://www.cmu.edu/student-affairs/theword/acad_standards/creative/academic_integrity.html	USA
London School of Economics and Political Science	http://www.lse.ac.uk/social-policy/student-hub/Plagiarism	UK
University of Washington	http://www.washington.edu/teaching/cheating-or-plagiarism/	USA
University of Edinburgh	https://www.ed.ac.uk/academic-services/students/conduct/academic-misconduct/plagiarism	UK
New York University	https://www.nyu.edu/about/policies-guidelines-compliance/policies-and-guidelines/academic-integrity-for-students-at-nyu.html	USA
Peking University	Could not find	China
Tsinghua University	Could not find	China
University of California, San Diego	http://senate.ucsd.edu/Operating-Procedures/Senate-Manual/Appendices/2	USA
University of Melbourne	https://academicintegrity.unimelb.edu.au/home	Australia
Georgia Institute of Technology	https://policylibrary.gatech.edu/student-affairs/academic-honor-code	USA
University of British Columbia	https://artsone.arts.ubc.ca/about-arts-one/ubc-policies/ubc-plagiarism-policy/	Canada
LMU Munich		Germany
King's College London	https://www.kcl.ac.uk/artshums/study/handbook/sguides/assessment/plagiarism.aspx	UK
University of Illinois at Urbana-Champaign	http://studentcode.illinois.edu/article1_part4_1-402.html	USA
École Polytechnique Fédérale de Lausanne	https://citation.epfl.ch/copyright/consequences	Switzerland

University	URL	Country
Karolinska Institute	https://ki.se/en/staff/checking-theses-for-plagiarism	Sweden
University of Hong Kong	http://www.rss.hku.hk/integrity	Hongkong
Technical University of Munich	https://www.gs.tum.de/en/supervisors/good-supervision/good-scientific-practice-plagiarism/	Germany
McGill University	https://www.mcgill.ca/students/srr/academicrights/integrity/cheating	Canada
University of Wisconsin-Madison	https://conduct.students.wisc.edu/academic-integrity/	USA
Hong Kong University of Science and Technology	http://www.rss.hku.hk/integrity/rcr/policy	HongKong
Heidelberg University	http://www.ub.uni-heidelberg.de/Englisch/service/plagiat.html	Germany
The University of Tokyo	http://www.cie.u-tokyo.ac.jp/RulesPertain.html	Japan
KU Leuven	https://www.kuleuven.be/english/education/plagiarism	Belgium
Australian National UniversityAustralia	http://www.anu.edu.au/students/program-administration/assessments-exams/academic-honesty-plagiarism	Australia
University of Texas at Austin	http://deanofstudents.utexas.edu/conduct/	USA
Brown University	https://www.brown.edu/academics/college/degree/index.php?q=policies/academic-code/	USA
Washington University in St Louis	https://wustl.edu/about/compliance-policies/academic-policies/undergraduate-student-academic-integrity-policy/	USA
Nanyang Technological University	http://www.ntu.edu.sg/ai/Pages/academic-integrity-policy.aspx	Singapore
University of California, Santa Barbara	http://judicialaffairs.sa.ucsb.edu/academicintegrity.aspx	USA
University of California, Davis	https://cieuniv.ucdavis.edu/student-life/what-is-plagiarism/	USA
Washington University in St Louis	https://wustl.edu/about/compliance-policies/academic-policies/undergraduate-student-academic-integrity-policy/	USA
Nanyang Technological University, Singapore	http://research.ntu.edu.sg/rieo/RI/Pages/index.aspx	Singapore
University of California, Santa Barbara	http://judicialaffairs.sa.ucsb.edu/academicintegrity.aspx	USA
University of California, Davis	https://cieuniv.ucdavis.edu/student-life/what-is-plagiarism/	USA
University of Manchester	http://www.staffnet.manchester.ac.uk/tlso/policy-guidance/assessment/process-of-assessment/academic-malpractice/academic-malpractice-advice/	UK
University of Minnesota	https://cla.umn.edu/hsjmc/about/plagiarism-fabrication-policy	USA
University of North Carolina at Chapel Hill	https://writingcenter.unc.edu/tips-and-tools/plagiarism/	USA
Chinese University of Hong Kong	https://www.cuhk.edu.hk/policy/academichonesty/Eng_htm_files_(2013-14)/index_page2.htm	Hong Kong
University of Amsterdam	https://student.uva.nl/en/content/az/plagiarism-and-fraud/plagiarism-and-fraud.html	Netherlands

University	URL	Country
Purdue University	https://www.purdue.edu/odos/osrr/academic-integrity/index.html	USA
University of Sydney	https://sydney.edu.au/students/academic-dishonesty-and-plagiarism.html	Australaia
Humboldt University of Berlin	Could not find	Germany
Delft University of Technology	https://www.tudelft.nl/en/about-tu-delft/strategy/strategy-documents-tu-delft/integrity-policy/scientific-integrity/	Netherlands
Wageningen University & Research	https://www.wur.nl/en/Research-Results/Chair-groups/Social-Sciences/Rural-Sociology-Group/Education/Plagiarism.htm	Netherlands
University of Queensland	https://my.uq.edu.au/information-and-services/manage-my-program/student-integrity-and-conduct/academic-integrity-and-student-conduct	Australia
University of Southern California	https://sjacs.usc.edu/students/academic-integrity/	USA
Leiden University	https://www.universiteitleiden.nl/en/research/quality-and-integrity/academic-integrity	Netherland
Utrecht University	https://students.uu.nl/en/practical-information/policies-and-procedures/fraud-and-plagiarism	Netherlands
University of Maryland, College Park	https://tltc.umd.edu/plagiarism-and-honor-code	USA
Boston University	https://www.bu.edu/academics/policies/academic-conduct-code/	USA
Ohio State University	https://u.osu.edu/cononlinecoursefaq/academic-misconduct-and-plagiarism/	USA
Erasmus University Rotterdam	https://www.eur.nl/en/about-eur/schools-and-llcs/eur-holding/integrity-policy	Netherlands
Paris Sciences & Lettres – PSL University	Could not find	France
Kyoto University	Could not find	Japan
Seoul National University	Could not find	South Korea
University of Bristol	https://www.bristol.ac.uk/library/support/findinginfo/plagiarism/	UK
Pennsylvania State University	http://tlt.psu.edu/plagiarism/links/penn-state-policies/	USA
McMaster University	https://www.mcmaster.ca/academicintegrity/students/typeofad/plagiarism/	Canada
RWTH Aachen University	http://www.ub.rwth-aachen.de/cms/UB/Forschung/Wissenschaftliches-Publizieren/Wissenswertes-fuer-Autoren/~iigo/Plagiate/?lidx=1	Germany
University of Glasgow	https://www.gla.ac.uk/myglasgow/senateoffice/studentcodes/staff/plagiarism/	UK
Monash University	https://www.monash.edu/students/academic/policies/academic-integrity	Australia
University of Freiburg	Could not find	Germany

15

Plagiarism and Guides to Good Scientific Practices: The Brazilian Perspective

Eduardo Graziosi Silva
João Carlos Gardini Santos
José Augusto Chaves Guimarães

1. INTRODUCTION

The advent of the information society, associated with the exponential growth of the Internet and of information dissemination tools, brought up an old problem of academic and scientific environments, but that was formerly difficult to identify: plagiarism. The issues surrounding plagiarism cover many legal aspects such as moral rights (inalienable, nontransferable, irrevocable having his name linked to the creation of intellectual work, for example) and economic rights (right to obtain economic values with commercialization of the work), as well as ethical aspects, especially with regard to scientific production.

Etymologically, plagiarism is a word of Latin origin (*plagium* – theft, kidnapping) and such practice can be conceptualized in a generic way, "[...] such as the presentation made by someone, as of his own authorship, of intellectual work (or part of it) produced by others." (Guimarães, 2018)[14] or as the "[...] misappropriation of third-party contents, ideas or works." (Krokoscz, 2014). On the other hand, in the academic and scientific sphere, plagiarism can be understood as "[...] the presentation of a scientific production (academic work, research project, undergraduate thesis[15], scientific article, essay, among others) original, when the same comes

---

14. All the quotes presented throughout this article were translated by the writers to provide the reader with better reading pace. As such, all of them can be found in their original source. See Reference section below.

15. Generally presented by undergraduates to obtain a Bachelor's degree by the end of their major.

from copy (literal or rewritten), whose original authorship is suppressed or disguised." (Alves, Casarin, & Fernandéz Molina, 2016).

There are many forms of plagiarism: a) total or integral plagiarism, characterized by the transcription, without citation of the source, of the whole of a text; b) partial plagiarism, in which there is the transcription of parts of one or several works camouflaged in the writing of the author-plagiarizer himself; c) conceptual plagiarism, evidenced when the author-plagiarizer presents as one or some concepts or a complete theory, but which in reality were elaborated by another person; d) mosaic plagiarism, most common among all, where there is simple substitution of the words of the original text without the indication of the source; and, lastly, e) the vague or incorrect reference in which the author-plagiarizer fails at the moment of elaborating the references of the works used for the development of his work (Kirkpatrick, 2001; Garschagen, 2006).

Several initiatives have been carried out in order to combating plagiarism by protecting copyright. At the international level, the literature records that the first copyright protection for a literary work was granted, in 1786, by the Senate of Venice to Marcus Antonius Coccius Sabellicus for his work *Decades rerum Venetarum*, a history of Venice. However, previously, in 1567, the same Institution granted to Titian the first copyright that is registered for the creation of an artistic work. Subsequently, the first copyright law was introduced, which was enacted in 1710 in England and became known as *The Statute of Anne*. This law established the first guidelines for the attribution of credits to authors for their intellectual creations, in addition to guaranteeing, for fourteen years, the author's right over his work (Canalli, Silva, & Canalli, 2018).

Two other laws that also contributed to guarantee the rights of the author on his intellectual creation as an important instrument to combat plagiarism were the Berne Convention, published in 1886, and the Universal Declaration of Human Rights, published in 1948. The latter, in its Article XXVII.2, states that "Every human being has the right to the protection of moral and material interests arising from any scientific or literary scientific production of which he is the author" (UN General Assembly, 1948, p. 15).

At the national level, in turn, the first legislation that dealt with the protection of author's rights dates from August 11, 1827, when, from the creation of the first Law courses in the country, in Olinda and São Paulo, respectively, professors were assured for ten years, the protection of their works. Currently, in order to protect copyright and, consequently, the fight against plagiarism, Law 9,610 of February 19, 1998 is in force in Brazil. It should be noted that this legislation has undergone two changes: the first occurred in 2013 with Law Nº. 12,853, which amended articles of Law Nº. 9,610 and reformulated the collective management of copyright, and the second occurred in 2015 with Constitutional Amendment Nº. 48, which amended and supplemented Article 215 of the Federal Constitution, laying the systematization of guidelines between the State and society in the cultural sphere.

However, the fight against plagiarism is not restricted only to the Legislative Power initiatives. In the scientific and academic spheres, for example, the establishment of chambers, committees, commissions of ethics and/or integrity of research to promote integrity in scientific research (Alves, 2016). Research promotion agencies, in turn, as responsible for the management of public resources for the development of science, devoted themselves to the publication of codes of ethics and scientific conduct, documents that are currently the main means of orientation and combat to plagiarism.

Codes of ethics and scientific conduct provide guiding guidelines for researchers in their activity so that they can avoid harm to themselves, to others, and to institutions. In Brazil, the following stand out: *Code of Good Scientific Practice by São Paulo Research Foundation* (FAPESP); *Report of the Commission for Research Integrity of the National Council for Scientific and Technological Development* (CNPq); and, lastly, *Rigor and Integrity in the Conduct of Scientific Research: a guide to recommendations of responsible practices by the Brazilian Academy of Sciences* (ABC).[16]

Considering the importance of these documents in the scientific making, a qualitative study of the exploratory type based on the documental research method was carried out. The study universe consisted of the codes of FAPESP, CNPq and ABC in order to verify the guidelines offered on plagiarism. Content analysis was used to study the excerpts from the abovementioned codes dealing with plagiarism, which were grouped into categories and subcategories.

2. CODES OF ETHICS AND SCIENTIFIC CONDUCT: THE CASE OF FAPESP, CNPQ AND THE BRAZILIAN ACADEMY OF SCIENCES

2.1. Code of Good Scientific Practice by FAPESP

Released in 2014, the Code of Good Scientific Practice by FAPESP "[...] establishes the ethical guidelines for the scientific activities of researchers who are beneficiaries of FAPESP grants and fellowships and for the exercise of the function of scientific evaluator by FAPESP's advisors." (Fundação de Amparo à Pesquisa do Estado de São Paulo, 2014, p. 15). It is applied both to public institutions and to private institutions that seek to benefit from the benefits provided by the research promotion agency and the scientific journals that receive their support. Its purpose is to establish general precepts that will be complemented by those involved in scientific research according to their peculiarities. Its content covers the introductory sections (*Letter of Routing from the Scientific Board and Preamble*); the *Guidelines for scientific activities*; *On poor scientific conduct*; *On the responsibility of research institutions*; and, lastly, *On the allegation, investigation and declaration of more scientific conduct*.

About the term plagiarism, we can find two indications. The first one, in the section that deals with bad scientific behavior, clarifies that plagiarism or the use of third-party ideas without proper reference and that is apt to confuse the reader's perception to the point of attributing the

---

16. Except of FAPESP's document which has a published version of 2012, the other two documents are originally written in Brazilian Portuguese: "Código de Boas Práticas Científicas da Fundação de Amparo à Pesquisa do Estado de São Paulo" (FAPESP); "Relatório da Comissão de Integridade de Pesquisa do Conselho Nacional de Desenvolvimento Científico e Tecnológico" (CNPq); "Rigor e Integridade na Condução da Pesquisa Científica: guia de recomendações de práticas responsáveis" (ABC).

original idea to the plagiarist is one of the most typical and frequent serious conduct of researchers (Fundação de Amparo à Pesquisa do Estado de São Paulo, 2014).

The second indication of plagiarism is in the section dealing with the allegation, investigation and declaration of misconduct, reaffirms plagiarism as a serious scientific misconduct and establishes that the preliminary assessment of the allegation of plagiarism should be conducted by a committee composed of by at least three people.

2.2. Research Integrity Commission Report by CNPq

CNPq, by means of RN-006/2011, published in Section 1, page 116 of the Official Gazette of March 3, 2012, instituted the Commission for Integrity in Scientific Activity (CIAC). Among the duties of the Commission is to examine dubious situations regarding the integrity of research carried out and / or published by researchers who, in the exercise of the activity, received any kind of benefits from the body. The performance of the Commission in the development of its attributions has generated the Research Integrity Commission Report by CNPq, which is subdivided into *Introduction (Introdução)*, *Definitions (of terms) (Definições)*, *Guidelines (Diretrizes)* and, lastly, References *(Referências)*.

The report emphasizes the presence of the terms plagiarism and self-plagiarism. The first is defined as the "[...] submission, as if it were his own, results or conclusions obtained earlier by another author, as well as full texts or a substantial part of foreign texts without the care detailed in Guidelines." (Conselho Nacional de Desenvolvimento Científico e Tecnológico, 2011, p. 3). In adittion, the document also clarifies that practices "[...] plagiarism who uses ideas or data obtained in analyzes of unpublished manuscripts or manuscripts to which he had access as a consultant, reviewer, editor, or the like." (Conselho Nacional de Desenvolvimento Científico e Tecnológico, 2011, p. 3).

Self-plagiarism, in turn, is defined as the "[...] total or partial presentation of texts already published by the same author, without due references to previous works" (Conselho Nacional de Desenvolvimento Científico e Tecnológico, 2011, p. 3). In order to avoid cases of self-plagiarism, the Report recommends that texts and works previously developed by the author be duly cited and referenced. For non-characterization of plagiarism, the document generally recommends that the author always give due credit to all sources that somehow directly substantiate his work and that any direct (or literal) quotation is indicated in quotation marks.

2.3. Brazilian Academy of Sciences (ABC)

ABC published, in 2013, the document "Rigor and integrity in conducting scientific research: a guide to responsible practical recommendations". This regulation is formed by *Introduction, Premises, Principles, Good practices, Misconduct and References*. On the one hand, the text of the document relates directly to the plagiarism quoted in the sections *Premises* and *Misconduct*, to the bad scientific conduct, and, on the other hand, to the lack of observance of the good practices in which, eventually, the researcher may incur.

In addition, the document clarifies that violations of the principles governing good scientific practice are liable to harm the advancement of both science and society and should therefore be investigated. In this sense, both plagiarism and self-plagiarism are two of the ways in which violations of good scientific practices may occur.

In the ABC document, plagiarism involves "[...] the appropriation of ideas and work of others without due credit" (Academia Brasileira de Ciências, 2013, p. 11) and self-plagiarism is related to "[...] republication of scientific results already released, like new, without giving information on prior publication." (Academia Brasileira de Ciências, 2013, p. 11).

3. METHODOLOGY

A qualitative exploratory approach was adopted based on the documental research method.

The selected study universe consisted of the documents Code of Good Scientific Practices by FAPESP, Report of the Commission of Research Integrity by CNPq and Rigor and integrity in the conduction of scientific research: guide of responsible practical recommendations by ABC. The selection of documents is due to the fact that they are national references of codes of ethics and scientific conduct.

As far as what concerns the research procedures, the categorical analysis of Bardin (2009) was used, through which three categories were highlighted: explanation, definition and orientation.

4. PRESENTATION AND DISCUSSION OF RESULTS

Table 1 presents the universe, unit of analysis, categories and subcategories identified in the codes of ethics and scientific conduct analyzed.

Table 1. Universe, unit of analysis, categories and subcategories identified in the codes of ethics and scientific conduct

Universe	Unit of analysis	Category	Subcategory
Brazilian Academy of Sciences	"Scientific misconduct mainly concern manufacturing, falsification and plagiarism, but also involves inattention to the good practices recognized in the research activity." (Academia Brasileira de Ciências, 2013, p. 5)	Explanation	Scientific misconduct
Brazilian Academy of Sciences	"c. **Plagiarism** involving the appropriation of ideas and the work of others without due credit;" (Academia Brasileira de Ciências, 2013, p. 11)	Definition	Scientific misconduct
Brazilian Academy of Sciences	"d. **Self-plagiarism** or republication of already published scientific results, as if they were new, without informing previous publication." (Academia Brasileira de Ciências, 2013, p. 11)	Definition	Scientific misconduct
CNPq	"More difficult to correct are the problems arising from plagiarism, where the true author, whether of discoveries or texts, may have its merit subtracted with possible professional losses." (Conselho Nacional de Desenvolvimento Científico e Tecnológico, 2011, p. 2)	Explanation	Scientific misconduct

CNPq	"In addition to such damaging consequences of counterfeiting and plagiarism, such practices may unduly favor their authors in order to gain advantages in their careers and in obtaining financial aid. In relation to this, the growing practice of self-plagiarism." (Conselho Nacional de Desenvolvimento Científico e Tecnológico, 2011, p. 2)	Explanation	Scientific misconduct
CNPq	"The existence of software capable of identifying already published excerpts from submitted manuscripts has facilitated the prevention of plagiarism and self-plagiarism." (Conselho Nacional de Desenvolvimento Científico e Tecnológico, 2011, p. 2)	Guidance	Prevention
CNPq	"Plagiarism: consists in the presentation, as if it were of its authorship, of results or conclusions previously obtained by another author, as well as of integral texts or of a substantial part of other texts without the care detailed in the Guidelines. It is also a plagiarism that uses ideas or data obtained in analyzes of unpublished manuscripts or manuscripts to which he had access as a consultant, reviser, editor, or the like." (Conselho Nacional de Desenvolvimento Científico e Tecnológico, 2011, p. 4)	Definition	Scientific misconduct
CNPq	"Self-plagiarism: consists of the total or partial presentation of texts already published by the same author, without due references to previous works." (Conselho Nacional de Desenvolvimento Científico e Tecnológico, 2011, p. 4)	Definition	Scientific misconduct
CNPq	"7: In order to avoid any characterization of self-plagiarism, the use of texts and previous works of the own author must be indicated, with the appropriate references and quotations." (Conselho Nacional de Desenvolvimento Científico e Tecnológico, 2011, p. 5)	Guidance	Prevention
FAPESP	"(c) *Plagiarism*, or the use of verbal, oral or written ideas or formulations of others without expressly and clearly giving them credit, so as to reasonably generate the perception that they are ideas or formulations of own authorship." (Fundação de Amparo à Pesquisa do Estado de São Paulo, 2014, p. 31)	Definition	Scientific misconduct
FAPESP	"Any allegation of fabrication, forgery or plagiarism (as defined in section 3 above) should be considered as a claim of serious scientific misconduct." (Fundação de Amparo à Pesquisa do Estado de São Paulo, 2014, p. 40)	Explanation	Scientific misconduct

From the content analysis, it was possible to identify the presence, in the analyzed sections, of three categories: Definition, Explanation and Guidance. The "Definition" category refers to the manifestation of the concept presented by codes of good scientific practice when referring to plagiarism and self-plagiarism. The category "Explanation", in turn, manifests the intelligibility of the Codes about good and bad scientific practices. Finally, the category "Guidance" refers to the guiding behaviors that researchers and scientists must observe when they carry out their activities, as well as to refer to software capable of preventing plagiarism and guiding corrective measures.

The Explanation category had four occurrences: one in the ABC document, two in CNPq and one in FAPESP. The subcategories identified in this case are related to cases of scientific misconduct, where situations are described about plagiarism and self-plagiarism, along with other conducts, such as fabrication and falsification of data. The Definition category, in turn, occurred five times, two in the ABC document, two in CNPq and one in FAPESP. While ABC and CNPq defined plagiarism and self-plagiarism, FAPESP defined only plagiarism. The identified subcategory was also Scientific Misconduct, because all definitions describe those behaviors.

The Guidance category occurred twice. Both are included in the document CNPq, where it is mentioned the use of softwares identifiers of excerpts from previously published texts and the use of references and citations as forms of prevention and combat to plagiarism. Both the use of the software and the use of references and quotations were included in the subcategory Prevention, since it is understood that both are measures that aim to curb the practice of plagiarism.

Thus, the most frequent category was Definition, which reveals the concern of the institutions to clarify precisely behaviors incompatible with scientific practice. The most frequent subcategory, in turn, was Scientific Misconduct, which occurred four times in conjunction with the Explanation category and five times in the Definition category, thus demonstrating the emphasis of codes of ethics and scientific conduct in clarifying and defining, respectively, behavior that undermines good scientific practice.

5. CONCLUSION

The growing use of technological tools for access and use of information combined with promotion criteria and academic merit based on the number of publications has contributed to the occurrence of behaviors hitherto difficult to identify in science, as plagiarism. The growing concern with plagiarism therefore mobilized actors in the scientific community to take action to prevent or at least minimize the impacts from such behavior in order to ensure the integrity of themselves. Research promotion agencies, as responsible for the distribution of public funds for the development and advancement of science, have devoted themselves to the publication of codes of ethics and scientific conduct that provide guidelines for promoting good scientific practice.

Regarding the plagiarism, the analysis of three Brazilian codes made possible to infer that the emphasis is on the definition and explanation of behavior incompatible with scientific work. ABC's document, for instance, defines plagiarism and self-plagiarism and explains that such behaviors, combined with the fabrication and falsification of data, as well as inattention to good scientific practices, are compromising in science. CNPq's document, in turn, also defines plagiarism and self-plagiarism, putting them side by side to other behaviors and situations harmful to the researcher. It is emphasized that it is the only document that provides guidelines on prevention of plagiarism, namely: the use of software identifiers and the use of references and citations. Finally, FAPESP's document defines only plagiarism and clarifies that along with manufacturing and falsification, it must also be considered scientific misconduct.

In order to better educate researchers, the documents analyzed should provide information to help them prevent and combat plagiarism. These guidelines are relevant to provide researchers with autonomy in decision-making in situations that are confronted with ethically unacceptable scientific behavior. It is therefore hoped that future editions of the documents will present such guidelines in order to promote good scientific practice and thus contribute not only to the development and advancement of science, but to spread ethics throughout society, which is the main beneficiary of science.

Last but not least, it is important to highlight that those tools for good scientific practice are not able to avoid plagiarism by themselves. For this, and educational approach is not only necessary but mandatory, by including the teaching of scientific good practices into the undergraduate and graduate programs, through an effective use of the mentioned tools.

REFERENCES

Academia Brasileira de Ciências (2013). *Rigor e integridade na condução da pesquisa científica: guia de recomendações de práticas responsáveis*. Rio de Janeiro: Academia Brasileira de Ciências. Retrieved from http://www.abc.org.br/IMG/pdf/doc-4311.pdf

Alves, A. P. M. (2016). *Competência informacional e o uso ético da informação na produção científica: o papel do bibliotecário na produção intelectual no ambiente acadêmico* (Doctoral dissertation). Faculdade de Filosofia e Ciências, Universidade Estadual Paulista, Marília. Retrieved from http://hdl.handle.net/11449/143419

Alves, A. P. M., Casarin, H. D. C. S., & Fernandéz Molina, J. C. (2016). Uso ético da informação e combate ao plágio: olhares para as bibliotecas universitárias brasileiras. *Informação & Sociedade: Estudos*, 26(1). Retrieved from http://www.periodicos.ufpb.br/ojs2/index.php/ies/article/view/27444/15531

Bardin, L. (2009). *Análise de conteúdo*. Lisboa: Edições 70.

Canalli, W. M., Silva, R. P., & Canalli, T. L. M. (2018). *Direitos autorais: uma breve história*. Retrieved from http://www.hcte.ufrj.br/downloads/sh/sh5/trabalhos%20orais%20completos/trabalho_046.pdf

Conselho Nacional de Desenvolvimento Científico e Tecnológico (2011). *Relatório da Comissão de Integridade de Pesquisa do CNPq*. Brasília: CNPq. Retrieved from http://www.cnpq.br/documents/10157/a8927840-2b8f-43b9-8962-5a2ccfa74dda

Fundação de Amparo à Pesquisa do Estado de São Paulo (2014). *Código de boas práticas científicas*. São Paulo: FAPESP. Retrieved from http://www.fapesp.br/boaspraticas/FAPESP-Codigo_de_Boas_Praticas_Cientificas_2014.pdf

Garschagen, B. (2006). *Universidade em tempos de plágio. EAD-L* [lista de discussão na internet]. Campinas: Unicamp/Centro de Computação. Retrieved from https://www.listas.unicamp.br/pipermail/ead-l/2006-January/068244.html

Guimarães, J. A. (2018). *Propetip 11: o plágio na produção acadêmica*. Retrieved from https://www2.unesp.br/portal#!/prope/apoio-ao-pesquisador/propetips/propetip-11/

Kirkpatrick, K. (2001). *Evitando plágio*. Retrieved from https://edisciplinas.usp.br/pluginfile.php/352423/mod_resource/content/1/O%20que%20%C3%A9%20pl%C3%A1gio.pdf

Krokoscz, M. (2014). A ditadura do plágio e a obsessão pela citação. *Revista da Rede de Enfermagem do Nordeste*, 15(4), 557-558. Retrieved from http://www.redalyc.org/articulo.oa?id=324032212001

UN General Assembly (1948). *Universal Declaration of Human Rights* (217 [III] A). Paris. Retrieved from http://www.onu.org.br/img/2014/09/DUDH.pdf

16
Understanding the Concept of Plagiarism among Iranian Students

Asefeh Asemi
Marzieh Sadat Hosseini

1. INTRODUCTION

A glimpse on the history of plagiarism shows that this phenomenon has an old history, and comes in a variety of shapes and methods. This phenomenon is continually undergoing change due the influence of the ICTs, and increasing importance of research and publication in gaining social status. Plagiarism means using a person or other people's work or ideas without citing them. In other words, when someone uses the writings of others without any citation in his/her writing, he/she commits plagiarism. Plagiarism can occur consciously or unconsciously. "When you really understand how to draw on other people's ideas and words, then the problem of plagiarism just disappears. It will be your own work that you hand in and you will get credit for it. You will be confident of your ability to write from sources and your tutors will feel the same" (Williams and Carroll, 2009). This is a very important issue in research processes, particularly at the level of higher education. Plagiarism of text can occur in a variety of forms. Hamp-Lyons and Courter (1984) have presented four major types of plagiarism, including outright copying, paraphrase plagiarism, patchwork plagiarism and stealing an apt term. The first type occurs when someone copies the other's record word by word and use it in his/her own writings, without any citation. In the second type, he/she changes some words and grammar of other person's writings and takes advantage of them in his/her writings. In the third type, portions of the work of others are used by the person. He/she sticks these portions together in a way which are related to his/her writings. The fourth type of plagiarism is when the person only uses short meaningful terms from another person in his writings because he/she considers them very good and associated with his/her text (Hamp-Lyons and Courter, 1984). In order to understand the various forms of plagiarism and prevent its occurrences consciously and unconsciously in the scientific literature, culture making and informing all writers is very important. Given that master and doctoral students are the most important groups in researching and writing scientific text, the ILS experts should be pioneer due to their field. With this aim the current research has investigated the understanding of plagiarism among Iranian ILS master student. Based on former studies there are different types of plagiarism. In the current research, it is tried to look at the understanding of five common types of plagiarism, described below, among ILS master student based on scientific literature: a. Outright copying; b. Paraphrase plagiarism; c. Patchwork plagiarism; d. Stealing an apt term; e. Self-plagiarism.

2. RESEARCH BACKGROUND

So far various studies have been conducted on the concept of plagiarism and its various dimensions. Following are some of the researchers whose subjects are associated with this work and are presented as background research. Among them, there is research by Khoshroo (2011) that examines the personal and situational reasons of plagiarism among Iranian master students of English language. The results showed that plagiarism is quite common among these students and they do not have an adequate understanding of different types of plagiarism. Also, there wasn't any significant correlation between the prevalence of plagiarism and demographic variables such as age and sex, and each variable such as college GPA, amount of working hours for weekly earnings, and insistence for high school grades. However, prevalence of plagiarism is negatively correlated with understanding of plagiarism and perceived seriousness. The main reasons for committing plagiarism by students are mainly related to educational issues. Azade (2009) in his article entitled "Examining the accuracy of citation in PhD thesis papers at Tehran University of Medical Sciences" studied the accuracy of citation of articles and their concordance with Vancouver Style in Tehran University of Medical Sciences' PhD theses. The findings showed that out of 357 citations just 136 citations were invoked without any citation errors, and only 35 citations had full compliance with the Vancouver style sheets. Also reasons such as lack of awareness about the importance and station of citations' homogeneity in scientific literature, students' carelessness in preparing citations, lack of access to primary sources and copying from other sources, lack of teachers' emphasis on the correctness of the citations, deficiency in paying attention to citations provided in the thesis by educational institutions, lack of benefiting from consulting expert librarians, and unfamiliarity with resource management software, cause errors of citation in thesis. Marshall and Garry (2006) examined English-speaking and non-English speaking students' understanding of intellectual property, plagiarism and copyright in particular, and found the differences between them in a research entitled "NESB and ESB students' attitudes and perceptions of plagiarism". The results showed that although plagiarism is more likely among non-English speaking students, in general it is very common among students. It indicated that students are not committed to the content they receive from the Internet and correct citation to them, and the cases of plagiarism are vague and unclear for them. Bradinova (2006) in his thesis titled "Exploring students and university teachers' perceptions of plagiarism" examined the University students and educators' understanding of plagiarism. The results showed that there aren't significant differences between students and teachers in understanding the meaning of plagiarism and attitude towards strategies to prevent it in terms of sex and age. Also, students who speak English and other languages understand the same concept of plagiarism and apply the same strategies to combat it. Yeo (2007) in a research titled "First-year university science and engineering students' understanding of plagiarism" examined the first-year university science and engineering students' understanding of plagiarism. Results showed that although students can provide a definition of plagiarism, they are not always and in all cases able to recognize its domain. Also some examples of plagiarism were regarded as less serious than others and in contradiction with the institution's policy. Students also generally favored more lenient penalties than provided for by policy. Therefore, first-year students have lots of problems with the understanding of plagiarism and its range, and should gain more information about academic honesty, plagiarism and should understand how to use knowledge of others. Ryan (2009) in a research titled "Undergraduate and Postgraduate Pharmacy Students' Perceptions of Plagiarism and Academic Honesty" examines the awareness and understanding of the policies for plagiarism in university and related penalties for its first and second commitment, among undergraduate and postgraduate students in pharmaceutical science. Findings indicated that students don't perceive plagiarism as a serious issue and the use of inappropriate strategies for sourcing and acknowledging material is common. Sentleng (2012) in a thesis titled "Plagiarism among undergraduate students in the Faculty of Applied Science at a South African higher education institution" investigated the reasons of tendency to plagiarism and awareness of organizational policies and existing guidance on Plagiarism in undergraduate students. The results showed that plagiarism among college undergraduate students in chemistry and mathematics are relatively common. 41 percent of the students considered plagiarism as a serious and important issue, but are still committing this. Also, 71 percent of students use the Internet for their homework, which probably is one of the most important resources in the incidence of plagiarism. Books and magazines can also be other resources that cause plagiarism among students. Sarlauskiene and Stabingis (2014) in a research titled "Understanding of plagiarism by the students in HEIs of Lithuania" revealed that students themselves confidently say they know what plagiarism is, but empirical study showed that understanding of plagiarism among participating students' is unambiguous as it is stated and in analyzed scientific publications, and this understanding does not satisfy academic community. Comprehensive and clear definition of plagiarism and its various types with practical examples could help the academic community to develop plagiarism prevention. Gunnarsson, Wlodek and Pettersson (2014) in a paper titled "Teaching international students how to avoid plagiarism: librarians and faculty in collaboration" indicated that international master students need basic education on how to cite and reference properly in order to avoid plagiarism. They have also found that the continued collaboration between the teacher and the librarian can approach the issue of correct use information from different points of view. Abdia, Idrisa, Alguliyevb and Liguliyevb (2015) in a paper titled "PDLK: Plagiarism detection using linguistic knowledge" presented a method to detect external plagiarism using the integration of semantic relations between words and their syntactic composition. They believed this method can improve the performance of plagiarism detection because it is able to avoid selecting the source text sentence whose similarity with suspicious text sentence is high but its meaning is different. The study of Chen and Chou (2015) aimed to respond to the growing educational concerns about plagiarism by comparing the perceptions held by faculty and college students. The results reveal that most students with an Arts or Communication major held a relatively adverse thinking toward plagiarism. Last, this study provides research-based strategies for school and faculty to reduce the likelihood of plagiarism. Babaii and Nejadghanbar (2017) investigated the ability of Iranian students of applied linguistics to discern plagiarism in writing, their perceptions of its ethical aspects, their characterizations of plagiarists, and their perspectives on why they commit plagiarism. It is concluded that they regarded unfamiliarity with the concept and nature of plagiarism as the main reason for committing it. Chien (2017) investigated Taiwanese college students' perceptions of plagiarism. Specifically, this study seeks to explore how perceptive students pursuing higher education in Taiwan are in recognizing plagiaristic writing, in what terms they perceive source use in writing as appropriate and inappropriate, and view why plagiarism occurs. Most of the students participating in the study had some basic understanding of plagiarism. They had some familiarity with the Western notion of plagiarism, but based on the writing exercise, more often than not they were not able to recognize plagiarism when it actually occurred. Students' understanding was generally, but not entirely, consistent with their source use behavior. More than half of the students considered that plagiarism is a cultural issue. However, there are also other factors that may lead to plagiarism. Cosma et. al. (2017) conducted a research with home students undertaking computing and joint computing subject degrees at higher education institutions throughout the UK, China, and South Cyprus. The survey results revealed that although students who were informed about plagiarism better understood what actions constitute plagiarism, some topics were still unclear among students regardless of the students' educational background and whether they had been previously informed about plagiarism. Kam, Hue, and Cheung (2017) investigated the secondary school students regarding academic plagiarism in Hong Kong. The participants were 257 Grade 10 and 11 students who were taking liberal studies. Quantitative analysis showed that the students were unfamiliar with what actions constituted plagiarism. The best predictor of attitudes was the perceived descriptive norm regarding plagiarism (i.e., perception of the frequency of plagiarism in one's environment). According to studies, different researches have been conducted about understanding and knowledge of academic honesty and plagiarism among students in different disciplines and different academic levels. But no research has been conducted on the understanding of the plagiarism in knowledge and information science master students in Iran. Therefore, this study investigates the Iranian KIS master students' understanding of five types of plagiarism, including outright copying, paraphrase plagiarism, patchwork plagiarism, stealing an apt term, self-plagiarism.

3. RESEARCH THEORETICAL FRAMEWORK

Knowledge and information professionals have an important mission in the realization of various forms of plagiarism and prevent it to occur consciously and unconsciously in the scientific literature. One of their most important tasks is culture making and sufficient informing of all writers in this case. Therefore, before any action, we should check the professionals' understanding of plagiarism. The existing level of librarians and professionals' understanding of plagiarism would be clarified by the examination of their understanding of this concept. These results can be used to detect the gap between existing and desired condition. As long as professionals remain unaware of their existing status, they cannot properly plan to achieve the desired status. The current study is conducted to meet this goal so that it can be a guide for information professionals for successful making of a plagiarism-free culture in this field. If the scientific community wants to improve academic honesty, they must first attempt to train specialists in this field and make pervasive the basic concepts of academic honesty and plagiarism by the training given to them. Many components can be considered and evaluated in the examination of master students in KIS' understanding of plagiarism. According to research background and component studied in earlier studies by researchers to find students' knowledge and understanding of plagiarism, five types of plagiarism have been studied in this study. This section briefly describes the five components have been discussed above.

3.1. Outright Copying

Outright copying means to copy the direct word of the other person's work/research without mentioning his/her name as a source (Mirdehghan, 2009, 11). To prevent this type of plagiarism, we should note the following:

- Whenever we want to use the exact phrase or sentence from someone in our writings, it must be placed inside quotation marks, and then its source must be mentioned;
- Whenever we want to add an explanation to a direct Quotation, we should put it inside quotation mark;
- Whenever we want to use an exact paragraph in our writings, we should shrink the font size, use indented words and put them in quotation marks;
- The last point about outright copying is that we can only bring a certain amount of a source identically in our writings. For example, according to American Psychological Association Writing Style rules, only 11 lines can be literally brought in your writings in a direct quote from a dissertation or book.

3.2. Paraphrase Plagiarism

In this type of plagiarism, the person doesn't copy the source directly, but changes the sentences and rewrites the paragraph a little without citing the original author (Sotude, 2010, p 33). To prevent this type of plagiarism, we should note the following:

- For indirect quotation of a sentence or phrase in our writings, we must act in a way that the original concept remains; at the same time, we should use our own words to express subject, instead of copying the text;
- In an indirect quote, the changed sentences and phrases should not be much longer or shorter than the original text, but they should be about the same length of the original text;

- Another point is that in the indirect quotation of words or sentences from a writer who has taken them from another source, the main author of the article with the name of the author who adapted from him/her should be mention;
- In an indirect quote, when we want to get several writers' sentences together, we should bring our meaningful sentences between sentences to connect them to each other, and offer citation just when we use the exact sentences;
- The other thing about indirect quotations that it should be noted is that in such cases, only a certain percentage of resources can be used and referred to in our posts.

3.3. Patchwork Plagiarism

In Patchwork plagiarism, the writer copies the important parts of several different sources and makes minor variation in sentences and sticks them together in such a way that is related (Sotude, 2010, p 33). For example, if we want to bring the sentences of different authors in our writings, we shouldn't change the meaning of sentences or the number and combination of words, but we should stick them together –with the citation- so that they'd be coordinated with our text. In quotation of various authors' sentences and to prevent this type of plagiarism, we should:

- Not change/manipulate the others' sentences and not to present them as a new knowledge;
- Specify parts of the text that are taken from other texts exactly and referring to them;
- Not distort the concept and meaning of sentences taken from the works of others;
- Not stick various texts together so that their joint message will disappear.

3.4. Stealing an Apt Term

In stealing an apt term, the writer uses the short meaningful statements made by others in his/her works, because he/she considers them relevant to his/her writing, without referring to the original text (Hamp-Lyons and Courter, 1984). To prevent this type of plagiarism, noting the following points are necessary:

- Referring to the original text - even if it is very short term - with proper Citations within the text;
- Not to change the meaning of terms used and their analysis;
- Using footnotes in order to refer to the main text.

3.5. Self-plagiarism

In self-plagiarism, the researcher uses data, findings of his/her earlier published writings to present a new article and does not tell readers of the formerly published article (Khaki Sedigh, 2010, p39). To prevent this type of plagiarism, we should note the following:

- Not to submit a paper written with the same data simultaneously over a magazine (parallel submit);

- Not to combine two or more of published articles in conferences in order to publish a new paper in the another conference;
- Referring to former and primary articles in our new articles, and citing them clearly;
- Not to change the former articles' data and publish it as a new paper (extension publish);
- Not to publish fragmented data from one of the earlier studies in separate papers (research fraction).

4. RESEARCH METHODOLOGY

Method of this research was descriptive-survey. In this research, researcher-made questionnaire is used for data collection, to achieve the objectives of study by answering its' questions. The statistical population of the study consisted of all KIS master students in Iran. For data collection, the web-based questionnaires were sent to all members of a special discussion group of KIS in the Ferdowsi University of Mashhad, after validity and reliability confirmation. After two months, 200 students randomly filled the questionnaire and were selected as statistical sample. After data collection, data analysis was performed at two levels: descriptive statistics and inferential level. For descriptive data analysis frequency distribution tables and relevant charts were used, and in inferential level, one sample t-test for equality of the mean of a variable with a hypothetical mean was used.

5. RESEARCH RESULTS

Answers were analyzed based on data obtained from 5 main components of study and 14 questions in multiple options formats. In this analysis, means in each part were compared with a number of correct choices to find the Iranian KIS master students' understanding of plagiarism. Results are presented below in descriptive and inferential level.

5.1. Data description

Percentages of correct answers to questions of Iranian KIS master students' understanding of components respectively discussed are showed below:

Table 1. Descriptive findings of examining the Iranian KIS master students' understanding of research components

Results	% Correct Answers to the Questions	Components
Less than Average	47/6%	Outright Copying
Less than Average	30/1%	Paraphrase Plagiarism
More than Average	66/3%	Patchwork Plagiarism
More than Average	58/8%	Stealing an Apt Term
More than Average	70/87%	Self-Plagiarism

5.2. Data inference

5.2.1 Iranian KIS master students' understanding of outright copying

Five questions - with five correct options – were put in the questionnaire in order to investigate the Iranian KIS master students' understanding of outright copying. Based on the results showed in Table (2) the probability is 0/179 and is more than 0/05, and Zero hypothesis is not rejected in this significance level. Therefore we can confirm that students score at least half the optimal score for an understanding of outright copying concept.

Table 2. T-test for examining the Iranian KIS master students' understanding of outright copying

Variable	Probability	Test Parameter	mean	df
Understanding of Outright Copying	0/179	-1/349	2/38	199

5.2.2. Iranian KIS master students' understanding of paraphrase plagiarism

Five questions - with six correct options – were put in the questionnaire in order to investigate the Iranian KIS master students' understanding of paraphrase plagiarism. Based on the results showed in Table (3) probability is 0/000 and less than 0/05 and Zero hypotheses are rejected in this significance level. Also, the mean is 2/26 and it is less than 3. Therefore, we can confirm that students score less than half of optimal score for an understanding of paraphrase plagiarism concept.

Table 3. T-test for examining the Iranian KIS master students' understanding of paraphrase plagiarism

Variable	Probability	Test Parameter	mean	df
Understanding of Paraphrase Plagiarism	0/000	-10/176	2/26	199

5.2.3. Iranian KIS master students' understanding of patchwork plagiarism

Two questions - with four correct options – were put in the questionnaire in order to investigate the Iranian KIS master students' understanding of patchwork plagiarism. Based on the results showed in Table (4) the probability is 0/000 and less than 0/05 and Zero hypotheses are rejected in this significance level. Also, the mean is 2/37 and more than 2. Therefore, we can confirm that Students score a little more than half of the optimal score for an understanding of patchwork plagiarism concept.

Table 4. T-test for examining the Iranian KIS master students' understanding of patchwork plagiarism

Variable	Probability	Test Parameter	mean	df
Understanding of Patchwork Plagiarism	0/000	5/305	2/37	199

5.2.4. Iranian KIS master students' understanding of stealing an apt term

Two questions - with four correct options – were put in the questionnaire in order to investigate the Iranian KIS master students' understanding of stealing an apt term. Based on the results showed in Table (5) the probability is 0/673 and less than 0/05 and Zero hypotheses are not rejected in this significance level. Therefore, we can confirm that students score at least half the optimal score for an understanding of stealing an apt term concept.

Table 5. T-test for examining the Iranian KIS master students' understanding of stealing an apt term

Variable	Probability	Test Parameter	mean	df
Understanding of Stealing an Apt Term	0/673	-0/423	1/97	199

5.2.5. Iranian KIS master students' understanding of self-plagiarism

One question - with three correct options – was put in the questionnaire in order to investigate the Iranian KIS master students' understanding of self-plagiarism. Based on the results showed in Table (6) the probability is 0/000 and less than 0/05 and Zero hypotheses are rejected in this significance level. Also, the mean is 1/26 and less than 1/5. Therefore, we can confirm that Students score less than half of optimal score for an understanding of self-plagiarism concept.

Table 6. T-test for examining the Iranian KIS master students' understanding of self-plagiarism

Variable	Probability	Test Parameter	mean	df
Understanding of Self-Plagiarism	0/000	-4/299	1/26	199

5.2.6. The overall objective of the research: Iranian KIS master students' understanding of plagiarism concept

Overall, based on the results showed in Table (7) the probability is 0/000 and less than 0/05 and Zero hypotheses are rejected in this significance level. Also, the mean is 10/17 and less than 11. Therefore, we can confirm that students score less than half of optimal score for an understanding of plagiarism concept.

Table 7. T-test for examining the Iranian KIS master students' understanding of plagiarism concept

Variable	Probability	Test Parameter	mean	df
Understanding of Self-Plagiarism	0/000	-3/63	10/77	199

6. EXPLANATION, ANALYSIS AND CONCLUSION

Iranian KIS master students' understanding of plagiarism concept is a little less than the desired level. Findings of Yeo's research about First-year university science and engineering students' understanding of plagiarism in 2007 shows that although students can give a definition of plagiarism they are not always and in all cases able to recognize its domain. Also, they have lots of problems with understanding of plagiarism and its range. These findings are consistent with results of the current study. Also, Marshall and Garry (2006) showed that plagiarism is very common among students, and students have no commitment to the content they receive from the Internet, and the concept of plagiarism is vague and unclear to them. These results are consistent with the findings current studies too. Findings of Ryan's research in 2009 showed that Undergraduate and Postgraduate Pharmacy Students' understanding of Plagiarism and Academic Honesty is very poor and students use inappropriate strategies for a citation to sources and others' work. These findings confirm the results of current study too. Results of Sentleng's research in 2012 about plagiarism among undergraduate-students shows that Plagiarism among these students is common and just 41 percent of them considered plagiarism as a serious and important issue. These results are consistent with the current studies' findings too. Many studies, conducted in recent years worldwide about students' understanding of plagiarism concept, show that their understanding is relatively low. This problem can be related to weakness of their training and their unfamiliarity with the concept of plagiarism. Concepts related to plagiarism and how to avoid it are not taught in any of their courses completely and clearly. A few courses that can familiarize students with correct methods of Citations are scientific writing methods, research methods, research seminars and similar courses and issues. These however have a very limited impact on awareness of students. Academic pressure on students to offer written assignment regardless of the scientific criteria and contents' authenticity are some of the reasons for students' little familiarity with concepts of plagiarism and citation. Inability to write and students' accustomedness to use others' work instead of thinking on the subject and then to write are other reasons for their plagiarism. Bad institutionalization of scientific fraud and misconduct among students and lack of adequate supervision by the professors and their Universities can be other reasons which make students feel no need to learn the issues related to plagiarism and do not attempt to learn about them. Also, lack of social patterns and expansion of social frauds and students' placing in such an environment can lead to lack of attention and need to learn about correct writing..

REFERENCES

Abdia, A., Idrisa, N., Alguliyevb, R.M., Aliguliyevb, R.M (2015). PDLK: Plagiarism detection using linguistic knowledge. *Expert Systems with Applications*, 42(22), 8936–8946. http://www.sciencedirect.com/science/article/pii/S0957417415005084

Azade, F., Gharib, M. & Wa'ez, R. (2009). Examining the accuracy of citation in PhD thesis papers at Tehran University of Medical Sciences [Persian]. *Payavard-e-Salamat*, 3 (1&2), 9-17. http://payavard.tums.ac.ir/article-1-119-fa.html

Babaii, E. and Nejadghanbar, H. (2017). Plagiarism among Iranian Graduate Students of Language Studies: Perspectives and Causes. *Ethics & Behavior*, 27(3). 240-258. www.tandfonline.com/doi/full/10.1080/10508422.2016.1138864

Bradinova, M. (2006). *Exploring students and university teachers' perceptions of plagiarism*. Unpublished doctoral dissertation, university of Pennsylvania, Indiana.

Chen, Y. and Chou, Ch. (2017). Are We on the Same Page? College Students' and Faculty's Perception of Student Plagiarism in Taiwan. *Ethics & Behavior*, 27(1). 53-73. www.tandfonline.com/doi/abs/10.1080/10508422.2015.1123630

Chien, Sh. (2017). Taiwanese College Students' Perceptions of Plagiarism: Cultural and Educational Considerations. *Ethics & Behavior*, 27(2). 118-139. https://doi.org/10.1080/10508422.2015.1136219

Cosma, G., Joy, M., Sinclair, J., Andreou, M., Zhang, D., Cook, B., and Boyatt, R. (2017). Perceptual Comparison of Source-Code Plagiarism within Students from UK, China, and South Cyprus Higher Education Institutions. *Trans. Comput. Educ.* 17(2). https://doi.org/10.1145/3059871

Gunnarsson, J., Wlodek J.K. & Pettersson, A. (2014). Teaching International Students How to Avoid Plagiarism: Librarians and Faculty in Collaboration. *Journal of Academic librarianship*, 40. 413-417. www.sciencedirect.com/science/article/pii/S0099133314000603

Hamp-Lyons, L. and Courter, K.B. (1984). *Research Matters*. Rowley, MA: Newbury House.

Kam, Ch.Ch.S., Hue, M.T., Cheung, H.Y. (2017). Plagiarism of Chinese Secondary School Students in Hong Kong. *Ethics & Behavior*, (0)0. 1-20. https://doi.org/10.1080/10508422.2017.1333909

Khaki Sedigh, A. (2010). *Introduction to research ethics and engineering ethics* [Persian].Tehran: Khaje Nasir University. ieee.org.ir/wp-content/uploads/2015/11/PlagiarismAwareness.pdf

Khoshroo, F. (2011). *Examination of the personal and situational reasons of plagiarism among Iranian master students of English language* [Persian]. Master's thesis. Library and information science. https://ganj.irandoc.ac.ir/articles/529605

Marshall, S., and Garry, M. (2006). NESB and ESB students' attitudes and perceptions of plagiarism. *International Journal for Educational Integrity*, 2(1), 26-37.

Mir Dehghan, M.N. (2009). Plagiarism: Prevention with education in the growth of research structure [Persian].*Mahname-e- Mohandesi Farhangi*, 4(33 & 34), 10-17. https://www.ojs.unisa.edu.au/index.php/IJEI/article/view/25

Ryan, G.,Bonanno H.,Krass, I.,Scouller, K., Smith, L. (2009).Undergraduate and Postgraduate Pharmacy Students' Perceptions of Plagiarism and Academic Honesty. *American Journal of Pharmacological Education*, 73(6), 105. https://www.ncbi.nlm.nih.gov/pmc/articles/PMC2769527

Sarlauskiene, L., Stabingis, L. (2014). Understanding of Plagiarism by the Students in HEIs of Lithuania. *Procedia - Social and Behavioral Sciences*, 110, 638–646. www.sciencedirect.com/science/article/pii/S1877042813055481

Sentleng, M. P. (2012). Plagiarism among undergraduate students in the Faculty of Applied Science at a South African higher education institution.*South African Journal of Libraries and Information Science*, 78(1). 57-67. http://dx.doi.org/10.7553/78-1-47

Sotude, H., Rafi', N., & Mirzai, Z. (2010). Look at the plagiarism and strategies for prevention and follow-up [Persian]. *Faslname-e- Ketabdari va Etela' resani*, 52, 27-50. http://www.sid.ir/Fa/Journal/ViewPaper.aspx?id=178694

Yeo, S. (2007). First-year university science and engineering students' understanding of plagiarism. *Higher Education Research & Development*, 26(2), 199-216. www.tandfonline.com/doi/pdf/10.1080/07294360701310813

Williams, K. and Carroll, R. (2009). *Referencing and Understanding Plagiarism*. China: Palgrave MacMillan. https://www.goodreads.com/book/show/8581387-referencing-and-understanding-plagiarism

17

Awareness and Attitude of Agricultural Students Towards Plagiarism

Nirmal Singh
Sanjeev Kumar
Dhiraj Kumar

1. INTRODUCTION

Academic integrity is of utmost importance to ensure and maintain the quality and standards of education and research. However, there are incidences when the work is copied crossing the limits of fair dealing, and without giving credit to the original author. This act of copying a work, wholly or partially, and then pretending to be its original author is called plagiarism (Icaza, 2007). According to Oxford Dictionary (2018) "plagiarism is the practice of taking someone else's work or ideas and passing them off as one's own". Stealing someone's original idea, whether using different wording or not, is just as severe of an offense of plagiarism (Charbonneau, 2018).

Plagiarism is a curse on academic integrity. This serious offense in academia is a major ethical concern attaining attention of intellectuals around the globe (Jeergal et al., 2015) (Rathore et al., 2015). Hu and Lei (2015) say that the grave academic misconduct of plagiarism is associated with condemnatory labels including deception, cheating, academic crime, intellectual dishonesty, etc. Even the world famous writers, journalists and thinkers, including William Shakespeare, Laurence Sterne, Samuel Taylor Coleridge, Oscar Wilde, Martin Luther King, Jr., George Harrison, Alex Haley and Jayson Blair, have been accused of copying others' writings in unethical ways (Hannah, 2015). However, with proliferation of literature and advancements in plagiarism detection tools, the increasing number of cases of plagiarism are being reported. Marshell and Garry (2005) went to say that "there hardly seems to be a day now that does not include the report of yet another incidence of plagiarism in either public or academic life". In present information age "students freely associate with information: hunt it, discover it and share it without much thought of Copyright" (Satija, 2015). However, the impact of the Internet on acts of plagiarism has been a debatable issue. On the one hand the easy availability and accessibility of information in multiple format over the Internet is being cited as a major reason for plagiarism (Murtaza et al., 2013) (Jones et al., 2010) (Ukpebor and Ogbebor, 2013). On the other hand, the plagiarism detection tools have made it possible to detect every bit of plagiarism. The laws/ regulations to handle the cases of plagiarism vary from nation to nation and even from institutions to institution. The unethical act of plagiarizing can lead to severe consequences including dismissal from universities and other research institutions, article rejections or retractions from journals, and decreased credibility as a researcher (Panter, 2018).

There may be various factors provoking the students to plagiarise including expectations of parents and teachers, pressure to score more, academic competition with others, hectic academic schedule, pressure to complete assignments within stipulated period, etc. Therefore, before coming up with a policy to curve plagiarism, it is important to know the awareness of students towards plagiarism, their perception and attitude towards this academic misconduct and the reasons behind their plagiarizing. A survey of students can be a useful step in this direction.

2. AN INTRODUCTION TO PUNJAB AGRICULTURAL UNIVERSITY, LUDHIANA

The Punjab Agricultural University, Ludhiana has its geneses to the small experimental farm established at Lyallpur, now in Pakistan in 1901. After partition of United India, following the loss of Lyallpur, Agricultural College and Research Institute was established at Amritsar in 1948.Later on, the college was shifted to Ludhiana. In 1962, it was upgraded to the status of Agricultural University with objective of serving the state of erstwhile Punjab. But in 1966, the erstwhile state of Punjab was divided into three states on linguistic grounds. As a result the Haryana Agricultural University was carved of Punjab Agricultural University by an act of the Parliament in February 1970. Similarly, Himachal Pradesh Krishi Vishvavidyalaya was established in July 1970. The PAU is also mother institution of Guru Angad Dev Veterinary & Animal Sciences University, Ludhiana as in 2006 the College of Veterinary Science, PAU was upgraded to become veterinary university. The campus of PAU is spread across 1510 acres of land. University is serving the integrated function of teaching, research and extension in agriculture, agricultural engineering, home science and allied disciplines. The university has played a significant role in in increasing food grain production in the state and was adjudged the 'Best Agricultural University' in 1995 for its exceptional accomplishments in agricultural research, education and extension. The university has four constituent colleges including College of Agriculture, College of Agricultural Engineering, College of Home Science and College of Basic Sciences & Humanities. Presently there are 3 schools and 32 departments in all four colleges offering 43 masters' and 29 Ph.D. programmes (http://web.pau.edu/index.php?_act=manageLink&DO=firstLink&intSubID=12)

3. REVIEW OF LITERATURE

Many studies have been conducted worldwide to ascertain the awareness, attitude and perceptions of academicians about plagiarism, reasons for plagiarizing and ways to prevent it. A review of selective studies found relevant for the present problem is given here:

Dawson and Overfield (2006) conducted a study of bioscience undergraduate students at ManchesterMetropolitanUniversity, United Kingdom to investigate students' perceptions of what constitutes plagiarism. The results of study revealed that students were uncertain about several aspects of plagiarism, including downloading of material from the Internet. Students were unclear about the boundaries between plagiarism and acceptable practice. Similar results of confusion about many aspects of plagiarism were found among students of University of Florida by Radunovich *et al* (2009). Sarlauskienea and Stabingisa (2014), in a survey of 119 students from various universities in Lithuania also found that though students claimed to have understanding of plagiarism, but only a few were able to describe it properly.

Students of public and private universities of Pakistan had a low level of awareness about plagiarism and university plagiarism policies (Ramzan *et al*, 2012). Many respondents even admitted to have plagiarized written materials intentionally. Plagiarism was also found as a critical problem among students of two universities of Tanzania (Anney and Mosha, 2015). Though the students had an understanding of plagiarism, but they still copied from other sources without acknowledging the original authors. The access of the Internet, shortage of books, student's laziness and poor academic writing skills were found to be the main reasons to plagiarize. The study recommended software for detecting plagiarism. In a similar study of students and teachers of Stockholm University, lack of interest in the topic of study was found as one of the common reasons to plagiarize (Razera, 2011) and it was recommended to design the course in an attractive way. This study also reported some differences regarding what is allowed and not allowed in terms of plagiarism. Introduction of course on academic writing can play a vital role in prevention of plagiarism among students as a statistically significant difference was found in plagiarism behaviour after the article writing workshop between participating and non-participating students in Tarbiat Modares University (Fealy *et al*, 2015).

The above studies reveal the gap in knowledge of students towards plagiarism. Researchers found various reasons for this immoral act.

4. PURPOSE OF STUDY

The study aimed to find the followings:

1. The attitude of agricultural students toward plagiarism.
2. Their perceptions about plagiarism and
3. To suggest the methods and ways to discourage and reduce the academic plagiarism

5. METHODOLOGY

The descriptive survey design was used to investigate the awareness, attitude and perception of agricultural students towards plagiarism pursuing postgraduate programmes at Punjab Agricultural University, Ludhiana. The academicians have developed various tools to examine the perceptions of students and researchers about plagiarism. For the purpose of present study, a part of the questionnaire developed by Razera (2011) was adopted. The questionnaire consisted of three sections. Section-A aimed to collect the demographic information of students including their year of study, gender, age and academic performance in terms of Overall Credit Point Average (OCPA). Section-B comprised of nine statements aimed to know the attitude of students towards plagiarism. Section C consisted of statements to know the perceptions of students towards plagiarism and means and ways to overcome this academic blasphemy.

Purposive sampling method was used for selecting the sample of study. Copies of questionnaire were distributed to total 200 postgraduate students of Punjab Agricultural University, Ludhiana, during their visit to University Library. In section B, respondents were required to give responses for each of the nine statements on five point Likert scale representing the degree of their agreement with the statements. The responses for these statements were assigned scores for data analysis. Total 122 copies of questionnaire were received back as complete and relevant for analysis leading to the response rate of 61%. The data were analyzed using percentage, frequencies and via Statistical Package for Social Sciences (SPSS). The t-test was applied to assess the difference between opinion of students towards statements to examine their attitude towards plagiarism based on their gender and year of postgraduate programme. The correlation coefficient was arrived at to find the correlation between attitude of students towards plagiarism, their age and academic performance as depicted by their OCPA.

6. DISCUSSION AND ANALYSIS

6.1. Demographics details of respondents

The total 122 respondents comprised of 78 (63.93%) students pursuing first year of postgraduate programmes and 44 (36.07%) students of second year of post-graduation. Of the respondents, 80 (65.58%) were males and 42 (34.42%) were females. Age of students varied from between 20 to 36 years, including 108 students (88.52%) in the age group of 20-25 years and 14 (11.48%) students ageing above 25 years. Three (2.45%) students had OCPA <6; 22 (18.03%) had between 6-7; 62 (50.81%) had 7-8 and the OCPA of remaining 35 (28.69%) students varied 8-9.

6.2. Attitude about plagiarism

The data collection tool consisted of nine statements to know the attitude of students towards plagiarism. The students were required to choose one option out of the five available from 'Strongly Disagree' to 'Strongly Agree' for each statement. The responses of the students for each statement are presented in table 1:

Table 1. Attitude of students towards plagiarism

S. No.	Statement	SD	D	NAD	A	SA
1	To buy an essay from a so-called "paper mill" (an Internet site which sells papers) and hand the paper in as if it was yours	25 (20.49)	19 (15.57)	18 (14.75)	34 (27.87)	26 (21.31)
2	To submit someone else's work as if it was yours	35 (28.69)	14 (11.48)	11 (9.02)	18 (14.75)	44 (36.07)
3	To submit an essay that a friend wrote and gave you the permission to use it as if it was yours	12 (9.84)	30 (24.59)	34 (27.87)	34 (27.87)	12 (9.84)
4	To literally take a piece of text from a book and submit it in as yours without indicating a source	22 (18.03)	22 (18.03)	21 (17.21)	28 (22.95)	29 (23.77)
5	To take a piece from a known source, then make some small language changes in the text, but only indicate the source (i.e. no reference in the text)	6 (4.92)	34 (27.87)	30 (24.59)	41 (33.61)	11 (9.02)
6	To use most of the content from someone else's original text but change the order. There is a reference in the text (e.g. Sjögren, 1999) and the original source appears in a list.	17 (13.93)	17 (13.93)	28 (22.95)	41 (33.61)	19 (15.57)
7	To write a paragraph by bringing together shorter pieces of 10-15 words from a number of various sources and add some of your own words to form a paragraph. All original sources listed in the list without reference to the text	13 (10.66)	30 (24.59)	29 (23.77)	31 (25.41)	19 (15.57)
8	To extract your main points from a text you read, but write it in your own words. The new version looks different, both in detail and because it uses different examples. A reference to the text (e.g. Sjögren, 1999) is used and the original source is listed in the bibliography.	26 (21.31)	25 (20.49)	17 (13.93)	32 (26.23)	22 (18.03)
9	To quote a paragraph as well as to italicize it and cite the source with a PAGE REFERENCE in the text, in a footnote and in the bibliography.	25 (20.49)	23 (18.85)	17 (13.93)	35 (28.69)	22 (18.03)

The statements at serial numbers 1 to 7 represented the cases of plagiarism. For statement 1 i.e. 'To buy an essay from a so-called "paper mill" (an Internet site which sells papers) and hand the paper in as if it was yours', 49.18% students either agreed or strongly agreed that it is a case of plagiarism. Around 14.75% students neither agreed nor disagreed for the statement. Remaining 36.06% respondents either disagreed or strongly disagreed to accept the statement as a case of plagiarism. Similarly 50.82% students either agreed or strongly agreed that 'To submit someone else's work as if it was yours' is a clear example of plagiarism. On the other hand, only 37.71 respondents agreed or strongly agreed that 'To submit an essay that a friend wrote and gave you the permission to use it as if it was yours' represents plagiarism. Nearly 27.87% students were not sure if it is a case of plagiarism or not. Around 46.72% students agreed/ strongly agreed with statement 4 i.e. 'To literally take a piece of text from a book and submit it in as yours without indicating a source' to be a case of plagiarism. With respect to statement 5 'To take a piece from a known source, then make some small language changes in the text, but only indicate the source (i.e. no reference in the text)', 42.63% students accepted it as representing a case of plagiarism. Similarly for statement 6, i. e. 'To use most of the content from someone else's original text but change the order. There is a reference in the text (e.g. Sjögren, 1999) and the original source appears in a list.' and statement 7 'To write a paragraph by bringing together shorter pieces of 10-15 words from a number of various sources and add some of your own words to form a paragraph. All original sources listed in the list without reference to the text', 49.18% and 40.98% either agreed or strongly agreed for these to be depicting plagiarism. Statements 8 and 9 did not represent plagiarism and 41.80% and 39.34% students disagreed that these were instances of plagiarism.

The responses of students make obvious that except for the statement 'To submit someone else's work as if it was yours', majority of respondents were not aware about the instances of plagiarism. Hence, serious steps need to be taken to make students aware about what causes plagiarism. The students were not aware about the importance of giving in-text citation and complete reference to the referred sources of information. A gap was found in their knowledge about ethical writing, as students feel once the original writer of a class assignment allow them to use his/ her work, they can claim this as their own work. The results revealed a strong need for sensitizing the students about what constitutes plagiarism.

6.3. Statistical analysis of results with respect to demographics

The correlation-coefficient was calculated using SPSS 22 to find the relation between students awareness about plagiarism assessed through 9 statements and their age and academic performance in terms of Overall Credit Point Average. The results revealed no significant relation between the age of students and their awareness about plagiarism. Similarly, no significant relation was found between the academic performance of students and their responses about instances of plagiarism (Table 2). In other words, the awareness of students about plagiarism was found to be independent of their age and academic performance.

Table 2. Correlation between awareness about plagiarism and age and academic performance of students

S. No.	Statement	r with Age	r with OCPA
1	To buy an essay from a so-called "paper mill" (an Internet site which sells papers) and hand the paper in as if it was yours	.099	-.137
2	To submit someone else's work as if it was yours	.124	.052
3	To submit an essay that a friend wrote and gave you the permission to use it as if it was yours	.036	-.069
4	To literally take a piece of text from a book and submit it in as yours without indicating a source	.083	.100
5	To take a piece from a known source, then make some small language changes in the text, but only indicate the source (i.e. no reference in the text)	.038	.010

6	To use most of the content from someone else's original text but change the order. There is a reference in the text (e.g. Sjögren, 1999) and the original source appears in a list.	-.163	-.062
7	To write a paragraph by bringing together shorter pieces of 10-15 words from a number of various sources and add some of your own words to form a paragraph. All original sources listed in the list without reference to the text	.040	-.072
8	To extract your main points from a text you read, but write it in your own words. The new version looks different, both in detail and because it uses different examples. A reference to the text (e.g. Sjögren, 1999) is used and the original source is listed in the bibliography.	-.145	-.115
9	To quote a paragraph as well as to italicize it and cite the source with a PAGE REFERENCE in the text, in a footnote and in the bibliography.	-.169	-.052

The t-test was conducted to statistically find the variation in awareness of students towards plagiarism based on their gender and course level. The results revealed no significant differences in results of male and female students. Further no statistically significant difference was found in awareness of students towards plagiarism based on their course level (table 3).

Table 3. Difference between awareness about plagiarism based on gender and course level

S. No.	Statement	t-test Gender		t-test Course level	
		t	P	T	P
1	To buy an essay from a so-called "paper mill" (an Internet site which sells papers) and hand the paper in as if it was yours	1.432	.155	-1.023	.308
2	To submit someone else's work as if it was yours	.855	.394	-.901	.369
3	To submit an essay that a friend wrote and gave you the permission to use it as if it was yours	.227	.821	-.582	.562
4	To literally take a piece of text from a book and submit it in as yours without indicating a source	1.312	.192	-1.152	.251
5	To take a piece from a known source, then make some small language changes in the text, but only indicate the source (i.e. no reference in the text)	.150	.881	1.607	.111
6	To use most of the content from someone else's original text but change the order. There is a reference in the text (e.g. Sjögren, 1999) and the original source appears in a list.	.844	.400	-1.024	.308
7	To write a paragraph by bringing together shorter pieces of 10-15 words from a number of various sources and add some of your own words to form a paragraph. All original sources listed in the list without reference to the text	-.232	.817	1.629	.106
8	To extract your main points from a text you read, but write it in your own words. The new version looks different, both in detail and because it uses different examples. A reference to the text (e.g. Sjögren, 1999) is used and the original source is listed in the bibliography.	.351	.726	1.004	.317
9	To quote a paragraph as well as to italicize it and cite the source with a PAGE REFERENCE in the text, in a footnote and in the bibliography.	.676	.500	.814	.417

6.4. Students' perceptions about plagiarism

The respondents were required to express their perceptions towards plagiarism based on 11 statements given in questionnaire. Majority of the students (60.66%) responded that major cause of plagiarism was that the students do not know how to write scientifically (table 4). Around 48.36% students accepted that they feel that they cannot express anything as well in their own words. Generally, it is thought that the Internet has resulted into an increase in academic plagiarism. The responses of 42.62% students supported this notion as they responded that they see plagiarism as an easy way out especially today with the spread of computers and the Internet. However, this finding is contrary to the findings of Nirmal Singh (2017), who revealed that the Internet has not influenced the plagiarism among veterinary students. Shockingly, 40.98% respondents revealed that students do not understand that studying is aimed at independent and critical thinking. Nearly 40.98% respondents cited lack of knowledge about what is allowed and what is not allowed in academic writings. At the same time 40.16% students responded of lacking interest in the topic of study as one of the reasons for plagiarism. The pressure to pass course at any price, laziness, lack of time, high course demands and competition among students with respect to grades are the other reasons cited by students as factors encouraging plagiarism among students.

Table 4. Perceptions of students

S. No.	Particular	No. of Students	Percentage
1	The students do not understand that studying is aimed at independent and critical thinking	50	40.98
2	The students feel that he/she cannot express anything as well in his/her own words.	59	48.36
3	The students do not know how to write scientifically	74	60.66
4	The students lacks knowledge about what is allowed and what is not allowed.	50	40.98
5	The course demands are too high	27	22.13
6	There is a competition among students with respect to grades	27	22.13
7	The students want to pass the course at any price	40	32.79
8	The students lacks interest in the topic of study	49	40.16
9	The students see plagiarism as an easy way out especially today, with the spread of computers and the Internet	52	42.62
10	The students lack time.	35	28.69
11	The students are lazy.	38	31.15

6.5. Measures for prevention of plagiarism

The structured data collection tool consisted of multiple statements representing measures for prevention of plagiarism. Around 60.66% students suggested the course on academic writing as a measure for prevention of plagiarism. Conducting such courses would be fundamental not only for reducing the instances of plagiarism but for enhancing the level of academic writing too.

Nearly 54.92% respondents suggested that teachers should openly discuss plagiarism with students. This would boost the morale of students for honest academic writing and will help them to clear their doubts, if any. About 54.10% respondents suggested for training in the type of assignments where plagiarism usually occurs to give them better self-esteem. Nearly 50.82% students suggested for reduction in students' course workload so that they may not be in a pressure to plagiarize. Around 43.44% students desired that they should be informed about the rules regarding plagiarism on every course and examination. Another 43.44% students recommended that students should be informed that their work will be checked for plagiarism. This will create a fear for plagiarism in students.

S. No.	Particular	No. of Students	Percentage
1	Assignments should be formulated differently for different students.	52	42.62
2	Students should get better training in the type of assignments where plagiarism usually occurs to give them better self esteem	66	54.10
3	Students should have better knowledge about academic writing, for example, by attending a course in academic writing	74	60.66
4	Students should learn what is allowed and not allowed through education and open discussions	45	36.89
5	On every course and examination the students should be informed about the rules regarding plagiarism	53	43.44
6	Teachers should openly discuss plagiarism with students	67	54.92
7	The penalty for those who committed plagiarism should be more severe	20	16.39
8	Electronic plagiarism detection tools should be used	46	37.70
9	Students should be informed that their work will be checked for plagiarism	53	43.44
10	The students' course workload should be reduced	62	50.82
11	Students should receive proper instructions on writing assignments in time so that time pressure is avoided	55	45.08
12	Any other	13	10.57

7. CONCLUSION

This is very un-doubtful that agricultural students lack awareness about plagiarism. There is a strong need for sensitizing them about what constitutes plagiarism, how it can be a big hurdle in their academic development and how to avoid plagiarism. This can be achieved by imparting them a course on ethical academic writing, especially about usage of the Internet based information. This will not only make them aware about the ethics of academic writing but also boost their morale to express their ideas in their own words.

REFERENCES

Anney, V. N. and Mosha, M. A. (2015). Student's plagiarisms in higher learning institutions in the era of improved Internet access: case study of developing countries. *Journal of Education and Practice*, 6(13). https://files.eric.ed.gov/fulltext/EJ1080502.pdf

Charbonneau, Jacleen. Understanding plagiarism and its dangers. https://www.collegexpress.com/articles-and-advice/majors-and-academics/articles/college-academics/understanding-plagiarism-and-its-dangers/

Dawson, Maureen M. and Overfield, Joyce A. (2006). Plagiarism: do students know what it is? *Bioscience Education*, 8(1). https://www.tandfonline.com/doi/full/10.3108/beej.8.1

Fealy, S., Bighlari, N. and Rad, Gholamreza P. (2012). Agricultural students' attitude and behavior on plagiarism in Tarbiat Modares University. *Quarterly Journal of Research and Planning in Higher Education*, 18(3). Abstract accessed from:http://journal.irphe.ir/browse.php?a_id=1652&sid=1&slc_lang=en

Hannah, J. (2015). History of plagiarism. Available at: https://prezi.com/h2mje6xznk6d/untitled-prezi/.

Hu, G. and Lei, J. (2015). Chinese University students' perceptions of plagiarism, ethics & behaviour. *Ethics and Behaviour*, 25:3, 233-255, DOI: 10.1080/10508422.2014.923313

Icaza, Maria de (2007). The arts and copyright: learn from the past, create the future. World Intellectual Property Organization, Geneva, p. 48.

Jeergal, P. A., Surekha, R., Sharma, P., Anila, K., Jeergal, V. A. and Rani, T. (2015). Prevalence, perception and attitude of dental students towards academic dishonesty and ways to overcome cheating behaviors. *Journal of Advanced Clinical & Research Insights*, 2, 2-6.

Jones, Karl O.; Reid, Juliet and Bartlett, Rebecca (2008). Cyber cheating in an information technology age". *Digithum*, issue 10 [article online]. DOI: http://dx.doi.org/10.7238/d.v0i10.508

Marshall, Stephen and Garry, Maryanne (2005). NESB and ESB students' attitudes and perceptions of plagiarism. Paper based on a paper presented at the 2nd Asia-Pacific Educational Integrity Conference (Newcastle, 2-3 December 2005). http://citeseerx.ist.psu.edu/viewdoc/download?doi=10.1.1.624.5928&rep=rep1&type=pdf

Murtaza, G., Zafar, S., Bashir, I. and Hussain, I. (2013). Evaluation of student's perception and behaviour towards plagiarism in Pakistani universities. *Acta Bioethica*, 19 (1), 125-130.

Nirmal Singh, (2017) "Level of awareness among veterinary students of GADVASU towards plagiarism: a case study", *The Electronic Library*, 35(5),899-915, https://doi.org/10.1108/EL-06-2016-0132

Oxford Dictionary (2018). Definition of plagiarism in English. https://en.oxforddictionaries.com/definition/plagiarism

Panter, Michaela. Defining Plagiarism. https://www.aje.com/en/arc/editing-tip-defining-plagiarism/

Radunovich, H., Baugh, E. and Turner, E. (2009). An examination of students' knowledge of what constitutes plagiarism. *NACTA Journal*, 53(4), 30-35. https://www.jstor.org/stable/43765409?seq=1#page_scan_tab_contents

Ramzan, M., Munir, M. A. Siddique, N. and Asif, M. (2012). Awareness about plagiarism amongst university students in Pakistan. *Higher Education*, 64(1), 73-84.

Rathore et al. (2015), Exploring the attitudes of medical faculty members and students in Pakistan towards plagiarism: a cross sectional survey. *Peer J.*, 3:e1031; DOI 10.7717/peerj.1031

Razera, Diana (2011). Awareness, attitude and perception of plagiarism among students and and teachers at Stockholm University. Department of Computer and Systems Sciences, Stockholm University, Sweden (Master of Science Thesis). http://www.diva-portal.org/smash/get/diva2:432681/FULLTEXT01.pdf

Sarlauskienea, L. and Stabingisa, L. (2014). Understanding of plagiarism by the students in HEIs of Lithuania. *Procedia - Social and Behavioral Sciences*, 110, 638-646.

Satija, M. P. (2015). Preventing the plague of plagiarism. *Library Herald*, 53(4), 367-68.

Ukpebor, C. O. and Ogbebor, A. (2013). Internet and plagiarism: awareness, attitude and perception of students of secondary schools. *International Research: Journal of Library & Information Science*, 3(2).

18

Academic Plagiarism : An Overview of the Policy and Preventive Measures in Pakistan

Kanwal Ameen
Faiqa Mansoor

1. INTRODUCTION

Plagiarism has never been an accepted norm and measures have always been taken to control it. The practice of plagiarism does not only affect the quality of research, creating loss of writing and thinking skills among researchers, but also the credibility of the institutions and societies associated with such researchers. The introduction of the copyright laws in 1710 and the subsequent recognition of intellectual property rights in 1967 are examples of significant attempts made by governments to control and discourage the unfair use of information in the printing and publication businesses (Sharkey & Culp, 2005).

Scripting, a simple yet comprehensive definition of plagiarism is difficult. One may find many definitions of the word plagiarism in dictionaries and on academic institutions websites, but these may become confusing when one tries to segregate different examples of information use and writing practices (Cogdell & Aidulis, 2008). Bretag and Mahmood (2009) supported the definition provided by the WPA (Council of Writing Program Administrators, 2003) on its website as simple and wide-ranging. The Council declared that "in an instructional setting, plagiarism occurs when a writer deliberately uses someone else's language, ideas, or other original (not common-knowledge) material without acknowledging its source." The use of the word 'deliberately' is helpful in excluding cases of unintentional similarities.

Moreover, the role of 'intent' is very important in labelling an inappropriate usage of information as plagiarism as in certain disciplines like fine arts making an imitation of great works is still used as a technique to learn different painting styles (Auer & Krupar 2001). Cultural contexts, that include linguistic competence of a researcher, prevailing academic literacy standards in a society, and institutional governance practices, are also important to determine the intent in a plagiarism instance (Bretag & Mahmud, 2009). Mundava and Chaudhuri (2007) mentioned that the latest concept of plagiarism as an academic integrity offence has been developed in English speaking countries where the authors have the right to own their phrases or ideas and it is unacceptable to use them without acknowledging the author while in the non-English speaking countries, information is considered to be owned by the society in general and anyone can use it without giving credit to the original source. Therefore, it is argued that while interpreting the concept of plagiarism in other than the western academic culture, the academic should not neglect the differences of cultures and the concept of plagiarism should be defined in the cultural context (Yusof, 2009).

However, ironically due to stereotype perspectives prevailing in societies and irresponsible media coverage at times, the embarrassment a researcher or an institution will have to face in case of plagiarism allegations does not lessen despite the fact that cultural and academic contexts might be involved behind it. Consequently, academic institutions all over the world have become conscious towards the issue and are implementing strict policies and taking measures to protect academic integrity.

2. THE CASE OF PAKISTAN

2.1. A Snapshot of the Literature Produced

The majority of the studies conducted in Pakistan on plagiarism were aimed at exploring the knowledge and attitudes of students towards plagiarism. Their findings indicate that the lack of conceptual awareness among students regarding plagiarism (Shirazi, Jafarey, & Moazam, 2010) and the lack of awareness towards institutional policies against plagiarism were found to be high among students (Murtaza, Zafar, Bashir, & Hussain, 2013). Moreover, as the students were mostly found unaware of the negative implications of plagiarism towards their intellect and careers (Siddiqui & Mushtaq, 2015) resultantly, they do not take plagiarism seriously (Ramzan, Munir, Siddique, & Asif, 2012).

The inconsistencies in the implementation of plagiarism policies at student level may equally be blamed for the prevalence of plagiarism in Pakistan (Saeed, Aamir, & Ramzan, 2011). Shukr (2014) found that in the medical field, the lack of teaching on professional ethics and the inadequate training regarding academic honesty was major contributing factor for plagiarism pervasiveness. Similarly, for students, the impact of the surrounding environment including peer pressure and the attitude of the teacher towards academic integrity found to be critical in both, increasing (Tanveer, Gill, & Ahmed, 2013) and decreasing the tendency to cheat (Soroya, 2014).

The scholars stressed that efforts to create awareness among academia towards plagiarism and its countering policies should be accelerated by the institutions along with generating opportunities to enhance one's required skills to adopt a strong ethical writing behaviour (Aslam & Nazir, 2011; Murtaza et al., 2013; Shirazi et al., 2010; Siddiqui & Mushtaq, 2015).In this regard, the universities should establish academic integrity centres and such centres can be a part of the universities' central library (Soroya, 2014). Moreover, the use of Turnitin software may be encouraged to enhance the students' ability in avoiding unnecessary use of other's words (Rana & Tuba, 2015). The educational strategies should be revised with special emphasis on creating a "value-based culture" of academic integrity and fully augmented with across the board implementation of policies (Khan, 2012).

2.2. Role of Higher Education Commission (HEC), Pakistan

The HEC, Pakistan, was established in 2002 by devolving the University Grant Commission of Pakistan. It took revolutionary steps to promote research and development activities in Pakistani universities with a special emphasis on quality maintenance in each activity. The Quality Assurance Agency (QAA) was established in 2005 by the HEC for policy-making and as a monitoring body to provide assistance to universities in maintaining ethical standards and quality in research and development activities.

2.2.1. The Policy

The first steps to control plagiarism were taken in 2007 by the HEC, Pakistan, with the introduction of a detailed plagiarism policy for its recognized universities (Higher Education Commission Pakistan, n.d.-a) and making it available online. The definition of the act of plagiarism was adopted from the Concise Oxford Dictionary in the policy preamble as, "taking and using the thoughts, writings, and inventions of another person as one's own". However, it is also acknowledged in the policy that such definitions are incomplete to explain the different types of plagiarism and to ascertain guilt or innocence in some cases. The purpose of the policy is described as to ensure credit, respect, and recognition of research for the authors on their original scholarly publications and not with merely replicating the efforts of others to achieve career development and make financial gains. For this, it was mentioned that the menace of plagiarism should be "curbed through exemplary punitive actions," along with recognizing the need to protect the researchers against bogus or false complaints. The academic institutions and organizations were made responsible to implement the policy in two aspects as its objectives:

1. To apprise students, teachers, and researchers and staff about Plagiarism and how it can be avoided; and
2. To discourage plagiarism by regulating and authorizing punitive actions against those found guilty of the act of plagiarism.

The policy provided a modified text of "Little Book of Plagiarism" published by Leeds Metropolitan University as an 'annexure' to facilitate its institutions in creating awareness about plagiarism (Higher Education Commission Pakistan, n.d.-b). The universities were strictly instructed that if they could not apply this policy for all of their students, teachers, researchers and staff members, their degrees will be derecognized by the HEC. Furthermore, it was also made clear that if a university fails to take recommended action against an offender, the HEC would itself take action.

The policy rationally suggests that in order to impose penalties, the intellectual standing of the offender must be kept under consideration and gradual increase in penalty should be organized in subsequent attempts of the offence. The levels of punishments for a teacher/researcher/staff and for students should be categorized separately. The suggested penalties in the policy are summarized in Table 1 under different categories.

Table 1. Penalties suggested in HEC plagiarism policy for teachers, students and co-authors

Level of Penalty	For Teachers, researchers and staff members	Students	Co-Authors/Declarations
Major (In cases of word for word plagiarism)	1. Dismissal from service and may "Black Listed" for eligibility for any future employment at an academic organization 2. "Black Listing" published in the print media or on different websites	1. Expelled from the University and may restrain for a period from joining any institution of Higher Education in Pakistan. 2. The degree may be withdrawn if AT ANY TIME it is proven that the work is plagiarized. 3. The verdict may be notified on print media or on different websites. 4. Financial grants may be stopped.	1. Access to the published paper may be removed from the web page and legal action will be taken. 2. The author(s) will be asked to write a formal letter of apology to the authors of the Original paper.
Moderate (In case of paraphrasing plagiarism)	1. Demotion to the next lower grade along with "Black Listing" published in the print media or on different websites	1. Relegated to a lower class. 2. A failure grade in the subject. 3. Fined an amount.	1. If the paper is submitted but not published yet, the paper will be rejected by the Editor-in-Chief or the Program Chair without further. 2. Warnings may be issued.
Minor (In case a few paragraphs copied from an external source without giving reference to that work)	1. Warnings And for a specified period 2. freezing of all research grants, funding, travel grants 3. the promotions/annual increments of the offender may be stopped 4. may be stopped from supervision of PhD students, scholarship, fellowship or any other funded program	1. Written warning	

The policy also mentions that in the case of a thesis the responsibility of plagiarism will be of the student and not of the supervisor or members of the Supervisory Committee. However, the HEC Plagiarism Standing committee decided in its meeting held on September 24, 2016 that if plagiarism established in the thesis of a PhD/MS/MPhil scholar the supervisor will also be held responsible for this act and will be black listed for five (05) years. The National Quality Assurance Committee in its 22nd meeting held on January 09, 2017 endorsed these decisions and the universities were notified (Higher Education Commission Pakistan, 2017).

The co-authors, if claiming benefits on the base of that paper, were deemed to be equally responsible for any plagiarism committed in a published or presented to a journal or at a conference. The editors of journals in Pakistan were also instructed to get a declaration from all authors that the work they were submitting was not plagiarized. In case of a false allegation, the policy instructs that disciplinary action against the complainant must be taken by his parent organization on the recommendation of the head of the institution of the victim.

2.2.2. Use of Plagiarism Detection Software

The HEC provided free access of Turnitin software in public sector universities in 2007, and made it mandatory for them to have scrutinized all their research work of PhD and international publications for possible instance of plagiarism through this software before final submission of the research work (Piracha, 2011). Later on, the MPhil research works were also included in the circle. The HEC instructed the universities to designate their focal persons for the facilitation and administration of this service and researchers were made to get plagiarism clearance certificates from the designated authorities in order to have their work submitted.

Mansoor and Ameen (2016) reported that universities mostly designated a focal person from the community such as a member from faculty or quality enhancement cell (QEC) or Information Technology centre, or central library etc. to administer the software service. The focal persons are responsible for not only issuing a plagiarism free clearance certificate to a researcher for, but also to manage the login accounts generated for instructors and organize training sessions for instructors on the operational usage of the software. Initially, the free access of Turnitin software was only for the HEC public sector universities, however later on some private sector universities were also provided with its free access while other private sector universities purchased the software license. Mansoor and Ameen (2016) reported that in the year 2014 out of 100 responding universities of their survey 77 public and private sector universities were using Turnitin software.

3. ANTI-PLAGIARISM AWARENESS PRACTICES

The universities' anti-plagiarism awareness and guidance practices indicate that most of the universities were using classrooms lectures to provide anti-plagiarism awareness and guidance among students. Other mediums such as the university's website, student manual/booklets, handouts etc. were rarely used (Mansoor & Ameen, 2016). After classroom advice, the second most used channel to provide informal anti-plagiarism guidance was found at the universities' central libraries (Mansoor & Ameen, 2016). This indicated that, although universities are making some efforts in this regard, the systematic, tangible and more formal practices were yet required to meet the objectives. The university libraries have an important role in this regards to play through offering seminars on ethical use of information.

4. CONCLUSION

The matter of addressing academic plagiarism received significant attention in the academic environment of Pakistan after 2007, mainly due to HEC. Previously it was dealt as a moral value like practising other values. It became mandatory for all HEC recognized universities in Pakistan since then to check their research output for possible instances of both intentional or un-intentional higher ratio of similarities in the text of a given work using the similarity index software 'Turnitin' (usually called as anti-plagiarism software) report plagiarism cases, and impose penalties in order to address the problem. The literature indicates a strong need to further accelerate the efforts regarding conceptual awareness and providing training for ethical use of information. Furthermore, the inconsistencies in policies interpretation and implementation should be addressed.

We can safely claim that Pakistan has taken the lead in the South Asian region in controlling the academic plagiarism through various measures, whereas recommendations to develop similar mechanisms in its neighbouring countries given by their higher education institutions were only initiated after 2012. (Bailey, 2013; University Grant Commission India, 2012).

REFERENCES

Aslam, M. S. & Nazir, M. S. (2011). The impact of personality traits on academic dishonesty among Pakistani students. *The Journal of Commerce*, 3(2), 50-61. http://www.ciitlahore.edu.pk/Papers/Abstracts/146-8588087886673289558.pdf

Bailey, J. (2013). Expanding Plagiarism Policies for Doctoral Theses in India [Web Log message]. Retrieved from http://www.ithenticate.com/plagiarism-detection-blog/bid/96726/Expanding-Plagiarism-Policies-for-Doctoral-Theses-in-India#.VS6QsNyUex1

Bretag, T. & Mahmud, S. (2009). A model for determining student plagiarism: electronic detection and academic judgement. *Journal of University Teaching & Learning Practice*, 6(1), 6. http://ro.uow.edu.au/cgi/viewcontent.cgi?article=1076&context=jutlp

Cogdell, B. & Aidulis, D. (2008). Dealing with plagiarism as an ethical issue. In T. S. Roberts (Ed.), *Student plagiarism in an online world: Problems and solutions* (pp. 38-59). Hershey: Information Science Reference.

Council of Writing Program Administrators. (2003). Defining and Avoiding Plagiarism: The WPA Statement on Best Practices. Retrieved 2014, from http://wpacouncil.org/positions/WPAplagiarism.pdf

Higher Education Commission Pakistan. (n.d.-a). HEC plagiarism policy. from http://hec.gov.pk/english/services/faculty/Documents/Plagiarism/Plagiarism%20Policy.pdf

Higher Education Commission Pakistan. (n.d.-b). The little book of plagiarism. from http://www.hec.gov.pk/english/services/faculty/Documents/Plagiarism/Little%20Book%20of%20Plagiarism.pdf

Higher Education Commission Pakistan. (2017). Responsibility on the supervisor of plagiarized PhD/MS/MP. (Official Notification Ref. 1-22 (NQAC)/QAD/2017/HEC/07-364 dated March 24, 2017)

Khan, M. A. (2012). An empirical study of students' perception of ethical behaviour in higher education institutions in Pakistan. *Actual Problems of Economics/Àêòóàëüí³ ïðîáëåè åêîíîì³êè*, 132(6), 328-338. http://www.irbis-nbuv.gov.ua/cgi-bin/irbis_nbuv/cgiirbis_64.exe?C21COM=2&I21DBN=UJRN&P21DBN=UJRN&IMAGE_FILE_DOWNLOAD=1&Image_file_name=PDF/ape_2012_6_45.pdf

Mansoor, F. & Ameen, K. (2016). Promoting Academic Integrity in South Asian Research Culture: The Case of Pakistani Academic Institutions. *South Asian Studies*, 31(2), 77.

Mundava, M., & Chaudhuri, J. (2007). Understanding plagiarism The role of librarians at the University of Tennessee in assisting students to practice fair use of information. *College & Research Libraries News*, 68(3), 170-173. http://crln.acrl.org/content/68/3/170.full.pdf

Murtaza, G., Zafar, S., Bashir, I. & Hussain, I. (2013). Evaluation of student's perception and behavior towards plagiarism in Pakistani universities. *Acta Bioethica*, 19(1), 125-130. http://www.semanariorepublicano.uchile.cl/index.php/AB/article/download/27106/28737

Piracha, H. A. (2011). Plagiarism at a glance: a case study of University of the Punjab. *Journal of the Bangladesh Association of Young Researchers*, 1(1), 127-132. http://www.banglajol.info/index.php/JBAYR/article/view/6842

Ramzan, M., Munir, M. A., Siddique, N. & Asif, M. (2012). Awareness about plagiarism amongst university students in Pakistan. *Higher Education*, 64(1), pp.73-84. http://www.academia.edu/download/46004663/Awareness_about_plagiarism_amongst_unive20160527-26252-y0wuja.pdf

Rana, N. A. & Tuba, A. (2015). Diffusing ICT to Enhance Students' Academic Writing Skills: An experimental study at a Business Institute in Karachi, Pakistan. *International Journal of English and Education*, 4(2), 340-351. http://ijee.org/yahoo_site_admin/assets/docs/29.19011810.pdf

Saeed, S., Aamir, R. & Ramzan, M. (2011). Plagiarism and its implications on higher education in developing countries. *International Journal of Teaching and Case Studies*, 3(2), 123-130. doi:http://dx.doi.org/10.1504/IJTCS.2011.039552

Sharkey, J. R. & Culp, F. B. (2005). Cyberplagiarism and the library: Issues and solutions. *The Reference Librarian*, 44(91-92), 103-116. http://ir.library.illinoisstate.edu/cgi/viewcontent.cgi?article=1043&context=fpml doi:http://dx.doi.org/10.1300/J120v44n91_08

Shirazi, B., Jafarey, A. M. & Moazam, F. (2010). Plagiarism and the medical fraternity: A study of knowledge and attitudes. *J Pak Med Assoc*, 60(4), 269-273. http://jpma.pakcyber.biz/PdfDownload/1996.pdf

Siddiqui, A. A. & Mushtaq, S. (2015). Plagiarism free academic enviroment [Editorial]. *Pakistan Journal of Medicine and Dentistry*, 4(3).

Soroya, M. S. (2014). *Impact of student-teacher relationship on academic integrity in Pakistani universities*. (Unpublished doctoral dissertation), University of the Punjab, Lahore, Pakistan.

Sutherland-Smith, W. (2005). Pandora's box: Academic perceptions of student plagiarism in writing. *Journal of English for Academic Purposes*, 4(1), 83-95. http://citeseerx.ist.psu.edu/viewdoc/download?doi=10.1.1.457.1598&rep=rep1&type=pdf

Tanveer, M. A., Gill, H. & Ahmed, I. (2013). Why Business Students Cheat? A study from Pakistan. *International Journal of African and Asian Studies*, 2, 66-71. http://www.iiste.org/Journals/index.php/JAAS/article/view/9118/9337

University Grant Commission India. (2012). Inclusive and Qualitative expansion of higher education 12th Five-Year Plan, 2012-17 (pp. 149). New Delhi: University Grants Commission.

Yusof, D. (2009). A different perspective on plagiarism. *The Internet TESL Journal*, 15(2). http://iteslj.org/Articles/Yusof-Plagiarism.html

19

Ethical Policies of LIS e-Journals Listed in the UGC Approved List

Dinesh K Gupta
Vijendra Kumar[17]

1. INTRODUCTION

A news item that appeared in the *Economic Times* (23rd June 2018)[18] elaborates cases of journals as falsely claiming to be on white lists, fabricating citation scores for papers, stating implausible time frames for peer review (claims of rapid review are often associated with questionable journals) and brazenly listing as sitting on their editorial boards scholars who are not in fact doing so. The top ranked journal '*Nature*' reports about the recruitment of fake editors in predatory journals in place of established experts in the subject (Sorokowski et al, 2017). Reader's Digest discloses about a highly cited paper which was never published. Similarly, *Economic Times* (*17th March 2018*) reports that as might be expected, countries with weaker misconduct policies than America's are China and India.

Studies report about the predatory nature of Indian journals (Seethapathy et al, 2016; Pulla, 2016).Azeez (2017) reports negative trends in the quality of journals, due to paid publication, publication without a peer review system, plagiarism and unethical practices have become quite common these days. Patwardhan et al. (2018) made a critical analysis of the UGC approved list and suggests that 'over 88% of the non-indexed journals in the university source component of the UGC-approved list, included on the basis of suggestions from different universities, could be of low quality. In view of these results, the current UGC-approved list of

---

17. The authors acknowledge the discussions had with Dr. G. Mahesh, Senior Principal Scientist, CSIR-NISCAIR.
18. Some science journals that claim to peer review papers do not do so: One estimate puts the number of papers in questionable journals at 400,000 (2018, June 23). The Economist. Retrieved from: http://media.economist.com/news/science-and-technology/21744818-one-estimate-puts-number-papers-questionable-journals-400000-some. (on 28th June 2018)

journals needs serious re-consideration. New regulations to curtail unethical practices in scientific publishing along with organization of awareness programmes about publication ethics at Indian universities and research institutes are urgently needed'.

With these studies it is quite clear that ethical norms in journal publication are not being followed. There is no question on the intentions of the UGC API but the way beneficiaries and publishers dealt with the emerged situation largely remained unethical.However, Graf (2007) considers that 'academic publishing depends, to a great extent, on trust. Editors trust peer reviewers to provide fair assessments, authors trust editors to select appropriate peer reviewers, and readers put their trust in the peer-review process. Academic publishing also occurs in an environment of powerful intellectual, financial, and sometimes political interests that may collide or compete. Good decisions and strong editorial processes designed to manage these interests will foster a sustainable and efficient publishing system, which will benefit academic societies, journal editors, authors, research funders, readers, and publishers. Good publication practices do not develop by chance, and will become established only if they are actively promoted'.

Various journals and publishers (Elsevier, 2018; De Gruyter, 2015; 12. PsychOpen Publishing Psychology, 2011; Electronic Physician, 2018) define ethical responsibilities of editor's, reviewer's, author's and publisher's which is demonstrated in the Table 1.

Table 1. Ethical Responsibilities

Editor's Responsibilities	Reviewer's Responsibilities	Author's Responsibilities	Publisher's Responsibilities
Accountability	Contribution to editorial decisions	Reporting standards	Handling of unethical publishing behaviour
Fairness	Promptness	Originality and Plagiarism	Access to journal content
Confidentiality	Confidentiality	Multiple, redundant or concurrent publication	Fraudulent publication
Disclosure, conflicts of interest, and other issues	Standards of objectivity	Acknowledgement of sources	Plagiarism the publisher
Involvement and cooperation in investigations	Acknowledgement of sources	Authorship of a manuscript	Ensures the autonomy of editorial decisions
Publication decisions	Disclosure and conflict of	Data access and retention interest	Protects intellectual property and copyright
Peer review process	Suggest for alternative reviewers to editor	Disclosure and conflicts of interest	Maintaining Standard
Digital Archiving	Authenticity of content and references	Fundamental errors in published works	
Procedures for dealing with unethical behavior	Must aware of copyright infringement and plagiarism	Publication and Submission fee	
		Open Access Policy	
		Hazards and human or animal subjects	

2. UGC API LINK WITH JOURNAL PUBLICATIONS

UGC linked research contributions of university and college teachers with recruitment and promotion and developed a process of attaining API points. Paper publication in the journals remained the top criteria in this category. A mechanism for identifying quality journals (with due weightage for Refereed Journals, Journals having ISSN, Covered in subject based databases, Impact Factor) was suggested in the UGC Regulations-2010 (University Grants Commission, 2017a) and universities were asked to develop subject-wise list and their availability on the university website. However universities failed to do so. As a result, the UGC brought out a list (dynamic) of 38653 journals from three databases, namely Web of Science (WOS), Scopus, and ICI for use of selection and promotion of university and college teachers (University Grants Commission, 2017b). Approved journal list came up hoping that 'UGC has taken the right step in bringing out the journal list which is supposedly to be a dynamic list. This step will bring about a positive change in overall academic environment. This would improve Indian research outputs and standing at the international level and importantly keeps questionable journals at bay' (Gupta et al., 2017).

Later on, the UGC invited lists of journals to be added in the list in the respective subjects from the universities and large numbers of journals were added/deleted with a separate list of ceased journals was created in due course of time. The UGC also asked 'for any complaint about inclusion of predatory, fake or questionable journals is received from universities / academic fraternity. As such, all complaints regarding inclusion of predatory, fake or questionable journals in the UGC-approved list of journals should be routed through universities or through research guide or faculty in a university'[19].

UGC developed criteria to include a journal in lieu of meeting out of primary and secondary criteria. To meet out the primary criteria, the journal has a website which provides full postal and email addresses of Chief Editor and Editors, and at least some of these addresses are verifiable official addresses. To meet out second criteria, journal to get 6 score in Science, Social Sciences and Multi-disciplinary category and 5 score in Humanities on the checklist of 8 scores with plus-minus marking. The third point in the check list 'The journal has a well-defined Ethics policy' offers plus one mark for having ethical policy and minus one for not having an ethical policy for a journal[20]. Each of the journals was scrutinized on different criteria and recently, on 2nd May 2018, 4305 journals were removed on failing to meet out various criteria brought out by the UGC[21]. In a most recent move, the HRD Minister the country announced to employ Turnitin for plagiarism check for the research work produced in the country (BS Web Desk, 2018).

19. Notification on Predatory/Fake/Questionable Journals, (UGC). Retrieved from: https://www.ugc.ac.in/journallist/predatory.pdf. (on 5th May 2018).
20. Scope, Coverage and Methodology Used for Preparing the UGC-approved List of Journals, (UGC). Retrieved from: https://www.ugc.ac.in/journallist/methodology.pdf (on 15th March 2018).
21. Journals Removed from UGC-Approved List of Journals, (UGC). Retrieved from: https://www.ugc.ac.in/journallist/Removed_Journals.pdf (on 5th May 2018).

As in lieu of the ethics in higher education, fair conduct of research and prevention of misconduct, as per UGC (Promotion of Academic Integrity and Prevention of Plagiarism in Higher Educational Institutions) Regulations, 2017 (draft), students, researchers and faculty members should not perform any academic misconduct by the theft of intellectual property in any manner (University Grants Commission, 2017).

Shafi (2014) considers that the online version acted as a stimulator for the growth but issues of quality remain. There is negligible number of journals from learned societies and a few from associations are of average quality. But a new breed of journals owned by .com community evidently for commercial ends is growing in number. These journals are an easy avenue for those authors eager to get their mediocre or poor papers published.

3. LIS JOURNALS AND ETHICAL ISSUES: A REVIEW

A large number of studies from a wide range of disciplines and sub disciplines have tried to explain ethical issues associated with the publication of journals.From the library and information science field, the following major studies address this issue: 'In Library and information science journals, all expect that journals in the discipline adhere to high ethical standards and employ state-of-the art editorial and publishing practices. In addition, authors submitting work for editorial and peer review similarly expect to be treated fairly, ethically, and consistently throughout the review and publishing process. They seek publications that will provide them with the best possible opportunity to reach their desired audience in the present and into the future (Shafi, 2014).

Shafi (2014)considers that the ethics of editors and authors has become a more serious problem, as the number of flawed papers is increasing exponentially. The checks and vigilance have become more mechanical with the availability of anti-plagiarism software. The errant authors make many excuses including fixing responsibility on a junior author. It has also become a matter of least concern of authorities and no mechanism is in place to enforce punishments. The conflict of interest is less evident in LIS unlike other disciplines like medicine, marketing or biotechnology where papers are sponsored or published to highlight key features of their products for commercial gains.

Mungilal (2018) argues that LIS professionals also do research and publish journal articles and books in their field. Proper ethical processes have to be followed in publishing process and plagiarism should be avoided. An article submitted to one journal should not simultaneously be submitted to another journal.

Pujar (2014)observes that quality of content and unethical practices of publishing followed by some journals is a worrying factor for the sustainable growth of open access journals.

Vishwakarmaand Mukherjee (2014) emphasise that it is important to note that no journal has yet mentioned the publication ethics they follow while publishing article. In fact such practice may be common in publishing of journals in developing countries. COPE forum and SHERPA/ROMEO project have an intension to spread publication ethics among editors and journal publishers.

Jeevan (2014) finds that Supply always tries to meet the demand of the market. The ground reality is that without much infrastructure and editorial acumen, it is relatively easy to float a journal, and that too an e- only open access journal some pocketing page charges from authors. There are also other models such as subscription to fund the cost and profit required. Our country has a huge market of academics who want to publish and search for easy outlets guaranteeing quick publication. Some of these journals may demand payment for publication.

Sen (2017) observes that research misconduct is a growing problem. The focus is largely is on plagiarism, data falsification, data fabrication and the like. Duplicating publications can also be attributed as a kind of self-plagiarism that can have serious consequences. The primary responsibility is that of the authors. Journal editors and reviewers also have to be more vigilant and have to put measures in place to avoid publishing duplicate articles.

Gupta & Kumar (communicated) finds that about 60% of the journals removed from UGC list in the subject Library and Information Science started after 2008.

As a consequence of linking API with the recruitment and promotion, large numbers of new journal publishers, societies, editors, reviewers, authors and publications havemushroomed. Most of them do not seem to have even the requisite knowledge or exposure of publishing, writing, reviewing, editing, etc., and seem to have complete disregard of ethical practices. In light of UGC's focus on journals to have ethical policy, it will useful to see the current status of ethical policy in place for the journals in the UGC approved list.

4. SCOPE AND METHODOLOGY

Presently, there are 293 journals available in the approved list of the UGC having 40 journals from India with 14 e-journals from Library and Information Science (Gupta & Kumar, submitted for publciation, Table 2).In this study, the websites of the 14 LIS e-journals were visited to examine the availability of the ethical policy of the respective journal. In cases, where the ethical policy was given, the same was studied understand the ethical policy adopted by the journal. Such ethical policies are discussed in the following sections:

Table 2. List of Indian LIS e-journals with Publisher Name

S.N.	Journal Name	Publisher
1	Annals of Library and Information Studies	National Institute of Science Communication and Information Resources (NISCAIR)
2	DESIDOC Journal of Library and Information Technology	Defence Scientific Information & Documentation Centre (DESIDOC)
3	Gyankosh : Journal of Library and Information Management	Gyankosh : Journal of Library and Information Management
4	International Journal of Information Library and Society	Publishing India Group
5	International Journal of Information Studies and Libraries	Publishing India Group
6	International Journal of Library, Information, Networks and Knowledge	Scientific Society of Advance Research and Social Change

7	Journal of Advancements in Library Sciences	STM Journals
8	Journal of Scientometric research	phcog.net
9	Journal of Indian Library Association	Indian Library Association, Delhi
10	Library Herald	Indianjournals.com
11	Library Progress (International)	Bulletin of Pure and Applied Sciences
12	Pearl: Journal of Library & Information Science	Indianjournals.com
13	SRELS Journal of Library Management	Informatics Publishing Ltd Bangalore
14	World Digital Libraries: An International Journal	The Energy & Resources Institute (TERI) Delhi

5. DISCUSSION

Author Guidelines : Publication of an article in a journal requires some guidelines to be followed by the author(s). It is helpful for streamlining the processes for paper submission, fair and impartial referral process, availability of uniform services to the authors, and commitment towards ethical processes and improving overall quality. While looking at the Indian LIS e-journals, it is found that most of the journals have such guidelines.

Editorial Policies : All submissions go to the editor/editorial staff for further processing for acceptance or rejection of the paper submitted for publication in the journal. Editorial policy can help the authors and reviewers in adhering while submitting and reviewing the papers, respectively. It may cover aspects such as authorship (including conflict resolution), contribution of each individuals in the paper in case of joint authorship, confidentiality of work, integrity of the process, changes in the content, corrections in the papers, etc. While looking at the Indian LIS e-journals, it is found that seven of the papers have some aspects dealing with the editorial policies, while six journals don't make any mention about this.

Open Access and Licensing : Open access movement is gaining momentum throughout the world. Some countries in Europe have come forward with Open Science policy in coming years. Each journal should have its policy toward open access. While looking at the Indian LIS e-journals, it is found that only one journal is available in the DOAJ while other four journals have papers in open access and rest of the journals have restricted access to content. A journal in the restricted access makes charges from the authors in putting the content in open access. Journals don't provide any information about availability of papers in repository of the institute author works. Only a few journals adopt use of publications in licensing in Creative Commons.

Timeline for Publishing : Time frame for publishing a paper in any journal is not pre-determined. However, in absence of such framework, publication delay is obvious and does not imbibe transparency and any delay on account of the journal may adversely affect the scientific dissemination of information. No doubt, each of the processes from reviewing, correcting, proof reading, copy editing involve many people and time taken in each process in each paper cannot be standardized. However, if any journal mentions date of submission, date(s) of revision, date of acceptance, etc. indicate time taken at each stage. Such information will develop confidence of the contributors and contributors can assess the time taken based on the published papers. While looking at the Indian LIS e-journals, three of the journals make mention of such dates while others don't follow such practice.

Publishing Charges : This is a crucial area of journal publishing as such information is difficult to find for a researcher. Many a times such information is not given at the website of the journal and sometimes charges are levied for different purposes, e.g. compulsion for subscribing journal for a year or two, charges for keeping the journal in open access, charges for processing of paper, etc. While looking at the publishing charges for Indian LIS e-journals, only a few make mentions.

Submission Mode : While looking at the submission mode of Indian LIS e-journals, it is found that eleven of the journals have online submission of paper for publishing in the journals. Three other journals accept papers through e-mail. Some of the journals in online mode use OJS platform for manuscript submission and journal management. Some others do have their own website/arrangement with commercial database providers to submit and manage the journal.

Plagiarism/Ethical Policy : Plagiarism policy demands authors not to allow copying of text from one publication to other publication in any form including duplication in publication, fabrication, and manipulation of facts. Plagiarism policy must inculcate clear intentions and allow good practices to be followed while such case appears. While looking at the Indian LIS e-journals, it is found that these journals use different nomenclatures for such policies and have scattered/minimum information relating to plagiarism and ethics. There are journals which have developed ethical policy after introduction of UGC approved list of journals.

Ethical Policy : Different journals have different way to deal with publication ethics. The practices followed in Indian LIS e-journals are given below:

The SRELS Journal of Information Studies has ethical policy with the title 'Publication ethics' which mentions that 'articles not in accordance with publication ethics and malpractices will be removed from publication if detected at any time. Plagiarism and research fabrication such as making up of data, manipulation of existing data, tables etc. and ethical clearance on the use of humans or animals for the study will also be checked. The journal reserves the right to use plagiarism detecting software to screen submitted papers at any time and suspected plagiarism or duplicate publishing will be reported immediately'. Also makes mention of authors, reviewer's, and editor's responsibilities in this section. The publisher also makes mention of the COPE's best practice guidelines for dealing with ethical issues in a journal.

The Journal of Advances in Library Sciences which is a part of STM Journals mention common ethical policy for journals with 'Publication Ethics & Malpractice Statement' section and listed the ethical responsibilities of the Editors, Peer-reviewers and Authors to meet the journal standards. Publishing behaviour and Unethical Behavior/Misconduct are also covered.

The Journal of Scientometric Research has Publication Ethics and Publication Malpractice Statement' largely follows the large part, on the guidelines and standards developed by the Committee on Publication Ethics (COPE) (http://publicationethics.org/). The relevant duties and expectations of authors, reviewers, and editors of the journal.

International Journal of Information Studies and Libraries has Ethics policy for Journal Publicationwhich asks to agree upon standards of expected ethical behaviour for all partiesinvolved in the act of publishing: the author, the journal editor, the peer reviewer, the publisher and thesociety of society-owned or sponsored journals.

The International Journal of Library, Information, Networks and Knowledge has code of ethics' which mentions that from the researchers' point of view it becomes a personal obligation of our profession that we all maintain a highest ethical and professional conduct and asks to agree the 10 points mentioned therein.

The DESIDOC journal of Information Technology does not have ethical policy 'as such but various ethical issues are covered in publishing policy, as author responsibilities, Digital image integrity and standards, Correction and retraction policy, duplication in publications, etc.

There is a need for all journals to bring out clear ethical policy and followed by all parties involved in publishing of a journal.

6. CONCLUSION

In the past two years, the UGC has taken up steps to streamline the list of journals in order to keep faculty researches published in good journals. Ethical issues are important for the journals which make difference- what is good journal and what is not on various aspects of journal publishing. In this process, role of authors, reviewers, editors, and publishers remains to be liable for any misconduct in the whole process and which bring any deviation from ethical principles. Though, there are no as such 'ethical principles' in practice but none of the act should be against norms for being good. But, it is important to agree upon standards of expected ethical behavior for all parties involved.While studying LIS e-journals, it is found that some journals have brought out ethical policy on their website but this is largely levied on the author responsibilities rather than editor's or publisher's commitments for accepting ethical principle in writing and bring into practice.

REFERENCES

Azeez, A.E.P. (2017). Academic writing and publishing in India: is quality a touchstone?.*Journal of Community Positive Practices*, 17(1), 13. Retrieved from: https://www.questia.com/library/journal/1P4-1929695303/academic-writing-and-publishing-in-india-is-quality. (on 28th June 2018)

BS Web Desk (2018). MHRD allows universities to use 'Turnitin' software to curb PhD plagiarism (2018, June 30). *Business Standard*. Retrieved from: https://www.business-standard.com/article/education/mhrd-allows-universities-to-use-turnitin-software-to-curb-phd-plagiarism-118062700113_1.html. (on 30th June 2018)

De Gruyter (2015). Publication ethics and publication malpractice statement. Retrieved from: https://www.degruyter.com/staticfiles/pdfs/140117_Publication_ethics_and_publication_malpractice_FINAL.pdf (on 21th June 2018)

Economic Times. (2018) Are research papers less accurate and truthful than in the past? Retrieved from: https://www.economist.com/science-and-technology/2018/03/17/are-research-papers-less-accurate-and-truthful-than-in-the-past. (on 28th June 2018)

Electronic Physician (2018). Publication ethics and publication malpractice statement. Retrieved from:http://www.ephysician.ir/index.php/26-about-electronic-physician/142-publication-ethics-and-publication-malpractice-statement (on 21th June 2018)

Elsevier (2018). Publishing Ethics. Retrieved from: https://www.elsevier.com/about/policies/publishing-ethics (on 24th June 2018)

Graf, C., Wager, E., Bowman, A., Fiack, S., Scott-Lichter, D., &Robinson, A. (2007). Best practice guidelines on publication ethics: a publisher's perspective, *Int J ClinPract*, 61 (Suppl. 152), 1–26. Retrieved from: https://www.ncbi.nlm.nih.gov/pmc/articles/PMC1804120/(on 28th June 2018)

Gupta, D. K. & Kumar, V. (Communicated) A Study of the Removed Library and Information Science Journals from the UGC Approved List. *SRELS Journal of Information Management.* (Communicated).

Gupta, D. K. & Kumar, V. (Submitted for publication). Indian e- journals in library and information science: a study based on coverage in UGC approved list. *Annals of Library and Information Studies*

Gupta, D. K., Kumar, V.&Kabra, N. (2017). Library and information science journals on the UGC API list: a Study, *Annals of Library and Information Studies*, 64(1), 76-92.

Jeevan, V. K.J., (2014). Quality improvement and quantity enhancement of Indian LIS journals. *Annals of Library and Information Studies*, 61(3), 217-226.

Laliberte, M. (2017). This Article Has Been Cited 400 Times—but It Doesn't Exist, Reader's Digest. Retrieved from https://www.rd.com/culture/fake-article-cited-400-times/ (on 28th June 2018)

Munigal, A. (2018). Suggested code of ethics and professional conduct for library and information science professionals in India. *Annals of Library and Information Studies*,65(1), 70-76

Patwardhan, B., Nagarkar, S., Gadre, S.R., Lakhotia, S. C., Katoch, V.M. & Moher, D. (2018). A critical analysis of the 'UGC-approved list of journals. *Current Science*, 114(6), 1299-1303. Retrieved from: http://www.currentscience.ac.in/Volumes/114/06/1299.pdf (on 28th June 2018)

PsychOpen publishing psychology (2011). Publication Ethics and Publication Malpractice Statement. Retrieved from: https://www.psychopen.eu/fileadmin/user_upload/documents/guidelines/publication_ethics_and_publication_malpractice_statement.pdf (on 21th June 2018)

Pujar, S.M. (2014). Open access journals in library and information science: a study. *Annals of Library and Information Studies*, 61(3), 199-202.

Pulla, P. (2016, December 16). Predatory publishers gain foothold in Indian academia's upper echelon. *Science*, 1, p.80. Retrieved from: http://www.sciencemag.org/news/2016/12/predatory-publishers-gain-foothold-indian-academia-s-upper-echelon(on 28th June 2018)

Seethapathy, G.S., Santhosh Kumar, J.U. and Hareesha, A.S. (2016). India's scientific publication in predatory journals: need for regulating quality of Indian science and education. *Current Science*, 111(11), 1759–1764. Retrieved from: http://www.currentscience.ac.in/Volumes/111/11/1759.pdf(on 28th June 2018)

Sen, B.K., (2017). An ethical question of LIS profession. *Annals of Library and Information Studies*,64(4), 280-281.

Shafi, S.M., (2014). LIS journals in India: a critical analysis. *Annals of Library and Information Studies*,61(3), 240-242.

Sorokowski, P., Kulczycki, E., Sorokowska, A. and Pisanski, K. (2017, March 22). Predatory journals recruit fake editor. *Nature*, 543(7646). Retrieved from at: https://www.nature.com/news/predatory-journals-recruit-fake-editor-1.21662. (on 28th June 2018)

University Grants Commission (2017). University Grants Commission (Promotion of Academic Integrity and Prevention of Plagiarism in Higher Education Institutions) Regulations – 2017 (Draft) (2017, September 1). Retrieved from: https://www.ugc.ac.in/pdfnews/8864815_UGC-Public-Notice-on-Draft-UGC-Regulations,-2017.pdf(on 24th January 2018)

University Grants Commission (2017a). UGC Regulations on Minimum Qualifications for Appointment of Teachers and other Academic Staffin Universities and Colleges and Measures for the Maintenance of Standards in Higher Education 2010. Retrieved from: http://www.ugc.ac.in/page/UGC-Regulations.aspx. (on 24th January 2018)

University Grants Commission (2017b). UGC Notice reg.: UGC approved List of Journals for the purpose of Career Advancement Scheme (CAS) and Direct Recruitment of Teachers and other academic staff as required under the UGC (Minimum Qualifications for Appointment of Teachers and other Academic Staff in Universities and Colleges) (Published on 11/01/2017). Retrieved from: http://ugc.ac.in/ugc_notices.aspx?id=1604 (on 11th January 2017)

Vishwakarma, P., & Bhaskar, M., (2014). Developing qualitative indicators for journal evaluation: case study of library science journals of SAARC countries. *DESIDOC Journal of Library & Information Technology*, 34(2), 152-161.

20

Controlling Plague of Plagiarism in Indian Academic Institutions: Draft UGC Plagiarism Regulations 2018

Ramesh C. Gaur

1. INTRODUCTION

No research can be done without referring to earlier works by various Researchers in the concerned field. In our education system, students are required to submit projects, assignments, presentations, reports, theses, dissertations and other academic write-ups as partial requirement for award of a degree. Teachers, researchers and students also contribute to various publications such as Journals, monographs and other research publications. For all of the above, researchers are required to refer to a number of resources, both online as well as offline.

In our schooling system, students are given holidays' homework, assignments, and project work etc. Most of the times, these assignments require help either from parents or other resources mainly Internet or published books, journals etc. Generally, these students copy the idea and also the texts from these sources. Most of the assignments submitted by the students to the school teacher do not acknowledge or give credit to the original creator of the information because these students do not know about citations. Moreover, teachers themselves either because they do not know it or, if they know it, they do not feel it important to educate students about the need to give credit to the sources. This encourages a copy-paste culture, and sometimes students get the impression that they are allowed to do so, and that it is perfectly legal to do so.

After schooling, when students arrive in a College or in a University, they get engaged in various research and academic writings. However, in our education system, there is still no way or provision to create awareness about plagiarism or issues associated with it. Till M. Phil or PhD, we do not have any process to educate students about the menace of plagiarism.

Nowadays, when students get registered in PhD, they are required to undergo a pre- PhD course work, and later they are required to attend Research Methodology workshop etc. Most of these programmes also do not have the course contents to educate them or to create awareness about plagiarism. Most of these students are not familiar with reference management tools, citations and other issues related to plagiarism.

2. CURRENT INDIAN SCENARIO

The Hindu, dated July 6, 2014, reported that one PhD student along with a Sr. Scientist in CSIR, IMTECH Chandigarh published three papers in PLoS ONE using fake data. Indian Express reported on 11th July 2016 that an article by three eminent scientists was retracted from the journal 'Applied Microbiology and Biotechnology'. DNA on 4th March, 2014 reported that two Professors from Zoology Department, working at a College affiliated to University of Pune, had been stripped off their status as a PhD guides, and two increments had been stopped after they were found guilty of plagiarism. A female student of Veer Narmad South Gujarat University committed suicide after plagiarism was detected in her M.Phil Dissertation. This was reported on 7th August, 2013 by The Times of India. As per The Times of India news of the 22nd of August, 2013, a Professor in a reputed institution in Gurgaon was terminated on charges of plagiarism. Recently a case has been filed against a Professor in JNU as reported in Media. In September, 2014 the Ministry of Human Resource Development setup a committee to look into the allegations of copyright violation and plagiarism against Delhi University Professors. In one of the cases, the Vice-Chancellor of a University in Uttarakhand was charged by seven Professors from Stanford University, USA for copying their papers.

Detailed accounts of these cases are available on the Internet. There are many such cases available in the public domain. Most of the Media reports reflect that charges are being levelled against teachers, students of even very reputed institutions in India. Concerns were raised by many Academicians and Researchers on the same. Moreover, Universities, colleges and other academic institutions do not have a policy or guidelines to deal with plagiarism. Keeping the above in view, the Ministry of Human Resource Development agreed to constitute a committee to draft Plagiarism Regulations in 2016.The Committee had several drafts and discussions from 2016 to 2018. Finally, in May, 2018, UGC Committee submitted the final draft of the Plagiarism Regulations 2018 to UGC, which was later sent to Ministry of HRD for approval. In June, 2018, the Ministry approved the Plagiarism Regulations 2018, which are expected to be notified soon. Once this is done,it will be mandatory for all colleges and Universities to draft a Plagiarism policy based on these regulations.

3. WHAT IS PLAGIARISM?

Generally speaking, plagiarism is an act of passing off someone else's work as one's own i.e. it is an act of stealing someone's idea, contents etc. It can be intentional as well as unintentional. This kind of research misconduct occurs due to deviations from practices commonly accepted in academic and research activities, generally in proposing, performing, reviewing or reporting research and other creative activities. It has several connotations as follows:

(a) **Fabrication** : It is an international act of making up data or results and recording or reporting them. Under such cases, researchers use fake data instead of real data.

(b) **Falsification** : Falsification is an act of manipulating research materials, equipments or processes or changing or omitting data or results without scientific or statistical justification so that the research is not accurately represented in the research record. Here a researcher may manipulate data, materials and methods to get desired results.

(c) **Fake Peer Reviews** : Recently it was reported on retraction watch.com that 107 papers from a Springer Journal an article titled 'Tumor Biology' was retracted as it was based on fake reviews

(d) **Unintentional plagiarism** : Due to lack of awareness about reference management system or citation methods, a researcher might commit some errors which may results in plagiarism. This may be due to quoting accessibly, failing to use your own voice, careless paraphrasing, or the Researcher may be unfamiliar with International styles of documentation or may not know how to integrate ideas of others, or to document properly. Most of the International Journals and other publications are published in English. In India, students/ researchers come from different backgrounds and regions. So at the time of writing in English, they are not very confident. They try to mix up ideas of others by copy-pasting and hence end up committing mistakes. Unintentional plagiarism is most common in research writings.

3.1. Self plagiarism

Many authors in India often believe that they can use their previous writings as and when required. However, the same International conventions and rules apply on use of your own writings. You need to cite the sources even if you are the author, and can use your writings either by quoting or paraphrasing or summarising. In all these cases, you need to cite the sources. The only exception is use of research papers in theses & dissertation. A PhD/M. Phil student can include his/her paper in theses/dissertations provided that paper is on topic of research and has been published during the period of research, and the researcher is the first author. Otherwise it has to be used as other references.

4. PLAGIARISM DETECTION

Despite all the rules and regulations, it may be possible that some unintentional plagiarism may occur in writings. In order to ensure it as plagiarism free, it is better to check the contents using some plagiarism detection tool. A number of plagiarism detection tools, commercial as well as open sources, are in practice. Most commonly used softwares in India are Turnitin and Urkund. ITHENTICATE is also used by many organizations. ITHENTICATEand Turnitin are from the same company. The basic difference in the two is that one is more used in academic institutions while the other is useful for research institutions. Turnitin has an interconnected student-teacher module which is useful for supervisors to check the contents of PhD, M. Phil and other research works directly. ITHENTICATE is more useful for research institutions and publishing houses. Urkund has been made available to various Universities and other Academic Institutions by INFLIBNET Centre. There are a number of other softwares available to check Plagiarism. However, the quality of plagiarism detection software depends upon the subject coverage. Thus, the report generated using Open Source Software may not be so accurate. Other plagiarism detection tools available are Plagium, Dupli Checker, Plagiarism Checker, Plagiarismdetect, Plagiarisma.net, Eve Plagiarism and Detection System.

Another important issue in plagiarism detection is analysing similarities. No plagiarism detection tool will tell you what and where plagiarism occurs in your contents; it just gives a similarity percentage i.e. the contents which are similar to contents available on internet. Some of these similarities may be coincidental. However, it is advised that each similarity should be verified from the original source. Generally speaking, any similarities beyond four consecutive words need to be cited. However, sometimes this range may be from four to fourteen words, depending on the kind of contents and types of similarities. Another important feature of similarities report is exclusion i.e. what to exclude at the time of checking the contents like small matches, references and bibliography etc. One should know that all contents based on quotations and references may be included or excluded while checking. These similarities can be checked using the following ways:

(i) All coincidental small matches or common knowledge may be ignored. However, you should be sure about it.

(ii) Contents from other sources can be used as quotations or paraphrase or as summary. So each and every similarity should be verified and, as such, proper citation should be recorded.

(iii) In case you wish that all such similarities may be deleted it is advisable to rewrite in your own language. However, even if you wish to rewrite it in your own language even then the original source should be cited.

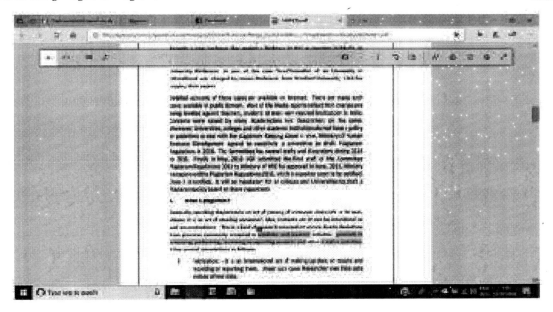

4.1. What percentages of similarities are allowed?

Whenever you interact with Indian researchers on plagiarism, the most common question asked by almost everyone is: what percentage of similarities is allowed? Generally speaking, similarities should be zero percent. However, sometimes it may not be possible due to certain coincidental small matches and common knowledge etc. Efforts should be made to make such similarities at the minimum. However, in case of a good original writings, it should not be more than five to six percent.

5. PLAGIARISM AVOIDANCE

The best method to avoid plagiarism is simply by being honest. First of all, every researcher should go through the respective guidelines before writing a paper, thesis or a book. Many times a researcher is not aware of guidelines to be followed in their research writings. A researcher should also have in place a proper infrastructure such as grammar tools, reference management tools and plagiarism detection tools. An Orientation workshop on what is plagiarism, how to detect and avoid it should be organized for the researcher in a particular institution. The Researcher should also know the authenticated and reliable library resources at their disposal. They should know that use of any already plagiarised resource may create problem for them. They should be advised to register themselves at various research forums, like research gate and academia etc. They should register themselves at ORCID. Every University, college and research institute should have a plagiarism policy in place. The plagiarism policy should provide them with a list of resources to use, list of library resources, penalties and consequences in a detailed manner to help them in improving their research writings. Author workshops should be conducted. They should be encouraged to initiate mutual dialogue with other researchers. Some of the important reference management tools are listed below:

Citation Machine : This site helps researchers and professionals to properly cite sources used. Users can select from APA, MLA, Chicago, and Turabian citation styles.

CrossRef : A collaborative, membership-based association of scholarly publishers, CrossRef calls itself "the citation linking backbone for all scholarly information in electronic form" and serves as a platform for the scholarly community to have easier access to research content.

EasyBib : On EasyBib, users can find easy-to-use citation, note taking, and research tools as well as resources on MLA, APA, and Chicago citation styles. The platform also provides tools and information to help educators teach their students how to be effective researchers.

EndNote : This reference manager allows users to search databases, collect PDFs, organize sources, build and format bibliographies, and share research. The platform is offered in three versions: EndNote X7 (desktop and online), EndNote for iPad, and EndNote basic (free, online-only).

Mendeley : Mendeley is a free reference manager that allows students and researchers to cite as they write, as well as read and annotate PDFs on any device.

OWL - Research and Citation Resources : Purdue OWL offers guides and information on research and proper citation. Find information on APA, MLA, and Chicago styles.

Zotero : An online, free, and easy-to-use tool to help users collect, organize, cite, and share research sources, Zotero can interact with all types of online resources and allows users to automatically extract and save bibliographic references.

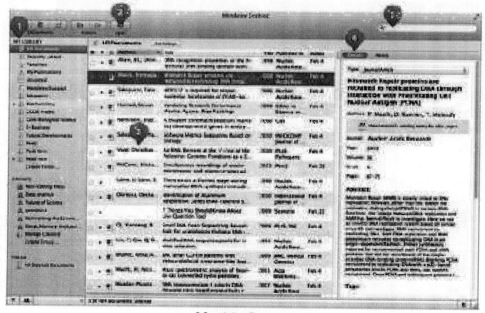

Mendeley Desktop

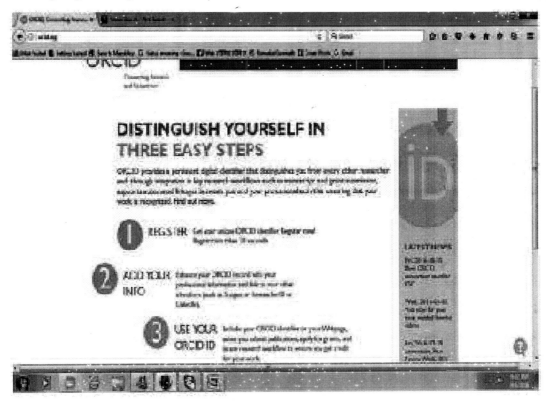

6. UGC PLAGIARISM REGULATION 2018

To deal with the problem of plagiarism, and also to provide guidelines to various universities and colleges for creating awareness and also to lay down a policy on plagiarism, the University Grants Commission (UGC) as per the instructions of Ministry of Human Resource Development, Government of India formed a committee to draft Plagiarism Regulations. After several meetings and brainstorming Sessions in 2016, 2017 & 2018, the committee drafted comprehensive plagiarism regulations. Now these draft regulations have also been approved by the Ministry of Human Resource Development, Government of India and soon it is going to be notified by the UGC for further implementation by academic institutions.

7. SALIENT FEATURES OF THE UGC PLAGIARISM REGULATION 2018

These regulations will be mandatory guidelines to be followed in Universities and Colleges in India. Every Higher Educational Institution has to frame a policy based on these guidelines. Some of the important tasks to be undertaken by these institutions in this regard are as follows:

(i) Awareness : Every University and College will have to organize training workshops and programmes to create awareness about what is plagiarism, how to detect plagiarism, and its avoidance for the faculty, staff and students.

(ii) Training in use of Reference Management Tools : In all research writings, a reference list is to be provided. Based on a subject discipline, a researcher has to prepare reference list using a citation style such as APA or MLA etc. So a researcher should have knowledge of such styles. Moreover, a number of online reference management tools such as Endnote, Mandatory and Zotero etc. are available for use.

(iii) Infrastructure : Every Higher Educational Institution has to create a proper infrastructure for detection and avoidance of plagiarism. Suitable plagiarism detection software is to be provided for checking contents such as theses, research papers and books etc. A training programme to understand use of such tools is to be organized. A number of plagiarism detection tools are available. INFLIBNET Centre is also providing access to such tools to many Universities in India. Institutions should create a mechanism to ensure checking of all contents.

(iv) Introduction of new course work on Plagiarism and Research Ethics. Academic Institutions should include a compulsory course-work/module at UG/PG level on Academic Integrity and Publication Ethics.

(v) Formation of Committees : Every Higher Educational Institution has to constitute the following two committees as per the guidelines given in these regulations:

(a) Departmental Academic Integrity Panel (DAIP)
(b) Institutional Academic Integrity Panel (IAIP)

Also, proper information regarding formation of these committees is to be circulated to all concerned.

8. PENALTIES

In these regulations plagiarism has been levelled and according to each level penalties have been proposed. These are minimum penalties for respective offence. However, institutions are free to set higher norms according to their needs. Up to 10% similarities in form of small matches, coincidental words, and common knowledge have been left out from penalties. The penalties have been divided into three levels 10-40%, 40-60%, and 60% and above. Penalties range from warming to cancellation of degree for students and maximum dismissal from service in case of faculty and staff.

9. CONCLUSIONS

The draft plagiarism regulations committee has tried to put in place realistic workable, achievable and flexible guidelines to help universities and colleges in ensuring quality research publications. It is the responsibility of the faculty, students, researchers and administrators to ensure that these regulations are implemented in the right spirit. One has to understand that plagiarism destroys the academic reputation of the researcher, University/ Institution and the reputation of a country also. It is not helpful in creating a proper original research publication. Original research leads to innovations and enhances development of a country. It is more helpful in building a good career. So the best way to avoid plagiarism is to be honest and to believe in yourself to write a good original research publication. India is amongst the top 5 countries in terms of number of papers published. However in terms of contributing original research, same is not applied. India is even not included in the list of top 10 countries in case of citations. Plagiarism may be one of the reasons for poor quality research papers. Plagiarism is should not be considered just an ethical issue; it needs to be dealt with in a proper way. It can be controlled with proper awareness, training, and by using the emerging tools and technologies. UGC plagiarism regulations 2018 once in place will be instrumental in creating an ideal research environment and controlling plagiarism.

REFERENCES

MSU Procedures Concerning Allegations of Misconduct in Research and Creative Activities,http://rio.msu.edu/June_2009_Procedures.pdf

http://orei.unimelb.edu.au/content/fabrication-falsification-plagiarism

Draft UGC Plagiarism Regulations 2018 (unpublished)

21

The Pressures and Perils of Overachieving - An Inquiry into the Kaavya Viswanathan Case

Gurpartap S. Khairah
Nirmal Singh

In the year 2006, an India born Tamilian, US citizen nineteen years young girl shot to fame when she received a huge advance for her book from a reputed publisher, Little, Brown and Company. The girl was Kaavya Viswanathan and the book that had received widespread acclaim was 'How Opal Mehta got kissed, got wild, and got a life'. This chic-lit book was published among huge fanfare and everyone looked at it as a publishing phenomenon. This anticipation proved to be right but in a completely wrong sense. Within a week of its release instances of plagiarism followed by those of blatant copying were levelled at the young writer. All those having stakes in the book became offensive, then defensive and finally apologetic. The infamous novel was withdrawn but by then it had succeeded in stirring up a hornet's nest of controversy between outright plagiarism and cryptomensia. The incident shed new light on the unethical practice of plagiarism but even more interesting was the aspect of the ways and means of defending 'unintentional' plagiarism. Also of interest is the validation of terms brought into use by the accused. The 'why' of the whole episode also needs to be examined in detail. The incident remains a watershed in the annals of plagiarism and needs to be discussed at length to determine what really constitutes plagiarism.

'In the beginning was the Word, and the Word was with God and the Word was God' (John 1:1-3). This line from the Old Testament puts the 'word' on a holy pedestal, comparing it straight with God. But over the years the sanctity of the word has diminished. Everyone, at one stage or another, has 'borrowed' from some other sources. It isn't the borrowing that's unethical or offensive; being conscious of it does mitigate the offense. What makes the act odious is not acknowledging it and passing the material as one's own. Such people, it appears, rely solely on luck, hoping that no one would notice the similarities, or having noted it that they would take it lightly and not do anything about it. Many a time luck does favour the bravados; their misdoings go undetected, or merely ignored as trivial. But many others are not so fortunate, and when they are found out all hell breaks loose. This is what happened with the young prodigy Kaavya Viswanathan. Her story was the stuff that fairy tales are made off. But soon it became apparent that this particular fairy tale had a nightmarish twist to it.

The witticism 'Great poets imitate and improve whereas small ones steal and spoil' seems to be an apt summarization for the Kaavya Viswanathan's infamous case. The young girl who shot into short-lived limelight with incredible advance amounts rumoured to be five *lac* US dollars and contracts for her two books and a Hollywood movie also came in for brickbats when charges of plagiarism were not only levelled against her but were also proven. Advocators of Kaavya - albeit her publisher, agent and lawyers - thought up new and impressive sounding terms protecting her case, but those others who were one removed from her harboured their own misgivings and opinion about the whole case.

But the seeds of this infamous episode were not sown overnight; their origins can be traced right back to Kaavya's childhood. It was obvious that she was a precocious child. Her ambitious and proud parents invested lot of time and money in her right education to get her into an Ivy League institution — that she eventually did with aplomb (Lampert,2008,20). Her mother had given up her flourishing practice as a gynaecologist and devoted herself for the nurturing of her daughter's exceptional talent as she had shown excellent aptitude in everything she put her hand to. She "started cello lessons at 5, studied four foreign languages beginning at 6, had near-perfect SAT scores and was president of three honors societies in high school" (Smith, 2006a). This unusual talent predicted huge success for the young child who was clearly seen as a prodigy. Much praise was lavished upon the young girl from many quarters including from the celebrated author Amitav Ghosh who saw 'astonishing poise' in the budding writer. Such attention became the cause of trying to aspire for the skies at any cost. The pressure on the young girl to prove herself and to achieve must have been overwhelming. She devised her own means to handle it. Thus, it came hardly as a surprise when she wrote a novel and it was this well-received. What came later was a source of shock, not surprise.

Similarities in the text were traced to two novels by Megan McCafferty (*First Timers and Second Helpings*) but Kaavya denied the charges. When accosted with the problem she turned hostile and replied with a brazen 'No comment. I don't know what you are talking about' (Zhou 2006b). In the first instance, Kaavya claimed that the story of 'Opal Mehta' had been inspired from own childhood and what she had seen around her while she was growing up (Kapadia, 2006). The inspiration behind 'Opal Mehta' and her struggles was allegedly dredged up from her own life and her "own experiences of applying to college... (and) were also themed about a young woman from New Jersey trying to get into an Ivy League college in Columbia" (Smith, 2006b). This sounded plausible as she did have that particular experience.

Interestingly, in an interview when she was asked to name her favourite writers, Kaavya did not mention Megan McCafferty at all. She cited Amitav Ghosh and Kazuo Ishiguro as her favourite authors. But later when the controversy erupted and similarities had been pointed out, she did bend a little. Kaavya admitted that Megan too had been her all-time favourite writers. She admitted to "reading McCafferty's books in high school days." Again with an attempt at innocence, she said that "I wasn't aware of how much I may have internalized Ms. McCafferty's words." Having admitted that, when told that the publishers might initiate legal action against her, she once again resorted to her stance of it all being "unintentional and unconscious" (Smith, 2006b) and even wondered why they would take such action against something that was "a genuine, genuine mistake... [as she had] never looked at them while I was writing 'Opal.' They're on my bookshelf at home" (Zhou, 2006b). The fears and pressures at this stage of her career, when it was all at the brink, can only be imagined. Here was a young girl, barely out of her teens, being promised the skies – after all, not everyone is offered huge monetary advances, movie contracts. That she was out on a ledge to hold onto it by means, fair or foul, is understandable. She acknowledged her debt to the writer and also talked about issuing an apology and going into damage control mode by assuring McCafferty that the objectionable text would be expunged from her to be immediately revised novel.

But in spite of her changed apologetic stand, she was in for no reprieve from any corner. Her case went from bad to worse almost instantly. It was later brought to attention that Kaavya had not only 'internalised' from the novels of one writer alone but her text bore striking 'similarities' to other novels by different writers. It soon appeared that passages from Salman Rushdie's *Haroun and the Sea of Stories* had also been seemingly 'internalised'.

More excuses were wrought up and it was claimed that she had a photographic memory and all the 'copying' might have been an unconscious and unfortunate recall. The theory didn't fit well when it came out as a case of 'total recall'. It then became apparent that her claims of having memorized and reproduced entire passages were nothing but fabrications to save skin. It was obvious that she had also lifted passages from different writers of the same genre. Books like Sophie Kinsella's "Can You Keep a Secret?", Meg Cabot's "The Princess Diaries" and Tanuja Desai Hidier's "Born Confused" (www.Vivlish.com, 2006) (Fahrenthold, 2006) had been used liberally by Kaavya during the writing of her own novel. It was at this point that Kaavya's stand of being innocent came down like a house of cards. This was the point of no return for her. She knew that it would be impossible to deny using as many as 40 passages unintentionally and unconsciously. Publishers too called her apology as 'troubling and disingenuous'. Quoting the similarity in more than 40 passages in Ms. Viswanathan's book and McCafferty's, Steve Ross of Crown Publishing House said that as the book contains "identical language and/or common scene or dialogue structure from Megan McCafferty's first two books... [and] based on the scope and character of the similarities, it is inconceivable that this was a display of youthful innocence or an unconscious or unintentional act." (Smith, 2006b; www.Vivlish.com, 2006; Zhou, 2006b)

Those who had praised her, namely many other notable writers like Salman Rushdie and Amitav Ghosh also changed sides when blatant instances of 'copying' were levelled and later proven. Salman Rushdie said that he could not believe her claims of being innocent as he could not believe "the idea that this could have been accidentally or innocently done" (http://www.rediff.com/news/report/kaavya/20060502.htm).

Everything that had been offered to the young author – advances, book and movie contracts – were withdrawn swiftly as were the copies of the ill-fated novel, leaving Kaavya high and dry. Her case highlights the many aspects of plagiarism and the myriad excuses one could think up to 'defend' one's case. Right from Carl Jung's concept of 'collective unconscious' to 'cryptomensia', Kaayva's case traversed every term in the book. To this day, it remains arguably the most highlighted instance of plagiarism and the shifting stands adopted by the writer. The swift rather instant retribution that followed should serve as an example to deter everyone who wishes to write anything – research paper, memoir, biography, novel – from plagiarism. But what needs to be done for writers is to take the edge off by reducing the pressure upon the writers. If resorted to just for the sake of convenience and comfort – after all copying is damn easier than creative writing – it should be dealt with swiftly and with action strict enough to deter others from doing the same. But if done after buckling due to mounting pressures and the fear of loss of the offered incentives, it is time to think of the system that is at work behind the scenes. It is imaginable that someone would lie to save face and the lucrative deal. Perhaps, if the pressure of making something of oneself were taken off, people would be inspired to think and write original works to earn genuine credit, and fame, if any.

REFERENCES

Fahrenthold, David A. (2006). Publisher Pulls Young Author's Suspect Novel, By Washington Post Staff Writer, Friday, April 28, 2006, Washington Post.

Kapadia, Payal (2006) "[Interview with Kaavya Viswannathan]" *Outlook* 1May 2008. https://www.outlookindia.com/magazine/story/kaavya-viswanathan/231130

Lampert, Lynn D. (2008) *Combating student plagiarism; An academic librarian's guide.* Oxford: Chandos, pp.17-23

Smith, Dinitia (2006a). Teenager gets a life, and writes about it. *New York Times*, April 10, 2006. https://www.nytimes.com/2006/04/10/arts/teenager-gets-a-life-and-writes-about-it.html

Smith, Dinitia (2006b). Aggrieved Publisher Rejects Young Novelist's Apology. *New York Times*, April 26, 2006. https://www.nytimes.com/2006/04/26/books/aggrieved-publisher-rejects-young-novelists-apology.html

Zhou, David (2006a). Examples of Similar Passages between Viswanathan's Book and McCafferty's Two Novels. *Harvard Crimson*, April 23, 2006. https://www.thecrimson.com/article/2006/4/23/examples-of-similar-passages-between-viswanathans/

Zhou, David (2006b). College Looking Into Plagiarism Accusations: Viswanathan tells NBC's Today Show she is "taking a few days off" from Harvard The Crimson. *Harvard Crimson*, April 27, 2006. https://www.thecrimson.com/article/2006/4/27/college-looking-into-plagiarism-accusations-the/

www.Vivlish.com (2006). Viswanathan yet another faker. http://tarnishedlady.typepad.com/tarnishedlady/2006/05/viswanathan_yet.html

22

Anti-Plagiarism Software Check to the Doctoral Theses in Indian Universities and Institutions

S. T. Kale

1. INTRODUCTION

The information age makes a huge use of internet based information and web 2.0 tools are more interactive where making copy of other documents not difficult for information users among them students are mainstream factor for information use across the World. The plagiarism has increased many folds and considered to be a misdeed for the doctoral theses and other academic works in the universities and institution to uphold academic degree. Plagiarism originated in early 17th century from the Latin word *plagiarius*. The Oxford Dictionary defines plagiarism as "The practice of someone else's work or ideas passing them as one's own". The United States Office of Research Integrity (ORI) defines plagiarism as "Both the theft and misappropriation of intellectual property and the substantial unattributed textual copying of another's work" Different forms of plagiarism took place became more ambiguous have to protect from plagiarism. Most common forms of plagiarism in the writings are *ghost writer* making a copy of another work's word for word and verbatim to this without being of citing the original document. *The photocopy* writer has to make copy of significant portion of another writings from one and single source without modification and acknowledgment to the source used. *The Potluck Paper* writer attempt of copying from several other sources with a few changes have made of paragraphs and sentences retaining most of the original phrasing. *The Self-Stealer* writer borrows idea generously from own previous works and common threat to all above not putting the original source (Bansal, 2018). Above types of plagiarism generally found in the academic writings consisting of journal papers, conference- seminars papers, project reports, books and theses and dissertations etc. Most stealers even don't know that plagiarism is a crime both legally and ethically which is common in India even common in developed countries and other part of World. (McCabe, 2010). In this context especially doctoral theses are known to be first unpublished (sometime may published its findings in primary publications) record of original research and development or description of a new application or a new interpretation of old theme to be written for doctoral research. It is an important document category and outcome of deliberate efforts made by the research scholar usually expected to explain original pieces of evidence in the concerned field of discipline. Meanwhile mainstream Indian university departments suffered from bad exercises mostly nonexistence of academic norms followed, the standards of research degree deteriorated measurably. "Most of research work suffers from number of ills mere repetition of earlier work, over exploration of a given ideas, unethical practices such as plagiarism" (Das, 2015) "The process of scrutiny, validation and approval of doctoral dissertations is confined to few experts identified by the university on recommendation of theses supervisors it was not opened to the scientific community at large and quality sacrificed" (University Grants Commission, 2005). Moreover, doctoral theses after its approval in most of university libraries in India remain a closed access rather than available for the further research to avoid unnecessary duplication and repetition. India is presently producing 27671 doctoral theses (UGC, 2017) both in English and other regional languages and sustain this work original is present day task and policy of apex bodies in India targeting to maintain originality in the doctoral theses and other academic writings. The regulation published in Gazette of India issued by the University Grants Commission titled "UGC Minimum Standard and Procedure for award of M.Phil. and PhD degree regulation 2009" under UGC Act 1956 circulated to all universities, deemed to be universities, Institutions of National Importance and affiliated colleges offered research degree both regular and distance education mode mandated to run course work and training to scholars, admission procedure, eligibility of supervisor, evaluation and assessment methods and deposition of softcopy of thesis to Shodhganga repository within the period of 30 days (UGC, 2009). One such regulation has been published in the gazette of India issued by UGC titled "University Grants Commission (Minimum Standards and Procedure for Award of M.PHIL./PH.D Degrees) Regulations, 2016" provided that "institutions shall evolve a mechanism using well-developed software and gadgets to detect plagiarism while submitting for evaluation the dissertation/ thesis ... vouching that there is no plagiarism"(UGC, 2016, p.11). Prior to this, setting up the ETD labs and digitization of retrospective theses were the issues at University Grants Commission that were already implemented in most of the Indian Universities as a significant infrastructural provision for the plagiarism detection.

2. COPYRIGHT IN INDIA

The plagiarism and other similar misconducts are considered as a fraud and illegal in almost all the countries the world which have copyright legislation. We have copyright legislation enactment parallel to the other developed countries and according to this the original ideas and thoughts discovered by any individual or group are protected because these ideas or thoughts are considered intellectual property thereby protecting authorship and other such rights from unlawfulness and other misconducts. This protection is valid for expression of idea and not the idea itself and if found infringed the law provided punishment in diverse range according to severity of misconduct. At the same time the law gives liberty to the general public to use other's work for scholarship under fair use dealing. The fair use is doctrine that tolerates limited use of copyrighted material without consent of copyright owner for research, education and social benefit. Most of the time releases funds for this discovery from government treasury basically collected from public and discoveries to certain extent tolerated for the public. Authorship and creativity require deliberate efforts and hard work hence time span for copyright protection in India according to this law is lifetime of author and a term of 60 years after his/her death. After expiry the work is open for public under public domain one may use it without authorization not for profit purpose. The plagiarism is somewhat different from copyrights infringement.

3. PLAGIARISM CHECK METHOD IN INDIA

The anti-plagiarism software enables scanning of documents against billions of online sources such as web pages, local database and databases of journals and periodicals and online scholarly publications and similarity is generated to estimate the percentage of matches. The software tool looks matches a string of eight to ten words (Jones, 2008). "It extracts the text portions and looks through them for matching words in phrases of a specified minimum length. When it finds matching files that share enough words in a number of phrases, a report generated which contain the document text with the matching phrases underlined". Omission is possible while calculating similarity of documents. Many software systems both licensing and free are available however performance always depends on large databases size and capability of tool. Wan-Yu Lin "introduced a frame work that identify online plagiarism by exploiting lexical, syntactic and semantic features that includes duplication-gram, reordering and alignment of words, POS and phrase tags, and semantic similarity of sentences." Efstathios Stamatatos "proposed a method based on structural information provided by occurrences of a small list of stop words. The research elaborated that stop word n-grams are able to capture local syntactic similarities between suspicious and original documents and algorithm for detecting the exact boundaries of plagiarized and source passages was proposed." Most Indian universities 30% plagiarism in theses considering admissible beyond 30% stealing in the doctoral theses treated as plagiarized while some other excludes plagiarism threshold in the range of 15 – 25 %. The INFLIBNET (UGC) recommended URKUND Plagiarism Checker the anti-plagiarism tool developed by Prio Info center AB being used by more than 250 universities and colleges in India and more than 3000 institutes worldwide like Europe, US, Asia and the Middle East parts. The service had it origin from academic field where "Some teachers hit on the idea of creating a web-based service that could help them to detect student cheating and plagiarism came to be set up in autumn 2000" The INFLIBNET Centre chosen URKUND a global tender offering anti-plagiarism service to the Indian universities that having memorandum of understanding (MOU) with INFLIBNET eligible who have a status under 2 f and 12 (B) of

University Grants Commission Act (e-Galactic, n.d.). URKUND enable checking of documents from three central source areas are materials such as web pages, published materials in the form of journals and other scholarly material by large publication houses and previously submitted student's assignments. The UGC 2015 onward anti plagiarism made mandatory to all eligible universities in India to check doctoral theses for plagiarism detection purpose using Urkund software. This software mark text of theses if copied 30 consecutive words from the writings of others not acknowledged with quotation marks. It identifies mere quotation marks rather than standards and rules of specified by various citation styles. TURNITIN plagiarism checker is another anti-plagiarism software is cloud based service developed by i-paradigm to advance the student learning and evaluation is now being using over 15000 institutions and universities in 140 countries in the world processing about 300000 papers per day and 600000 papers per pick days support nineteen languages" (Suseela, 2016). More than 80% of UK universities applying Turnitin tool (Jones, 2008). Many US universities give priority to apply the Turnitin tool. Textual similarities of Indian languages are concern Turnitin and Urkund both are unable for searches for the plagiarism detection in Indian languages. The INFLIBNET an early stage of scanning of doctoral theses in Indian universities already used Turnitin & i-Thenticate for scanning for similarity index in the doctoral theses of hundreds of universities in India on trial basis in 2014. Institutions in the category of institution of national importance are using this Turnitin tool to detect the plagiarism / similarity check.

4. REVIEW OF LITERATURE

"A survey conducted in 2005 as part of Centre of Academic Integrity's Assessment project reveals that 40% of students admitted to engaging in plagiarism as compared to 10% reported in 1999" (CAI 2005). "Another mass survey conducted by a Rutgers University professor in 2003 reports 38% of students involved in online plagiarism these alarming figures show a gradual increase and new generation is more aware of technology than ever before" (Rutgers, 2003) "Plagiarism now is not confined to mere cut and paste; synonymizing and translation technologies are giving a new dimension to plagiarism" (Maurer, Kappe & Bilal Zaka, 2006). The Institute of Electrical and Electronics Engineers (2017) published list of authors prohibited not to submit their manuscripts for publication all IEEE journals due to the alleged plagiarized noticed in accordance with violation of section 8.2.4.C of the IEEE PSPB operations Manual. In 1228 authors list most authors are from the countries of India, China, Pakistan, Bangladesh, Korea and other parts of World. Further the list revealed majority authors prohibited from India are working at various private engineering colleges and university departments (The Institute of Electrical and Electronics Engineers, 2017). The country scenario of most resent plagiarized cases both allegation and confirmed by the judiciaries in India is presented here as an example to sought for the current picture in order to testify the facts. A doctoral research supervisor at University of Mysore was suspended for the period five years by allegation of plagiarism, a student under his supervision submitted doctoral thesis to the university is 27% plagiarized from various sources published earlier shown after scanning of anti-plagiarism tool used by the university. The appeal for relief is filed in the high court against suspension in which presented fact that the 30% plagiarism is acceptable under the university rule, high court then invalidated the order of Mysore University for suspension of research supervisor on the ground that "Admissibility of plagiarism to the extent of 30 percent if permitted, the same requires to be examined by the syndicate with reference to the rules and the regulations framed by the university to that effect." (Prasad, 2017). Another case in the Panjabi University Patiala the allegation to the submitted doctoral thesis on "Changing Trends in Contemporary Hindi Cinema" is plagiarized from previously published articles including Wikipedia information. The university approved anti-plagiarism check software shown the thesis has 21% plagiarism and research supervisor has given clean cheat from the allegation that "Software-generated report could not be taken for granted and human judgment is needed to determine the copying" (Khaira, 2017). A complaint for the blame of plagiarism in the University of Mumbai with a copy to the chancellor and Governor of Maharashtra against the professor of econometrics working at school of Economics and Public Policy at University of Mumbai, described that the doctoral thesis submitted by the professor where complainant stated that the professor has made illegal stealing of some part from his wife's doctoral thesis. An alleged professor denied accusation of plagiarism and claimed that the present lifting is part of his own paper published earlier and his wife borrowed ideas from working paper indicated that self-plagiarism, certain extent is allowed for the next research writings further he says university has no clear plagiarism policy and framework. (Correspondent, Hindustan Times, 2018). A case of the country's leading Jawaharlal Nehru University (JNU) teacher working as an assistant professor in Political Geography at Centre of International Politics Organization and Disarmament (CIPOD) School of International Studies who has discharged additionally members of certain administrative committees has accused copying almost verbatim to his M. Phil. dissertation titled "Broader Management problems in South American Geopolitics : an Assessment " from San Diego and David R. Mares' University of California . The whole text of dissertation has been scanned through anti-plagiarism tool Turnitin the result gone up to 45% dissertation text is copied without proper acknowledgement to San Diego and David R. Mares' work (Mahaprashasta, 2018). The complaint by research scholar same university against a teacher designated assistant professor working at Centre for the Study of Discrimination and Exclusion, School of Social Sciences accused plagiarism of her doctoral thesis titled "Role of Tourism in Economic and Social Development of Thailand" copying 73% from the original sources after scanned through Turnitin anti-plagiarism tool. Moreover, a doctoral thesis titled "Political Radicalism in Pre-Islamic Revolutionary Persian Literature of Iran with Special Reference to the writings of Dr. Ali Shariati." completed in 2000 accused by a teacher presently working as an associated professor at Jawaharlal Nehru University New Delhi. The doctoral thesis found plagiarized verbatim from fifteen different sources published previously. The appeal is filed by Jawaharlal Nehru University based research scholar to the Delhi High court "bench sought an explanation from the professor, and listed the matter for further inquiry during earlier hearing court stated "Plagiarism cannot be tolerated by any professor. If they indulge in this kind of practice, criminal action can be taken against them" (Singh, 2018). A research scholar submitted thesis titled "A History of Educational Progress of scheduled tribes in Thane district 1947-2000" to the Mumbai

University in 2002 and complaint to the University of Mumbai against scholar that made copy exactly of earlier submitted work by another researcher. To look into the matter the University of Mumbai has constituted a committee after enquiry against accused and his supervisor both are debarred not given relief against committee decision by the Bombay high court and banned the research scholar and his supervisor for the PhD programme for the period of five years. (Thomas, 2015). Sunderland-smith and Carr (2008) argued that "The software would high light passages of text and identify those passages as plagiarized, Turnitin not to be considered as plagiarism detection system it is merely text matching system". Further academics "expected the would need very little input in identification of plagiarism" "It is still the role of academic to review the report to determine if plagiarism has actually occurred, because Turnitin does not differentiate between correctly cited references and unacknowledged copying. Also one must be aware that there is difference between incorrect referencing and intentional plagiarism, this judgment can only be made by a human and not by software" Tejani (2018) research gate based scientist gives particular towards use of anti-plagiarism software that "Urkund is not reliable to check plagiarism that he had checked paper with Urkund and Turnitin the result was shocking Urkund shown 5% similarity whereas Turnitin revealed 90% similarity for the same text of a paper." Puri (2017) "The tool when posed with a multi-lingual document containing English, Hindi and Punjabi text failed to provide the accurate results for testing purpose, a sample research paper consisting of Hindi, Punjabi and English was downloaded from Internet and submitted to the Turnitin platform. Logically, this paper was supposed to give 100% plagiarism as the paper itself was downloaded from Internet; however, it calculated only 72% similarity. On further investigations, it was found that the Turnitin engine only detected the English words, but failed to recognize the Punjabi and Hindi text at all." Satija (2015) explained that "Every university and research center must adopt a zero tolerance policy for unfair means in research and writing" Same think described by most scientists and researchers on research-gate attitude zero tolerance plagiarism policy has to be adopted by the institutions and universities in the World and plagiarism is not acceptable in any percentage.

5. OBJECTIVES OF STUDY

- To review some recent doctoral research controversies on high plagiarism percentage, tolerance limit, related issues and present them as an effect of anti-plagiarism check on doctoral degree programs in the country.
- Anti-plagiarism check of the doctoral theses of dissimilar subjects of Indian universities written in English language and those doctoral theses not written in English language obliviously written in various Indian regional languages how the software tool can facilitate the scanning process by the recommended software tool for the doctoral theses written in different regional languages.
- Similarly some of the doctoral theses are in the form of scan images enlisted in Open DOAR and elsewhere on internet. Is the software tool is able to scan such doctoral theses text for plagiarism detection purpose?

- To testify present software tool accepted by the UGC on behalf of Indian universities for scanning of PhD theses for plagiarism detection showing different level of plagiarism percentage when compared to other established software tool.

6. METHODOLOGY

Policy documents (from 142 universities listed in appendix) in the form of ordinances, policy papers, newspapers reviews, regulations, reports of universities, plagiarism checking guidelines were analyzed to draw the findings purpose. Further review of doctoral research set-up in consideration of the minimum Standard and Procedure for award of M.Phil.and PhD degree regulation 2009 and "Minimum Standards and Procedure for Award of M.PHIL./PH.D Degrees Regulations 2016 issued by the University Grants Commission in the context of deposition soft copy of thesis in Shodhganga theses repository and applying the mechanism using well-developed software gadget to detect plagiarism while submitting for evaluation to the university concerned in India vouching that there is no plagiarism.

7. DISCUSSION

Following analysis has been made to show a tangible picture on various current plagiarism related issues.

8. DOCTORAL THESES ONLINE

There are 795 universities in India among them 385 universities (48%) have completed memorandum of understanding with INFLIBNET Centre for deposition of softcopy of thesis to Shodhganga repository, and 325 universities (41%) are actually contributing to make their doctoral theses online through Shodhganga theses repositories, so far it has hosted 193570 doctoral theses (as on 7th June 2018) figure mounting incessantly one of the fast growing repository in the World to make their theses online in full text open access. Such large part of database size is the basic infrastructure for plagiarism check through software tool to prevent absolute similarity in the theses. (Information and Library Network center [INFLIBNET], 2018).

9. TOLERANCE LIMIT OF PLAGIARISM

While evaluating the doctoral theses in the universities in India, different prevailing tolerance limits for plagiarism have been found out for acceptance of plagiarism/ similarities percentage in the theses. Among them Punjab University "As per norms, around 10-15 per cent similarity is allowed in research papers, but the percentage can be higher depending upon the bibliography" (Minhas, 2016). Some other universities have a rule of tolerance percentage allowed below 30% while beyond 30% the thesis text would have to be considered as plagiarized. Plagiarism percentage accepted in the universities are University of Mysore 30%, University of Mumbai 30%, Bharatidasan University 30% Guwahati University 20%, Visvesvaraya Technological University Belgum 25%, Madras University Chennai 20% for science disciplines and 30% for the mathematics, arts, humanities, social sciences, commerce and management disciplines, MGR Medical University Channai 25%, Pondicherry University 15%, and Jagannath

University Jaipur 20%, Acharya Nagarjuna University Guntur 30%, Swami Ramanand Thirth Marathawada University Nanded 30%, Alagappa University Karaikudi 30%, Central University of Karnataka Gulbarga 30% and Kuvempu University Shimoga 30%.

10. ORIENTATION PROGRAMS AND COURSE WORK

The universities as per UGC regulation conducting the course work for new scholars before commencing doctoral research. The course work is prior training of some duration understanding basic methods of research like understanding review of literature, techniques of data collection, computer application in research, methods for plagiarism free writing and use of citation methods and anti-plagiarism software functionality etc. Some universities organized specialized one day orientation programs in universities jointly by the INFLIBNET center among them are Jawaharlal University New Delhi, Guru Nanak Dev University Amritsar, Bundelkhand University Jhansi, Anna University, Pondicherry University, University of Calicut, and Tezpur University etc.

11. PLAGIARISM POLICIES PRIOR TO UGC REGULATION

There are some universities and intuitions of national importance were existed in India which had separate plagiarism policies at their university and institution level. The University of Pune, Jawaharlal Nehru University New Delhi, Indian Institute Technology Delhi, Indian Institute Technology Mumbai, Indian Institute Technology Kharagpur, Calicut University, Gujarat University Ahmadabad, Punjab University Chandigarh, Jagannath University, Jaipur have had their own plagiarism policies prior to the enforcement of UGC regulations.

12. RESULTS

1. The formation of Shodhganga national theses repository has made positive impact on plagiarism check/matching similarity index in the doctoral theses submitted to the Indian universities because this has completed a database of millions of doctoral theses mandated to deposit a softcopy of doctoral thesis to the INFLIBNET by the UGC regulation 2009. The Indian universities and institutions find similarity index using software tool recommended, any new works submitting to the universities in India prohibiting from false work and absolute copying of doctoral theses. The Shodhganga repository presently hosted 193850 doctoral theses (as on 11.06.2018) from 325 universities in India made a basic infrastructure of database of millions of doctoral theses to curb plagiarism and related concern is a milestone.

2. It is observed that Some Ph.D controversies in the Indian Universities already gone to the law courts in India that the text in the concerned PhD thesis has plagiarized from another sources. The appellant has given relief from punishment by concerned high courts and commented that "Admissibility of plagiarism to the extent of 30 percent if permitted, the same requires to be examined by the syndicate with reference to the rules and the regulations framed by the university to that effect" in another case "Software-

generated report could not be taken for granted and human judgment is needed to determine the copying." Jones (2008) already pointed that "there are some problems with the text matching algorithm, the result obtained thus far from the use of turnitin software have revealed occasions where text highlighted can be considered as innocent... " Sunderland -Smith and Carr (2005) observed that "the software would highlight passages of text and identify those passages as plagiarized, it must be made clear the Turnitin should not be really plagiarism detection system is merely text matching system"

3. There is disagreement on tolerance of plagiarism percentage accepted by the Indian universities, as per norms most universities declared tolerance plagiarism limit up to 30% whereas few other universities allowed tolerance limits in range of 15-25% for the introduction and review of literature uses the definitions and common theories and mathematical equations are the common knowledge to earlier published literature may be plagiarized to certain extent. While analyzing web document through Google search engine no written evidences were found from the most of the universities in India to justify the minimum similarity percentage accepted in the doctoral thesis. Whereas INFLIBNET Centre who is responsible as monitoring and coordinating agency to the all universities pronounces not recommend any percentage criteria for minimum plagiarism percentage as permitted in the thesis during scanning of PhD text by the software tool, the criteria depends on individual university and research guides. There are different opinions on tolerance limit of plagiarism in the world. However, majority of scientists and researchers in the world articulated that the plagiarism has to be at zero level some other said it should below 10% due to some repetition of thoughts and ideas mostly the definitions and thought expressed in the review of literature.

4. There is disparity in calculating the similarity index while scanning the thesis and research paper by the recommended URKUND anti- plagiarism tool if comparing with other similar software tool like turnitin. Example here quoted that same work prepare for doctoral degree at SGB Amravati University on nanotechnology application checked by UGC recommended URKUND plagiarism checker by University Library shown 6% similarity index to the thesis then same thesis text if scanned by the turnitin tool the result was 0% plagiarism, again its checked by free internet tool the result calculates differs. Another specimen quoted here to justify percentage of similarity discovered by the software tool that Tejani (2018) scanned a paper through Urkund shown 5% similarity whereas equal work if checked by Turnitin revealed 90% similarity. These disparities of text matching percentage for the same document need to be justifying removing confusion in scholars. These dissimilar plagiarism percentages occurring due to different database size used and uses of mind different range of matches a string of words looks during scanning by different software tools,

5. An Anti-plagiarism software tool is able to process only English language text and there are also many universities in India which have provision to submit their doctoral thesis in the languages other than English Such institutions are not using these machines for

scanning purpose to curb plagiarism /similarity index. Plagiarisms of such theses are unknown. These regional languages PhD theses so far have not become part of anti-plagiarism check program of country effectively. Moreover, huge doctoral theses written in English and in regional languages, some are scanned images files of respective doctoral theses accepted by the Indian universities much earlier are now hosted in Shodhganga theses repository and Open-DOAR listed repositories of universities and research institutions in India. The question arises here is that such theses are even online text but due to technical error and deficiencies of inability to identify by the software tools are not able to match similarity percentages to current doctoral theses during scanning.

6. Plagiarism detection software merely understand on double quotation marks and exclude the text during scanning that are quoted in quotation marks which are not commensurate with citation rules set by the typical citation style guides (APA, MLA etc.). Any well-known citation style plays imperative role in describing the sources as evidences in the form of structure entry for reference list and in text citation for the research writings.

REFERENCES

Bansal, Stuti. (2018). Plagiarism: A basic idea. Retrieved from http://www.legalserviceindia.com/article/l222-Plagiarism.html

Center for Academic Integrity Duke University.(2006).Academic honesty CAI research. Retrieved fromhttp://www.waunakee.k12.wi.us/hs/departments/lmtc/Assignments/McConnellScenarios/AcadHonesty_5Article.pdf

Das, Santanu (2015). 'Indian higher education: the context of research universities', *University News*, 53, p.3.

e-Galactic, (n.d.). URKUND –Plagiarism Checker. Retrieved from http://egalactic.in/urkund.html

HT Correspondent. (2018, March 6). Mumbai professor accused of plagiarism in PhD. *Hindustan Time*. Retrieved from https://www.hindustantimes.com/mumbai-news/mumbai-professor-accused-of-plagiarism-in-phd-thesis/story-x5l9Ah5E1zZfHJPaf26ACJ.html

Information and Library Network. (2018). Shodhganga: A reservoir of Indian theses. Retrieved from http://shodhganga.inflibnet.ac.in/

Institute of Electrical and Electronics Engineers.(2017). IEEE prohibited authors list.Retrieved fromhttp://grouper.ieee.org/groups/npec/NPEC%20Docs/IEEE%20Prohibited%20Authors%20List%207-2017.pdf

Jones, Karl. (2008). Practical Issues for academics using the turnitin plagiarism detection software. International conference on computer systems and technologies. Retrieved from https://www.researchgate.net/profile/Karl_Jones2/publication/220795552_Practical_issues_for_academics_using_the_Turnitin_plagiarism_detection_software/links/0c9605320c356cf097000000/Practical-issues-for-academics-using-the-Turnitin-plagiarism-detection-software.pdf

Khaira, Harinder Singh. (2017, May 10). Plagiarism complaint in PhD thesis lands researcher, supervisor in soup. The Tribune. Retrieved from http://www.tribuneindia.com/news/chandigarh/education/plagiarism-complaint-in-phd-thesis-lands-researcher-supervisor-in-soup/404899.html

Mahaprashasta, Ajay Ashirwas. (2018, April 3). New JNU appointees caught in plagiarism charges. *The WIRE*. Retrieved from https://thewire.in/education/jnu-scholars-plagiarism-vc

Maurer Hermann, Kappe Frank & Zaka Bilal (2006).*Journal of Universal Computer Science*, (12) 8, 1050-1084 submitted: 10/8/06, accepted: 25/8/06, appeared: 28/8/06

Minhas, Vikram. (2016 February 10). Panjab University to use anti-plagiarism software.*The Indian Express*.Retrieved fromhttp://indianexpress.com/article/cities/chandigarh/panjab-university-to-use-anti-plagiarismsoftwarepanjab-university-panjab-university-anti-plagiarism-software-anti-plagiarism-software-urkund-inflibnet/

Prasad, Shayam S. (2017, March 24). Plagiarism for PhD thesis OK as long as its limited to 30%. *Bangalore Mirror*. Retrieved from https://bangaloremirror.indiatimes.com/bangalore/others/plagiarism-for-phd-thesis-ok-as-long-as-its-limited-to-30/articleshow/57799614.cms

Prabhakar, Siddharth. (2017, June 23). University of Madras makes plagiarism software must. *The Times of India*. Retrieved from https://timesofindia.indiatimes.com/city/chennai/university-of-madras-makes-plagiarism-software-must/articleshow/59280245.cms

Puri, Rajeev. (2016). Development of automated software for plagiarism detection in Punjabi text (Doctoral thesis, I.K. Gujral Punjab Technical University, Jalandhar, India). Retrieved from http://hdl.handle.net/10603/194819

Satija, M.P. (2015). Preventing the plague of plagiarism. *Library Herald*, 53(4), 363-378.doi:10.5958/0976 - 2469.2969.2015.00033.017.

Singh, Pritam Pal. (2018). Plagiarism can invite criminal action: Delhi HC. *The Indian Express*. Retrieved from http://indianexpress.com/article/cities/delhi/plagiarism-can-invite-criminal-action-delhi-hc-5136715/

Suseela, V. J. (2016). Plagiarism: The academic dishonesty the significance of anti-plagiarism software (Tools) in plagiarism detection.*PEARL - A Journal of Library and Information Science*, 10(1), 11-23. doi:10.5958/0975-6922.2016.00002.4

Sunderland –Smith, W. and Carr, R. (2008). Turnitin.com: Teacher perspective of anti-plagiarism software in raising the issue of educational integrity, *Journal of University Teaching and Learning Practice*, (2) 3.

Thomas, Shibu. (2015, February, 12). Plagiarism row: No Bombay high court relief for PhD student, guide. *The Times of India*. Retrieved from https://timesofindia.indiatimes.com/city/mumbai/Plagiarism-row-No-Bombay-high-court-relief-for-PhD-student-guide/articleshow/46205330.cms

Tejani, Ghanshyam G. (2018). Urkund not reliable to check plagiarism in engineering field Retrieved from https://www.researchgate.net/post/is_urkund_a_reliable_plagiarism_checking_software_for_researchers_in_engineering_field

United States Office of Research Integrity. (2018). ORI Policy on Plagiarism. Retrieved from https://ori.hhs.gov/ori-policy-plagiarism

University Grants Commission. (2005). UGC submission of Metadata and Full-text of Doctoral Theses in Electronic Format Regulations, Retrieved from http://etheses.saurashtrauniversity.edu/doc/regulation.pdf

University Grants Commission.(2016). Annual report 2016-17. Retrieved fromhttps://www.ugc.ac.in/pdfnews/9764381_Complete-AR-2016-17-English.pdf

University Grants Commission. (2005). Background Information, Current Scenario, Major Issues & Data Standards, Retrieved from http://etheses.saurashtrauniversity.edu/doc/part_1.pdf

Lin, Wan-Yu, Peng, Nanyun, Yen, Chun-Chao, Lin, Shou-de. (2012, July 12-14). Online Plagiarismdetection through exploiting lexical, syntactic, and semantic information. Paper presented at the 50th Annual Meeting of the Association for computational linguistics, pages 45–150, Jeju, Republic of Korea.

APPENDIX

List of Universities having anti-plagiarism check and Tolerance Limit (Plagiarism accepted level)

Sr No	University	State	Anti-Plagi.Tool	Tolerance%
1	Acharya Nagarjuna UniversityGuntur	Andhra Pradesh	Urkund	30%
2	Alagappa University Karaikudi	Tamil Nadu	Urkund	30%
3	Aligarh Muslim University Aligarh	Uttar Pradesh	Urkund	
4	Anna University, Chennai	Tamil Nadu	Urkund	
5	Annamalai UniversityChidambaram	Tamil Nadu	Urkund	
6	Assam University Silchar	Assam	Urkund	
7	AIHSHEW Coimboture	Tamil Nadu	Urkund	
8	Baba Ghulam Shah Badshah University Rajouri	Jammu & Kashmir	Urkund	
9	Babasaheb Bhimrao Ambedkar University Lucknow	Uttar Pradesh	Urkund	
10	Banaras Hindu University, Varanasi	Uttar Pradesh	Urkund	
11	Bangalore University,	Karnataka	Urkund	
12	Bharathiar University Coimbatore	Tamil Nadu	Urkund	
13	Bharathidasan University, Tiruchirappally,	Tamil Nadu	Urkund	
14	Birla Institute of Technology and Science, Pilani	Rajasthan	Urkund	
15	BPS MahilaVishwavidyalayaKhanpurKalan	Haryana	Urkund	
16	Bundelkhand UniversityJhansi	Uttar Pradesh	Urkund	
17	Central University of Gujarat Gandhinagar	Gujarat	Urkund	
18	Central University of Haryana Mahendergarh	Haryana	Urkund	
19	Central University of Himachal Pradesh Dharamshala	Himachal Pradesh	Urkund	
20	Central University of Jammu	Jammu & Kashmir	Urkund	
21	Central University of KarnatakaGulbarga	Karnataka	Urkund	30%
22	Central University of Kerala, Kasaragod	Kerala	Urkund	
23	Central University of OrissaKoraput	Orissa	Urkund	
24	Central University of PunjabBathinda	Punjab	Urkund	
25	Central University of Rajasthan Bandar Sindri Ajmer	Rajasthan	Urkund	
26	Chaudhary Charan Singh UniversityMeerut	Uttar Pradesh	Urkund	
27	ChhatrapatiShahuJiMaharaj UniversityKanpur	Uttar Pradesh	Urkund	
28	Cochin University of Science &Technology,Cochin	Kerala	Urkund	
29	Dayalbag Educational Institute Agra	Uttar Pradesh	Urkund	
30	Deccan College Post Graduate & Research Institute Pune	Maharashtra	Urkund / Turnitin	
31	Delhi Technological University New Delhi	New Delhi	Urkund	
32	Devi Ahilya Vishwavidyalaya Indore	Madhya Pradesh	Urkund	
33	Dibrugarh University, Dibrugarh	Assam	Urkund	

Sr No	University	State	Anti-Plagi.Tool	Tolerance%
34	Doon UniversityDehradun	Uttarakhand	Urkund	
35	Dr. Harisingh Gour VishwavidyalayaSagar	Madhya Pradesh	Urkund	
36	Dr. Babasaheb Ambedkar Technological University Lonere	Maharashtra	Urkund	
37	Dr. Babasaheb Ambedkar Marathwada University Aurangabad,	Maharashtra	Urkund	
38	English and Foreign Language University Hyderabad	Andhra Pradesh	Urkund	
39	Gandhigram Rural Institute Dindigul	Tamil Nadu		
40	Gandhi Institute of Technology and Management Visakhapatnam	Andhra Pradesh	Urkund	
41	Gauhati University Guwahati	Assam	Urkund	
42	Goa University	Goa	Urkund	
43	Gujarat National Law Univesrity Ahemedabad	Gujarat	Urkund	
44	Gujarat University Ahmedabad	Gujarat	Urkund	
45	Gujarat Vidyapith Ahmedabad	Gujarat	Urkund	
46	Gulbarga University Gulbarga	Karnataka	Urkund	
47	Guru Ghasidas Vishwavidyalaya, Bilaspur	Chhattisgarh	Urkund	
48	Guru Gobind Singh Indraprastha University	New Delhi	Urkund	
49	Guru Jambheshwar University of Science & Technology, Hisar	Haryana	Urkund	
50	Guru Nanak Dev University, Amritsar	Punjab	Urkund	
51	Hemchandracharya North Gujarat University Patan	Gujarat	Urkund	
52	Himachal Pradesh UniversityShimla	Himachal Pradesh	Urkund	
53	HNB Garhwal University Srinagar	Uttarkhand	Urkund	
54	Indira Gandhi National Open University New Delhi	New Delhi	Urkund	
55	Indraprastha Institute of Information Technology New Delhi	New Delhi	Urkund	
56	Institute of Chemical Technology, Mumbai,	Maharashtra	Urkund	
57	Jain Vishva Bharati InstituteLadnun	Rajasthan	Urkund	
58	Jamia Hamdard University, Hamdard Nagar	New Delhi	Urkund	
59	Jawaharlal Nehru Technological University Anantapur	Andhra Pradesh	Urkund	
60	Jawaharlal Nehru Technological University, Hyderabad	Andhra Pradesh	Urkund	
61	Jawaharlal Nehru University	New Delhi	Urkund	
62	Jiwaji University Gwalior	Madhya Pradesh	Urkund	
63	Kannur UniversityKannur	Kerala	Urkund	
64	Karnataka UniversityDharwad	Karnataka	Urkund	
65	Karnataka State Women's University Vijyapur	Karnataka	Urkund	

Sr No	University	State	Anti-Plagi.Tool	Tolerance%
66	Kavi KulaguruKalidas Sanskrit University Ramtek	Maharashtra	Urkund	
67	Kumaun University Nainital	Uttarakhand	Urkund	
68	Kuvempu University Shimoga	Karnataka	Urkund	30%
69	M.S.University of Baroda Vadodara	Gujarat	Urkund	
70	Madras university, Chennai	Tamil Nadu	Urkund	20-30%
71	Madurai Kamaraj UniversityMadurai	Tamil Nadu	Urkund	
72	Maharaja Krishna Kumarsinhji Bhavnagar University, Bhavnagar	Gujarat	Urkund	
73	Maharishi Dayanand Saraswati UniversityAjmer	Rajasthan	Urkund	
74	Maharshi Dayanand University Rohtak	Haryana	Urkund	
75	Mahatma Gandhi Antarrashtriya Hindi Vishwavidyalaya Wardha	Maharashtra	Urkund	
76	Mahatma Gandhi University, Kottayam	Kerala	Urkund	
77	Mangalore University Mangalagangotri	Karnataka	Urkund	
78	Manipur University Imphal	Manipur	Urkund	
79	Manonmaniam Sundaranar University Tirunelveli	Tamil Nadu	Urkund	
80	Mizoram University Aizawl	Mizoram	Urkund	
81	Mohanlal Sukhadia University Udaipur	Rajasthan	Urkund	
82	Mother Teresa Women's University	Tamil Nadu	Urkund	
83	Nagaland University, Kohima	Nagaland	Urkund	
84	North Maharashtra University Jalgaon	Maharashtra	Urkund	
85	North-Eastern Hill University, Shillong	Meghalaya	Urkund	
86	Osmania University Hyderabad	Andhra Pradesh	Urkund	
87	PanditRavishanker Shukla University Raipur	Chattisgarh	Urkund	
88	Panjab University Chandigarh	Punjab	Urkund	10-15%
89	Periyar University, Salem	Tamil Nadu	Urkund	
90	Pondicherry University	Pondicherry	Urkund	
91	Punjabi UniversityPatiala	Punjab	Urkund	
92	Rabindra Bharati University, Kolkata	West Bengal	Urkund	
93	Rajiv Gandhi Prodyogiki Vishwavidyalya, Bhopal	Madhya Pradesh	Urkund	
94	Rajiv Gandhi University Itanagar	Arunachal Pradesh	Urkund	
95	Rani Channamma University, Belagavi	Karnataka	Urkund	
96	Sambalpur UniversityJyotiVihar	Orissa	Urkund	
97	Sant Gadge Baba Amravati University Amravati	Maharashtra	Urkund	
98	Sardar Patel University Vallabh Vidyanagar	Gujarat	Urkund	
99	Saurashtra University, Rajkot	Gujarat	Urkund	
100	Shivaji University Kolhapur	Maharashtra	Urkund	

Sr No	University	State	Anti-Plagi.Tool	Tolerance%
101	Shri Lal Bahadur Shashtri Rashtriya Sanskrit Vidya. Delhi	New Delhi	Urkund	
102	Shri Mata Vaishno Devi University Katra	Jammu & Kashmir	Urkund	
103	Sikkim UniversityGangtok	Sikkim	Urkund	
104	SNDT Women's University Mumbai	Maharashtra	Urkund	
105	Solapur University, Solapur	Maharashtra	Urkund	
106	South Asian University, New Delhi	New Delhi	Urkund	
107	SreeSankaracharya University of Sanskrit Kalady	Kerala	Urkund	
108	Sri Chandrasekharendra Saraswathi Viswa Mahavidyalaya Kanchipuram	Tamil Nadu	Urkund	
109	Sri Krishnadevaraya University, Anantpur,	Andhra Pradesh	Urkund	
110	Sri Venkateswara University, Tirupati	Andhra Pradesh	Urkund	
111	Swami Ramanand Teerth Marathwada University Nanded	Maharashtra	Urkund	30%
112	Tamil University, Thanjavur	Tamil Nadu	Urkund	
113	Tata Institute of Social Sciences, Mumbai	Maharashtra	Urkund	
114	Tezpur University Tezpur	Assam	Urkund	
115	Tamil Nadu Dr.Ambedkar Law University Chennai	Tamil Nadu	Urkund	
116	Tilak Maharashtra Vidyapeeth Pune	Maharashtra	Urkund	
117	Tripura University Agartala	Tripura	Urkund	
118	Tumkur University, Tumkur	Karnataka	Urkund	
119	University of Burdwan	West Bengal	Urkund	
120	University of Allahabad	Uttar Pradesh	Urkund	
121	University of Calicut, Kerala,	Kerala	Urkund	
122	University of Delhi, New Delhi	New Delhi	Urkund	
123	University of Hyderabad, Hyderabad	Andhra Pradesh	Urkund	
124	University of Jammu	Jammu	Urkund	
125	University of Kalyani Kalyani	West Bengal	Urkund	
126	University of Kashmir Srinagar	Jammu & Kashmir	Urkund	
127	University of Kerala Thiruvanathapuram	Kerala	Urkund	
128	University of Lucknow, Lucknow	Uttar Pradesh	Urkund	
129	University of Mumbai	Maharashtra	Urkund	
130	University of Mysore	Karnataka	Urkund / Turnitin	
131	University of North Bengal Darjeeling	West Bengal	Urkund	
132	University of Pune	Maharashtra	Urkund / Turnitin	
133	University of RajasthanJaipur	Rajasthan	Urkund	
134	Uttarakhand Technical University Sudhowala	Uttarakhand	Urkund	
135	V.B.S Purvanchal University, Jaunpur	Uttar Pradesh	Urkund	

Sr No	University	State	Anti-Plagi.Tool	Tolerance%
136	Veer Narmad South Gujarat UniversitySurat,	Gujarat	Urkund	
137	Veer Surendra Sai University of Technology, Burla, Sambalpur	Orissa	Urkund	
138	Visva-Bharati University Santiniketan	West Bengal	Urkund	
139	WB National University of Juridical Sciences Kolkata	West Bengal	Urkund	
140	Yashwantrao Chavan Maharashtra Open University, Nashik	Maharashtra	Urkund	
141	YMCA University of Science and Technology Faridabad	Haryana	Urkund	
142	Visvesvaraya Technological University Belgum	Karnataka	Urkund	

23
Information on Plagiarism at the University of Bradford

University of Bradford Library[22]

1. WHAT IS PLAGIARISM?

The Oxford English Dictionary (Simpson and Weiner, 1989) defines plagiarism as "the wrongful appropriation or purloining, and publication as one's own, of the ideas, or the expression of the ideas [...] of another".

Plagiarism is cheating in your academic assignments by using other people's work without telling us that you are doing it, so that it looks as if you are the one who created the work. If you learn anything from a resource you read, you must show where you found it out from, even if you are not using exactly the same words as they wrote. You must be careful to give people credit for anything that they produce, for example:

- Facts they discovered.
- Ideas they discussed.
- Photographs they took.
- Computer code they wrote.
- Designs or diagrams they drew.
- Models they built.

You must always give credit to people who create, among others:

- Books.
- Websites.
- Newspaper articles.

---
[22]. Reprinted with permission from https://www.bradford.ac.uk/library/help/plagiarism/ with minor changes.

- Television programmes.
- Journal articles.

If you are using a website (or some other source) where no person is named as having written it, you must still acknowledge that you found the information on a website. Always make it clear to the person marking your assignment whether you are referring to your own work or that of someone else. When you acknowledge the sources of your information, you will not just stay out of trouble. You will also gain marks by:

- Showing that you have put in the time and effort to find and read relevant resources.
- Providing evidence to support your arguments.
- Enabling your tutors to check the accuracy and dependability of your sources.
- It also makes it possible for other people to follow up your area of research.

What is not plagiarism? You can use other people's work for your course as long as you make it clear that you did not create it. As Isaac Newton wrote in a letter to Robert Hooke (5 Feb 1657) "If I have seen further, it is only by standing on the shoulders of giants".

University of Bradford policies on plagiarism cover the University of Bradford's position on plagiarism. In your previous work, you may have been held to very similar standards to ours, or very different ones. It is vital that all your assignments submitted for University of Bradford courses follow our regulations, which are based on the standards for academic writing in the UK Higher Education community. Any set of rules has its own underlying logic and follows from a particular way of thinking about how the world should work. The University of Bradford's standards about plagiarism are based on the consensus of the UK Higher Education community about how to use work that other people created. You may be used to standards that are based on a different understanding of how to use things that you read, but your work for University assignments needs to follow our rules. (For more information on the University of Bradford policies on plagiarism, see the pages on Breaches of Assessment Regulations https://www.bradford.ac.uk/student-academic-services/breaches-appeals-complaints/breaches/information-for-students/).

2. TYPES OF PLAGIARISM

(a) Academic Integrity

This section introduces the concepts of good and bad Academic Practice or Academic Integrity.

Good academic practice is about adopting strategies and behaviour that allow you to complete your university studies independently and honestly, and writing assignments in an appropriate academic style. It will also get you better marks!

Bad academic practice includes dishonesty, cheating and plagiarism and also work that is badly prepared and rushed. The rest of this page shows examples of bad academic practice and how to avoid it.

(b) Direct copying

This sort of plagiarism is taking the exact words somebody else wrote, (in a website, a book, another student's work, or any other source) and putting that into your assignment, without pointing out that you are using someone else's words.

(c) Word-switching

This sort of plagiarism means taking someone else's writing and changing words here and there, or taking little bits of sentences, without pointing out that you are using someone else's ideas and sentence structure.

(d) Concealing sources

Not making it obvious where you are drawing on somebody else's work will be regarded as plagiarism. This includes:

- Taking somebody else's ideas and putting them into your words without telling us where you got the ideas.
- Using a source several times, but only pointing it out once.

If you use ideas from the same source several times in a piece of work, you should place a citation each time you use the source.

(e) Working with other students

You must always do your assignments yourself. So:

- Copying another student's work is plagiarism.
- Submitting all or part of another student's work as your own is plagiarism.
- Sharing written work is plagiarism.
- Paying somebody to do your work for you is plagiarism.
- In an individual assignment, writing the assignment with other people is plagiarism. (Group assignments are different!).
- If you need help with English language, you should go to official University sources such as the Academic Skills Advice service or the Language Centre, rather than asking friends for help.
- Asking another student to translate your ideas into English, or getting their help to write your assignment is plagiarism.

Unless you are told to work in a group, you must work alone. If you want to talk to your friends about the work, do it before you start writing. The work you submit must be your own!

It is acceptable to:

- Discuss work with other students.
- Get advice on information sources from other students.
- Work in a group when told to do so by your lecturer.

(f) Buying assignments

Buying your assignment is the most severe form of plagiarism. If you are found to have purchased your assignment, you will usually be excluded from the University.

For more details on the penalties for buying assignments, consult the Breaches of Assessment Regulations: Academic Misconduct document (https://www.bradford.ac.uk/student-academic-services/breaches-appeals-complaints/).

(g) Re-using your previous work

Re-using work from a previous assignment without making it clear what you are doing deceives the lecturer who is marking this piece of work, and is regarded as plagiarism. If you re-submit all or part of a previous piece of work it is poor academic practice as you are trying to get two sets of marks for one piece of work. You will not be set an identical assignment twice – even if the title looks similar you are expected to develop your ideas and arguments rather than simply cutting and pasting previous work

You can re-use previous work in the following ways:

- Using results from a previous assignment and referencing them as you would any other source.
- Re-reading and re-interpreting sources used on a previous assignment.
- Building on ideas from a previous assignment.

You should NOT cut and paste large parts of a previous assignment into a new one.

Sometimes you are told to re-use work for different assignments. For example, you might:

- Have an assignment where you write an essay plan, then another assignment where you write the full essay.
- Have an assignment where you write a literature review, then another assignment where you write a dissertation that includes the review.

This is acceptable because the lecturer knows that you are doing it.

3. AVOIDING PLAGIARISM

Why reference?

- To acknowledge the sources of your information
- To gain marks by:
    — Providing evidence to support your arguments
    — Enabling your tutors to check the accuracy and dependability of your sources
- It also enables others to follow up your area of research

What is a reference? A reference is the way that you acknowledge your use of other people's work. There are two parts:

Information on Plagiarism at the University of Bradford

- The citation is a pointer in the text of your work, saying that you are using someone else's ideas.
- The reference gives the full details of where the information came from. You put it in a reference list at the end of your work

The following is a basic example of a citation and reference in Harvard format. Your course may require references to be formatted in a slightly different way. Go to the Library's referencing page (https://www.brad.ac.uk/library/help/referencing/) to find the referencing guide for your course.

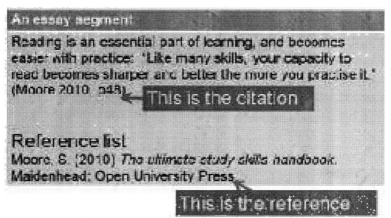

The citation consists of the family name of the author followed by the year of publication in brackets. So if you were citing a work written by Albert Einstein in 1945 it would be cited as (Einstein, 1945). For a direct quotation, you also include the page from which the quoted material was taken.

An example of a citation and a reference in numeric format. The citation consists of a number indicating the order in which the citation appear in the essay.

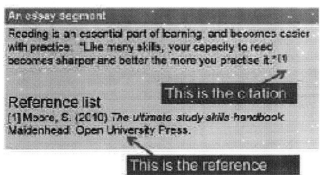

Avoiding Plagiarism

Always make it clear when you are using somebody else's work.

You need to point out in the body of your assignment every time you draw on something that you did not create or discover yourself, and separately give the full details of everything used so that your lecturer can find your sources. This is called 'citing and referencing'. The Library has made available online guides to referencing for each subject.

Citing and referencing is an integral part of writing your assignments. Make sure you cite and reference every source you use while you are doing the writing. Do not think of it as a separate job and leave it until the end: you could end up missing some places where you need to cite, or running out of time to do it properly.

The headings below give some details on how you will need to do your work to make sure that you do not plagiarise.

Note-taking

When you are reading for an assignment, keep full records of all the things you use. This includes the author, title, page numbers and so on for books and the web address and so on for websites. Read the Library's guides on citing that tell you which details you need to write down.

Make it clear to yourself in your notes where each piece of information you are taking down comes from. That way, when you come to do your writing you will be able to put in the pointers that tell your lecturer where you found out everything.

The library has a lot of books on study skills for University students, which include how to make notes that will be effective in doing your writing. Academic Skills Advice have created online guides on note-taking for you to consult.

Time management

Make sure that you give yourself enough time to find the sources you should be reading, read them thoroughly so that you understand them, do your own writing, and revise and change your work if you need to, without panicking. You will probably need more time than you think. The sort of reading and writing that you have to do at University level is different from what you have done before: you need to develop the skills for choosing trustworthy sources, scanning a source for information, reading critically and drawing on many pieces of information to write a logical assignment.

When reading, you need to make notes which include all of the information you will need to reference the source correctly. If you do this you will not have to find the source again when you are writing your assignment.

You also need to know that your lecturers have a lot of work to do and you will not always be able to get hold of them quickly. Do not leave it until near the deadline to ask them for comments on your work, or you might have no time for changes if they are needed.

The library has a number of books on study skills for University students, which include how to manage your time. The Academic Skills Unit has online guides to time management.

Information on Plagiarism at the University of Bradford 285

If English is not your first language, it will take you longer to do your reading and writing, especially if you are also not used to the critical and analytical way that British universities expect you to read. The advisers in the Academic Skills Advice service and the International Study Centre can help you come up with strategies to use your time well.

Quotation vs. paraphrasing

Quotation: quoting is when you use the exact words of someone else's work.

You must make it plain exactly which words you are quoting, and acknowledge the source that they came from.

Please note that direct quotation of words is strongly discouraged in science subjects and engineering.

Items such as charts, diagrams, photographs and code which are directly copied from someone else's work also count as direct quotes.

A quotation looks like this:

"Academic writing is not an uncomplicated task. It involves a wide range of different kinds of skills and if you are going to do it properly, it means that you have to know clearly what is required of you and how to deliver it." (Moore, 2010, p 96.)

Notice the quotation marks telling us where the quoting starts and finishes and the exact page number from which the quote is taken.

(From Moore, S. (2010) The ultimate study skills handbook. Maidenhead: Open University Press).

Paraphrasing : Paraphrasing takes place when you read someone else's work, think about it, and rewrite or summarise it in your own words, keeping the facts and ideas of the original source.

It is considered good academic practice to paraphrase, because it shows you have understood the original work. Some departments want you to paraphrase anything you use and never to directly quote at all. You must acknowledge the source of anything you paraphrase or summarise, because you did not come up with the facts by yourself.

A paraphrase looks like this:

To succeed in academic writing, you need several different skills, including understanding what you are supposed to do. (Moore, 2010).

There are no quotation marks, but the source of the information is still shown.

Source : Moore, S. (2010) The ultimate study skills handbook. Maidenhead: Open University Press.

Remember : if you learn and subsequently use anything from a resource you have read you must acknowledge where it came from even if you are not using the same words as the original source.

Direct Quotation in the Sciences : If you are studying a science subject you should never use direct quotation but instead always put ideas into your own words (paraphrasing). You still need to acknowledge sources you have paraphrased.

You will still need to label items such as images, graphs and tables of data that have been copied from other sources as direct quotations

4. FREQUENTLY ASKED QUESTIONS ABOUT PLAGIARISM

(a) What's so wrong with plagiarising?

In a nutshell, plagiarism is illegal and it is also:

- NOT FAIR to the students who do their own work.
- NOT FAIR to the people who actually created the source that a plagiariser uses - they deserve to get the credit for their hard work.
- NOT FAIR to employers - they deserve to know that a Bradford graduate has really learnt everything they need to know, not just copied from other people. If we allowed this to happen, our degrees themselves would become devalued.
- depriving yourself from expressing a point of view or argument about a subject under discussion.

(b) What if there is no name on something I read?

You still need to show that you are using something you did not originally create. You can put in the author's name as 'Unknown' or 'Anonymous'. This includes images, websites, statistics and computer code. You may also have a source where the author is an organisation, for instance, a report written by a government department. In these cases it is fine to use the organisation as an author.

(c) There is no author or date on this website, how do I reference it?

Consider the following:

- You may have to search around the website to find some details. For instance, see if there is a "home" or "about us" page.
- If you cannot find an individual author, it is perfectly acceptable to cite the organisation producing the website as the author.
- Check for copyright dates and the date the site was last updated if you cannot find a date of composition.
- If you cannot find a date or an author, should you really be referencing the source?

(d) What about websites that have been put up to be used by anybody?

There are many websites that have been written to be freely used by people who need information. It is fine to use them, providing your lecturer is happy that they are good quality

Information on Plagiarism at the University of Bradford

and reliable. However, you still found out the information from looking at the website, not by doing all the research yourself, so you need to point this out.

You must always give credit to people who create:
- Books.
- Websites.
- Newspaper articles.
- Models.
- Television programmes.
- Journal articles.

...or any other source from which you have used information.

(e) I've read a book that discussed something another person wrote, but I haven't read the original work. How do I reference that?

This is called 'secondary referencing', and the referencing guide for your department will tell you how to do it. you need to acknowledge both the source you have read and the original source of the information.

But be careful! Particularly in science subjects, it is not a good idea to do this. You should always try to get hold of the original source and read it yourself. Without reading the original source, you cannot know if the discussion or summary you have read is reporting the original source correctly. For example, they might be leaving out details that are not important to them but matter for what you want to discuss.

Referencing guides for different subject areas (https://www.bradford.ac.uk/library/help/referencing/) are available online.

(f) What happens if I have an idea that someone else has had independently? Will I be accused of plagiarism even though I did not know about the other person's idea?

It is very unlikely that you will come up with exactly the same idea as somebody else. However:
- Your lecturers can tell the difference between a student talking about their own idea and a student talking about something they have read. Your idea will be written in your own voice, and draw on examples and information from your own background.
- The more reading you do, the more familiar you will become with what people in your subject area have written. If you do find that someone else has had an idea that is very similar to yours, you should cite it and then write about how your idea is different.

(g) Everyone knows this, do I really need to reference it?

'Common knowledge' is basic things that anybody might know and there is no need to say where you learnt it. It can be difficult to tell if something is 'common knowledge' or not.

- To avoid plagiarism, if you have had to look something up, it is safer to assume it is not common knowledge and to tell us where you found it.
- Things that your lecturers say in lectures are usually common knowledge for your subject.
- If you are not sure whether something is 'common knowledge', try and find a source to back up your information.

(h) I'm not sure how to reference this thing I've used. Might I get in trouble for a badly done reference? Should I just leave it out?

You do need to provide a reference to anything that you have taken information from. If you make a good try at a reference (following the pattern of how references generally work in your subject), you might lose a mark or two for not getting it exactly right, but if you leave the reference out you will definitely be concealing a source, which is a form of plagiarism.

Try to construct a reference for your source, giving enough information to enable your lecturer to trace the source.

Library guides for referencing are available online (https://www.bradford.ac.uk/library/help/referencing/).

(i) I understand that I need to give people credit for ideas they created, but this is a fact about the world. How can someone own that?

There are two reasons why you need to give references for statistics, results from experiments, and other sources that are factual information. One reason is that somebody else did the work to discover and prove those facts, or did all the calculations to provide the statistics. If you do not reference, you look like you are trying to claim that you discovered this information yourself when in fact you simply read the results of someone else's work.

The other reason is about the reliability of whatever you are quoting. How does your lecturer know that the fact you are talking about is accurate? If you tell us where you found out this information, the person marking your work can look at the source of the data and be sure that it is a good academic source.

(j) I speak English as a foreign language. Can other students translate for me?

Always seek help from official University sources only, rather than your friends. Your Bradford degree will be taken by employers as proof you are fluent in English. We must ensure you are!

(k) I've run out of time for my assignment, what should I do?

Try to manage your time carefully

- Note when all your assessments are due
- Work out how much time YOU take to do assignments: you may take more or less time than your friends!

Remember that it is better to get a bad mark for a poor piece of work than no mark for cheating!

For hints and tips on managing your time, see the Personal development, planning & goal setting resources from the Academic Skills Advice service (https://www.bradford.ac.uk/academic-skills/).

(l) My assignment is not a piece of written work. How do I avoid plagiarism?

These pages concentrate on written work. Plagiarism in visual and material media, computer code, music, film etc is a complex and specialist subject. Ask your lecturer for further guidance as they are experts in their particular discipline.

5. QUESTIONS ABOUT TURNITIN

(a) What is Turnitin?

Turnitin is a tool that:

- helps your lecturers by indicating parts in your assignments that use very similar words to other documents in their database.
- generates a report based on the percentage of similarities between your assignment and other works in the database. This is called the Originality Report.
- will allow you to see the Originality Reports depending how your lecturer set up the assignment.

Read more about Turnitin (https://www.brad.ac.uk/elearning/Plagiarism/Student-Guide-to-TurnitinUK/page_01.htm=.

(b) Can I see the Turnitin report on my piece of work?

The University's guideline is that you should generally be allowed to see a report on one draft before your final submission. The module co-ordinator will have created the correct settings for Turnitin when they set up the assignment submission link in Blackboard. Look in your handbook or ask the module co-ordinator to find out how to submit the draft and see the report.

(c) I got a high number in a Turnitin report. What does that mean?

Turnitin is not a plagiarism detector. It is a tool that helps your lecturers by showing parts of your assignments that use very similar words to other documents in their database. Your lecturer will look at the report and use their judgment to see if the number reflects a real problem with how you have done the assignment. For example, they will ignore groups of words that very commonly appear together (like "University of Bradford Faculty of Social Sciences"). Also, they look to see if you have pointed out that you are using somebody else's work. It is acceptable to have a section in your assignment that is a quote from a website, a book or a source of any kind, providing that you reference it so that the lecturer knows it is a quote.

(d) What percentage of similarity should I get in a Turnitin report?

There is no set number that you have to aim for. A main reason for that is that different kinds of assignments work differently. For example, in a literature review, you are supposed to read and quote from a lot of different sources, but in a lab report, it is expected to be all about work you did yourself. You would expect to see a higher amount of similarities in the literature review than in the lab report.

Rather than worrying about percentages, it is more important to make sure that you are citing and referencing correctly, so that all the similarities are ones that you have pointed out as references. If you want to know more about Turnitin reports, ask the person who set the assignment (usually the module co-ordinator).

6. PENALTIES FOR PLAGIARISM

Penalties for plagiarism depend on the amount which has been plagiarised and whether there are previous offences, but include:

- Repeating the piece of work with a maximum possible mark of 40% for the piece of work in question.
- Repeating the piece of work with a maximum possible mark of 40% for the whole module.
- Repeating the piece of work with a maximum possible mark of 0% for the whole module.
- Permanent exclusion from the University.

You can find more details on the penalties for plagiarism on the Student and Academic Services web pages (https://www.bradford.ac.uk/student-academic-services/breaches-appeals-complaints/breaches/information-for-students/).

7. QUICK TIPS

Follow these tips to maintain academic integrity and avoid plagiarism:

- Keep good notes.
- Manage your time well.
- Reference correctly.
- If in doubt, give a reference.
- Use other people's work but make sure you acknowledge it.
- Only work in groups when told to do so.
- Acknowledge your sources, even if they are anonymous.

REFERENCES

Simpson, J. and Weiner, E. (eds). (1989). *The Oxford English Dictionary*. 2nd ed. Oxford: Oxford University Press.

APPENDIX 1

UNIVERSITY GRANTS COMMISSION (PROMOTION OF ACADEMIC INTEGRITY AND PREVENTION OF PLAGIARISM IN HIGHER EDUCATIONAL INSTITUTIONS) REGULATIONS, 2018

University Grants Commission
New Delhi, the 23rd July, 2018

F. 1-18/2010(CPP-II).—

Preamble

Whereas, University Grants Commission (UGC), as per UGC Act, 1956, is mandated to coordinate and determine the standards of higher education;

And whereas, assessment of academic and research work done leading to the partial fulfillment for the award of degrees at Masters and Research level, by a student or a faculty or a researcher or a staff, in the form of thesis, dissertation and publication of research papers, chapters in books, full-fledged books and any other similar work, reflects the extent to which elements of academic integrity and originality are observed in various relevant processes adopted by Higher Educational Institutions (HEIs);

Therefore, in exercise of the powers conferred by clause (j) of Section 12 read with clauses (f) and (g) of subsection (1) of Section 26 of the University Grants Commission Act, 1956, the University Grants Commission here by makes the following regulations:-

1. Short title, application and commencement –

(a) These regulations shall be called the University Grants Commission (Promotion of Academic Integrity and Prevention of Plagiarism in Higher Educational Institutions) Regulations, 2018.

(b) They shall apply to the students, faculty, researchers and staff of all Higher Educational Institutions in the country.

(c) These regulations shall come into force from the date of their notification in the Official Gazette.

2. Definitions -

In these regulations, unless the context otherwise requires—

(a) "Academic Integrity" is the intellectual honesty in proposing, performing and reporting any activity, which leads to the creation of intellectual property;

(b) "Author" includes a student or a faculty or a researcher or staff of Higher Educational Institution (HEI) who claims to be the creator of the work under consideration;

(c) "Commission" means the University Grants Commission as defined in the University Grants Commission Act, 1956;

(d) "Common Knowledge" means a well known fact, quote, figure or information that is known to most of thepeople;

(e) "Degree" means any such degree specified by the University Grants Commission, by notification in the Official Gazette, under section 22 of the University Grants Commission Act, 1956;

(f) "Departmental Academic Integrity Panel" shall mean the body constituted at the departmental level to investigate allegations of plagiarism;

(g) "Faculty" refers to a person who is teaching and/or guiding students enrolled in an HEI in any capacitywhatsoever i.e. regular, ad-hoc, guest, temporary, visiting etc;

(h) "Higher Educational Institution (HEI)" means a university recognized under section 2(f) of the UGCAct,1956 or an institution deemed to be university under section 3 of the UGC Act, 1956 or an affiliating college/ institution or a constituent unit of a university;

(i) "Information" includes data, message, text, images, sound, voice, codes, computer programs, software and databases or microfilm or computer generated microfiche;

(j) "Institutional Academic Integrity Panel" shall mean the body constituted at Institutional level to consider recommendations of the departmental academic integrity panel and take appropriate decisions in respect of allegations of plagiarism and decide on penalties to be imposed. In exceptional cases, it shall investigate allegations of plagiarism at the institutional level;

(k) "Notification" means a notification published in the Official Gazette and the expression "notify" with itscognate meanings and grammatical variation shall be construed accordingly;

(l) "Plagiarism" means the practice of taking someone else's work or idea and passing them as one's own.

(m) "Programme" means a programme of study leading to the award of a masters and research level degree;

(n) "Researcher" refers to a person conducting academic / scientific research in HEIs;

(o) "Script" includes research paper, thesis, dissertation, chapters in books, full-fledged books and any othersimilar work, submitted for assessment / opinion leading to the award of master and research level degreesor publication in print or electronic media by students or faculty or researcher or staff of an HEI; however, this shall exclude assignments / term papers / project reports / course work / essays and answer scripts etc.;

(p) "Source" means the published primary and secondary material from any source whatsoever and includes written information and opinions gained directly from other people, including eminent scholars, public figures and practitioners in any form whatsoever as also data and information in the electronic form be it audio, video, image or text; Information being given the same meaning as defined under Section 2 (1) (v) ofthe Information Technology Act, 2000 and reproduced here in Regulation 2 (l);

(q) "Staff" refers to all non-teaching staff working in HEIs in any capacity whatsoever i.e. regular, temporary, contractual, outsourced etc.;

(r) "Student" means a person duly admitted and pursuing a programme of study including a research programme in any mode of study (full time or part-time or distance mode);

(s) "University" means a university established or incorporated by or under a Central Act, a Provincial Act or a State Act, and includes an institution deemed to be university under section 3 of the UGC Act, 1956;

(t) "Year" means the academic session in which a proven offence has been committed.

Words and expressions used and not defined in these regulations but defined in the University Grants Commission Act,1956 shall have the meanings respectively assigned to them in UGC Act, 1956.

3. Objectives

3.1 To create awareness about responsible conduct of research, thesis, dissertation, promotion of academic integrity and prevention of misconduct including plagiarism in academic writing among student, faculty, researcher and staff.

3.2 To establish institutional mechanism through education and training to facilitate responsible conduct ofresearch, thesis, dissertation, promotion of academic integrity and deterrence from plagiarism.

1.3. To develop systems to detect plagiarism and to set up mechanisms to prevent plagiarism and punish a student, faculty, researcher or staff of HEI committing the act of plagiarism.

4. Duties of HEI

Every HEI should establish the mechanism as prescribed in these regulations, to enhance awareness about responsible conduct of research and academic activities, to promote academic integrity and to prevent plagiarism.

5. Awareness Programs and Trainings

(a) HEI shall instruct students, faculty, researcher and staff about proper attribution, seeking permission of the author wherever necessary, acknowledgement of source compatible with the needs and specificities of disciplines and in accordance with rules, international conventions and regulations governing the source.

(b) HEI shall conduct sensitization seminars/ awareness programs every semester on responsible conduct of research, thesis, dissertation, promotion of academic integrity and ethics in education for students, faculty, researcher and staff.

(c) HEI shall :
   i. Include the cardinal principles of academic integrity in the curricula of Undergraduate (UG)/Postgraduate (PG)/Master's degree etc. as a compulsory course work/module.

ii. Include elements of responsible conduct of research and publication ethics as a compulsory course work/module for Masters and Research Scholars.

iii. Include elements of responsible conduct of research and publication ethics in Orientation and Refresher Courses organized for faculty and staff members of the HEI.

iv. Train student, faculty, researcher and staff for using plagiarism detection tools and reference management tools.

v. Establish facility equipped with modern technologies for detection of plagiarism.

vi. Encourage student, faculty, researcher and staff to register on international researcher's Registry systems.

6. Curbing Plagiarism

(a) HEI shall declare and implement the technology based mechanism using appropriate software so as to ensurethat documents such as thesis, dissertation, publications or any other such documents are free of plagiarism atthe time of their submission.

(b) The mechanism as defined at (a) above shall be made accessible to all engaged in research work including student, faculty, researcher and staff etc.

(c) Every student submitting a thesis, dissertation, or any other such documents to the HEI shall submit an undertaking indicating that the document has been prepared by him or her and that the document is his/her original work and free of any plagiarism.

(d) The undertaking shall include the fact that the document has been duly checked through a Plagiarism detection tool approved by the HEI.

(e) HEI shall develop a policy on plagiarism and get it approved by its relevant statutory bodies/authorities. The approved policy shall be placed on the homepage of the HEI website.

(f) Each supervisor shall submit a certificate indicating that the work done by the researcher under him / her is plagiarism free.

(g) HEI shall submit to INFLIBNET soft copies of all Masters, Research program's dissertations and thesis within a month after the award of degrees for hosting in the digital repository under the "Shodh Ganga e-repository".

(h) HEI shall create Institutional Repository on institute website which shall include dissertation / thesis / paper /publication and other in-house publications.

7. Similarity checks for exclusion from Plagiarism

The similarity checks for plagiarism shall exclude the following:

(a) All quoted work reproduced with all necessary permission and/or attribution.

(b) All references, bibliography, table of content, preface and acknowledgements.

(c) All generic terms, laws, standard symbols and standards equations.

Note : The research work carried out by the student, faculty, researcher and staff shall be based on original ideas, which shall include abstract, summary, hypothesis, observations, results, conclusions and recommendations only and shall not have any similarities. It shall exclude a common knowledge or coincidental terms, up to fourteen (14) consecutive words.

8. Levels of Plagiarism

Plagiarism would be quantified into following levels in ascending order of severity for the purpose of its definition:

i. Level 0: Similarities upto 10% - Minor similarities, no penalty
ii. Level 1: Similarities above 10% to 40%
iii. Level 2: Similarities above 40% to 60%
iv. Level 3: Similarities above 60%

9. Detection/Reporting/Handling of Plagiarism

If any member of the academic community suspects with appropriate proof that a case of plagiarism has happened in any document, he or she shall report it to the Departmental Academic Integrity Panel (DAIP). Upon receipt of such acomplaint or allegation the DAIP shall investigate the matter and submit its recommendations to the Institutional Academic Integrity Panel (IAIP) of the HEI.

The authorities of HEI can also take *suomotu* notice of an act of plagiarism and initiate proceedings under these regulations. Similarly, proceedings can also be initiated by the HEI on the basis of findings of an examiner. All such cases will be investigated by the IAIP.

10. Departmental Academic Integrity Panel (DAIP)

i. All Departments in HEI shall notify a DAIP whose composition shall be as given below:
   a. Chairman - Head of the Department
   b. Member - Senior academician from outside the department, to be nominated by the head of HEI.
   c. Member - A person well versed with anti plagiarism tools, to be nominated by the Head of the Department.

   The tenure of the members in respect of points 'b' and 'c' shall be two years. The quorum for the meetings shall be 2 out of 3 members (including Chairman).

ii. The DAIP shall follow the principles of natural justice while deciding about the allegation of plagiarism against the student, faculty, researcher and staff.

iii. The DAIP shall have the power to assess the level of plagiarism and recommend penalty(ies) accordingly.

iv. The DAIP after investigation shall submit its report with the recommendation on penalties to be imposed to the IAIP within a period of 45 days from the date of receipt of complaint / initiation of the proceedings.

11. Institutional Academic Integrity Panel (IAIP)

i. HEI shall notify a IAIP whose composition shall be as given below:
   a. Chairman - Pro-VC/Dean/Senior Academician of the HEI.
   b. Member - Senior Academician other than Chairman, to be nominated by the Head of HEI.
   c. Member - One member nominated by the Head of HEI from outside the HEI
   d. Member - A person well versed with anti-plagiarism tools, to be nominated by the Head of the HEI.

   The Chairman of DAIP and IAIP shall not be the same. The tenure of the Committee members including Chairman shall be three years. The quorum for the meetings shall be 3 out of 4 members (including Chairman).

ii. The IAIP shall consider the recommendations of DAIP.

iii. The IAIP shall also investigate cases of plagiarism as per the provisions mentioned in these regulations.

iv. The IAIP shall follow the principles of natural justice while deciding about the allegation of plagiarism against the student, faculty, researcher and staff of HEI.

v. The IAIP shall have the power to review the recommendations of DAIP including penalties with due justification.

vi. The IAIP shall send the report after investigation and the recommendation on penalties to be imposed to the Head of the HEI within a period of 45 days from the date of receipt of recommendation of DAIP/complaint / initiation of the proceedings.

vii. The IAIP shall provide a copy of the report to the person(s) against whom inquiry report is submitted.

12. Penalties

Penalties in the cases of plagiarism shall be imposed on students pursuing studies at the level of Masters and Research programs and on researcher, faculty & staff of the HEI only after academic misconduct on the part of the individual has been established without doubt, when all avenues of appeal have been exhausted and individual in question has been provided enough opportunity to defend himself or herself in a fair or transparent manner.

12.1. Penalties in case of plagiarism in submission of thesis and dissertations

Institutional Academic Integrity Panel (IAIP) shall impose penalty considering the severity of the Plagiarism.

i. Level 0: Similarities upto 10% - Minor Similarities, no penalty.

ii. Level 1: Similarities above 10% to 40% - Such student shall be asked to submit a revised script within astipulated time period not exceeding 6 months.

iii. Level 2: Similarities above 40% to 60% - Such student shall be debarred from submitting a revised script for aperiod of one year.

iv. Level 3: Similarities above 60% -Such student registration for that programme shall be cancelled.

Note 1 : Penalty on repeated plagiarism- Such student shall be punished for the plagiarism of one level higher than the previous level committed by him/her. In case where plagiarism of highest level is committed then the punishment for the same shall be operative.

Note 2 : Penalty in case where the degree/credit has already been obtained - If plagiarism is proved on a date later than the date of award of degree or credit as the case may be then his/her degree or credit shall be put in abeyance for a period recommended by the IAIP and approved by the Head of the Institution.

12.2. Penalties in case of plagiarism in academic and research publications

I. Level 0: Similarities up to 10% - Minor similarities, no penalty.

II. Level 1: Similarities above 10% to 40%
   (i) Shall be asked to withdraw manuscript.

III. Level 2: Similarities above 40% to 60%
   (i) Shall be asked to withdraw manuscript.
   (ii) Shall be denied a right to one annual increment.
   (iii) Shall not be allowed to be a supervisor to any new Master's, M.Phil., Ph.D. Student/scholar for a period of two years.

IV. Level 3: Similarities above 60%
   (i) Shall be asked to withdraw manuscript.
   (ii) Shall be denied a right to two successive annual increments.
   (iii) Shall not be allowed to be a supervisor to any new Master's, M.Phil., Ph.D. Student/scholar for a period of three years.

Note 1 : Penalty on repeated plagiarism - Shall be asked to withdraw manuscript and shall be punished for the plagiarism of one level higher than the lower level committed by him/her. In case where plagiarism of highest level is committed then the punishment for the same shall be operative. In case level 3 offence is repeated then the disciplinary action including suspension/termination as per service rules shall be taken by the HEI.

Note 2 : Penalty in case where the benefit or credit has already been obtained - If plagiarism is proved on a date later than the date of benefit or credit obtained as the case may be then his/her benefit or credit shall be put in abeyance for a period recommended by IAIP and approved by the Head of the Institution.

Note 3 : HEIs shall create a mechanism so as to ensure that each of the paper publication/thesis/dissertation by the student, faculty, researcher or staff of the HEI is checked for plagiarism at the time of forwarding/submission.

Note 4 : If there is any complaint of plagiarism against the Head of an HEI, a suitable action, in line with these regulations, shall be taken by the Controlling Authority of the HEI.

Note 5 : If there is any complaint of plagiarism against the Head of Department/Authorities at the institutional level, asuitable action, in line with these regulations, shall be recommended by the IAIP and approved by the Competent Authority.

Note 6 : If there is any complaint of plagiarism against any member of DAIP or IAIP, then such member shall excuse himself / herself from the meeting(s) where his/her case is being discussed/investigated.

13. Removal of Difficulty

UGC reserves the right to remove difficulty/difficulties in the course of implementations of these Regulations inconsultation with the Government of India/ Ministry of Human Resource Development.

Prof. RAJNISH JAIN, Secy.

[ADVT.-III/4/Exty./161/18]

APPENDIX 2

IFLA STATEMENT ON COPYRIGHT EDUCATION AND COPYRIGHT LITERACY
International Federation of Library Associations and Institutions (IFLA)[23]

This IFLA policy statement, aimed at governments (including intergovernmental organisations), libraries, library associations and library educators, looks to explain the concept of copyright literacy, its importance within the broader work of libraries, and make recommendations for improvements.

Copyright laws with appropriate limitations and exceptions are critical to the work of libraries, enabling activities such as access, lending, copying and preservation. Having few or no adequate provisions for libraries creates serious restrictions on the ability of our institutions to carry out their mission of giving access to information legally.

Nonetheless, the experience of users is shaped as much by the way in which libraries interpret and apply the rules, as by the text of the law itself.

IFLA's *Code of Ethics for Librarians and Other Information Workers*[24] underlines that alongside the responsibility to recognise intellectual property rights, there is a parallel duty not to impose unnecessary restrictions on users' right to access information. In short, libraries should use all possibilities provided by the law to give access and enable learning.

To do this, librarians and other information workers need to be copyright literate, in order both to carry out their own functions and duties, and to support colleagues and users, in the most effective way possible.

Copyright literacy can be defined as sufficient copyright knowledge to be able to take well informed decisions on how to use copyrighted materials[25]. It includes understanding the structure, functioning and implications of the copyright system, as laws, practices, and user expectations evolve. Copyright education is the process of developing and updating copyright literacy.

Copyright literacy is an issue for all types of library. Public and school libraries, for

---

23. Available at: https://www.ifla.org/files/assets/clm/statements/ifla-statement-on-copyright-literacy.pdf
24. IFLA Code of Ethics for Librarians and Other Information Workers (2012): https://www.ifla.org/publications/node/11092. The Code of Ethics also underlines a duty to advocate for stronger user rights in future. It is worth noting that experts have also noted a 'latent flexibility' within copyright law – Hudson (https://kclpure.kcl.ac.uk/portal/en/persons/emily-hudson(5a070bc2-4fd2-4ea5-9fc1-cdcb986c0806).html) (2019, forthcoming).
25. "Acquiring and demonstrating the appropriate knowledge, skills and behaviours to enable the ethical creation and use of copyright material", Secker and Morrison, (2016) p.211. Morrison and Secker define it as the "increasing range of knowledge, skills and behaviours that individuals require when working with copyright content in the digital age" (Morrison and Secker, 2015). Arguably, a copyright-literate person also understands the wider policy debate around copyright, and whilst not necessarily engaging directly in copyright advocacy is able to relate their own approach to the history and development of copyright laws. This involves an awareness of the inherent tensions between the various stakeholders.

example, may need to advise library users, staff and others on what they can copy or use, make accessible format copies of works for people with disabilities, or provide educational services (including activities such as maker spaces).

Libraries with more extensive services may, amongst other things, run repositories, carry out mass-digitisation programmes, engage in document supply, oversee legal deposit, and negotiate contracts for digital content. All require knowledge of copyright, including its application to new uses or types of material. Lack of knowledge may result in mis-application of the law, and lead either to infringement, or overly restrictive limits on what users can do.

In all institutions, librarians may well also be seen as the copyright experts, and become reference points forthose around them. Their approach and attitude are likely to influence others, and affect the guidance given toa wide range of users. Librarians additionally have the opportunity to shape institutional policies, for example,on open access, and promote approaches that are consistent with library missions and in accordance with the *IFLA Code of Ethics for Librarians and Other Information Workers*.

Nonetheless, extensive research[26] shows that knowledge of copyright among librarians is highly variable andthat there is a great need and demand for copyright training within the profession. Having a named (orinformal) external copyright expert on whom librarians can call represents a helpful approach to dealing withthe most complex questions. However, a greater level of copyright literacy within the profession as a wholewill mean that more users' questions can be answered in a quick, confident and well-informed way.

This notwithstanding, it remains the case that, in the long-term, copyright reforms are essential, both at thenational and global level, to guarantee meaningful access to information, preserve collections, provideeducation in libraries, and enable creation by library users, amongst other activities. Given that for manycountries, reforms are not a realistic prospect in the short term, better understanding and application of the lawas it stands represents the best prospect for enhancing user rights quickly and legally.

This does not and should not take away from the need for reform, and may help identify the most pressingneeds. Indeed, the more librarians become experienced in copyright issues, the more likely they feel confidentin collaborating and working towards copyright reform.

Recommendations

Based on the above, IFLA makes the following recommendations to governments, libraries, libraryassociations and library educators:

Governments (and intergovernmental organisations, where appropriate) should:
- Provide for limitations on liability for librarians and other information workers both when they areacting in good faith for library purposes and supporting the activities of their users, as well as safeharbours in the digital environment. Such a step will give

---

26. copyrightliteracy.org offers a bibliography around the theme: https://copyrightliteracy.org/about-2/internationalcopyright-literacy

librarians greater confidence in applying thelaw.
- Ensure that government-sponsored copyright education programmes, both for librarians and for thebroader public, give due attention to exceptions, limitations and other user rights. Such programmeshould focus on what users can - rather than cannot - do, in order to avoid creating fear or concernwhen using copyrighted materials. Public money should support campaigns that both identify therights of rightholders and the opportunities for users.
- In the longer term, ensure that copyright laws provide for a simple and easy-to-apply framework oflimitations and exceptions that enable libraries to fulfil their mission and mandates and assistindividual library users in understanding the appropriate use of copyrighted content, notably throughsimple, targeted guides.

Libraries should:
- Comply with the law as it stands, and whilst respecting the legitimate interests of rightsholders,maximise access to information and preservation of their collections.
- Recognise and value the development and updating of copyright literacy among staff.
- Engage in and use any opportunities to ensure that institutional policies and practices relevant tocopyright facilitate access to information, within the limits of the law.
- In line with the *IFLA Code of Ethics for Librarians and Other Information Workers*, advocate forstronger exceptions and limitations in order to maximise access to information.
- Offer workshops and training for staff and users on copyright and related issues, especially when lawsare amended.
- Ensure that all professional library staff have a basic knowledge of copyright law, and considerdesignating a specialist copyright librarian, for example regarding questions of copyright in otherjurisdictions.

Library associations should:
- Ensure that comprehensive copyright literacy is included in competencies for library professionals,working with library educators, and explore the possibilities to provide guidelines or certification.
- Advocate for stronger exceptions and limitations in order to maximise access to information.
- Act as fora for the exchange of expertise and best practice to raise the standard of provision ofcopyright education and, where possible, produce practical guides on copyright literacy forpractitioners, as well as workshops and conferences.
- Collect and publish empirical data on copyright literacy initiatives for both pre- and in-servicetraining to ensure continuous improvement of the copyright education programmes.

Such data willalso support advocacy activities.

Library educators should:
- Ensure that there is adequate coverage of copyright in the curriculum to address those topics that arecritical to library work (including the national and international context, as appropriate). Sucheducation and training must reflect the context in which students will apply knowledge, focus also onpositive rights (such as text and data mining or fair use, where relevant), and furthermore couldconsider other legal questions, such as privacy and liability.
- Work with relevant professional associations to ensure that curricular inclusion of copyright literacy isa requirement for accreditation.

Endorsed by the IFLA Governing Board on 20 August 2018.

Bibliography

Nirmal Kumar Swain
Harish Chander

BOOKS

1900

1. Deahl, JasperNewton. (1900). *Imitation in Education: Its Nature, Scope, and Significance*. New York: Macmillan, Reissued as a scanned book on Google in 2006

1989

2. Mailon, Thomas. (1989). *Stolen Words: Forays into the Origins and Ravages of Plagiarism*. New York: Ticknor and Fields.

1992

3. LaFollette, Marcel. (1992). *Stealing into Print: Fraud, Plagiarism, and Misconduct in Scientific Publishing*. Berkeley and London: University of California Press.

1999

4. Howard, Rebecca Moore. (1999). *Standing in the Shadow of Giants: Plagiarists, Authors & Collaborators*. Stanford, CT: Ablex.

2001

5. Buranen, Lisa and Roy, A.M. (Eds.) (2001). *Perspectives on Plagiarism and Intellectual Property in a postmodern world*. Albany: SUNY Press.

6. Randall, Marilyn. (2001). *Pragmatic plagiarism: Authorship, profit, power*. Toronto: University of Toronto Press.

7. Whitley, Bernard E. and Keith-Spiegel, P. (2001). *Academic Dishonesty: An Educator's Guide*. Mahwah, NJ: Erlbaum.

2002

8. Carroll, J. (2002). *A Handbook for Deterring Plagiarism in Higher Education*, Oxford: Oxford University Press.

9. Harris, Robert A. (2002). *Using sources effectively: strengthening your writing and avoiding plagiarism.* Los Angeles, CA: Pyrczak Publishing.

2004

10. Lessig, Lawrence (2004). *Free Culture: How Big Media Uses Technology and the Law to Lock Down Culture and Control Creativity.* New York: Penguin.

2007

11. Posner, Richard A. (2007). *The little book of plagiarism.* New York: Pantheon Books.
12. Stern, Linda. (2007). *What every student should know about avoiding plagiarism.* New York: Pearson/Longman.

2008

13. Eisner, Caroline and Vicinus, Martha. (Eds.) (2008) *Originality, Imitation, Plagiarism: TeachingWriting in the Digital Age.* Ann Arbor: The University of MichiganPress .253p DOI: http://dx.doi.org/10.3998/dcbooks.5653382.0001.00
14. Howard, R. M. & Robillard, A. (2008). *Pluralizing plagiarism: identities, contexts, pedagogies.* Heinemann, Portsmouth, NH.
15. Lampert, L.D. (2008). *Combating Student Plagiarism: An Academic Librarian's Guide,*Oxford:Chandos Publishing.
16. Lipson, C. (2008). *Doing honest work in college: How to prepare citations, avoid plagiarism, and achieve real academic success* (2nd ed.). Chicago: University of Chicago Press.

2009

17. Haviland, C.P., & Mullin, J.A. (Eds.) (2009). *Who owns this text?: plagiarism, authorship, and disciplinary cultures.* Utah State University Press, Logan, UT.

2010

18. Anderson, Katie Elson andCvetkovic, V. Bowman(2010). *Stop plagiarism: A guide to understanding and prevention.*Chicago, IL: ALA, 220p.
19. Neville, Colin. (2010).*The complete guide to referencing and avoiding plagiarism.* Maidenhead: Open University Press/McGraw Hill.

2011

20. Rocco, T.S. & Hatcher, T. (Eds.) (2011). *The handbook of scholarly writing and publishing.* Jossey-Bass, San Francisco, CA.

2015

21. Brandt, D. (2015). *The rise of writing: redefining mass literacy.* Cambridge University Press, Cambridge, UK.
22. Patra. M. and Jena, S.K. (Eds.) (2015). *Combating plagiarism: A new role for librarians.* New Delhi: S K Book Agency.

ARTICLES, BOOK CHAPTERS, AND OTHER PAPERS

1908

23. Goudy, H. (1908). Plagiarism-A fine art. *Juridical Review*, 20, 302.

1971

24. Corbett, Edward P. J. (1971). The Theory and Practiceof Imitation in Classical Rhetoric. *CollegeComposition and Communication* 22(3):243–50.

1988

25. Weinrib, Arnold S. (1988)"Information and property" *University of Toronto Law Journal* .38 117-150.

1992

26. Howard, R.M. (1992). A plagiarism pentimento. *Journal of Teach Writ*, 11(2):233–245.

1993

27. Muir, A. & Oppenheim, C. (1993). Electrocopying, the Publishers Association and Academic Libraries. *Journal of Librarianship and Information Science*, 25(175), 175-186.

28. Wolk, R. S. (1993). "Dr. research": A quick fix for plagiarists. *Journal of Information Ethics*, 2(1), 63-71,96.

1994

29. Anderson, J. (1994). Fraud in research 1986-1992: An annotated bibliography.*Journal of Information Ethics*, 3(2), 64-98.

30. Kozak, E. M. (1994). Towards a definition of plagiarism: The Bray/Oates controversy revisited. *Journal of Information Ethics*, 3(1), 70-75.

31. Marcel, C. L. (1994). Avoiding plagiarism: Some thoughts on use, attribution, and acknowledgment. *Journal of Information Ethics*, 3(2), 25-35.

32. Martin, B. (1994). Plagiarism: A misplaced emphasis. *Journal of Information Ethics*, 3(2), 36-47.

33. McCutchen, Charles W. (1994). Plagiarism: A Tale of Telltale Words. *Journal of Information Ethics*, 3(2), 48-50.

34. Norman, S. (1994). Copyright Issues. *IFLA Journal*, 20(3), 357-359.

35. Roig, M. and Ballew, C. (1994). Attitudes toward cheating of self and others by college students and professors. *Psychological Record*, 44, 3 12.

36. Wollan, Laurin A, Jr. (1994). Plagiarism and the art of copying. *Journal of Information Ethics*, 3 (1), 58-64.

37. Wright, N. D. (1994). Reviews – stealing into print: Fraud, plagiarism, and misconduct in scientific publishing by Marcel C. LaFollette / research fraud in the behavioral and

biomedical sciences edited by David J. Miller and Lichel Hersen. *The Library Quarterly*, 64(2), 221.

1995

38. Howard, Rebecca Moore. (1995). Plagiarisms, Authorships, and the Academic Death Penalty. *College English*, 57(7):788–806.
39. Parrish, Debra. (1995). Scientific misconduct and the plagiarism cases. *Journal of College and University Law*, 21, 3 517-54.
40. Samuelson, P. (1995) Copyright and Digital Libraries. *Communications of the ACM*, 38(3), 15-21, 110.

1996

41. Houston, B. (1996). Scientific deception: An overview and guide to the literature of misconduct and fraud in scientific research. *Reference Reviews*, 10(3), 20.
42. Knoll, E. (1996). Glory days or the lure of scientific misconduct. *Journal of Information Ethics*, 5(1), 9-14.
43. Meredith, B. (1996). Document Supply in the Electronic World: The Publishers' View. *Interlending & Document Supply*, 24(3), 6-11.
44. Protti, M. (1996). Policing fraud and deceit: The legal aspects of misconduct in scientific inquiry. *Journal of Information Ethics*, 5(1), 59-71,95.
45. Williams, W. (1996). Words for the taking: The hunt for a plagiarist. *Library Journal*, 121(20), 120.

1997

46. Eisenschitz, T. & Turner, P. (1997). Rights and Responsibilities in the Digital Age. *Problems with Stronger Copyright in an Information Society*, 23(3), 209-223.
47. Maxwell, L. & Mccain, T.A. (1997). Gateway or Gatekeeper: The Implications of Copyright and Digitalization on Education. *Communication Education*, 46(3), 141-157.
48. McCabe, D.L. & Trevino, L.K. (1997). Individual and contextual influences on academic dishonesty: a multi campus investigation. *Res High Educ* 38(3):379–396.
49. Rees, H. (1997). The legal aspects of electronic information access. *COFHE Bulletin*, (82), 5-6.

1998

50. Bjorner, S. (1998). Giving credit where credit is due. *Online*, 22(1), 12.
51. Bourdon, C. (1998). Stop, thief! *American Libraries*, 29(11), 68.
52. Clement, O. A. (1998). Book piracy and nigerian copyright law. *Library Management*, 19(1), 22-25.
53. Hauptman, R. (1998). Research misconduct: Issues, implications, and strategies. *Journal of Academic Librarianship*, 24(3), 253-254.

54. Stebelman, S. (1998). Cybercheating: Dishonesty goes digital. *American Libraries*, 29(8), 48-50.

55. Thompson, C. (1998). You've always been a plagiarist. *Journal of Information Ethics*, 7(1), 49-53.

1999

56. Davies, J. (1999). Publishers and Copyright Licensing. *Interlending& Document Supply*, 27(2), 60-64.

57. Eysenck, H. J. (1999). Why do scientists cheat? *Journal of Information Ethics*, 8(2), 27-35.

58. Austin, M.Jill& Brown, Linda D. (1999). Internet Plagiarism: Developing Strategies to Curb Student Academic Dishonesty. *The Internet and Higher Education*, 2(1), 21-33

59. Oddie, C. (1999). Copyright Protection in the Digital Age. *Information Management & Computer Security*, 7(5), 239-240.

2000

60. Crews, K. D. & Harper, G. K. (2000). The Immunity Dilemma: Are State Colleges and Universities Still Liable for Copyright Infringements? *Journal of the American Society for Information Science*,50(14), 1350-1352.

61. LaFollette, M. C. (2000). Observations on fraud and scientific integrity in a digital environment. *Journal of the American Society for Information Science*, 51(14), 1334-1337.

62. Logan, D. K. (2000). Imitation on the web: Flattery, fair use, or felony? *Knowledge Quest*, 28(5), 16.

63. Pearce, D. (2000). Libraries and Copyright. *Australian Academic & Research Libraries*, 31(3), 43-64.

64. Pedley, P. (2000). Copyright and Libraries. In P. Pedley (Ed.) *Copyright for Library and Information Service Professionals* (2nd ed., pp. 8-13). London: Europa Publications.

65. Procter, M. (2000). How not to plagiarize. *School Libraries in Canada*, 20(2), 7-8.

66. Yushkiavitshus, H. (2000). Intellectual Freedom in Libraries in Eastern Europe. *IFLA Journal*, 26, 288-292.

2001

67. Atkins, Thomas andNelson, G. (2001). Plagiarism and the Internet: Turning Tables. *English Journal*, 90, 101-104.

68. Auer, N. J. and Krupar, E. M. (2001). Mouse click plagiarism: the role of technology in plagiarism and the librarians' role in combating it. *Library Trends*, 49 (3), 415 35.

69. Carbone, N. (2001). Turnitin.Com, a pedagogic placebo for plagiarism, *Bedford/ St.Martin's Tech Notes*,http://www.macmillanhighered.com /catalog/static /bsm/

technotes/techtiparchive/ttip060501.htm.

70. Goldstein, P. (2001). The Legal Traditions. In P. Goldstein (Ed.), *International Copyright: Principles, Law and Practice* (pp. 26-33). Cary, USA: Oxford University Press.

71. Nicole, J. A., & Ellen, M. K. (2001). Mouse click plagiarism: The role of technology in plagiarism and the librarian's role in combating it. *Library Trends*, 49(3), 415-435.

72. Rao, S.S. (2001). IPR in the Ensuing Global Digital Economy. *Library Hi Tech*, 19(2), 179-184.

73. Roig, M. (2001). Plagiarism and paraphrasing criteria of college and university professors. *Ethics & Behavior*, 11(3), 307-323.

2002

74. Bird, S. J. (2002). Self-plagiarism and dual and redundant publications: what is the problem?.*Sci. Eng. Ethics*, 8(4), 543-544.

75. Brandt, D Scott. (2002). Copyright's (not so) little cousin, plagiarism. *Computers in Libraries*, 22 (5), 39-41.

76. Cox, R. J. (2002). Unfair use: Advice to unwitting authors. *Journal of Scholarly Publishing*, 34(1), 31-42.

77. Fialkoff, Francine. (2002). Too sensitized to plagiarism? *Library Journal*, 127 (20), 100.

78. Hannabuss, S. (2002). Inspiration or infringement: Parody and the law. *Library Review*, 51(1), 79-89.

79. Janowski, A. (2002). Plagiarism: prevention, not PROSECUTION. *Book Report*, 21(2), 14.

80. Lincoln, Margaret. (2002). Internet plagiarism. *MultiMedia Schools*, 9(1), 46-49.

81. Price, M. (2002). Beyond "gotcha!": Situating plagiarism in policy and pedagogy. *Coll Compos Commun*, 54(1):88–115.

82. Rice, D. A. (2002). Copyright as Talisman: Expanding 'Property' in Digital Works. *International Review of Law Computers & Technology*, 16(2), 113-32.

83. Samtani, A., Kiong, J. S., Young, L. L. & Neo, A. C. (2002). Copyright Infringement in Universities in Singapore: Problems and Possible Solutions. *The Journal of World Intellectual Property*, 5(5), 791-821.

84. Scanlon, P.M. and Neumann, D.R. (2002). Internet plagiarism among college students. *Journal of College Student Development*, 43, 374.

85. Stubley, P. (2002). What's yours is mine. *Information Management Report*, Aug, 1-4.

2003

86. Ashworth, P., Freewood, M. and Macdonald, R. (2003). The student life world and the meanings of plagiarism. *Journal of Phenomenological Psychology*, 34 (2), 257 78.

87. Cast, M. (2003). Plagiarism. *Nebraska Library Association Quarterly*, 34(4), 17-24.
88. Crockett, Angela D. (2003). Plagiarism. *Library Media Connection*, 22 (1), 117.
89. Givler, P. (2003). What good is copyright? *Journal of Scholarly Publishing*, 34(3), 140-145.
90. Hauptman, R. (2003). Words for the taking: The hunt for a plagiarist. *Journal of Information Ethics*, 83-84.
91. Hoad, T. C., & Zobel, J. (2003). Methods for identifying versioned and plagiarized documents. *Journal of the American Society for Information Science and Technology*, 54(3), 203-215.
92. Ludlow, B. L. (2003). Understanding Copyright and Intellectual Property in the Digital Age: Guidelines for Teacher Educators and their Students. *Teacher Education and Special Education: The Journal of the Teacher Education Division of the Council for Exceptional Children*, 26(2), 130-144.
93. Park, C. (2003). In other (people's) words: plagiarism by university students – literature and lessons. *Assessment and Evaluation in Higher Education*, 28 (5), 471-488.
94. Savage, W. W. (2003). My favourite plagiarist: Some reflections of an offended party. *Journal of Scholarly Publishing*, 34(4), 214-220.
95. Scribner, Mary Ellen. (2003). An ounce of prevention: Defeating plagiarism in the information age. *Library Media Connection*, 21 (5), 32-34.
96. Simmonds, P. (2003). Plagiarism and cyber-plagiarism: A guide to selected resources on the Web. *College and Research Libraries News*, 64(6), 385-389.
97. Siriginidi, S. R. (2003). Copyright: It's implication for electronic information. *Online Information Review*, 27(4), 264-275.
98. Strickland, L.S. (2003). Copyright's Digital Dilemma Today: Fair Use or Unfair Constraints? Part I: The Battle Over File Sharing. *Bulletin of the American Society for Science and Technology*, 30(1), 7-11.
99. Yamada, Kyoko (2003). What prevents ESL/EFL writers from avoiding plagiarism? Analyses of 10 North-American college websites, *System*, 32(2), 247-258.

2004

100. Atlas, M. C. (2004). Retraction policies of high-impact biomedical journals. *Journal of the Medical Library Association*, 92(2), 242-50.
101. Burke, M. (2004a). Deterring plagiarism: a new role for librarians. *Library Philosophy and Practice*, 6, Retrieved from: http://digitalcommons.unl.edu/libphilprac/10.
102. Burke, M. & Heron, S. J. (2004). Copyright Issues and "For-Profit" Libraries. *Journal of Interlibrary Loan, Document Delivery & Information Supply*, 14(4), 5-21.
103. Butler, R. P. (2004). Avoiding copyright violations when using the internet as an

information source. *Knowledge Quest*, 32(3), 33-34.

104. Ercegovac, Z. and Richardson, J. Jr. (2004). Academic dishonesty, plagiarism included, in the Digital Age: a literature review. *College & Research Libraries*, 65 (4), 301 19.

105. Fernández-Molina, J. C. (2004). Licensing Agreements for Information Resources and Copyright Limitations and Exceptions. *Journal of Information Science*, 30(4), 337-346.

106. Ferullo, D. L. (2004). Major Copyright Issues in Academic Libraries. *Journal of Library Administration*, 40(1-2), 23-40.

107. Fink, C. & Maskus, K. E. (2004). Why We Study Intellectual Property Rights and What We Have Learned. In C. Fink, & K. Maskus (Eds.), *Intellectual Property Protection: Effects on Market Structure, Trade and Foreign Direct Investment* (pp. 17-31). Herndon, USA: World Bank.

108. Gitanjali, B. (2004). Academic dishonesty in Indian medical colleges. *J. Postgraduate Med.*, 50(4), 281-284.

109. Gustafson, C. (2004). Is it cheating if everybody does it? *Library Media Connection*, 22(5), 24-25.

110. Johnson, D. (2004). The other side of plagiarism. *Library Media Connection*, 23 (1), 98.

111. Julieta, Dias Fisher & Hill, Ann (2004). Plagiarism in an electronic age. *Library Media Connection*, 23 (3), 18-19.

112. Martin, B. (2004). Plagiarism: Policy against cheating or policy for learning?.*Nexus (Newsletter of the Australian Sociological Association)*,16(2), 15-16.

113. Seadle, M. (2004). Copyright in a Networked World: Ethics and Infringement. *Library Hi Tech*, 22(1), 106-110.

114. Shi, L. (2004). Textual borrowing in second-language writing. *Writ Commun* 21(2):171–200.

115. Sterngold, A. (2004). Confronting plagiarism. *Change*, 36, 16 21.

116. Tedford, R. (2004). Plagiarism Detection Programs: A Comparative Evaluation. *College & University Media Review* 9(2), 111-18.

117. Wood, G. (2004). Academic original sin: plagiarism, the internet, and librarians. *The Journal of Academic Librarianship*, 30(3), 237-242.

2005

118. Butler, R. P. (2005). Intellectual property defined. *Knowledge Quest*, 34(1), 41-42.

119. Dames, K. M. (2005). Copyright Clearances: The high stakes of fair use.*Online*, 29(6), 38-42.

120. Davidson, L. A. (2005). The End of Print: Digitization and its Consequence-Revolutionary Changes in Scholarly and Social Communication and in Scientific Research. *International Journal of Toxicology*, 24(25), 25-33.

121. Hayes, N. and Introna, L. D. (2005). Cultural values, plagiarism, and fairness: when plagiarism gets in the way of learning. *Ethics & Behavior*, 15 (3), 213 31.

122. Mahmood, K. & Ilyas, M. (2005). Copyright and Book Piracy in Pakistan. *IFLA Journal*, 31(4), 324-332.

123. Martin, D. (2005). Plagiarism and technology: a tool for coping with plagiarism. *Journal of Education for Business*, 80, 149 52.

124. Myers, S. (2005). Copyright and Online Learning: How Libraries can Help. *Kentucky Libraries*, 69(4), 14-17.

125. Okiy, R. B. (2005). Photocopying and the Awareness of Copyright in Tertiary Institutions in Nigeria. *Interlending & Document Supply*, 33(1), 49-52.

126. Purdy, J. (2005). Calling off the hounds: technology and the visibility of plagiarism. *Pedagogy: Crit App*, 5(2):275–295.

127. Reiner, L., & Smith, A. (2005). Professor copycat. *Journal of Academic Librarianship*, 31(3), 298.

128. Stokes, S. (2005). Why Digital Copyright Matters. In S. Stokes (Ed.) *Digital Copyright: Law and Practice* (pp. 37-54). Oxford: Hart Publishing Ltd.

129. Sutherland-Smith, W. (2005). Pandora's box: Academic perceptions of student plagiarism in writing. *J. English Academic Purposes*,4(1), 83-95.

130. Terry, Richard. (2005). Pope and plagiarism. *Modern Language Review*, 100(3), 593-608.

2006

131. Abasi, A. R., Akbari, N. & Graves, B. (2006). Discourse appropriation, construction of identities, and the complex issue of plagiarism: ESL students writing in graduate school. *J Second Lang Writ*, 15:102–117.

132. Barry, E.S. (2006). Can paraphrasing practice help students define plagiarism? *College Student Journal*, 40, 377 84.

133. Bernfeld, B. A. (2006). Free to Photocopy? *Legal Reference Services*. 25(2-3), 1-49.

134. Boden, Debbi & Carroll, Jude. (2006). Combating plagiarism through information literacy.*Library + Information Update*, 5(1-2), 40-41.

135. Boisvert, R.F. & Irwin, M.J. (2006). Plagiarism on the rise. *Communications ACM*, 49(6), 23-24.

136. Chalmers, I. (2006). Role of systematic reviews in detecting plagiarism: case of Asim Kurjak. *BMJ Brit Med J*, 333:594–596.

137. Dames, K. M. (2006, 11). Plagiarism: The new 'piracy'. *Information Today*, 23, 21-22.

138. Devlin, M. (2006). Policy, preparation, and prevention: Proactive minimization of student plagiarism. *J. Higher Edu. Policy Manag.*, 28(1), 45-58.

139. Doherty, W. (2006). Copyright Theft. *Industrial and Commercial Training*, 38(7), 371-378.

140. Henningsen, L. (2006). Harry Potter with Chinese Characteristics: Plagiarism between Orientalism and Occidentalism. *China Information*, 20(275), 275-311.

141. Hernon, P., & Schwartz, C. (2006). Peer review revisited. *Library and Information Science Research*, 28(1), 1-3.

142. Hoorn, E. & Graaf, M. V. (2006). Copyright Issues in Open Access Research Journals: The author's Perspectives. *D-Lib Magazine*, 12(2).

143. Isaacson, D. (2006). What makes a quotation familiar? *Reference & User Services Quarterly*, 46(2), 22-26.

144. Jackson, P. (2006). Plagiarism instruction online: assessing undergraduate students' ability to avoid plagiarism. *College & Research Libraries*, 67 (5), 418-428.

145. Joint, N. (2006). Teaching intellectual property rights as part of the information literacy syllabus. *Library Review*, 55(6), 330-336.

146. Mishra, R.K. and Ramesh, R. (2006). IPR, plagiarism and the text data security pyramid. *Annals of Library and Information Studies*, 11(5), 326-329.

147. Maxymuk, J. (2006). The persistent plague of plagiarism. *Bottom Line: Managing Library Finances*, 19(1), 44 7.

148. Pickard, J. (2006). Staff and student attitudes to plagiarism at University College Northampton. *Assessment & Evaluation in Higher Education*, 31(2), 215 32.

149. Seadle, M. (2006). Copyright in the Networked World: Copyright Police. *Library Hi Tech*, 24(1), 153-159.

150. Smith, H. K. (2006). Copyright Knowledge of Faculty at Two Academic Health Science Campuses: Results of a Survey. *Serials Review*, 32, 59-67.

151. Snyder, N., Garber, G. and Dobbs, A. (2006). Avoiding plagiarism: success strategies in Tennessee. *Tennessee Libraries*, 56 (2), 239 60.

152. Valentine, K. (2006). Plagiarism as literacy practice: recognizing and rethinking ethical binaries. *Coll Compos Commun* 58(1):89–109.

153. Wiebe, Todd J. (2006). College students, plagiarism, and the internet: the role of academic librarians in delivering education and awareness. *MLA Forum*, 5 (2).

154. Zhou, D. (2006, April 23). Examples of similar passages between Viswanathan's book and McCafferty's two novels. *The Harvard Crimson*. Retrieved from http://www.thecrimson.com/article/2006/4/23/examples-of-similar- passages-between-viswanathans/

2007

155. Abilock, D. (2007). Practicing what we teach. *Knowledge Quest*, 35(4), 6-10.

156. Badke, William. (2007). Give plagiarism the weight it deserves. *Online*, 31(5), 58-60.
157. Bretag, T. & Carapiet, S. (2007). A preliminary study to identify the extent of self-plagiarism in Australian academic research. *Plagiary* 2:92–103.
158. Dames, K Matthew. (2007). Understanding plagiarism and how it differs from copyright infrigement. *Computers in Libraries*, 27(6), 24-27.
159. Devlin, M. and Gray, K. (2007). In their own words: a qualitative study of the reasons Australian students plagiarize. *Higher Education Research & Development*, 26 (2), 181 98.
160. Duggan, Fiona (2007). Plagiarism: prevention, practice and policy, *Assessment & Evaluation in Higher Education*, 31(2),151-154
161. Embleton, Kimberly & Small Helfer, Doris (2007). The plague of plagiarism and academic dishonesty. *Searcher*, 15(6), 23-26.
162. Fallis, D. (2007). Information Ethics for Twenty-First Century Library Professionals. In K. E. Himma (Ed.), *Information Ethics* (pp. 23-36). Emeral Group Publishing Ltd.
163. Fawley, N. (2007). Plagiarism pitfalls: addressing cultural differences in the misuse of sources. *International Journal of Learning*, 14 (7), 71 4.
164. Ghai, S. K. (2007). Educational Publishing in India: Present Scenarios and Future Prospects. *Publishing Research Quarterly*, 23, 278-282.
165. Hamalainen, Maryellen. (2007). Useful tips on avoiding plagiarism. *Library Media Connection*, 25(6), 40-41.
166. Kartika, V. K. (2007). The Indian Rights Market. *Publishing Research Quarterly*, 23, 141-145.
167. Kulathuramaiyer, Narayanan & Maurer, Hermann. (2007). Fighting plagiarism and IPR violation: why is it so important? *Learned Publishing*, 20(4), 252-258.
168. Madray, A. (2007). Developing students' awareness of plagiarism: Crisis and opportunities. *Library Philosophy and Practice (e-journal)*, 134.http://digitalcommons.unl.edu/libphilprac/13
169. Mundava, Maud and Chaudhuri, Jayati. (2007). Understanding plagiarism. *College & Research Libraries News*, 68(3), 170-173.
170. Reddy, G. B. (2007). Infringement of Copyright and Doctrine of Fair Use. *DESIDOC Bulletin of Information Technology*, 24(4), 29-36.
171. Seadle, M. (2007). Copyright cultures. *Library Hi Tech*, 25(3), 430-435.
172. Williams, B. (2007). Trust, betrayal, and authorship: plagiarism and how we perceive students. *J Adolesc Adult Literacy*, 51(4): 350–354.
173. Yeo, S. (2007). First year university science and engineering students' understanding of plagiarism. *Higher Education Research & Development*, 26 (2), 199 216.

2008

174. Abasi, Ali R. & Graves, Barbara. (2008). Academic literacy and plagiarism: Conversations with international graduate students and disciplinary professors, *Journal of English for Academic Purposes*, 7 (4), 221-233

175. Adamsick, C. (2008). "Warez" the Copyright Violation? Digital Copyright Infringement: Legal Loopholes and Decentralization. *TechTrends*,52(6), 10-12.

176. Anderson, J. (2008). The little book of Plagiarism/Historians in trouble: Plagiarism,fraud, and politics in the ivory tower. *Journal of Information Ethics*, 17(2), 99-101.

177. Banerjee, D. S., & Banerjee, T. A. (2008). Optimal Enforcement and Anti-Copying Strategies to Counter Copyright Infringement. *The Japanese Economic Review*,59(4), 519-535.

178. Bloch, J. (2008). Plagiarism across cultures: is there a difference? In: Eisner C, Vicinus M. (Eds.) *Originality, imitation, and plagiarism: teaching writing in the digital age*. University of Michigan Press, Ann Arbor, MI.

179. Buchanan, Elizabeth. (2008). Library plagiarism policies. *Library & Information Science Research*, 30 (3), 235.

180. Chikate, R. V. and Patil, S. K. (2008). Citation analysis of the theses in LIS submitted to the university of Pune:a pilot study. *Library Philosophy and Practice*, 222, 1-15.

181. Culpepper, J. (2008). An interdisciplinary approach to preventing plagiarism: a librarian – social work educator collaboration. *Journal of Social Work Values and Ethics*, 5(1), 1 9.

182. Donahue, C. (2008). When copying is not copying: plagiarism and French composition scholarship. In Eisner C, Vicinus M (Eds) *Originality, imitation, and plagiarism: teaching writing in the digital age*. University of Michigan Press, Ann Arbor, MI.

183. Drinan, P. and Gallant, T. (2008). Plagiarism and academic integrity systems. *Journal of Library Administration*, 47(3/4), 125 40.

184. Ghai, S. K. (2008). Glimpses of Indian Publishing Today in the Words of Publishing Professionals. *Publishing Research Quarterly*, 24, 202-214.

185. Grossberg, M. (2008). History and the disciplining of plagiarism. In Eisner C, Vicinus M (Eds.) *Originality, imitation, and plagiarism: teaching writing in the digital age*. University of Michigan Press, Ann Arbor, MI.

186. Jabade, S. & Abhyankar, H. A. (2008). Model IPRinternalise – Integrating Intellectual Property Rights in Technical Education. *World Patent Information*, 30, 220-224.

187. Jamieson, S. (2008). One size does not fit all: plagiarism across the curriculum. InHoward RM, Robillard A (Eds.) *Pluralizing plagiarism: identities, contexts, pedagogies*. Heinemann, Portsmouth, N,H.

188. Ledwith, A. and Risquez, A. (2008). Using anti plagiarism software to promote academic

honesty in the context of peer reviewed assignments. *Studies in Higher Education*, 33(4), 371 84.

189. McCabe, D.L, Feghali, T & Abdallah, H. (2008). Academic dishonesty in the Middle East: individual and contextual factors. *Res High Educ* 43(3):451–467.

190. Nimsakont, Emily Dust. (2008). How can academic librarians educate students about plagiarism? *PNLA Quarterly*, 72(3), 10-12.

191. Ochoa, T.T. (2008). Copyright Protection for Works of Foreign Origin. In J. Klabbers, & M. Sellers (Eds.), *The Internationalization of Law and Legal Education* (pp. 167-190). Springer Science+Business Media.

192. Reyman, J. (2008). Rethinking plagiarism for technical communication. *Tech Commun*, 55(1):61–67.

193. Rowlands, I., Nicholas, D., Williams, P., Huntington, P., Fieldhouse, M., Gunter, B., Tenopir, C. (2008). The google generation: The informationbehavior of the researcher of the future. *Aslib Proceedings*, 60(4), 290-310.

194. Schlipp, J. (2008). Coaching Teaching Faculty: Copyright Awareness Programs in Academic Libraries. *Kentucky Libraries*, 72(3), 18-22.

195. Seadle, M. (2008). Copyright in the Networked World: The Technology of Enforcement. *Library Hi Tech*, 26(3), 498-504.

196. Selwyn, N. (2008). Not necessarily a bad thing …: A study of online plagiarism amongst undergraduate students. *Assessment & Evaluation in Higher Education*, 33 (5), 465-479.

197. Sreekumar, M. G. (2008). Open Access: the New Frontier Connecting the Learning Commons Through Hassle-Free and Seamless Scholarly Communication. *World Digital Libraries*, 1(1), 61-76.

198. Yeo, S. (2008). First year university science and engineering students' understanding of plagiarism. *Higher Education and Research Development Society of Australasia*, 26(2), 199-216.

199. Zwagerman, S. (2008). The scarlet P: plagiarism, panopticism, and the rhetoric of academic integrity. *Coll Compos Commun* 59(4):676–710.

2009

200. Brandt, D. (2009). When people write for pay. *JAC* 29(1/2):165–197.

201. Bretag, T. and Mahmud, S. (2009). A model for determining student plagiarism: electronic detection and academic judgement. *Journal of University Teaching and Learning Practice*, 6(1), 49 60.

202. Clarida, R. W. (2009). Electronic Copyright Rights: Do You Have What You Need? *Publishing Research Quarterly*, 25, 199-204.

203. Dames, K. M. (2009, 06). Why the frame of 'piracy' matters. *Information Today*, 26, 22-23.

204. Fishman, T. (2009). "we know it when we see it" is not good enough: toward a standard definition of plagiarism that transcends theft, fraud, and copyright. Paper presented at the *4th Asia Pacific conference on educational integrity*, University of Wollongong NSW Australia, http://www.bmartin.cc/pubs/09-4apcei/4apcei-Fishman.pdf.

205. Kapitzke, C. (2009). Rethinking copyrights for the library through creative commons licensing. *Library Trends*, 58(1), 95-108.

206. Koshy, S. (2009). A case of miscommunication? Obstacles to effective implementation of a plagiarism detection system in a multicultural university, *University of Wollongong in Dubai working paper*. http://ro.uow.edu.au/dubaiwp/3/.

207. Lincoln, M. (2009). Ethical behavior in the information age. *Knowledge Quest*, 37(5), 34-37.

208. Mukherjee, B. (2009). Scholarly communication: A journey from print to web. *Library Philosophy and Practice*, 1-8.

209. Neelakantan, S. (2009). In India, plagiarism is on the rise – publish, perish, or pitfer? *Global Post*. 2009. Retrieved from https://www.pri.org/stories/2009-10-18/india-plagiarism-rise.

210. Orthaber, S. (2009). Detecting and preventing internet plagiarism in a foreign language e learning course. *International Journal of Advanced Corporate Learning*, 2(2), 20 4.

211. Potter, J. (2009). New Issues, New Developments and New Challenges for Negotiating the International Rights Contract. *Publishing Research Quarterly*, 25,12-23.

212. Power, L.G. (2009). University students' perceptions of plagiarism. *Journal of Higher Education*, 80(6), 643 62.

213. Purdy, J. (2009). Anxiety and the archive: understanding plagiarism detection services as digital archives. *Comput Compos*, 26:65–77.

214. Sharma, A. (2009). Indian Perspective of Fair Dealing Under Copyright Law: Lex Lata or Lex Ferenda? *Journal of Intellectual Property Rights*, 14, 523-531.

215. Smerillo, D. (2009). Selling Translation Rights to an American Publisher. *Publishing Research Quarterly*, 25, 181-190.

2010

216. Carreiro, E. (2010). Electronic Books: How Digital Devices and Supplementary New Technologies are Changing the Face of the Publishing Industry. *Publishing Research Quarterly*, 26, 219-235.

217. Charles L, McLafferty & Karen M, Foust. (2010). Electronic Plagiarism as a College Instructor's Nightmare—Prevention and Detection, *Journal of Education for Business*, 79(3), 186-190

218. Choi, P., Bae, S. H. & Jun, J. (2010). Digital Piracy and Firms Strategic Interactions: The Effects of Public Copy Protection and DRM Similarity. *Information Economics and Policy*, 22, 354-364.

219. Collins. S. (2010). Digital Fair: Prosumption and the Fair Use Defence. *Journal of Consumer Culture*, 10(37), 37-55.

220. Cummings, C. & Gunnells, E. G. (2010). Copyright and Fair Use inHigher Education. In 3rd (Ed.), *Encyclopedia of Library and Information Sciences* (Vol. 1, pp. 1282-1289). London, UK: Taylor & Francis.

221. Gabriel, T. (2010, August 1). Plagiarism Lines Blur for Students in Digital Age. *The New York Times*. Retrieved from http://www.nytimes.com/

222. Gilmore J, Strickland D, Timmerman B, Maher M, & Feldon, D. (2010). Weeds in the flower garden: an exploration of plagiarism in graduate students' research proposals and its connection to enculturation, ESL, and contextual factors. *IJEI* 6(1):13–28.

223. Green, D. A. (2010). Copyright Revolt. *Index on Censorship*, 39(1), 143-148.

224. Heitman, E. & Litewka, S. (2010). International perspectives on plagiarism and considerations for teaching international trainees. *Urologic Oncology: Seminars Original Investigations*, 29(1), 104-108.

225. Howard, R.M. and Watson, M. (2010). The scholarship of plagiarism: where we've been, where we are, what's needed next. *WPA: Writing Program Administration*, 33(3), 116-124.

226. Larivière, V., & Gingras, Y. (2010). On the prevalence and scientific impact of duplicate publications in different scientific fields (1980-2007). *Journal of Documentation*, 66(2), 179-190.

227. Levine, M. (2010). Opening Up Content in Hathi Trust: Using Hathi Trust Permissions Agreements to Make Authors' Work available. *Research Library Issues*, 269, 14-19.

228. Mok, M. S. & Sohn, S.Y. (2010). Conjoint Analysis for Intellectual Property Education. *World Patent Information*, 32, 129-134.

229. O'Dwyer, M., Risquez, A. and Ledwith, A. (2010). Entrepreneurship educationand plagiarism: tell me lies, tell me sweet little lies. *Journal of Small Business and Enterprise Development*, 17, 641 51.

230. Paton, G. (2010, September 2). Foreign students 'cheating on university applications'. *Telegraph*. Retrieved from http://www.telegraph.co.uk/

231. Prenafeta, J. (2010). Protecting Copyright Through Semantic Technology. *Publishing Research Quarterly*, 26, 249-254.

232. Qiu, J. (2010). Publish or perish in China. *Nature*, 467, 142-143.

233. Satyanarayana, K. (2010). Plagiarism: a scourge afflicting the Indian science. *Indian Journal of Medical Research*, 131 (3), 373 6.

234. Spoo, R. A. (2010). Intellectual Property and Vietnam's Higher Education System. In G. E. Harman (Ed.), *Reforming Higher Education in Vietnam* (pp. 117-127).SpringerScience+Business Media.

235. Stapleton, P. (2010). Gauging the effectiveness of anti-plagiarism software: an empirical study of second language graduate writers. *J Engl Acad Purp* 11:125–133.

236. Tshepo, Batane (2010). Turning to Turnitin to Fight Plagiarism among University Students,*Journal of Educational Technology & Society*, 13(2), 1-12

237. Vathitphund, T. (2010). Access to Knowledge Difficulties in Developing Countries: A Balanced Access to Copyrighted Works in the Digital Environment. *International Review of Law, Computers & Technology*, 24(1), 7-16.

2011

238. Adnan, H. M. (2011). Xerox Makes Everybody a Publisher: Problems of BookPhotocopying and Ways to Control it in Malaysia. *Publishing Research Quarterly*, 27, 268-276.

239. Anderson, M.S. & Steneck, N. H. (2011). The problem of plagiarism. *Urologic Oncology:Seminars Original Investigations*, 29(1), 90-94.

240. Anson, C. (2011). Fraudulent practices: academic misrepresentations of plagiarism in the name of good pedagogy. *Comp Stud*, 39(2), 29–43.

241. Arai, Y. (2011). Civil and Criminal Penalties for Copyright Infringement. *Information Economics and Policy*, 23, 270-280.

242. Babu, T.A., Joseph, N.M. & Sharmila, V. (2011). Academic dishonesty among undergraduates from private medical schools in India: are we on the right track?.*Medical Teacher*, 33(9), 759-761.

243. Bowdoin, D. (2011). Copyright's Immoral Rights? *Visual Resources*, 27(4),361-369.

244. Butler, Marian. (2011). *Strategies to help organize your writing and avoid plagiarism* Retrieved from http://www.uq.edu.au/student-services/sites/uq.edu.au.student-services/files/imported/Avoid_Plagiarism.pdf

245. Childress, D. (2011). Citation tools in academic libraries: Best practices for reference and instruction. *Reference & User Services Quarterly*, 51(2), 143-152.

246. Fernández-Molina, J. C. (2011). Copyright and E-learning: Professors' Level of Knowledge About the New Spanish Law. *Aslib Proceedings: New Information Perspectives*, 63(4), 340-353.

247. Gibson, Nancy Snyder and Chester Fangman, Christina. (2011). The librarian's role in combating plagiarism. *Reference Services Review*, 39(1),132-150.

248. Jauhar, A. (2011). All Talk and No Bite: Copyright Infringement and Piracy Trends in India. *Computer Law & Security Review*, 27, 537-541.

249. Kose, O. and Arikan, A. (2011). Reducing plagiarism by using online software: an experimental study. *Contemporary Online Language Education Journal*, 1, 122-129.

250. Parry, M. (2011, April 28). Plagiarism goes social. *The Chronicle of Higher Education*. Retrieved from http://chronicle.com/

251. Paxhia, S. (2011). The Challenges of Higher Education Digital Publishing. *Publishing Research Quarterly*, 27, 321-326.

252. Satija, M. P. (2011). Plagiarism: A Tempting Snake. *Library Progress*, 31(1),99-106.

253. Seadle, M. (2011). Archiving in the Networked World. *Library Hi Tech*,29(4), 655-662.

254. Sharma, B.B. & Singh, V. (2011).Ethics in writing: Learning to stay away from plagiarism and scientific misconduct. *Lung India: Official Organ Indian Chest Society*, 28(2), 148-150.

255. Stenis, Paul. (2011). Stop plagiarism: A guide to understanding and prevention. *Reference & User Services Quarterly*,50(4), 406-407.

256. Weisberg, M. (2011). Student Attitudes and Behaviors Towards Digital Textbooks. *Publishing Research Quarterly*, 27, 188-196.

257. Xalabarder, R. (2011). Copyright Issues in E-Learning. In Ferran, & J. Minguillon (Eds.), *Content Management for E-Learning* (pp. 87-109). Springer Science+Business Media.

258. Yoon, C. (2011). Theory of Planned Behaviour and Ethics Theory in Digital Piracy: An Integrated Model. *Journal of Business Ethics*, 100, 405-417.

259. Zimerman, M. (2011). E-Books and Piracy: Implications/Issues for Academic Libraries. *New Library World*, 112(1/2), 67-75.

2012

260. Anderson, J. (2012). Intellectual property, fee or free? *Journal of Information Ethics*, 21(2), 114-121.

261. Choolhun, N. (2012). The only way is information literacy. *Legal Information Management*, 12(1), 44-50.

262. Dominguez-Aroca, M. (2012). Fighting against plagiarism from university libraries. *Profesional De La Informacion*, 21(5), 498-503.

263. Edwards, L., Klien, B., Lee, D., Moss, G., & Philip, E. (2012). Framing the Consumer: Copyright Regulation and the Public. *Convergence: The International Journal of Research into New Media Technologies*,19(1), 9-24.

264. Evering L.C. & Moorman, G. (2012). Rethinking plagiarism in the digital age. *J Adolesc Adult Lit* 56(1):35–44

265. Favale, M. (2012). The Right of Access in Digital Copyright: Right of the Owner or Right of the User? *The Journal of World Intellectual Property*, 15(4), 1-25.

266. Gayathri Devi S & Navalgund, C.U. (2012) Plagiarism: a rising degree of plague

questioning ethics, policies and technology. *SRELS Jl of Info Mgmt* 49(1): 69-73.

267. Honig, B. & Beti, A. (2012). The fox in the hen house: a critical examination of plagiarism among members of the academyof management. *Acad Manag Learn Edu*, 11(1):101–123.

268. Isiakpona, C. D. (2012). Undergraduate students' perception of copyright infringement: A case study of the university of ibadan, oyo state, Nigeria. *Library Philosophy and Practice*, 1-9.

269. Speight, D. & Darroch, J. (2012). Clarifying Copyright. *Legal Information Management*, 12(3), 209-13.

270. Tsui, H-C. & Wang, T-M. (2012). Piracy and Social Norm of Anti-Piracy. *International Journal of Social Economics*, 39(12), 922-932.

271. Xia, J. (2012). Diffusionism and open access. *Journal of Documentation*, 68(1), 72-99.

272. Zafron, Michelle. (2012). Good intentions: providing students with skills to avoid accidental plagiarism. *Medical Reference Services Quarterly*, 31(2), 225-229.

273. Zimerman, Martin. (2012). Plagiarism and international students in academic libraries. *New Library World*, 113 (5/6), 290-299.

2013

274. Bell, Mary Ann. (2013). Plagued by Plagiarism? Here Are Some Antidotes.*Internet @ Schools*, 20(1), 24-25.

275. Bouhnik, D., & Deshen, M. (2013). Unethical behavior of youth in the internet environment.*International Journal of Technology, Knowledge and Society*, 9(2), 109-124.

276. Eleonora, Dagienë (2013). Findings of the Survey on Prevention of Plagiarism in Lithuanian Research Journals. *Procedia - Social and Behavioral Sciences*, 110 (24), 1283-1294.

277. George, S., Costigan, A., & O'Hara, M. (2013). Placing the library at the heart of plagiarism prevention: The university of bradford experience. *New Review of Academic Librarianship*, 19(2), 141-160.

278. Greenstein, S., Lerner, J. & Stern, S. (2013). Digitization, Innovation, and Copyright: What is the Agenda? *Strategic Organization*, 11(1), 110-121.

279. Kathleen, Lourdes Obille. (2013). Can information literacy develop intellectual honesty? *Journal of Philippine Librarianship*, 33 (1), 47-57.

280. King, D. (2013). Hollywood's copyright wars: From edison to the internet. *Portal: Libraries and the Academy*, 13(1), 116-118.

281. Liesegang, T. J. (2013). The Continued Movement for Open Access to Peer-Reviewed Literature. *American Journal of Ophthalmology*, 156(3), 423-432.

282. Liu, Y., & Rousseau, R. (2013). Interestingness and the essence of citation. *Journal of Documentation*, 69(4), 580-589.

283. Lu, B. (2013). Reconstructing Copyright from 'Copy-Centric' to 'Dissemination-Centric' in the Digital Age. *Journal of Information Science*, 39(4),479-493.

284. Martin, B. R. (2013). Whither Research Integrity? Plagiarism, Self-Plagiarism and Coercive Citation. *Research Policy*, 42(5), 1005-1014.

285. Mingaleva, Z. & Mirskikh, I. (2013). The Protection of Intellectual Property in Educational Process. *Procedia - Social and Behavioral Sciences*, 83, 1059-1062.

286. Pedersen, A.M. (2013). Thinking globally about plagiarism: international academic writers' perspectives. In Donnelly M, Ingalls R, Morse TA, Post JC, Stockdell-Giesler AM (Eds.) *Critical conversations about plagiarism*. Parlor Press, Anderson, SC.

287. Rezanejad, A. and Rezaei, S. (2013). Academic Dishonesty at Universities: The Case of Plagiarism Among Iranian Language Students. *Journal of Academic Ethics*, 11(4), 275-295.

288. Scott, Rachel and Schnabel, Jennifer. (2013). Plagiarist Patrol: How Librarians Can Collaborate with Online Instructors to Promote the Ethical Use of Information. *Tennessee Libraries*, 63(2).

289. Smith, K. & Davis, S. (2013). Copyright in a Digital Age: Conflict, Risk, and Reward. *The Serials Librarian: From the Printed Page to the Digital Age*, 64(1-4), 57-66.

290. Spring, Hannah & Adams, Rachel. (2013). Combating plagiarism: the role of the health librarian. *Health Information and Libraries Journal*, 30 (4), 337-342.

291. Sun, Y. (2013). Do journal authors plagiarize? Using plagiarism detection software to uncover matching text acrossdisciplines. *J Engl Acad Purp* 12:264–272.

292. Volpe, T., & Schopfel, J. (2013). Dissemination of knowledge and copyright: An historical case study. *Journal of Information, Communication & Ethics in Society*, 11(3), 144-155.

293. Wu, W-P. & Yang, H-L. (2013). A Comparative Study of College Students' Ethical Perception Concerning Internet Piracy. *Quality & Quantity*, 47(1), 111-120.

2014

294. Adam, A.R. (2014). Plagiarism detection algorithm using natural language processing based on grammar analyzing. *Journal of Theoretical & Applied Information Technology*, 63(1),168-180.

295. Dejong, S. M. (2014). Academic Honesty. In *Blogs and Tweets, Texting and Friending* (pp. 95-105). New York: Academic Press.

296. Duncan, S., M.S.L.S. (2014). Research ethics: A philosophical guide to the responsible conduct of research. *Journal of the Medical Library Association*, 102(2), 131-132.

297. Forsyth, R. S., & Sharoff, S. (2014). Document dissimilarity within and across languages: A benchmarking study. *Literary and Linguistic Computing*, 29(1), 6-22.

298. García-Romero, A. & Estrada-Lorenzo, J. M. (2014). A bibliometric analysis of plagiarism and self-plagiarism through Déjà vu. *Scientometrics*, 101(1), 381-396.

299. Gunnarsson, J., Kulesza, W. J., & Pettersson, A. (2014). Teaching international students how to avoid plagiarism: Librarians and faculty in collaboration. *The Journal of Academic Librarianship*, 40(3-4), 413-417.

300. Rudd, M, & Hodges, A. (2014). Isn't everyone a plagiarist?: teaching plagiarism is teaching culture. In: Seawright L (Ed.) *Going global: transnational perspectives on globalization, language, and education*. Cambridge scholars publishing, Newcastle upon Tyne, UK.

301. Singh, H.P. & Guram, N. (2014). Knowledge and attitude of dental professionals of North India toward plagiarism. *North Am. J. Med. Sci.*, 6(1), 6-11.

302. Singh, Jnanendra Naryan. (2014). Literature review on Copyright Infringement and Protection. *Library Herald*, 52(2):158-181.

303. Wager, E. (2014). Defining and responding to plagiarism. *Learned Publishing*,27(1), 33-42. doi: 10.1087/20140105

2015

304. Fahnrich, Birte, Danyi, Claudia Janssen, and Nothhaft, Howard. (2015) The German Plagiarism Crisis: Defending and explaining the working of Scholarship on the Front Stage. *Jl of Communication Management* 19(1): 20-38.

305. Hadjiargyrou, Michael. (2015). Scientific Misconduct: How Best to Punish Those Who Consciously Violate Our Profession's Integrity? *Journal of Information Ethics*, 24(2), 23-30.

306. Juyal, D., Thawani, V. & Thaledi, S. (2015). Plagiarism: An egregious form of misconduct. *North Am. J. Med. Sci.*, 7(2), 77-80.

307. Resnik, D. B., Wager, E., & Kissling, G. E. (2015). Retraction policies of top scientific journals ranked by impact factor. *Journal of the Medical Library Association*, 103(3), 136-139.

308. Sabir, H., Kumbhare, S., Parate, A., Kumar, R. & Das, S. (2015). Scientific misconduct: A perspective from India. *Med., Health Care Philosophy*, 18(2), 177-184.

309. Satija, M.P. (2015). Preventing the Plague of plagiarism. *Library Herald*, 52 (4), 363-378.

310. Scholzel, H and Nothhaft, H. (2015). Swarming for Democracy—Karl—Theodor Guttenberg's Plagiarism Case, the Court of Public Opinion and the Parliament of Things. In Coombs, W.T., Falkheimer, J. Hide, M. and Philip,Y.(Eds) *Strategic Communication, Social Media and Democracy: The Challenge of Digital naturals*. London Routledge.

311. Velmurugan, C. & Radhakrishnan, N. (2015). Literature output of plagiarism: a Scientometric approach through Web of Science. In *Combating Plagiarism: a new role for Librarian*, edited by M. Patra & S. K. Jena, SK Book Agency, New Delhi,78-88.

2016

312. Ahmad,Minaj Uddin, Begum, DilaraandHaq, Nomanul. (2016). Plagiarism:' to do or not to do is the real question. InMalhan, I.V. et al..., (Eds.) *Transformation of LIS education: Libraries and information servicesfor knowledge society*. New Delhi: Ess Ess Publications,pp.458-465.

313. Johnson, W. G. (2016). Copyright updates for K-12 librarians. *Knowledge Quest*, 45(2), 26-32.

314. Kokol, P., Zavrsnik, D. & Vosner, H. B. (2016). Creating a self-plagiarism research topic typology through bibliometric visualisation. *J. Academic Ethics*, 14(3), 221-230.

315. Lukose, L. P. (2016). Copyright issues in legal research and writing. *Journal of Intellectual Property Rights*, 21(5), 275.

316. Martin, B. (2016). Plagiarism, misrepresentation, and exploitation by established professionals: power and tactics. In Bretag T. (Ed.) *Handbook of academic integrity*. Springer, Singapore.

317. Ojala, M. (2016, 06). Copyright in the twilight zone. *Information Today*, 33, 10-11.

318. Panda, S. K. (2016). Shodhganga - a national level open access ETD repository of Indian electronic theses: Current status and discussions. *Library Hi Tech News*, 33(1), 23-26.

319. Suseela, V.J. (2016). Plagiarism: The Academic Dishonesty The Significance of Anti-plagiarism Software (Tools) in Plagiarism Detection. *PEARL - A Journal of Library and Information Science*, 10 (1), 11-23.

320. Yadav, S. Rawal, G. & Baxi, M. (2016). Plagiarism-A serious scientific misconduct. *Int. J. Health Sci. Res.*, 6(2), 364-366.

2017

321. Chang, Christina Ling-hsing & Chen, J. Q. (2017). The information ethics perception gaps between Chinese and American students. *Information Technology & People*, 30(2), 473-502.

322. Hodges, A., Bickham, T., Schmidt, E. and Searight, L. (2017). Challenging the profiles of a plagiarist: a study of abstracts submitted to an international interdisciplinary conference. *International Journal for Educational Integrity* 13(7).

323. Hoffman, N., Beatty, S., Feng, P., & Lee, J. (2017). Teaching research skills through embedded librarianship. *Reference Services Review*, 45(2), 211-226.

324. Jajpura, Lalit, Bhupinder Singh, and Nayak,Rajkishore. (2017). An Introduction to intelectual propertyrights and their importance in Indian context. *Jl of IntellectualProperty Rights*, 22(1): 32-41.

325. McKinzie, Steve. (2017). Teaching plagiarism prevention to college students: An ethics based approach. *Journal of Academic Librarianship*, 43(2), 156-157.

326. Muller, Karen. (2017). Teaching Plagiarism Prevention to College Students: An Ethics-Based Approach. *American Libraries*, 48(3/4,) 74.

327. Nirmal Singh. (2017). Level of awareness among veterinary students of GADVASU towards plagiarism: a case study. *The Electronic Library*, 35 (5), 899-915.

2018

328. Chauhan, S.K. (2018). Research on palgiarism in India during 2002-2016: A bibliometric study. *DESIDOC Journal of Library & Information Technology*,38 (2), 69-74.

329. Chen, W., Xing, Qin-Rui, Wang, H., & Wang, T. (2018). Retracted publications in the biomedical literature with authors from mainland China. *Scientometrics*, 114(1), 217-227.

330. Kubilius, R. (2018). Publication ethics, Today's challenges: Navigating and combating questionable practices. *Against the Grain*, 30(1), 51.

331. Manish Kumar and Srivastava, Garima Gaur (2018). Plagiarism awareness: A study of Jamia Millia Islamia, Delhi. *Journal of Library and Information Science*, 43(1), 163-174.

332. Myers, Carla. (2018). Plagiarism and copyright: Best practices for classroom education.*College & Undergraduate Libraries*, 25(1), 91-99.

333. Panneerselvem, P. (2018). Prevention of Plagiarism atB S Abdur Rehman Crescent College of Science and Technology: A case study.*International Journal of Next Generation Library and Technologies*, 4(2) May 2018,8p.

334. Schopfel, J., & Rasuli, B. (2018). Are electronic theses and dissertations (still) grey literature in the digital age? A FAIR debate. *The Electronic Library*, 36(2), 208-219.

335. Tikam, Madhuri (2018) Connection, collaboration and community:Creative commons" Int. Ji of Lib.& Info Serv. 7(1):30-43

336. Yanti Idaya Aspura, M. K., Noorhidawati, A., & Abrizah, A. (2018). An analysis of Malaysian retracted papers: Misconduct or mistakes? *Scientometrics*, 115(3), 1315-1328.

WEBSITES

http://www.queensu.ca/academicintegrity/students/avoiding-plagiarismcheating/dos-and-donts

http://www.queensu.ca/academicintegrity/students/avoiding-plagiarismcheating/dos-and-donts

https://www.um.edu.mt/__data/assets/pdf_file/0018/261324/avdplagiarism.pdf

https://www.um.edu.mt/__data/assets/pdf_file/0018/261324/avdplagiarism.pdf

Author Index to the Bibliography

References are to the serial numbers

Abasi, A. R.	131, 174	Bell, Mary Ann.	274	Chen, W.	329
Abdallah, H.	189	Bernfeld, B. A.	133	Chester Fangman, Christina	247
Abhyankar, H. A.	186	Beti, A.	267	Chikate, R. V.	180
Abilock, D.	155	Bhupinder Singh	324	Childress, D.	245
Abrizah, A.	336	Bickham, T.	322	Choi, P.	218
Adam, A.R.	294	Bird, S. J.	74	Choolhun, N.	261
Adams, Rachel	290	Bjorner, S.	50	Chang, Christina Ling-hsing	321
Adamsick, C.	175	Bloch, J.	178	Clarida, R. W.	202
Adnan, H. M.	238	Boden, Debbi	134	Clement, O. A.	52
Ahmad, Minaj Uddin	312	Boisvert, R.F.	135	Collins. S.	219
Akbari, N.	131	Bouhnik, D.	275	Corbett, Edward P. J.	24
Anderson, J.	29, 176, 260	Bourdon, C.	51	Costigan, A.	277
Anderson. Katie Elson	18	Bowdoin, D.	243	Cox, R. J.	76
Anderson, M.S.	239	Brandt, D Scott.	75	Crews, K. D.	60
Anson, C.	240	Brandt, D.	21,200	Crockett, Angela D.	88
Arai, Y.	241	Bretag, T.	157,201	Culpepper, J.	181
Arikan, A.	249	Brown, Linda D.	58	Cummings, C.	220
Ashworth, P.	86	Buchanan, Elizabeth.	179	Cvetkovic, V. Bowman	18
Atkins, Thomas	67	Buranen, Lisa	5	Dames, K Matthew	158
Atlas, M. C.	100	Burke, M.	101,102	Dames, K. M.	119, 137, 203
Auer, N. J.	68	Butler, Marian.	244	Danyi, Claudia Janssen	304
Austin, M. Jill	58	Butler, R. P.	103,118	Darroch, J.	269
Babu, T.A.	242	Carapiet, S.	157	Das, S.	308
Badke, William.	156	Carbone, N.	69	Davidson, L. A.	120
Bae, S. H.	218	Carreiro, E.	216	Davies, J.	56
Ballew, C.	35	Carroll, J.	8,134	Davis, S.	289
Banerjee, D. S.	177	Cast, M.	87	Deahl, JasperNewton	1
Banerjee, T. A.	177	Chalmers, I.	136	Dejong, S. M.	295
Barry, E.S.	132	Charles L, McLafferty	217	Deshen, M.	275
Baxi, M.	320	Chaudhuri, Jayati	169	Devlin, M.	138,159
Beatty, S.	323	Chauhan, S.K.	328	Dobbs, A.	151
Begum, Dilara	312	Chen, J. Q.	321	Doherty, W.	139

Dominguez-Aroca, M.	262	Graaf, M. V.	142	Janowski, A.	79
Donahue, C.	182	Graves, B.	131, 174	Jauhar, A.	248
Drinan, P.	183	Gray, K.	159	Jena, S.K	22
Duggan, Fiona	160	Green, D. A.	223	Johnson, D.	110
Duncan, S., M.S.L.S.	296	Greenstein, S.	278	Johnson, W. G.	313
Edwards, L.	263	Grossberg, M.	185	Joint, N.	145
Eisenschitz, T	46	Gunnarsson, J.	299	Joseph, N.M.	242
Eisner, Caroline	13	Gunnells, E. G.	220	Julieta, Dias Fisher	111
Eleonora, Dagienë	276	Gunter, B.	193	Jun, J.	218
Ellen, M. K.	71	Guram, N.	301	Juyal, D.	306
Embleton, Kimberly	161	Gustafson, C.	109	Kapitzke, C.	205
Ercegovac, Z.	104	Hadjiargyrou, Michael.	305	Karen M, Foust	217
Estrada-Lorenzo, J. M.	298	Hamalainen, Maryellen.	165	Kartika, V. K.	166
Evering L.C.	264	Hannabuss, S.	78	Kathleen, Lourdes Obille	279
Eysenck, H. J.	57	Haq, Nomanul	312	Keith-Spiegel, P.	7
Fahnrich, Birte	304	Harper, G. K.	60	King, D.	280
Fallis, D.	162	Harris, Robert A.	9	Kiong, J. S.	83
Favale, M.	265	Hatcher, T.	20	Kissling, G. E.	307
Fawley, N.	163	Hauptman, R..	53, 90	Klien, B.	263
Feghali, T	189	Haviland, C.P.	17	Knoll, E.	42
Feldon, D.	222	Hayes, N.	121	Kokol, P.	314
Feng, P.	323	Heitman, E.	224	Kose, O.	249
Fernández-Molina, J. C.	105, 246	Henningsen, L.	140	Koshy, S.	206
Ferullo, D. L.	106	Hernon, P.	141	Kozak, E. M.	30
Fialkoff, Francine.	77	Heron, S. J.	102	Krupar, E. M.	68
Fieldhouse, M.	193	Hill, Ann	111	Kubilius, R.	330
Fink, C.	107	Hoad, T. C.	91	Kulathuramaiyer, Narayanan	167
Fishman, T.	204	Hodges, A.	300, 322	Kulesza, W. J.	299
Forsyth, R. S.	297	Hoffman, N.	323	Kumar, R.	308
Freewood, M.	86	Honig, B.	267	Kumbhare, S.	308
Gabriel, T.	221	Hoorn, E.	142	LaFollette, M. C.	61
Gallant, T.	183	Houston, B.	41	LaFollette, Marcel	3
Garber, G.	151	Howard, R. M.	14, 26, 225	Lampert, L.D.	15
García-Romero, A.	298	Howard, Rebecca Moore.	4, 38	Larivière, V.	226
Gayathri Devi S	266	Huntington, P.	193	Ledwith, A.	188, 229
George, S.	277	Ilyas, M.	122	Lee, D.	263
Ghai, S. K.	164, 184	Introna, L. D.	121	Lee, J.	323
Gibson, Nancy Snyder	247	Irwin, M.J.	135	Lerner, J.	278
Gilmore, J.	222	Isaacson, D.	143	Lessig, Lawrence	10
Gingras, Y.	226	Isiakpona, C. D.	268	Levine, M.	227
Gitanjali, B.	108	Jabade, S.	186	Liesegang, T. J.	281
Givler, P.	89	Jackson, P.	144	Lincoln, M.	80, 207
Goldstein, P.	70	Jajpura, Lalit	324	Lipson, C.	16
Goudy, H.	23	Jamieson, S.	187	Litewka, S.	224

Author Index

Liu, Y.	282	Neville, Colin.	19	Ramesh, R.	146
Logan, D. K.	62	Nicholas, D.	193	Randall, Marilyn.	6
Lu, B.	283	Nicole, J. A.	71	Rao, S.S.	72
Ludlow, B. L	92	Nimsakont, Emily Dust.	190	Rasuli, B.	334
Lukose, L. P.	315	Nirmal Singh	327	Rawal, G.	320
Macdonald, R.	86	Noorhidawati, A.	336	Reddy, G. B.	170
Madray, A.	168	Norman, S.	34	Rees, H.	49
Maher, M.	222	Nothhaft, H.	310	Reiner, L.,	127
Mahmood, K.	122	Nothhaft, Howard	304	Resnik, D. B.	307
Mahmud, S.	201	Ochoa, T.T..	191	Reyman, J.	192
Mallon, Thomas.	2	Oddie, C.	59	Rezaei, S.	287
Manish Kumar	331	O'Dwyer, M.	229	Rezanejad, A.	287
Marcel, C. L.	31	O'Hara, M.	277	Rice, D. A.	82
Martin, B.	32, 112, 316	Ojala, M.	317	Richardson, J. Jr.	104
Martin, B. R .	284	Okiy, R. B.	125	Risquez, A.	188, 229
Martin, D.	123	Oppenheim, C.	27	Robillard, A.	14
Maskus, K. E.	107	Orthaber, S.	210	Rocco, T.S.	20
Maurer, Hermann	167	Panda, S. K.	318	Roig, M.	35
Maxwell, L.	47	Panneerselvem, P.	333	Roig, M.	73
Maxymuk, J.	147	Parate, A.	308	Rousseau, R.	282
McCabe, D.L	48, 189	Park, C.	93	Rowlands, I.	193
Mccain, T.A.	47	Parrish, Debra.	39	Roy, A.M.	5
McCutchen, Charles W.	33	Parry, M.	250	Rudd, M.	300
McKinzie, Steve	325	Patil, S. K.	180	Sabir, H.	308
Meredith, B.	43	Paton, G.	230	Samtani, A.	83
Mingaleva, Z.	285	Patra. M.	22	Samuelson, P.	40
Mirskikh, I.	285	Paxhia, S.	251	Satija, M. P.	252, 309
Mishra, R.K.	146	Pearce, D.	63	Satyanarayana, K.	233
Mok, M. S.	228	Pedersen, A.M.	286	Savage, W. W.	94
Moorman, G.	264	Pedley, P.	64	Scanlon, P.M.	84
Moss, G.	263	Pettersson, A.	299	Schlipp, J.	194
Muir, A.	27	Philip, E.	263	Schmidt, E.	322
Mukherjee, B.	208	Pickard, J.	148	Schnabel, Jennifer	288
Muller, Karen	326	Posner, Richard A	11	Scholzel, H.	310
Mullin, J.A.	17	Potter, J.	211	Schopfel, J.	292, 334
Mundava, Maud	169	Power, L.G.	212	Schwartz, C.	141
Myers, Carla	332	Prenafeta, J.	231	Scott, Rachel	288
Myers, S.	124	Price, M.	81	Scribner, Mary Ellen.	95
Navalgund, C.U.	266	Procter, M.	65	Seadle, M.	113, 149, 171, 195, 253
Nayak,Rajkishore	324	Protti, M.	44	Searight, L.	322
Neelakantan, S.	209	Purdy, J.	126, 213	Selwyn, N.	196
Nelson, G.	67	Qin-Rui Xing	329	Sharma, A.	214
Neo, A. C.	83	Qiu, J.	232	Sharma, B.B.	254
Neumann, D.R.	84	Radhakrishnan, N.	311	Sharmila, V.	242

Sharoff, S.	297	Stubley, P.	85	Whitley, Bernard E.	7
Shi, L.	114	Sun, Y.	291	Wiebe, Todd J.	153
Simmonds, P.	96	Suseela, V.J.	319	Williams, B.	172
Singh, H.P.	301	Sutherland-Smith, W.	129	Williams, P.	193
Singh, Jnanendra Naryan	302	Tedford, R.	116	Williams, W.	45
Singh, V.	254	Tenopir, C.	193	Wolk, R. S.	28
Siriginidi, S. R.	97	Terry, Richard.	130	Wollan, Laurin A, Jr.	36
Small Helfer, Doris	161	Thaledi, S.	306	Wood, G.	117
Smerillo, D.	215	Thawani, V.	306	Wright, N. D	37
Smith, A.	127	Thompson, C.	55	Wu, W-P.	293
Smith, H. K.	150	Tikam, M.	335	Xalabarder, R.	257
Smith, K.	289	Timmerman, B.	222	Xia, J.	271
Snyder, N.	151	Trevino, L.K	48	Yadav, S.	320
Sohn, S.Y.	228	Tshepo, Batane	236	Yamada, Kyoko	99
Speight, D.	269	Tsui, H-C.	270	Yang, H-L.	293
Spoo, R. A.	234	Turner, P.	46	Yanti Idaya Aspura, M. K.	336
Spring, Hannah	290	Valentine, K.	152	Yeo, S.	173
Sreekumar, M. G.	197	Vathitphund, T.	237	Yeo, S.	198
Srivastava, Garima Gaur	331	Velmurugan, C.	311	Yoon, C.	258
Stapleton, P.	235	Vicinus, Martha	13	Young, L. L.	83
Stebelman, S.	54	Volpe, T.	292	Yushkiavitshus, H.	66
Steneck, N. H.	239	Vosner, H. B.	314	Zafron, Michelle.	272
Stenis, Paul.	255	Wager, E .	303, 307	Zavrsnik, D.	314
Stern, Linda.	12	Wang, H.	329	Zhou, D.	154
Stern, S.	278	Wang, T.	329	Zimerman, M.	259
Sterngold, A.	115	Wang, T-M.	270	Zimerman, Martin.	273
Stokes, S..	128	Watson, M.	225	Zobel, J.	91
Strickland, D.	222	Weinrib, Arnold S.	25	Zwagerman, S.	199
Strickland, L.S.	98	Weisberg, M.	256		

Glossary

Apocrypha

Apocrypha are works, usually written, of unknown or doubtful authorship or of origin. It is attributing work(s) to a person who probably may not have written them. "The adjective apocryphal is commonly used in modern English to refer to any text or story considered to be of dubious veracity or authority" (Wikipedia). Now it has been proved that many of the works commonly attributed to William Shakespeare were not written by him. It usually happens in religious literature and scriptures. In the modern world when a pulp fiction writer becomes very popular then by the publisher many fiction works are issued in her/his name, even after author's death to encash the popularity of the dead author. Apocrypha is different than folk literature though the latter is also mostly anonymous *See also* **Folklore**; **Misattribution**.

Attribution *see* **Source attribution.**

Author

Author is a person, or a group of persons or a corporate body (whether known or anonymous) responsible for the content creation of a literary, artistic or scientific work and who also holds moral, ethical and legal responsibility for its content. In the modern world concept of authorship extends to any creator such as photographer, cartographer, painter, sculpture, architect, physical space planner, choreographer, musician, fashion designer, software designer, cartoonist, and other such creative being. Attribution to any of these authors is necessary by the subsequent creators even if the author be anonymous or a corporate body. *See also* **Copyright;Copyright holder**

Citing vs. Quoting

Quoting is reproducing somebody's expressions with full attribution in exactly the same words set apart usually by quotations marks or other typographical devices such as setting off in a new paragraph or in italicized typeface; Citing is referring to someone's ideas, thoughts or expressions in one's own words in a summarized or paraphrased way. Full attribution is necessary in both the cases. By citing or quoting others the author gets endorsement or discusses his/her ideas. *See also* **Paraphrasing.**

Copyleft

A concept created by Richard Stallman, founder of the Free Software Foundation, originally intended for the protection of free software. Copyleft is an extension of copyright in which distribution terms are added to the copyrighted material to make it free (in the sense of respecting the four essential freedoms of the free software definition) also ensuring future modifications and extensions from further restrictions. Copyleft is implemented in practice through licenses. Copyleft licenses grant users the freedom of using, studying, copying and sharing, and modifying and redistributing the licensed materials. The most important copyleft license for software is the GNU General Public License (GPL). Alternative copyleft licenses with equivalent or similar terms also exist, such as the GNU Affero General Public License (AGPL), designed for programs to be used on servers, or the GNU Free Documentation License (FDL), intended for manuals, textbooks, and other documents. Lawrence Lessig's Creative Common Licenses were inspired by the concept of copyleft. However, not all Creative Common licenses are copyleft (just the CC BY-SA can be considered equivalent to copyleft). Even in the print media traditionally some books and pamphlets are knowingly not copyrighted and the users are encouraged to make free copies. But still attribution is needed to use them. See *also* **Open Access Initiative (OAI)**

Copyright

Over its long evolution and varied use, it is used as a noun, verb and adjective. Certain exclusive rights granted by the law (Copyright Act) to a writer or artist to have some control over the creation for a limited period. It is a legally created temporary monopoly. Though there is no such thing as international copyright law, but the copyrighted works in country are internationally protected if the parent country is a party to the Berne Convention which is an international agreement governing copyright agency located in Switzerland. Violation of the copyright of the creators by any unauthorized party is an un-cognizable offence. The Copyright law encourages the author and provides motivation with accruing monetary benefits, if any, and, of course, with name as the creator and to the public at large provides access with the rider of 'fair use' to the work may it ne literacy, scientific or artistic. At the same time copyright is a hindrance in preserving knowledge, especially in the digital environment. A worn-out printed book during its copyright period cannot be digitized even for its preservation purpose. *See also* **Author;Copyright exhaustionCopyright holder; Patent law**

Copyright exhaustion

Rights of the copyright holder are neither absolute nor permanent; rights of the public are inherent in it. When a copyright holder sells or permits the use of his/her creation then some rights of the creator are diminished or given away to the subscriber. That is copyright exhaustion. "Exhaustion is the notion that an IP rights holder relinquishes some control over a product once it sells or gives that product to a new owner. We say that those IP rights have been exhausted because the rights holder no longer control many of the uses the new owner may make of that product" (Perzanowski and Schultz, 2016, 25). Exhaustion process and law differ diagonally in the print and digital words. *See also* **Copyright holder.**

Copyright holder

A person or any organization such as a publishing, academic, research or administrative body to which copyright has been lawfully invested under the copyright act. Copyright is transferable wholly or partially to any person or organization under mutually agreed negotiable terms. *See also* **Author;Copyright;Copyright exhaustion**

Copyright infringement

It is the act of breach of copyright law by making unpermitted and unacknowledged use (in fact abuse) of someone's creation in an illegal or unethical manner. Infringement of copyright is either plagiarism or piracy.

Correction *see* **Retraction**

Creative Commons

The Creative Commons licenses are a legal device created by Law Professor Lawrence Lessig, inspired by Richard Stallman's concept of copyleft, that allows authors to redefine the automatic "all rights reserved" clause of the copyrighted materials so others can benefit from those rights. Creative Commons licenses are legal contracts that allow copyright holders surrender or to grant others the rights to copy, distribute, edit, remix or build upon their materials. There is a total of seven Creative Common licenses that combine different conditions and rights to granted in the contract, including attribution, identical legal terms of the future distributions (share alike), non-commerciality, and non-derivation. Users of Creative Commons licensed materials must be very careful of the rights granted and conditions to use the materials. Out of the seven Creative Common licenses, only three licenses (CC BY, CC BY-SA, and CC0) are considered free in the sense of freedom (as in Richard Stallman's).

Cryptomnesia

"In a world flooded with information, cryptomnesia is something all of us could be guilty of" —**Dolly Parton.**

An illusion of the mind related with partial amnesia results in a biased memory. It is a selective memory loss. Under cryptomnesia one remembers the facts, or ideas but forgets their source. For stressed mind ideas, not their source, have the priority of retention. Thus, with time a cryptomnesiac person unconsciously starts attributing those ideas to self. This leads to unintended plagiarism. *See also* **Publish or perish syndrome**

Digital Rights Management (DRM)

Nature of copyright for digital objects is different and complex due to their different properties, hence copyright laws as applied to digital objects are bit different than in the print or analog world. Management of such rights of the creator, publisher, distributor and ultimately of the subscriber's rights and obligations is known as digital rights management. Also called "Digital Restrictions Management" or "digital handcuffs" by activists such as Richard Stallman, the Free Software Foundation, and Defective by Design.org, it is in short "the practice of imposing technological restrictions that control what users can do with digital media" (*https://www.defectivebydesign.org/what_is_drm_digital_restrictions_management*). *See also* **Intellectual Property Rights (IPR)**

Fair use

No copyright law gives absolute rights to the author of the work. It has inbuilt provision for some taken for granted rights of the users, too. In context of copyright it refers to some granted and given rights of any and all users to make some genuine but limited and cautiously fair use of the work under the clause 'Fair Use'. Spirit of fair use is to allow excerpts from the work without permission to review, criticize, quote or use for teaching and research purpose. Fair use is not infringement of copyright. In some countries though these parameters of the fair use are mentioned, yet limits of fair use remain open to debate and interpretation of legal experts.

Folklore

It is an expressed body of popular legends, fables, myths, folk tales, proverbs, jokes, old wives' tales and stories of a community passed through the generations by word of mouth It also includes the traditional beliefs, superstitions, mythology, lore, oral history, tradition, folk tradition and mores myths or beliefs relating to a particular place, community andactivity. Authorship of such literature is lost in antiquity or attribution cannot be confirmed. So it is a common property of the community and reflects their values and attitude to life. Now a daysefforts are underway in every literate society to record them lest these are lost to coming generations under the onslaught of modernization. Quoting and citing any element of folk literature needs no attribution. Paraphrased mostly from the https://en.wikipedia.org/wiki/Folklore

Ghostwriting

It is writing for someone else. A ghostwriter is hired with money or other compensations to write literary or journalistic works, speeches or other texts that are officially credited to another person as the author. Highly placed politicians, public persons, and officials, as an open secret get their speeches, twitters, blog written by officially appointed ghost writers, but they are not charged with plagiarism. For a student, researcher or academician it is a corrupt practice considered as a blatant form of punishable academic misconduct. Technically it is not plagiarism as the ghostwriter is faceless.. In reality hired ghostwriters freely indulge in plagiarism as they have no fear of being caught or be accountable--— a ghostwriter can never be charged

Glossary

with plagiarism! (Partially based on *https://en.wikipedia.org/wiki/Ghostwriter*) *See also* **Proxy writing**

Information literacy

Information literacy is a trained capacity of an individual to feel the need of information and a set of skills to locate, validate sources, evaluate, and use effectively and ethically the needed information. Projected as a human right, the information literacy skills help a person to live and work in the society to the full potential. Information literacy is an essential skill for students, researchers and authors to be taught at the school level. Information literate person is a well-informed citizen to participate effectively, intelligently and actively in the society for promotion of democracy and its human progress. An information literate person is unlikely to commit unintended plagiarism—perhaps intended too.

Intellectual Property Rights (IPR)

It is an umbrella term for all sorts of copyrights, patents, trademarks and DRMs, though mostly used in context of patents and industrial creations. It subsumes DRMs. S*ee also* **Digital Rights Management (DRM); World Intellectual Property Organization (WIPO)**

International Union for Protection of Industrial Property

A self-funding agency of the United Nations, the WIPO, established in 1967, is the global forum for intellectual property services, policy, information and cooperation. Its mission is to lead the development of a balanced and effective international intellectual property (IP) system that enables innovation and creativity for the benefit of all. Having membership of 191 states and international organisations it works from headquarters at Geneva, Switzerland*See also* **World Intellectual Property Organization (WIPO)**

Marrakesh VIP Treaty

The Marrakesh VIP Treaty (Marrakesh Treaty to Facilitate Access to Published Works by Visually Impaired Persons and Persons with Print Disabilities, commonly known as MVT) is a treaty on copyright exceptions for visually impaired persons, adopted in Marrakesh, Morocco, on 28 June 2013. It allows domestic exceptions for the creation of accessible versions ofcopyrighted works as well as imports and exports. It means any copyrighted material can be converted into Braille script and other document formats accessible to visually impaired persons(VIP) without infringement of copyright. India was the first country in ratify the treaty, being the 20th ratification (necessary to take into effect) received on 30 June 2016. The treaty entered into force on 30 September 2016, with the ratification of over 40 countries.

Misattribution

Like misinformation misattribution is attributing texts and ideas even events to something with which they really have no connection or association. It's making an incorrect attribution. *See also* **Sourceattribution**

Open Access Initiative (OAI)

Open Access to information is a condition of free access to scholarly research in the digital world. It is making the research publicly available to everyone—free of charge and without most copyright and licensing restrictions. It accelerates circulation of scientific research by allowing authors to reach a larger number of readers.

The OAI essentially is the result of a meeting organized by the Open Society Foundations to mark the tenth anniversary of Budapest Open Access Initiative (BOAI, February, 2002), which first defined Open Access. These recommendations include the development of Open Access policies in institutions of higher education and in funding agencies, the open licensing of scholarly works, the development of infrastructure such as Open Access repositories and creating standards of professional conduct for Open Access publishing. The recommendations also establish a new goal of achieving Open Access as the default method for distributing new peer-reviewed research in every field and in every country. Whatever be the type of open access license attribution is always necessary in citing or quoting them which otherwise will be clear plagiarism. Open Access Initiative only expects (not mandates) the users to make their publications available in this mode to perpetuate the movement in the interest of free and open flow of information and research. Open access journals have high impact factor. (Partially based on Wikipedia) *See also* **Copyleft; Sci-hub**

Open Science

It is Open Access Initiative applied to science. It is a practice of science and a movement to make scientific research, data and dissemination accessible at all levels of research and publications under terms that enable the reuse, redistribution and replication of research and its underlying data and methods. *See also* **Sci-hub**.

Originality report *see* **Similarity score**

Paraphrasing

Restating or summarizing someone's words into one's own words and style for brevity of words and thoughts, or for more contextual clarity, or even to present someone's ideas or expressions in an improved language and better literary style. Indeed, it is a highly skilled literary art. Unattributed paraphrasing amounts to plagiarism. Paraphrased texts need only citation, not quotation. *See also* **Citing vs. Quoting**

Patent law

It is copyright of inventions, trademarks, and industrial creations. While copyright for published texts is automatic, a patent has to be obtained by applying to a designated authority in the country which in turn applies internationally if the country is a signatory to the Patent Cooperation Treaty (PCT) of the WIPO. A letter of patent or patent right is granted on certain conditions, especially of originality, to the applicant whether an individual or a corporate body, whereas no such condition applies to obtain copyright for literary, artistic and other published works. *See also* **Copyright**

Piracy

Euphemism for the act of making unauthorized, usually an underground and clandestine activity, copies of literary, artistic works, whether printed or digital, which are still in copyright, usually for commercial gains or self-use. Pirated documents are counterfeited replicas of the originals. It is not plagiarism as pirated documents still have the attribution to the original author(s) and publishers. This is a serious copyright infringement causing financial losses and many other commercial damages to the publisher. A counterfeiter can be awarded financial punishment, or imprisonment, or both.

Authors such as Richard Stallman have discouraged the use of the term "piracy" to refer to copying (https://www.gnu.org/philosophy/words-to-avoid.en.html#Piracy). In this sense, a United States judge are stated that terms such as "piracy," "theft," and "stealing" are smear words. Neutral terms such as "unauthorized copying" (or "prohibited copying" when it is illegal) or even positive term such as "sharing information with your neighbor" are proposed as alternatives.

Plagiarism detection software

A computer software, both proprietary and open source, which helps to know the source of borrowed or stolen textual expressions in the new document, if any, and also counts the percentage of similarity between the suspected piece and the huge database of the anti-plagiarism software. A plagiarism software does not check for plagiarism in a piece of work. Instead, it only checks a work against the huge database held by the machine, and if there are instances where the new(suspected) writing is similar to or matches against any of the sources in the database, it gives data on overlapping with indication of the original sources. A database usually includes tremendously large number of web pages: both current and archived from the internet and a collection of documents, which comprises thousands of journals, ETDs, e-books, and webpages, databases and publications.Most of these are text matching systems and machines. *See also* **Similarity score**.

Proxy writing

Literal meaning of Proxy is authorized substitution, or somebody authorized to act on someone's behalf. Though not a very popular term in the lexicon of publication frauds, nevertheless it could mean something reverse of the ghost writing. Whereas the ghost writer remains behind the scene and totally incognito, a proxy writer can be someone to whom a publication is credited, mostly as a joint author, without having worked on it to earn that credit. It could be under force, an official obligation, or for some favors in return. In the Soviet Russia it was mandatory for every researcher to include name the head of the laboratory as one of the authors— though latter may not have done anything genuine to justify claim as on of the researcher of the piece. *See also* **Ghostwriting.**

Publish or perish syndrome

Among academics, the maxim "publish or perish" (i.e., author more and more research papers or suffer stagnation in your career) is a threatening reminder of publication linked promotions in higher education and research institutions. Many criticize it as a barbarian slogan which lays emphasis on quantity instead of quality and instigates academicians to resort to less than honest means to swell their needed number of publications. It may lead to despicable salami publishing to superficially enhance the number of publications. Apart from mental stress on the researcher this pressure is also widely believed as a cause of plagiarism and low-quality research. *See also* **Cryptomnesia**

PubPeer

Founded in 2012 by Brandon Stell and Boris Barbour Pubpeer.com is an online platform for post-publication peer review. It is a service run by the PubPeer a California based not-for-profit foundation for the benefit of its readers and commenters, who create its content. The overarching goal of the Foundation is to improve the quality of scientific research by enabling innovative approaches for community interaction. This post-publication has led to revelation of many academic misconducts and retraction of papers. Earlier the revelations of frauds were anonymous. Now the foundation has changed the policy to name the whistleblowers on demand. *See also* **Society for Scientific Values, India**

Retraction

Literal meaning of retraction is to take back your statement (either under pressure or voluntarily for any reason such as political, religious, offending feelings of someone or due to factual errors. The most common reasons for the retraction of research articles are scientific misconduct including plagiarism, serious errors, and duplicate/concurrent publishing (self-plagiarism). In case of publications the retraction may be initiated by the editors of a journal, or by the author(s) of the papers (or their institution). Retractions may or may not be accompanied by the author's further explanation as to how the original statement came to be made and/or what subsequent events, discoveries, or experiences led to the subsequent retraction. In some cases, retraction may be accompanied by apologies for previous error and/or expressions of gratitude to persons who disclosed the error to the author. Like original statements, retractions may in some cases be incorrect. In research, academic or a journalistic publications retraction of a published article indicates that the original article should not have been published and that its content should not be used or referred in future research except as a case study of retractions or research misconducts. it is just like convicting author(s) There have been numerous examples of retracted scientific publications and papers continue to be retracted. Retraction Watch provides updates on new retractions and discusses general issues in relation to retractions. (From *https://en.wikipedia.org/wiki/Retraction*) *See also* **Retraction index;Retraction Watch**

Retraction index

The retraction index is a measure of statistical probability of an article being retracted when published in a given journal. It is calculated by multiplying the number of retracted articles in a journal during a given time period by 1,000, and then dividing the result by the total number of articles published in that journal during the same period.

The term was coined in a 2011 by Ferric Fang and Arturo Casadevall, who also showed that there is a strong positive correlation between a journal's retraction index and its impact factor. It may be due to the fact that in an urge to get published in a reputed journal with a high impact factor an author may be tempted to push under the carpet some legal and ethical nuances of publishing and research. Being caught later will lead to retraction and thus increasing the retraction index of that journal. (Based on Wikipedia).

Retraction vs. Correction

The term retraction carries stronger connotation than the term correction. An alteration that changes the main point of the original statement is generally referred to as a retraction while an alteration that leaves the main point of a statement intact is usually referred to simply as a correction. A lesser withdrawal of content than a full retraction may be labeled a correction. Depending on the circumstances, either a retraction or correction is the appropriate remedy.

Retraction Watch

Launched by science writers Ivan Oransky and Adam Marcus in August 2010, Retraction Watch <https://retractionwatch.com> is a blog that reports on retractions of scientific papers and on related topics. The blog has demonstrated that retractions are more common than commonly assumed and in many cases the reasons for retraction are not reported publicly by the editors

Salami publication

Segmented publication, also called "salami publication" is one of the forms of self-plagiarism, is a distinct form of duplicated publication which is usually characterized by publishing the same paper in different media. It could also be making more papers from an earlier published paper having much in common. Such deliberate acts present a serious threat to publication ethics which constitute the ethical problem of self-plagiarism and ways to handle such cases. "Salami publication can be roughly defined as a publication of two or more articles derived from a single study. Articles of such type report on data collected from a single study split into several segments just large enough to gain reasonable results and conclusions, also known as "minimal publishable unit" (Smolèiæ, 2013). *See also* **Self-plagiarism**

Sci-hub

A website created by Alexandra Elbakyan that provides free access to more than 67 million copyrighted and non-free academic papers. It is presented as "the first pirate website in the world to provide mass and public access to tens of millions of research papers." The main ideas of the site are knowledge to all, removing barriers to the access to scientific knowledge based on income, social status, geographical location, and others; no copyright, advocating for the cancellation of intellectual property and copyright laws for scientific and education resources; and support for open access. Several publishers and associations such as Elsevier or American Chemical Society have filed lawsuits against Sci-hub.

Self-Plagiarism

Considered as a misconduct in research and publications It is using partly or wholly, thus recycling one's own pre-published works, to create new publications.

Though it is not theft of others' ideas, it nonetheless has created debatable issues in the scholarly publishing world as it leads to avoidable inflation in research communication. Writers often maintain that because they are the authors, they can reuse their work as they please; it couldn't be defined as "plagiarism" since they are not taking any words or ideas from someone else. However, the arguments continue on whether self-plagiarism is a serious misconduct, or misconduct at all. Salami publishing is a form of self-plagiarism. (*https://www.aje.com/en/arc/self-plagiarism-how-to-define-it-and-why-to-avoid-it/*) (*www.ithenticate.com/plagiarism.../What-Is-Self-Plagiarism-and-How-to-Avoid-It*). *See also* **Salami publication**

Similarity score

In the process of detecting plagiarism through machines some segments of a later work may match with some of the text in database held by the machine. The similarity score simply makes us aware of any overlapping areas in a later paper. It can then be used as data for a larger process, to determine if the match is or is not acceptable. Machines by comparison provides data only. Similarity Reports provide a quantified summary of matching or highly similar text found in a submitted paper Interpretation should be based on human judgment and on institutional policies. In a plagiarised work similarity may be of two types: Semantic similarity, and Syntactic similarity. The former is difficult to detect and measure. *See also* **Plagiarism detection software**.

Society for Scientific Values, India

Keeping the growing academic frauds in mind a group of the country's distinguished scientists with high international and national credentials, led by Prof. Avtar Paintal, FRS, set up the Society for Scientific Values in 1986 at New Delhi. The society has obviously no legal or administrative powers, but it enjoys high moral credibility as watchdog. It has taken up cases from time to time, where values intrinsic to science, "scientific ethics" have been compromised. The Society for Scientific (SSV) from time to time, organizes meetings with a specific purpose. It posts on the page the cases where it has come to a specific conclusion. The Society for Scientific Values, India (www.scientificvalues.org/society.html) works on issues related to scientific ethics and misconduct. Though it has no legal popover but as a watchdog keeps an eye on misconduct, fraud, and scientific integrity. It publishes SSV News and Views. *See also* **PubPeer**

Source attribution

In context of creative writing attribution means relating used or borrowed ideas or expressions to its real and ultimate source and appropriately giving credit to the creator or author. Non attribution of sourced ideas leads to plagiarism. *See also* **Misattribution**

World Intellectual Property Organization (WIPO)

Traced back to 1883, in 1893 it become the United International Bureau for the Protection of Intellectual Property (BIRPI), which was based in Bern, Switzerland. In the modern avatar WIPO was born in 1967 and came in force in April 1970 which became a specialized agency of the UN in 1974. The aims of WIPO are twofold. First, through international cooperation, WIPO promotes the protection of intellectual property. Second, WIPO supervises administrative cooperation between the Paris, Berne, and other intellectual unions regarding agreements on trademarks, patents, and the protection of artistic and literary works. WIPO's role in enforcing intellectual-property protections increased in the mid 1990s, when it signed a cooperation agreement with the World Trade Organization. As electronic commerce grew through the development of the Internet, WIPO was charged with helping to resolve disputes over the use of Internet domain names. WIPO's membership consists of more than 180 countries. More than 170 nongovernmental organizations maintain observer status. Its main policy-making body is the General Assembly, which convenes every two years. WIPO also holds a biennial conference, which determines the organization's budget and programs. *See also* **Intellectual Property Rights (IPR);International Union for Protection of Industrial Property**

About the Authors: Author-Title Index

Patrícia de Almeida

mebpatricia@gmail.com

Patrícia de Almeida holds a bachelor degree in Modern Languages and Literature - Portuguese Studies from the University of Porto (Portugal) and a masters in Education and Libraries from Universidade Portucalense (Portugal). She is a Portuguese teacher, school librarian, and member of the Centre for 20th Century Interdisciplinary Studies - CEIS20. She is currently pursuing her PhD in Information Science at the University of Coimbra, Portugal. Her main research interest is knowledge organization and management.

Contributed : Chapter 4: Ethical Use of Information: The Contribution of the Academic Libraries in the Prevention of Plagiarism, pp. 49-65.

Kanwal Ameen

kanwal.im@pu.edu.pk

Professor Kanwal Ameen is Chairperson, Dept. of Information Management. She has authored more than 140 publications which include scholarly journal articles, conference proceedings, books and book chapters. She is the Chief-Editor of Pakistan Journal of Information Management & Libraries and editorial advisory boards of international journals. She has served on prestigious international conferences' organising committees, have chaired their sessions, and has presented papers in quality peer reviewed conferences abroad. Prof. Kanwal has got a number of international and national awards/scholarships such as Research Fellowship as Professor, University of Tsukuba, Japan (2013), Fulbright Post-Doc, University of Missouri, Columbia (2009-2010) Fulbright Pre-Doc, University of Texas, Austin, Higher Education Commission of Pakistan's Best Teacher Award and Best Paper Award in Social Sciences, Pakistan Library Association's Life Time Achievements Award and Asian Library Leaders "Award for Professional Excellence – 2013", SRFLIS India.

Contributed : Chapter 18: Academic Plagiarism: An Overview of the Policy and Preventive Measures in Pakistan, pp. 231-237.

Asefeh Asemi

PhD, Full Professor in Department of Knowledge and Information Science, University of Isfahan, Isfahan, Iran (*asemi@edu.ui.ac.ir*)

Asefeh Asemi earned her PhD in Library and Information Science in 2006 from the University of Pune, India. In that year she joined the University of Isfahan (UI) as an assistant professor and worked as a Head of Department of Library and Information Science for more than 7 years. During this position, she founded Virtual MLIS Course at UI for the first time in her country. Also, she started Master and PhD courses in this department in different fields. Currently she is full professor at the Department of Knowledge and Information Science, UI. Professor Asemi does qualitative and quantitative research in Scientometrics, Information Science, Information Systems, Information Management, Knowledge Management, and Data Science.

Contributed : Chapter 16: Understanding the Concept of Plagiarism among Iranian Students, pp. 209-219.

Parveen Babbar

Deputy Librarian, Jawaharlal Nehru University, New Delhi, *parveenbabbar@gmail.com*

Dr. Parveen Babbar is presently Deputy Librarian at Jawaharlal Nehru University. Prior to this he has been Assistant Librarian in Library & Documentation Division at Indira Gandhi National Open University in New Delhi, India. He has been also associated with University of Delhi Professional Assistant and has more than twelve years of professional experience. He holds PhD. from University of Rajasthan, M.Phil. (Library & Information Science), MLISc, Masters of Computer Application and Masters of Business Administration. He had been Gold Medalist in MLISc from Delhi University, India. He had been Junior Research Fellow and has cleared JRF-NET exam from UGC, India. He has taken many projects of Library Automation & Digitization like CALPI Library Setup for Swiss Agency. He has written about 55 papers which have been published in National and International Journals and presented in National and International Conferences. He has also published 7 edited books as Conference Proceedings. He had been the speaker at various conferences including Invited Speaker at International M-Libraries Conference 2012 at The Open University, Milton Keynes, UK. He is a member of Special Libraries Association (SLA), USA and is presently member of Career Guidance/ Employment Committee of SLA Asian Chapter. He had also been the Treasurer and Webmaster in the Board of Asian Chapter, SLA. He has received many awards and scholarships including the 2013 Bonnie Hilditch International Librarian Award from SLA, Young Information Scientist Award 2012 by SIS, India, SLA Asian Librarian Award at the SLA 2010 Annual Conference in New Orleans, USA. He received the scholarship from Shastri Indo-Canadian Institute, 2009 and IFLA grant for the assignment in the year 2010. He is associated with several professional associations in various capacities in India and abroad including SLA, USA; Society for Library Professionals, India; Society for Information Science, India.

Contributed: Chapter 14: Policies and Guidelines for Academic Conduct in Universities: A Survey of the International Landscape, pp. 183-200.

John M. Budd

Professor Emeritus, School of Information Science & Learning Technologies, University of Missouri, Innovation (RRI) Framework, *BuddJ@missouri.edu*

John M. Budd is Professor Emeritus with the University of Missouri. He has also been on the faculties of Louisiana State University and the University of Arizona. He has had an abiding interest in the retraction of published works, particularly in the biomedical field and has written several works on this topic. He has also written quite extensively on scholarly communication and information ethics. He has been very active in the American Library Association, the Association for Library and Information Science Education, and the Association for Information Science and Technology. He is the author of approximately 150 publications and remains committed to the field of library and information science.

Contributed: Chapter 2: The Problem of Plagiarism in Retractions of Published Articles, pp. 21-28.

Helen de Castro S. Casarin

helen.castro@unesp.br

She graduated in Library Science from São Paulo State University, Masters in Education and PhD in Literature. Currently, she is Associate Professor at the Information Science Department of São Paulo State University and adviser of the Graduate Program in Information Science. Since 2012, she has coordinated a group on Information Literacy at the São Paulo State University library network. She is also a Research Productivity Fellow of the National Council for Scientific and Technological Development (CNPq), leader of the research group "Information Behavior and Information Literacy" and member of ISKO.

Contributed: Chapter 13: Role of Information Literacy in Curbing Plagiarism, pp. 175-182.

Harish Chander

Email: arora.hca@gmail.com

Harish Chander, presently serving as a Librarian, Punjab Institute of Textile Technology (PITT), Amritsar (India), is a promising scholar and researcher in the library science field. He did his Ph.D. and M.Phil. in LIS from the University of Delhi. Apart from a co-authored book he has published many research papers in peer reviewed journals in India and abroad He is the recipient of UGC JRF/NET and 'IATLIS- Prof. S.P. Narang Research Promotion Award'.

He is a life member of many professional bodies such as LA, IATLIS, DLA, PLA and SRFLIS.

Contributed: Bibliography, pp. 303-328.

Suresh K. Chauhan

Head, Learning Resource Center, Jaypee University of Information Technology, Waknaghat, Solan, Himachal Pradesh – 173234 (India), *sureshbabal@yahoo.com*; Mobile - +91 9555626161

Dr. Suresh K Chauhan obtained his MA, BLISc, MLISc and PhD from Panjab University Chandigarh. Presently, he is working as a Deputy Learning Resource Manaver (Deputy Librarian) and Heading Learning Resouce Centre of Jaypee University of Information Technology, Waknaghat, Solan (Himachal Pradesh). He has 20 years of working experience in various domains of Libraries. He worked as librarian at BML Munjal University, Gurgaon; GD Goenka University, Sohna and Jaipuria Institute of Management, Noida. He also worked with Information and Library Network (INFLIBNET) Centre, Gujarat and Centre For Research in Rural and Industrial Development (CRRID), Chandigarh. He has written many papers in professional journals, books and conferences. His areas of expertise include - bibliometrics/scientometrics, user centricity in libraries, E-resource management, Digital library and have special interest in exploring issues pertaining to plagiarism.

Contributed : Chapter 7: Measuring Plagiarism Research Output: A Bibliometric Analysis, pp. 95-105.

Gayatri Dwivedi

General Manager – Strategic Management at Welingkar Institute of Management Development and Research., Mumbai Also, she is Assistant Professor in Finance, *gd5gayatri@gmail.com*

Besides, she is active in the villages of Almora to help the socio-economic development of the place. Her activities include initiating farmers into non-farm activities and introducing them to better, progressive techniques of farming and just being with them- happily.

Contributed : Chapter 14: Policies and Guidelines for Academic Conduct in Universities: A Survey of the International Landscape, pp. 183-200.

Ramesh C. Gaur

PGDCA, MLISc, Ph.D. Fulbright Scholar (Virginia Tech, USA) Director (Library & Information in HAG Pay Scale) & Head, Kalanidhi Division, Indira Gandhi National Centre for Arts (IGNCA), (Autonomous body of Ministry of Culture, Government of India), Man Singh Road, New Delhi-110001, Mob: 9810066244 Ph.(Off) 011-23388333, e-mail; (1) *rcgaur66@gmail.com* (2) *gaur@ignca.nic.in*, website: *www.ignca.gov.in*, Profile: *http://ignca.gov.in/PDF_data/profile_of_dr_ramesh_c_gaur.pdf*

Dr. Ramesh C. Gaur is presently Director (Library & Information) & Head-Kala Nidhi Division at Indira Gandhi National Centre for the Arts (IGNCA), New Delhi, Ministry of Culture, Government of India. During the period October 2011-January 2018 he was the University Librarian, Jawaharlal Nehru University (JNU), New Delhi, India. He is Member of various national and International Committees such as International Advisory Committee-UNESCO Memory of the World Programme, IFLA-RSCAO, IFLA-ARL, International Centre on Documentary Heritage, South Korea and Member Board of Directors and Chair-NDLTD Conference Committee, National Coordinator-Experts Group on UNESCO Memory of the World Programme in India. He is aMember Governing Council INFLIBNET and National Committee on Implementationof e-Theses in India, UGC Draft Plagiarism Regulations Committee. He is Member of several national and international academic advisory boards and Library Advisory Committees. During 28 years ofprofessional career has authored 4 books, has published over 60 articles and delivered over 200 talks at various international national conferences / seminar etc. He has been associated in various capacities with all major Indian library associations and Professional committees. Dr Gaur has been duly recognised by various national and international bodies through 12 awards and recognitions. TURNITIN Honourable Mention- Global awards on Academic and Integrity is recognition to my contributions in the field. DigitisationandDigital Preservation of Cultural Heritage, Plagiarism, Open Access, Reengineering Management and Reference Management Tools are areas of his interests.

Contributed : Chapter 20: Controlling Plague of Plagiarism in Indian Academic Institutions: Draft UGC Plagiarism Regulations 2018, pp. 249-257.

José Augusto Chaves Guimarães

chaves.guimaraes@unesp.br

Full Professor at the Graduate School of Information Science (São Paulo State University – UNESP, Marília, Brazil). PhD in Communication Science (University of São Paulo, Brazil, 1993). MSc in Communication Science (University of São Paulo, Brazil, 1988). Bachelor in Library and Information Science (São Paulo State University – UNESP, Marilia, Brazil, 1981). Bachelor in Law (Faculdade de Direito de Marília, Brazil, 1982). Visiting Professor at University of Lille (2016). Former President of the Brazilian Chapter of the International Society for Knowledge Organization – ISKO-Brazil (2009-2013; 2015-2017). Associate Vice-Rector for Research of São Paulo State University – UNESP, Brazil. Former member of the Executive Board of ISKO (2012-2016).

Contributed : Chapter 15: Plagiarism and Guides to Good Scientific Practices: The Brazilian Perspective, pp. 201-208.

Sumeer Gul

Senior Assistant Professor, DLIS, University of Kashmir. Srinagar. Jammu & Kashmir, India. E-mail: *sumeersuheel@gmail.com*

Dr. Sumeer Gul works as a Senior Assistant Professor in the Department of Library and Information Science, University of Kashmir, India. He is associated as an author with reputed journals like *Scientometrics, Aslib Journal of Information Management, Data Technologies and Applications (Earlier Program), Online Information Review, The Electronic Library, European Journal of Integrative Medicine, VINE, Serials Librarian, Global Knowledge, Memory* and Communication (Earlier Library Review) etc. He is Associate Editor of journal, *Trends in Information Management* published by Department of Library & Information Science, University of Kashmir, India besides being Editor of the journal, *International Journal of Knowledge Management and Practices*.

Contributed : Chapter 9: Beleaguered and Tousled Research: Murky Waters of Plagiarism and Retractions, pp. 127-133.

Dinesh K Gupta

Professor, Department of Library and Information Science, Vardhman Mahaveer Open University, Kota – 324021, India; Email: *dineshkg.in@gmail.com / dineshkumargupta@vmou.ac.in*

Dinesh K. Gupta is Professor, Library & Information Sc. at Vardhaman Mahaveer Open University, Kota. He served as Member of Standing Committee of IFLA Education & Training Section, 2011-2015, IFLA Management and Marketing Section, 2003-2007 and 2007-2011 and also served as the Chair of the Jury of 'IFLA International Marketing Award' in 2009-2013. Served as a Member of the Selection Committee of South Asia LIS Award, 2012-2014. Published three IFLA books by official publisher K. G. Saur/ De Gruyter Saur (Munich, Germany). He is Member of the editorial board of the journals Library Management (Emerald); Annals of Library and Information Studies (CSIR-NISCAIR) etc. also served as Member of the Editorial Board IFLA Journal (Sage),2015-2017. He is PI for the MOOC on "Management of Libraries and Information Centres and Knowledge Centres" hosted on the portal Swayam.

Contributed : Chapter 19: Ethical Policies of LIS e-Journals Listed in the UGC Approved List, pp. 239-248.

Marzieh Sadat Hosseini

MKIS, Department of Knowledge and Information Science, University of Isfahan, Isfahan, Iran *mlm.hosseini@gmail.com.*

Marzieh Sadat Hosseini graduated in Master of Library and Information Science from University of Isfahan, Iran under supervising Prof. Asefeh Asemi. Her thesis was on "Understanding the Concept of Plagiarism among Iranian Students". She currently works as a librarian at the Public Library of Valiasr, Isfahan, Iran.

Contributed : Chapter 16: Understanding the Concept of Plagiarism among Iranian Students, pp. 209-219.

Taufat Hussain

Research Scholar, DLIS, University of Kashmir. Srinagar. Jammu & Kashmir, India. E-mail: *taufat.pathan@gmail.com*

Taufat Hussain is currently pursuing his PhD in the Department of Library and Information Science, University of Kashmir, India. He has a number of national and internal articles to his credit. He has also participated in a number of international and national conferences.

Contributed : Chapter 9: Beleaguered and Tousled Research: Murky Waters of Plagiarism and Retractions, pp. 127-133.

International Federation of Library Associations and Institutions (IFLA; http://www.ifla.org)

Global voice of the library and information profession, the IFLA is an independent, international, non-governmental, not-for-profit organization. Its basic aim is to promote high standards of provision and delivery of library and information services. It is the leading international body representing the interests of library professionals and their services throughout the world. Founded in 1927 in Edinburgh, Scotland, it has now more than 1,400 Members in over 140 countries around the world. It was registered in the Netherlands in 1971. The Royal Library, the national library of the Netherlands, in The Hague, provides the facilities for its headquarters. IFLA General Conference and Assembly 'World Library and Information Congress' is held usually in August in a different country each year wherein more than three thousand delegates meet to exchange experience and debate professional issues. Apart from its annual report and many occasional technical reports and books , it publishes the quarterly IFLA Journal which includes peer-reviewed articles on library and information services and the social political and economic issues that impact access to information through libraries.

Contributed : Appendix 2: IFLA Statement on Copyright Education and Copyright Literacy, pp.299-302

S.T. Kale

Librarian, J.D. Patil Sangludkar Mahavidyalaya, Daryapur, Amravati (Maharashtra, India), *kalesurendra@rediffmail.com*

S.T. Kaleis working as a librarian at J.D. Patil Sangludkar Mahavidyalaya Daryapur district Amravati (Maharashtra) a college affiliated to Sant Gadge Baba Amravati University Amravati. He obtained a master degree in commerce and Master in library and information science from Amravati University, Post Graduate Diploma in Library Automation & Networking (PGDLAN) from University of Hyderabad and Post Graduate Diploma in Digital Library and Information Management (PGDLIM) from Tata Institute of Social sciences (TISS) Mumbai. He has published 20 research papers at national and international journals and seminarsandconferences and visited France (University of Lille) andthe United States (George Masson University Washington DC) in connection to the presentation papers at ETD-2016 and ETD-2017 respectively organized by Networked Digital Library of Theses & Dissertations (NDLTD). He is the recipient ofUGC Travel Grant (2017) for attending ETD- 2016 (France) & NDLTD Travel Scholarship for ETD-2017 for visit to United State. He is now working on D-Space, KohaandSOUL 2.0 for automation purpose.Heis a life member of IASLIC.

Contributed : Chapter 22: Anti-Plagiarism Software Check to the Doctoral Theses in Indian Universities and Institutions, pp. 263-278.

H. K. Kaul

DELNET- Developing Library Network, JNU Campus, Nelson Mandela Road. Vasant Kunj, New Delhi-110070, Tel: 91-11-26741111, Mobile: 09891016667, E-mail: *hkkaul@gmail.com, director@delnet.ren.nic.in*, Web: *www.delnet.nic.in*

Dr. H. K. Kaul is Founder Director, DELNET—Developing Library Network, New Delhi. He was Chief Librarian of the India International Centre, New Delhi for about 40 years. He has been the Chairman of several committees of the Ministry of Communications and Information Technology, Ministry of Culture and DRDO. He was Member, National Mission on Libraries, Government of India, member of the Working Group on Libraries of the National Knowledge Commission, Indian National Commission for Unesco, and member of major national committees including Board of Management, National Library, Calcutta; Raja Rammohun Roy Library Foundation, Calcutta; Delhi Library Board; National Selection Committee, Fulbright Professional Fellowships in Information Science and Technology; among others. He has authored and edited sixty books including Library Networks: An Indian Experience, Library Resource Sharing and Networks, Empowering Libraries: Strategies for the Future; and Library and Information Networking – (20 vols. NACLIN 1998 – NACLIN 2017).

Contributed : Foreword, pp. vii-viii.

Gurpartap S. Khairah

gurpartap_gulzar@yahoo.com

Gurpartap S. Khairah is an Associate Professor teaching English at Hindu college, Amritsar. As a creative writer he has authored more than sixty short stories, some of which have been published in literary magazines of international repute, on online platforms and have also been aired on national Radio. He is the co-author of the book *Obsession – Eternal Stories of Life and Death* (2014) published by Tara Research Press, New Delhi, India. Apart from his interest in creative writing, Khairah also holds a keen interest in research. He has authored many research papers, published and presented at both National and International platforms. He did his Ph.D. on Graham Greene.

Contributed : Chapter 21: The Pressures and Perils of Overachieving - An Inquiry into the Kaavya Viswanathan Case, pp. 259-262.

Dhiraj Kumar

Mohinder Singh Randhawa Library, Punjab Agricultural University, Ludhiana. *dk1_malhotra@yahoo.com*

Dhiraj Kumar is working as a Library Assistant in the University Library, Guru Angad Dev Veterinary and Animal Sciences University, Ludhiana since July, 2010. He is Gold Medalist in B.Lib. & Inf. Sc., M.Lib. & Inf.Sc. and PGDLAN programmes. He has contributed about 20 papers in various international/national journals and conferences.

Contributed : Chapter 17: Awareness and Attitude of Agricultural Students Towards Plagiarism, pp. 221-230.

Sanjeev Kumar

Guru Angad Dev Veterinary and Animal Sciences University, Ludhiana, *srishti88@yahoo.com*

Sanjeev Kumar is working as Deputy Librarian, M S Randhawa Library, Punjab Agricultural University (PAU), Ludhiana since 2010. He served as College Librarian, MGN college of Education, Jalandhar from 1999-2004 and as Assistant Librarian, M S Randhawa Library, PAU, Ludhiana from 2004-2010. He is M.Sc (Botany) and M.Lib.Sc. His research interests include Library management and Library classification and cataloguing.

Contributed : Chapter 17: Awareness and Attitude of Agricultural Students Towards Plagiarism, pp. 221-230.

Vijendra Kumar

Assistant Professor, Department of Library and Information Science, University of Rajasthan, Jaipur – 302004, India; Email: *vijendrakumar@live.com*

Vijendra Kumar is presentlya UGC Junior Research Fellow pursuing Ph.D. fromthe Vardhaman Mahaveer Open University, Kota. He has served as Research Intern in CSIR-NISCAIR, New Delhi for two years. He was associated with the Indian National Centre for ISSN and *Annals of Library and Information Studies* (ALIS) journal. He was also engaged in the education and training activities of CSIR-NISCAIR. He has contributed in journals like *Current Science, ALIS, Desidoc JIT,* etc.

Contributed : Chapter 19: Ethical Policies of LIS e-Journals Listed in the UGC Approved List, pp. 239-248.

Helena Isabel Pereira Leitão

helenaleitao.1812@gmail.com

Helena Isabel Pereira Leitão is a librarian at the Library of the Faculty of Economics of the University of Coimbra where she acts in the areas of indexing, reference, and training of library users. She is currently a PhD student in Information Science at the Faculty of Arts of the University of Coimbra. She holds a Master's degree in Information, Communication and New Media (2015) and a degree in Information, Archival and Library Science (2012) from the same university. She is a collaborator of the Centre of 20th Century Interdisciplinary Studies (CEIS20) and her main research interests are knowledge organization systems, in particular scientific abstract, and information literacy in higher education libraries. The University Carlos III of Madrid awarded her in 2017 with the Catedra Luis de Camoes for the best communication by a young researcher in the VIII EDICIC 2017 Meeting.

Contributed : Chapter 4: Ethical Use of Information: The Contribution of the Academic Libraries in the Prevention of Plagiarism, pp. 49-65.

Faiqa Mansoor

faiqam@yahoo.com.

Dr. Faiqa Mansooristhe Deputy Chief Librarian in Central Library, University of the Punjab, Lahore, Pakistan and received her PhD degree in South Asian Studies from the same university. She explored the role of university libraries in prevention of plagiarism in her doctoral study and has got paper published.

Contributed : Chapter 18: Academic Plagiarism: An Overview of the Policy and Preventive Measures in Pakistan, pp. 225-237.

Daniel Martínez-Ávila

dmartinezavila@gmail.com

Dr. Daniel Martínez-Ávila is a professor at the Department of Information Science, São Paulo State University (UNESP), Marília, Brazil. He received his Ph.D. from Charles III University of Madrid (Spain) in 2012 under the supervision of former ISKO Spain President Rosa San Segundo and University of Wisconsin-Milwaukee Emeritus Professor Hope Olson. After completing his Ph.D., he was hired as Assistant Professor at the Department of Library Science and Documentation at Charles III University of Madrid (Spain). He was also hired as Researcher and Adjunct Instructor at the School of Information Studies at University of Wisconsin-Milwaukee in 2013. During his time in the United States, he worked with Professor Richard P. Smiraglia and taught courses on knowledge organization and information literacy. In 2014, he was hired as a tenured professor by the Graduate School of Information Science at São Paulo State University, Brazil. His main research interest is knowledge organization. He is a member of the ISKO Scientific Advisory Council and he has contributed to the ISKO Encyclopedia of Knowledge Organization both as an author and as an editor of Birger Hjørland's entry on Domain Analysis. He collaborated in the maintenance of the ISKO Knowledge Organization Literature database and he has also participated in the translation of the Universal Decimal Classification (UDC) database summary to Spanish. In addition, he has contributed papers to the latest UDC Seminar and North American, British, Spanish, Brazilian, French, and international ISKO chapters meetings and has published in top journals on knowledge organization around the world. Finally, he also collaborates and serves as International Coordinator at the Satija Research Foundation for Library and Information Science, India, and the Institute for Gender Studies (IEG) at University Carlos III of Madrid, Spain.

Contributed : Preface, pp. ix-x; Chapter 4: Ethical Use of Information: The Contribution of the Academic Libraries in the Prevention of Plagiarism, pp. 49-65.

Sanjaya Mishra

Education Specialist, e-Learning, Commonwealth of Learning, Burnaby, British Columbia, Canada. *smishra@col.org*

Dr Sanjaya Mishra is Education Specialist: eLearning at Commonwealth of Learning

(COL), Canada. Previously, he served COL as Director of the Commonwealth Educational Media Centre for Asia (CEMCA) from 1 July 2012 to 31 December 2014. Dr Mishra is one of the leading scholars in open, distance and online Learning. Prior to joining COL, he was Programme Specialist (ICT in Education, Science and Culture) at UNESCO, Paris.

Dr Mishra has over 25 years of experience in design, development and management of open and distance learning programmes. With a blend of academic and professional qualifications in library and information science, distance education, television production and training and development, he has been promoting the use of educational multimedia, eLearning, open educational resources (OER) and open access to scientific information around the world. During his service in different capacities at the Indira Gandhi National Open University (IGNOU), amongst many innovative activities and programmes, he developed the OER-based one-year Post-Graduate Diploma in eLearning.

As a staff developer and trainer, Dr Mishra has received the ISTD-Vivekanand National Award for Excellence in Human Resource Development and Training in 2007, and has facilitated over 1000 hours of training in distance education, information and communication technologies, educational multimedia, eLearning and Open Educational Resources in over 30 countries. He is involved in developing technology-enabled solutions for increasing the quality of and access to educational opportunities at all levels. Dr Mishra's vision is to unleash the potentials of every learner by providing an enabling environment for excellence through innovative use of educational technologies.

The Satija Research Foundation for Library and Information Science (*www.srflisindia.org*) conferred Dr Mishra with the Indian Library Leaders 2012 Award, and Dr Mishra received the Prof G Ram Reddy Social Scientist Award 2013 from Prof G Ram Reddy Memorial Trust for his contribution to distance education and OER. He has contributed over 200 publicationsin form of books, chapters, journal papers, conference presentations, book reviews and distance learning materials. At UNESCO, he facilitated the adoption of open access to scientific information and research. Dr Mishra has also previously served as Assistant Regional Director of one of IGNOU's Regional Centres and as a Programme Officer at CEMCA (2001-2003).

Contributed : Chapter 5: Does Open Access Promote Plagiarism?, pp. 67-76.

Ramesh Pandita

Assistant Librarian, Baba Ghulam Shah Badshah University, Rajouri, Jammu & Kashmir, India, E-mail: *rameshpandita90@gmail.com*

Ramesh Pandita obtained his BSc and BLIS from the University of Kashmir, Srinagar and M.Lib.Sc from the University of Jammu, Jammu. He is currently pursuing Ph.D in Library and Information Science from the Bharathiar University, Coimbatore. He has also to his credit, Master's Degree in Sociology and Master's Degree in Business Administration (International Business). Presently working as a Sr. Assistant Librarian at BGSB University, Rajouri, Jammu and Kashmir, India, he has more than 70 research papers and over 100 popular articles to his credit. His area of expertise include Biblometrics, Open Access, e-Documents, Library Automation and Networking, Library Administration and Management.

Contributed: Chapter 8: Plagiarism: A Growing Menace Across Academia, pp. 107-126.

Prabhash Narayana Rath

Deputy Librarian, Gokhale Institute of Politics and Economics, Pune, India. *prabhashrath@gmail.com*

Dr Prabhash Narayana Rath is presently working as Deputy Librarian, Gokhale Institute of Politics and Economics, Pune, India. He got his Ph.D. in Library and Information Science from the University of Calcutta for his thesis 'Development of Systematic Bibliographies in India'. In his two decades of professional experience, Dr. Rath has edited two books andauthored many publications in the form of journal articles, articles in edited books, and working papers. He has attended and presented papers in many conferences of national and international level. Dr. Rath was also actively involved in the activities of IASLIC in early 1990s and wasits Executive Council Member for 1993-1995. He was also Assistant Editor ofthe *Indian Library Science Abstracts* (ILSA) from 1990 to 1993. He was awarded a certificate of commendationin recognition to his contribution towards the modernization of libraries by IASLIC on the occasion of itsGolden Jubilee celebrations.

Besides academic and professional attainments, Dr Rath has served in various important administrative positions of Gokhale Institute of Politics and Economics and is presently the Officiating Registrar of the Institute. He is in the Editorial Board of *Social Science Spectrum*, an open access peer-reviewed journal devoted to study of different areas of social sciences. Dr Rathhas re-nominated as member of Indian Historical Records Committee of Government of India for the period 2017-2022.

Contributed : Chapter 5: Does Open Access Promote Plagiarism?, pp. 67-76.

R. Saha

Former Adviser, Department of Science and Technology, Government of India. *raghav.saha@gmail.com*

R Saha is a B Tech from IIT Kanpur in Aeronautical Engineering. He got his Master Degree from Cranfield University in England. He served the Government of India for 35 years in different capacities and handling different responsibilities including research and development and retired as Scientist G and Adviser from the Department of Science and Technology, Government of India. He has wide experience in technology evaluation and assessment, intellectual property rights management, regulatory processes and R&D policies and project implementation. He has been a pioneer in leading the national efforts in policy making and capacity building in the area of IPR. He planned and conducted two training programmes on IPR for developing countries drawing a participation of about 30 countries. He was invited as an international resource person to speak on IPR in Bangla Desh, Indonesia, Namibia, Sri

Lanka, Egypt, Oman, Malaysia, China, Philippines, Mauritius, Mexico and Uganda. He conducted more than 400 IPR workshops in India and other countries. 20 Patent Information Centres at state levels and 60 university IPR cells were set up in India under his leadership. He has been helping universities in developing their IPR policies. About 1000 patent applications were filed under his guidance on behalf of universities and R&D institutions. While in government he was actively engaged in law and policy making in the most crucial times after India signed the WTO agreement. He represented India in discussions at WIPO and, was involved in negotiating international agreements on IPR in the context of scientific research and development.

He was the MHRD Chair Professor in IPR at the Tezpur University, a Central university. He has been working on IPR issues related to SME in India. He completed a National Study on IPR and MSME in the Indian context on behalf of the World Intellectual Property Organization (WIPO) as a part of its Development Agenda. Presently, he advises many institutions like Confederation of Indian Industry (CII), IIT Delhi, IIT Kharagpur, C-DAC, NRDC, Indian Council of Medical Research and many government departments on IPR matters. He continues to teach IPR in various institutions. He is presently Senior Adviser to CII advising them on IPR policies and other substantial issues being faced by the Indian industry. He is also the Chairman of a committee set up by Department of Electronics and Information Technology, Government of India for providing IPR support to start ups and conducting awareness programmes.

Contributed : Chapter 10: Plagiarism in Research Publications and Violation of Law and Ethics, pp. 135-142.

Stavroula Sant-Geronikolou

ORCID ID: *https://orcid.org/0000-0002-4340-7463, 100302132@alumnos.uc3m.es*

Stavroula Sant-Geronikolou is aPhD student of Library and Information Sciences at the University of Madrid-Charles III (UC3M), currently conducting a short-term research stay at the University of West Attica. She holds a BA in French Literature from the National and Kapodistrian University of Athens, a Master's degree in Libraries and Digital Information Services (UC3M) and postgraduate certifications in Educational Technologies from Antonio de Nebrija University. Her thesis focuses onfactors potentially impacting library use data capitalization prospects. Her academic interests also include Open Science, Information Literacy, Learning Commons, Creative Industries and High Impact Practices.

Contributed : Chapter 6: Plagiarism and the New Norm in Scholarly Communication: The New Information Professionals and Open Access Advocacy Groups' Perspective, pp. 77-94.

João Carlos Gardini Santos

jcgardini@gmail.com

MSc student in Information Science (São Paulo State University - UNESP, Marília, Brazil). Bachelor in Library and Information Science (São Paulo State University - UNESP,

Marília, Brazil, 2017). Bachelor in Law (Faculdade de Direito da Alta Paulista, Tupã, Brazil, 2010). He is currently librarian at the Federal Institute of Education, Science and Technology of Mato Grosso do Sul (Nova Andradina, Brazil). He was a lawyer between 2011 and 2014.

Contributed : Chapter 15: Plagiarism and Guides to Good Scientific Practices: The Brazilian Perspective, pp. 201-208.

M.P. Satija

Former Professorand Emeritus Fellow, Guru Nanak Dev University, Amritsar, India. *Email:satija_mp@yahoo.com*

M P Satija retired as Professorand Head and later and UGC Emeritus Fellow from the Department of Library and Information Science, Guru Nanak Dev University, Amritsar, India, is in the library profession for the last four decades. As an author of more than twenty books, about 150 papers and numerous book reviews, course material on classification for distance education courses, and many conference papers published in India and abroad, he has collaborated with international experts namely, Dr. John Comaromi, Editor DDC (1979-1991), Ms Joan S. Mitchell, current editor DDC21-23, Dr. Ray Prytherch, Editor, Harrod's Glossary, Dr. S. P. Agrawal, former Director, National Social Science Documentation Centre, New Delhi. No wonder many bibliometric studies in India have found him a prolific author. Having done his Ph. D. on Ranganathan studies, he has been instrumental in interpreting and propagating Ranganathan's works and ideas to the new generation. He has written extensively on Classification, Book Numbers, Ranganathan Studies and Indian Library Literature.Internationally known for his expertise on Colon Classification and Indian state-of-the-art on classification in India and abroad, he is often invited to contribute papers in these areas for books and journals.

Contributed : Preface, pp. ix-x.; Chapter 1: Plagiarism: An Introduction, pp. 1-19.

Eduardo Graziosi Silva

eduardograziosi@gmail.com

On obtainingMSc in Information Science (São Paulo State University – UNESP, Marília, Brazil, 2018). Bachelor in Library and Information Science (Federal University of Sao Carlos – UFSCar, 2008),he is currently librarian at the School of Engineering of Sao Carlos at the University of Sao Paulo (EESC-USP) where he serves as a multitaskingHead of the User Service Section of the Library Service "Prof. Dr. Sérgio Rodrigues Fontes" and teacher in Content Mind, where he offers MOOC "CVLattes: how to create and keep up to date?".

Contributed : Chapter 15: Plagiarism and Guides to Good Scientific Practices: The Brazilian Perspective, pp. 201-208.

Maria da Graça de Melo Simões

gsimoes@fl.uc.pt

Maria da Graça de Melo Simões, PhD, is Associate Professor at the Department of

Philosophy, Communication and Information, Faculty of Letters, University of Coimbra, Portugal. Focusing her research and teaching interest on knowledge organization she has published several works related to these areas in books, scientific journals and conference proceedings.

Contributed : Chapter 4: Ethical Use of Information: The Contribution of the Academic Libraries in the Prevention of Plagiarism, pp. 49-65.

Nirmal Singh

nirmal02@yahoo.co.in

Dr. Nirmal Singh has been working as Assistant Librarian (Sr. Scale) at Guru Angad Dev Veterinary & Animal Sciences University, Ludhiana since August 2010. He has more than 10 years experience of working in different libraries. He has published more than 25 papers in national and international journals and contributedarticles for IFLA WIL Satellite Conferences, i.e. 2012 (University of Tampere, Tampere, Finland) and 2017 (University of Bratislava, Salovakia). His fields on interests include user studies, bibliometrics/ scientometrics and application of information technology in libraries. He is life member of Indian Association of Teachers of Library and Information Science (IATLIS).

Contributed : Chapter 17: Awareness and Attitude of Agricultural Students Towards Plagiarism, pp. 221-230.; Chapter 21: The Pressures and Perils of Overachieving - An Inquiry into the Kaavya Viswanathan Case, pp. 259-262.

Shivendra Singh

Senior Librarian, All India Institute of Medical Sciences, Patna, India, Ph. -+91-9815526163, E-mail : *shiv.mail@gmail.com*

Dr. Shivendra Singh is working as Senior Librarian in AIIMS, Patna. Prior to this he worked as Assistant Librarian at Baba Farid University of Health Sciences (BFUHS), Faridkot, Punjab and National Institute of Pharmaceutical Education and Research (NIPER), Mohali. He has worked with Institute of Management Technology (IMT), Ghaziabad and *Dainik Jagran*, Noida as Assistant Librarian. He is the recipient of the UNESCO prize in the category of National participant in appreciation of the commendable performance shown in the course assignments in UNESCO-DSIR-IIMK international workshop on GreenStone Digital Library software in 2006. Dr. Singh has published more than 40 research papers in both national and international journals.

Contributed : Chapter 8: Plagiarism: A Growing Menace Across Academia, pp. 107-126.

V. J. Suseela

Deputy Librarian (Retd.), Email - *vjsuseela@gmail.com*, Indira Gandhi Memorial Library, University of Hyderabad, Hyderabad, Telengana State – 46

Dr. (Mrs) V. J. Suseela recently retired as Deputy Librarian after serving the Indira Gandhi Memorial Library, University of Hyderabad for over three decades, including serving as a resource person for the PGDLAN program of the University. In her long and meritorious career she published about 65 research papers in national and international journals, jointly authored four books and attended numerous conferences. She has written course material for the BLIS students of the Dr B R Ambedakar Open university, Hyderabad. She is currently engaged in series of articles in Telugu on the topic of 'university library services' for the Grandhaalaya Sarvasvam Telugu LIS Periodical sponsored by Andhra Pradesh Library Association, Vijayawada (AP).

Contributed : Chapter 11: Plagiarism: An Academic Dishonesty. A Bibliometric Insight into the Spread of Problem, pp. 143-163.

Nirmal Kumar Swain

Associate Professor, Department of Lib & Inf Science, Vivekananda Library Building, Maharshi Dayanand University, Rohtak - 124001 India. Email : *drnkswain@gmail.com*

Philosopher by training, Dr. Swain earned his doctorate on copyright issues. In over a decade of teaching experience he has edited and authored a dozen books to his credit. Currently he is an Associate-Fellow at Indian Institute of Advanced Study, Shimla working on the theme, 'Academic Writings and Plagiarism' on which he has also delivered lectures at many universities

Some of the important awards he has received are, 1st prize in essay contest conducted by UNO State Committee, Meghalaya State, 1995; All India Indo-Kuwait Essay Competition Prize, 1995-96, conducted by Embassy of Kuwait, New Delhi; 3rd Prize in I.C.P.R. (under 25), Essay Contest-cum-Young Scholars Meet, 1995, Lucknow, prize in essay contest conducted by Forum of Free Enterprise, Mumbai, 1996 and a Gold Medal Certificate for the AVANTIKA Essay Contest, 2007.

Contributed : Bibliography, pp. 303-328.

Manorama Tripathi

Librarian, Jawaharlal Nehru University, New Delhi, *manoramatripathi2@yahoo.com*

Manorama Tripathi holds a doctorate in Library and Information Science fromthee Banaras Hindu University, Varanasi. At present, she is working as Librarian at the Central library, Jawaharlal Nehru University, New Delhi. Her work involves *inter alia*, teaching and promoting the use of print and electronic resources among the students, researchers and faculty members. Prior to joining JNU, she served Indira Gandhi National Open University New Delhi as Documentation Officer; University of Delhi, Delhi and Banaras Hindu University, Varanasi as a faculty member. She is a recipient of the best paper award from Raja RamMohun Roy Library Foundation. She has published 55+ research papers in national andinternational scholarly journals and conference volumes. She has done several presentations and delivered talks at CEC-UGC, Refresher and Orientation programmes of the universities across the country. She has visited many countries for participating in the international conferences. Her areas of research include information seeking behavior of researchers, innovative library services and scientometrics.

Contributed : Chapter 14: Policies and Guidelines for Academic Conduct in Universities: A Survey of the International Landscape, pp. 183-200.

Theodor Tudoroiu

Senior Lecturer, Department of Political Science, The University of the West Indies at St. Augustine, Email: *theodor.tudoroiu@sta.uwi.edu*, Phone:1(868) 347-7099,Fax:1(868) 663-4948, Mail address: The University of the West Indies, Department of Political Science, Faculty of Social Sciences, St. Augustine, Trinidad & Tobago, West Indies.

Theodor Tudoroiu is a Senior Lecturer at the Department of Political Science of the University of the West Indies at St. Augustine, Trinidad and Tobago. He holds an MA from the College of Europe, Bruges, Belgium, and a PhD from Université de Montréal. His work covers mainly topics related to international relations and regime change in the Commonwealth of Independent States, Eastern Europe and the Middle East. He is the author of The Revolutionary Totalitarian Personality (Palgrave Macmillan, 2016) and Brexit, President Trump, and the Changing Geopolitics of Eastern Europe (Palgrave Macmillan, 2018).

Contributed : Chapter 3: Plagiarism and High Politics: A Threat to Democracy, pp. 29-47.

V. Uma

Deputy Librarian, Email – *umav4966@gmail.com*, Indira Gandhi Memorial Library, University of Hyderabad, Hyderabad, Telengana State - 46

Dr. (Mrs) V. Uma is currently Deputy Librarian Indira Gandhi Memorial Library University of Hyderabad where she has served for over three decades including acting as a resource person for the PGDLAN program, Centre for Regional Studies and Academic Staff College, all of the University ofHyderabad . In addition she has occasionallylent her expertise to the Dr B R Ambedakar Open University, Hyderabad. She has published about 65 papers in national and international journals, participated in many conferences in addition to jointly editing four books, and has written course material for the BLIS students of the Dr B R Ambedakar Open University, Hyderabad. Life member of many professional organisations sheis recipient of the Mahila Siromani Award-2014.

Contributed : Chapter 11: Plagiarism: An Academic Dishonesty. A Bibliometric Insight into the Spread of Problem, pp. 143-163.

University Grants Commission (India)

The University Grants Commission (UGC) (*www.ugc.ac.in*) came into existence on 28th December, 1953 and became a statutory organization of the Government of India by an Act of Parliament in 1956, for the coordination, determination and maintenance of standards of teaching, examination and research in university education. In order to ensure effective region-wise coverage throughout the country, the UGC has decentralised its operations by setting up six regional centres at Pune, Hyderabad, Kolkata, Bhopal, Guwahati and Bangalore. The head office of the UGC is located at Bahadur Shah Zafar Marg in New Delhi, with two additional bureaus operating from 35, Feroze Shah Road and the South Campus of University of Delhi as well.

Contributed : Appendix 1: University Grants Commission (Promotion of Academic Integrity and Prevention of Plagiarism in Higher Educational Institutions) Regulations, 2018, pp. 291-298.

University of Bradford Library

The University of Bradford is a public university having two campuses in the city of Bradford, West Yorkshire, England. The university received its Royal Charter in 1966, making it the 40th university to be created in Britain. Of its about 11000 student strength, 22% come from over 110 different countries. It ranks quite high in the UK for graduate employment. At the same time university has a strong reputation for research and knowledge transfer as clear from its rank in the Top 50 English Universities based on research funding. Its Department of Peace Studies, established in 1973, is currently the world's largest university centre for the study of peace and conflict. Its J B Priestley library, which is open 24 hours, 360 days a year, has 530,000 volumes, more than 1,100 printed periodical titles and approximately 60,000 electronic journals.

The content of the chapter has been written by a group, including Sarah George and Jennifer Rowlandfrom the J B Priestly Library staff.

Contributed : Chapter 23: Information on Plagiarism at the University of Bradford, pp. 279-290.

Marta Ligia Pomim Valentim

marta.valentim@unesp.br

ProfessorValentim specializes in Information, Knowledge and Organizational Intelligence at Sao Paulo State University (UNESP). She earned her PhD in Communication Sciences from the School of Communications and Arts, University of São Paulo (ECA/USP). She teaches undergraduate and graduate courses at UNESP as full professor. She has scholarship for Research Productivity CNPq in the areas of organizational competitive intelligence; information management; knowledge management and informational culture. Leader of the Research Group 'Information, Knowledge and Organizational Intelligence'. She coordinates the research project 'Sharing and socialization processes of knowledge in business environments'. She is coordinator of the Graduate Program in Information Science at UNESP for the period 2017-2021. She hasauthored several books in the Information Science area. As a President of the Associação Brasileira de Educação em Ciência da Informação (ABECIN), 2016-2019 andVice President of the Asociación de Educación e Investigación en Ciencia de la Información de Iberoamérica y el Caribe (EDICIC), 2009-2011 she has done commendablework for these profesional bodies.

Contributed : Chapter 12: Reflections about Research Ethics in Contemporary Society, pp. 165-173.

Title Index

Academic Plagiarism: An Overview of the Policy and Preventive Measures in Pakistan/ Kanwal Ameen and Faiqa Mansoor, Chapter 18, pp. 231-238.

Anti-Plagiarism Software Check to the Doctoral Theses in Indian Universities and Institutions / S T Kale, Chapter 22, pp. 259-278.

Awareness and Attitude of Agricultural Students Towards Plagiarism / Nirmal Singh, Sanjeev Kumar and Dhiraj Kumar, Chapter 17, pp. 221-230.

Beleaguered and Tousled Research: Murky Waters of Plagiarism and Retractions / Sumeer Gul and Taufat Hussain, Chapter 9, pp. 127-134.

Bibliography / Nirmal Kumar Swain and Harish Chander, pp. 303-324.

Controlling Plague of Plagiarism in Indian Academic Institutions: Draft UGC Plagiarism Regulations 2018 / Ramesh C. Gaur, Chapter 20, pp. 249-258.

Does Open Access Promote Plagiarism? / Prabhash N. Rath and Sanjaya Mishra, Chapter 5, pp. 67-76.

Ethical Policies of LIS e-Journals Listed in the UGC Approved List / Dinesh K Gupta and Vijendra Kumar, Chapter 19, pp. 239-248.

Ethical Use of Information: The Contribution of the Academic Libraries in the Prevention of Plagiarism / Helena Isabel Pereira Leitão, Maria da Graça de Melo Simões, Patrícia de Almeida and Daniel Martínez-Ávila, Chapter 4, pp. 49-66.

Foreword / H. K. Kaul, pp. vii-viii.

Glossary, pp. 329-340.

IFLA Statement on Copyright Education and Copyright Literacy / Appendix 2, pp. 299-302.

Information on Plagiarism at the University of Bradford / Chapter 23, pp. 279-290.

Measuring Plagiarism Research Output: A Bibliometric Analysis / Suresh K Chauhan, Chapter 7, pp. 95-106.

Plagiarism and Guides to Good Scientific Practices: The Brazilian Perspective / Eduardo Graziosi Silva, João Carlos Gardini Santos, José Augusto Chaves Guimarães, Chapter 15, pp. 201-208.

Plagiarism and High Politics: A Threat to Democracy / Theodor Tudoroiu, Chapter 3, pp. 29-48.

Plagiarism and the New Norm in Scholarly Communication: The New Information Professionals and Open Access Advocacy Groups' Perspective / Stavroula Sant-Geronikolou, Chapter 6, pp. 77-94.

Plagiarism in Research Publications and Violation of Law and Ethics / R Saha, Chapter 10, pp. 135-142.

Plagiarism: A Growing Menace Across Academia / Ramesh Pandita and Shivendra Singh, Chapter 8, pp. 107-126.

Plagiarism: An Academic Dishonesty. A Bibliometric Insight into the Spread of Problem / V.J. Suseela and V. Uma, Chapter 11, pp. 143-164.

Plagiarism: An Introduction / M.P. Satija, Chapter 1, pp. 1-20.

Policies and Guidelines for Academic Conduct in Universities : A Survey of the International Landscape / Manorama Tripathi, Gayatri Dwivedi and Parveen Babbar, Chapter 14, pp. 183-200.

Preface / M.P. Satija and Daniel Martínez-Ávila, pp. xi-xii.

Reflections about Research Ethics in Contemporary Society / Marta Ligia Pomim Valentim, Chapter 12, pp. 164-174.

Role of Information Literacy in Curbing Plagiarism / Helen de Castro S. Casarin, Chapter 13, pp. 175-182.

The Pressures and Perils of Overachieving - An Inquiry into the Kaavya Viswanathan Case / Gurpartap S. Khairah and Nirmal Singh, Chapter 21, pp. 259-262.

The Problem of Plagiarism in Retractions of Published Articles / John M. Budd, Chapter 2, pp. 21-28.

Understanding the Concept of Plagiarism among Iranian Students / Asefeh Asemi and Marzieh Sadat Hosseini, Chapter 16, pp. 209-220.

University Grants Commission (Promotion of Academic Integrity and Prevention of Plagiarism in Higher Educational Institutions) Regulations, 2018 / Appendix 1, pp. 291-298.

Subject Index

* All terms and concepts are in context of plagiarism unless stated otherwise
* g stands for glossary (pages 329-339)
* Bibliography (pages 303-328) has not been indexed

Academic integrity, 188-190
Academic libraries, 49-65
    role in prevention, 50-60
Academicians, plagiarism among, 107-126, 183-200, 231-237
Agricultural students, survey of, 217-229
Apocrypha, g
Author defined, g, 291
Avoiding it, 12-15, 73, 175-182, 194-195, 229, 235-236, 253-254, 279-280, 282-286, 293-294
    editor's responsibility, 16
    see also Preventing it
Bacon, F., 13
Benefits of plagiarism, 5
Best practices, 195-196, 201-208
Bhutto, Zulfikar Ali, 5
Bibliography on, 303-328
    articles, 305-324
    books, 303-304
    websites, 324
Bibliometric analysis, 95-105, 143-163
Bradford University, 279-290
Brazil, 170-171, 201-208
Brazilian Academy of Sciences, 203-205
Budapest Initative, 69
Cases of, 7-8, 21, 97, 221
Causes of, 8-10, 26, 54, 80, 110, 116-117, 144, 184-185, 259-262

Citing, g
    retracted papers, 24-26
Committee on Publication Ethics, 21, 148, 70-71, 189
Copyleft, g, 4
Copyright, g, 111, 135
Copyright education, 299-302
Copyright exhaustion, g
Copyright holder, g
Copyright India, 135, 138 264-265
Copyright infringement, g, 5
Copyright literacy, 299-302
Copyright origin, 6
Copyright violation, 5
Correction, 27
Creative commons, g
Cryptomnesia, g, 8, 259, 262
Data falsification, 191
Definition of, 1, 50-51, 136-137, 221, 231, 291
    see also Meanings
Democracy and plagiarism 29-47
Detection software, g, 14, 96, 120-122, 139, 235, 251-253, 263-278, 265-266, 289
    limitations, 121-122
Digital rights management, g
Doctoral theses, 263-278
Duke University, 193-194
Economics of plagiarism, 138-139
Eliot, T.S., 3-4

Ethical use of information, 49-65
Ethics codes, 203-205, 240, 299
Examples of plagiarism, 137-138
Fair use, g
FAQs, 286-290
Folklore, g
Forms of, 1, 2, 202, 213-215, 280-282
Gaddafi, Saif, 29-30
Gates, Bill, 5
German education system, 34-35
Germany, 33-35
Ghosh, Amitav, 261-262
Ghost writing, g, 4, 115-116
Higher Education Commission, Pakistan, 233-235
Hungary, 35-36
IFLA recommendations, 299-302
Ill effects of, 11-12, 139-140, 185-186, 290, 297
    see also Penalty
Industrial Revolution, 6
INFLIBNET, 269
Information literacy, g, 175-182
Intellectual property rights, g, 110-111, 135
    see also Copyright; Patents
International sceanriuo,183-200
    Brazil, 201-208
    Germany, 33-35
    Hungary, 35-36
    India, 249-257, 217-229
    Iran, 209-219
    Pakistan, 231-237
    Rumania, 37-38
    Russia, 38-40
    U K, 279-290
Internet and plagiarism, 117-118
Iran, 209-219
IUP IP, g
Journals, ethical policies, 239-248
Jung,Carl, 262
Justification for, 2-4
KaavyaViswanathan
    see Viswanathan, Kaavya
Kuhlthau,C.K.,176
Library science-journals, 239-248
London of School of Economics, 29

Marrakesh Treaty, g
McCafferty, Megan, 260-261
Meanings of , 30-31, 50-51, 169, 201, 221, 279
    see also Definition
MEDLINE, 25
Milton, John, 3
Misattribution, g
Mizner,W., 3
Newton, I., 3
Office of Research Integrity, 111-112, 188, 263
Open access, 20-21, 67-76, 77-94
    vis-à-vis plagiarism,10-11, 67-74, 77-90
Open Access Advocacy Group, 77-94
Open access initiative, g, 69
Open science, g
Origins of, 30-31, 95-96, 201, 209-210
Pakistan, 10, 231-237
Paraphrasing, g, 213-214, 285
Patent law, g
PAU, Ludhiana, 222-229
Penalty for, 235-136, 256, 296-297
    see also Ill effects
Piracy, g, 2, 4-5
Policies for academic conduct, 96, 183-200, 233-234, 270
Ponta, Victor, 37-38, 41
Predatory journals, 70, 118-119, 239-240
Prevention of, 12-15, 49-65, 72-73, 140-142, 161-162, 175-182, 193-195,233-234, 249-257, 253-255, 279-280, 294
    see also Avoiding
Proxy writing, g
Publish or perish syndrome, g, 9
PubPeer, g
Putin, Vladimir, 38-40, 41
Reference management, 254
Rennaisance, 67
Research Data Management, 195-196
Research ethics, 165-173
Research misconduct, 184-185
Research on, 95-105
Retraction, g, 21-28, 81-83, 97, 127-131
    citation, 24-26
    correction, 27

Subject Index

Retraction index, g
Retraction watch, g
Romania, 37-38
Rushdie, Salman, 261-262
Russia, 38-40
Salami publication, g, 114-115, 214-215, 251
    see also Self-plagiarism
Schmitt, Pal, 35
Sci-hub, g
SCOPUS, 149
Self-plagiarism, g, 114-115, 214-215, 251
    see also Salami publication
Shakespeare, W., 95
Shodhganga, 269
Similarity score, g, 14-15, 119-120, 271, 294-295
Society for Scientific Values, g
Source attribution, g

Tolerance limit, 269-270, 295
Turnitin, 289
Toll-access journals, 72
UGC regulations-2018, 255-257, 291-298
Universities, 183-200, 279-290
    Indian, 236-278, 274-278
    Pakistani, 231-237
    U.K., 279-290
University Grants Commission, 107, 190, 239-248, 249-257, 270, 291-298
Viswanathan, Kaavya case, 259-262
What of plagiarism, 1-2, 108-109, 250-251
WIPO, g, 111
Writing Program Administrators, 50-54
Zu Guttenberg, Karl-Theodor, 33-35
Zurkowski, P., 175